OXFORD HISTORY OF
THE CHRISTIAN CHURCH

Edited by
Henry and Owen Chadwick

East and West: The Making of a Rift in the Church

From Apostolic Times until the Council of Florence

HENRY CHADWICK

OXFORD
UNIVERSITY PRESS

*This book has been printed digitally and produced in a standard specification
in order to ensure its continuing availability*

OXFORD
UNIVERSITY PRESS

Great Clarendon Street, Oxford OX2 6DP

Oxford University Press is a department of the University of Oxford.
It furthers the University's objective of excellence in research, scholarship,
and education by publishing worldwide in

Oxford New York

Auckland Cape Town Dar es Salaam Hong Kong Karachi
Kuala Lumpur Madrid Melbourne Mexico City Nairobi
New Delhi Shanghai Taipei Toronto
With offices in
Argentina Austria Brazil Chile Czech Republic France Greece
Guatemala Hungary Italy Japan South Korea Poland Portugal
Singapore Switzerland Thailand Turkey Ukraine Vietnam

Oxford is a registered trade mark of Oxford University Press
in the UK and in certain other countries

Published in the United States
by Oxford University Press Inc., New York

ISBN 978-0-19-928016-2

To my wife
Sine qua non

PREFATORY NOTE

Special thanks are due to support from the officers of Oxford University Press, especially Hilary O'Shea, Jenny Wagstaffe, Lucy Qureshi, and Dr Leofranc Holford-Strevens, and to many patient librarians in both Oxford and Cambridge.

H.C.

CONTENTS

ABBREVIATIONS

ACO	*Acta Conciliorum Oecumenicorum*
Acta Latina	*Acta Latina Concilii Florentini*, ed. G. Hofmann (Concilium Florentinum: documenta et scriptores, B vi; Rome, 1955)
An. Boll.	*Analecta Bollandiana*
Coleti	N. Coleti, *Sacrosancta concilia ad regiam editionem exacta*, 23 vols. (Venice, 1728–33)
Deusdedit	*Die Kanonessammlung des Kardinals Deusdedit*, ed. V. Wolf von Glanvell (Paderborn, 1905)
Greek Acts	*Quae supersunt actorum Graecorum Concilii Florentini*, ed. J. Gill, 2 vols. (Concilium Florentinum: documenta et scriptores, B v; Rome, 1953)
Hardouin	J. Hardouin, *Conciliorum collectio regia maxima*, 12 vols. (Paris, 1714–15)
Iconoclasm	A. Bryer and J. Herrin (eds.), *Iconoclasm: Papers Given at the Ninth Spring Symposium of Byzantine Studies, University of Birmingham, March 1975* (Birmingham, 1977)
JTS	*Journal of Theological Studies*
LW	Photius, *Epistulae et Amphilochia*, ed. V. Laourdas and L. G. Westerink, 6 vols. (Leipzig, 1983–9)
Mansi	J. D. Mansi, *Sacrorum conciliorum nova et amplissima collectio*, 55 vols. (Florence etc., 1759–1962)
MGH	Monumenta Germaniae Historica
Epp.	Epistulae
SRG	Scriptores rerum Germanicarum
PG	Patrologia Graeca
PL	Patrologia Latina
Reg.	*Registrum*
RP	G. A. Rhalles and M. Potlis, *Σύνταγμα τῶν θείων καὶ ἱερῶν κανόνων τῶν τε ἁγίων καὶ πανευφήμων Ἀποστόλων καὶ τῶν ἱερῶν οἰκυμενικῶν καὶ τοπικῶν Συνόδων καὶ τῶν κατὰ μέρος ἱερῶν Πατέρων*, 6 vols. (Athens, 1852–9)
Tanner	Norman P. Tanner, *Decrees of the Ecumenical Councils*, 2 vols. (London and Washington, DC, 1990)

TU   Texte und Untersuchungen
Will   J. K. C. Will, *Acta et scripta quae de controversiis ecclesiae Graecae et Latinae saeculo undecimo composita extant* (Leipzig and Marburg, 1861; repr. Frankfurt am Main, 1963)
ZSSR   *Zeitschrift der Savigny-Stiftung für Rechtsgeschichte*

I

INTRODUCTION

Religion when shared is one of the strongest of social bonds. When differences appear whether of rite or calendar or social custom or liturgy or, above all, basic allegiance, this powerful bonding becomes counterproductive and easily engenders deep divisions. Perhaps the monotheistic religions manifest these strong cleavages in an exceptional degree. In Judaism the differences between observant and reformed synagogues can produce strongly felt estrangements, so that to an observant Jewish believer it can be easier to talk freely with a Gentile Christian than with a liberal reformed rabbi. In Islam differences between Sunni and Shiite can lead to feelings of anger and alienation and even persecution. Christian history is scarred by splits—between Chalcedonian and Monophysite (or pre-Chalcedonian), or between Roman Catholic and Evangelical Protestant (there are Evangelical Catholics), or between Lutheran and Calvinist or between High Calvinist and Arminian.

But the greatest Christian split of all has been that between east and west, between Roman Catholic and eastern Orthodox. The medieval millennium saw both sharp disagreements and several high-minded endeavours to heal the breach. The points of difference still exist. Within the Roman Catholic Church divergences of deep significance have occurred and are still alive between (*a*) those for whom a sustained worldwide unity in a single communion is possible, indeed only conceivable and practicable, if and when the bishop of one Church at Rome blessed with the founding role of the apostles Peter and Paul in the capital of the then Gentile world is held to embody the one wholly reliable and authentic source of doctrine and rule of life, and (*b*) those for whom the necessarily limited apprehension of one man, however wise and saintly (as not all popes have been), offers too narrow a basis and for whom the common mind of a universal Church has to have a more conciliar and collegial expression.

2

EARLY CHRISTIAN DIVERSITY:
THE QUEST FOR COHERENCE

To the Christian community at Corinth in which diversity appeared more prominent than unity, the apostle Paul wrote (1 Cor. 11: 18) 'I hear that there are divisions among you.' The reader of the letter discovers that the divisions went deep. Were they really one body? The apostle certainly treats them as such. There is no hint that chapter 6, for instance, addressed to a group which believed the spirituality of grace to exempt them from observing rules against sexual licence, is not written to correct the same group as that addressed in chapter 7, where the ascetics were claiming that the spiritual experience of grace forbids sex even within marriage. The two incompatible parties are treated by St Paul as belonging together in Christ, but in need of discipline and correction. Yet later in the letter (11: 19) the diversity within the community is regarded as making it possible to judge who is right and who is wrong; there is no question of any and every opinion being acceptable merely because some group within the Christian society so professes. Dissent clarifies orthodoxy.

The Greek word *haeresis* ordinarily means a school of thought, a philosophical tendency, but does not necessarily carry a pejorative sense. In Christian usage it came to carry a negative connotation for a faction becoming a separate body, whether withdrawing itself or being extruded from the main community, or then by easy derivation for the characteristic doctrines maintained by the dissenting group. The original etymological sense of *haeresis* as meaning 'choice' reasserted itself and the term came to be used to affirm that the dissenters were deliberately, indeed obstinately in face of correction, preferring their private speculative opinions to the accepted mind of the community taken as a whole, whose coherence they seemed to threaten.

The first-century churches developed in different ways, and four distinct narratives of the life and teaching of Jesus were produced, one (John) being so different from the other three that in the second century there were serious disputes about its acceptance. Second-century tradition known to Papias of Hieropolis attributed to the apostle Matthew a collection of Jesus' sayings in Aramaic. A comparable collection was used in differing ways by the gospels which, after some disagreement on order, ended as the first and third in the list of four. The earliest of the four gospels was current, perhaps rightly, under the name of John Mark. The first gospel presupposes a church of Christian Jews, at least in the great majority, and stresses the continuity of Jesus with the Old Testament prophets and with Judaism; at the same time Jesus is presented as the New Moses teaching a final way to God.

At the opposite pole from Matthew stands Paul with his passionate claim to be called by the risen Christ to be apostle of the Gentiles and, correctly, understanding the acknowledgement of his standing as an apostle to be bound up with the acknowledgement of the legitimacy of his Gentile mission. His letters show that there were other missionaries in the Gentile world beside himself, and at Corinth there were parties in the local church claiming the authority of different leaders, Peter, Apollos, or Paul himself. The polemic in 1 Cor. 3: 11 against the notion that the Church can have any foundation other than Christ may well presuppose that the Peter party had been appealing to a saying of Jesus (Matt. 16: 18) associating Peter with the rock-foundation.

The Jews had rules designed to keep them apart from defilement, and meals with Gentiles were difficult. Table-fellowship for Jewish and Gentile believers in the Church was problematic in that it raised directly the question what authority the Old Testament law had for the people of God living under the new covenant of the Messiah. To abandon Jewish customs and feasts constituted a threat to Jewish identity, and the Church of Christian Jews embodied a Reform Judaism which observant conservatives were bound to regard with abhorrence, especially if Gentile proselytes were being stolen from the synagogues. Among Gentile believers some thought that the Law of Moses was so wholly superseded as to be incapable of Christian interpretation. Paul offered the Galatians a *via media* in the notion that the Law of Moses was a valued tutor until the coming of Messiah; but now the ethical norm was the following of the way of Jesus, a way to be expressed in love rather than in a fixed written code of rules, an inward life in the Spirit rather than one consisting of outward acts of charity and good works, though of course such acts were the spontaneous expression of the inward heart.

Authority for so profound a shift lay in the mystery of Christ, the prophet of Nazareth in whom the Father was present to reconcile the world to him and by his Spirit was now present in the community of God's people.

Two contrasting traditions came to interpret this last affirmation. On the one hand the Redeemer is seen as fully and spontaneously human in complete solidarity with the human race he came to cure and save. Origen reports (*Comm. on Matt.* 12. 6) that some second-century Christians did not wish to admit that Jesus was more than a mere man and appealed to St Matthew's gospel to legitimate this view. On the other hand the power of the

Redeemer to bring salvation presupposes a presence of the Spirit of the Creator himself. For Justin Martyr the adoration by the Magi of the infant Jesus proved Jesus to have been more than merely human at birth; he had not become a divine hero by adoption or reward for virtue.

When in the seventies of the second century the pagan critic of Christianity Celsus contrasted 'the great Church' with the fissiparous sects, mainly gnostic, of which he had considerable direct knowledge, the majority body was itself the result of a confluence of many streams distinguishable in the story of first- and early second-century Christianity. Celsus thought diversity one of the principal marks of the Christian movement, yet was impressed by their urge to stay together in what they called 'agape'. There were varieties of standpoint at an early stage in the development of the Church, as is evident from the Pauline epistles. The Roman Church of the second half of the second century was proud to honour the memory and the relics of the martyred apostles Peter and Paul, but a little more than a century earlier those two apostles had represented differing points of view, and the record of the epistle to the Galatians (2: 11 ff.). shows that the divergence was accompanied by a measure of feeling and high tension. The second-century Churches were sure they had inherited a universal body whose range according to Justin was already stretching out to the furthest limits of the empire. Apologists liked to contrast the dissensions of the philosophers with the unanimity of the Church, recipient of divine revelation in the word of God. In fact lively disagreements continued in the mid-second century, e.g. on whether St John's gospel and the Apocalypse of John were authentic apostolic texts, and on how the rather different picture of Jesus in St John's gospel could be reconciled with the synoptic gospels—evidently the latter had established their canonical status earlier. There were also plenty of debates about the problems discussed at Corinth in St Paul's time, above all the call to the celibate life and the second-class but accepted status of believers with spouses and families. Ascetic apocryphal texts such as the *Acts of Paul and Thecla* were popular reading.

The early Christians perhaps took a lead from St Paul (Phil. 1) in being remarkably tolerant of differences, a quality which facilitated their coherence and 'catholicity'. Even Origen in the third century once treats heretical sects as comparable to different schools in philosophy or medicine or Judaism (*c. Cels.* 3. 12–13). His contemporary Cyprian of Carthage even asserts the right of each individual bishop, in conscience before God, to make up his own mind on controversial questions in the baptismal controversy. Nevertheless doctrinal differences loomed larger in Christianity than in Judaism, and occupied the centre of the stage as they did not in pagan myths. Polytheistic cults were not mutually incompatible. But among the Christians theosophical speculation or gnosticism was rapidly felt to be a threat, partly because the sects liked to claim superiority to ordinary believers.

Gnosticism was an early arrival on the scene. Most of the groups were for the divine, not for the human redeemer, and in most cases disbelieved in the reality of Christ's human flesh. It seemed axiomatic that the divine could have no contact with anything so polluting. The first epistle of John has sharp polemic against those who deny the flesh of Jesus and is in effect the earliest document to insist that the redeemer must be both human and divine. To gnostics death on the cross seemed incompatible with divine presence. Early in the second century Ignatius of Antioch was in combat with Christian groups denying the physicality of the crucifixion. This theme had a long future among Manichees and Muslims.

In extreme form such gnostics held a doctrine which had affinities to late Platonism, though Neoplatonists (e.g. Porphyry, Simplicius) hated gnosticism as a rival. To Porphyry in the third century it was a principle that all the body's urges have to be avoided—*omne corpus fugiendum*—and the positive evaluation of the body presupposed by Christian understanding of creation and incarnation, not to mention the hope of individuality surviving death formulated as 'resurrection', seemed to him irreconcilable with a Platonic ethic and metaphysic.

Ancient authors, both pagan and Christian, generally assume that sacred texts bear an inner or allegorical meaning beyond the literal sense. Homer and Plato were understood to carry spiritual meanings lying hidden in texts that seemed to be about something else. Learned Jews allegorized the Israelite conquest of Canaan to mean the soul's conflict with the passions. Christians saw in the Old Testament both the prophets' vision of an extension of God's kingdom to the Gentile world and also a number of texts, in the law as well as in the prophets, which provided a clue to the redemptive work of Jesus.

There was a problem with allegory, namely that exegetes could differ widely in the meaning to be found in the text. Critics of Origen, whose biblical commentaries and homilies contain noble allegories of deep religious feeling, accused his method of being hopelessly subjective, 'mere divination'. It followed that allegorical interpretation of scripture could not be of much use in the settling of disagreements about the meaning of the Bible. Yet the Christian reading of the Old Testament, and of the Apocalypse of John of Patmos, was substantially dependent on insights concerning the inner meaning of the prophets.

In the books which by the time of Irenaeus (*c.*180) were becoming the New Testament there were difficult problems of interpretation, notably in the Pauline epistles in which 'there are some things hard to understand, which the ignorant and unstable twist to their own destruction as they do the other scriptures' (2 Pet. 3: 16).

Critics of Origen's interpretations were made particularly anxious by some of the meanings that he found which seemed too Platonic, especially his conviction that divine punishment is and will be therapy, not ultimately retributive. The total depravity of fallen humanity and indeed of fallen angels led by Satan was for him a gnostic doctrine. 'A totally wicked being could not be censured, only pitied as a poor wretch' (*Comm. on John* 20. 28). The salvability of the fallen angel called Lucifer or the devil alarmed those described by Clement of Alexandria as 'the orthodox'. For both Clement and Origen divine love and freedom of choice in all rational beings were ultimate principles. They therefore regarded the believing soul's state after death as an intermediate purification to make the believer fit for God's presence. Except for Gregory of Nyssa late in the fourth century that view seemed controversial to Greeks. In the Latin west Augustine of Hippo criticized Origen's universalism as holding 'long periods of real misery punctuated by short periods of illusory bliss' (*City of God* 12. 20). Nevertheless he himself realized that Paul's words about purging by fire (1 Cor. 3) stated an idea not far distant.

3

THE ROOTS OF DIVERGENCE

In Christian history the most intractable of all splits, especially because the early churches were associated with particular cities and locations, has been and is now that between the Greek east and the Latin west, each having a considerable diaspora today in territory associated with the other. To that split a multitude of factors, theological and non-theological, have contributed, and the roots can be discerned as early as the apostolic age. There was a difference between (a) those who understood the Church of Jesus' disciples to have its centre located in Jerusalem, where the community of believers, ethnically Jewish and continuing in observance of the Mosaic law, was led by members of the family of Jesus, perhaps in uneasy cooperation with the apostles, and (b) those who came to think of the Church, with St Paul, as a worldwide body largely consisting of Gentiles. For Paul and his Gentile converts it would be natural to think of the community in Rome, the Gentile capital, as a focus of authority parallel to that of Jerusalem. To keep Gentile and Jewish believers in one communion and fellowship was at no stage easy. St Matthew's gospel was evidently written for a largely Jewish Christian community, asserting its continuity with central traditions of Judaism, Jesus as the new Moses, the Messiah who has come and who therefore, in accordance with Isaiah's prophecies, includes the Gentiles in his kingdom. Yet that inclusion created uncomfortable relations with the scribes and Pharisees. In the epistle to the Ephesians, which is more an encyclical than a letter to one place, an early disciple of the apostle saw that the unity of this apparently heterogeneous society required an ecclesiology which took account both of the historical transmission of the faith from Jesus and the apostles and also of the prophetic or charismatic calling of a universal Church. That letter must soon have seemed an unrealistic dream.

In Paul's lifetime the collection of money which he organized among his new Gentile churches for the support of the impoverished believers at Jerusalem was intended to bond the solidarity between Gentile and Jewish Christians. The apostle had to beg the Roman Christians to intercede to God on his behalf that on arrival in Judaea he might be delivered from the unbelievers and that the 'saints' of the Church in Jerusalem would be willing to

accept the money (Rom. 15: 30–1). The chances that they might refuse it
were evidently high.

A substantial source of difficulty between Jewish and Gentile Christians
long remained the question whether Gentile believers had a duty or only an
optional right to observe Jewish ceremonies and feasts in the same way as
Jewish believers; or whether such observances implied recognition of the
permanently binding authority of the Mosaic law which, in the judgement
of the apostle Paul, was a grave error at least for Gentiles. Common meals for
Jews and Gentiles together could cause tensions. In the early stages of the
Gentile mission the most conciliatory course was no doubt that followed by
the apostle Peter when he was criticized by Paul for his compromises at
Antioch (Gal. 2: 11–12). Justin Martyr in the second century could regard
Jewish believers as in order if they kept traditional Jewish customs, but that
was not a unanimous view among the Gentile members of the Church.

The earliest Christian generations at least were undivided by language:
they spoke and wrote in Greek, the common tongue of the eastern
Mediterranean world, though in Jerusalem Paul (a Jew of the Dispersion)
would surprise a Roman army officer by his ability to speak Greek (Acts 21:
37). The scriptures used by the Christians consisted of the Alexandrian or
Septuagint version, which included books read in Greek-speaking synagogues but not in Aramaic-speaking communities in Palestine.

For a substantial period there was not a serious divergence of language
between eastern and western Christians. In 200 Tertullian in north Africa
was pioneering the writing of Latin theology, but was simultaneously publishing in Greek. By the middle of the third century Latin became the pre-
dominant speech of western Christians, but there long remained Greek
colonies at Rome, Carthage, the Rhône valley, and even Spain. Some in
South Italy and Sicily remained Greek-speaking for a millennium; refugees
from Persian and Arab attacks greatly increased the Greek-speaking population in the west in the sixth and seventh centuries.

Easter

Mid-second-century discussions between Asia Minor and Rome about the
correct way to calculate the date of Easter were partly caused by a difference
between those who took the festival to be commemorating the Passion and
those who were celebrating the anniversary of the Resurrection, but partly
also reflected a consciousness in Asia Minor that they were keeping the original custom by having their memorial on the day of the Jewish Passover. At
Rome the custom of celebrating the risen Lord on the first Sunday after the
full moon after the spring equinox was so established as to seem to have been
originated by St Peter and St Paul. The presence of Christians from Asia

Minor within the Roman community would have made the issue locally contentious, and about 190 Pope Victor proclaimed that dissent from the date for Roman Easter meant separation from the communion of the Roman see and of the common fellowship. What seemed autocratic to Smyrna was pastoral necessity at Rome. But for Victor it was not a merely local problem. As incumbent of the Church of Peter and Paul, had he not a right and a duty to speak for all his brethren and to prescribe for the universal Church? Nothing is more divisive than the observance of different calendars.

In the fifth century the church historian Socrates (5. 20–1) commented on the diversity of practice in different places, and thought that since the Saviour and his apostles had left no command to observe festivals, variety was to be expected and no sign of ill health in the churches. Polycarp of Smyrna and Anicetus of Rome would agree to differ without breach of communion. The traditions of Asia Minor and of Rome were both claimed to be apostolic in origin. Socrates judged a single date for Easter to be among the unnecessary things mentioned in the apostolic decree of Acts 15: 28. He thought well of a decision made by the Novatianist communities in Phrygia to allow freedom to individual churches.

Pope Victor in the second century took a different view, as did also the emperor Constantine at the Council of Nicaea in 325, regarding different dates in the Church calendar as potentially dangerous and divisive. The principal voice for peace and for the allowing of diversity was that of Irenaeus, who frankly regretted the Roman desire for uniformity. Disagreement was not only about the date of Easter but also about the length of the preceding fast (later to become Holy Week then Lent). Irenaeus boldly (or blandly) wrote that the very fact of 'difference concerning the fast enhances the unanimity of faith' (Eusebius, *HE* 5. 24. 13). Roman wish for uniformity also upset Cyprian's eastern correspondent Firmilian bishop of Caesarea (Cappadocia), who saw no reason to impose a single liturgical form on a diversity of churches.

Rome as Linchpin

The first epistle of Clement in the name of the Roman Church to the Christians of Corinth, Polycarp's journey to Rome to discuss the differing dates of Easter, and the testimony of Irenaeus to the expectation of other churches that the Roman community and its bishops would provide primacy of leadership in the struggle against gnostic or other heresy, all illustrate the point that this local church, with its resources and possession of the bones of the martyred apostles Peter and Paul, rapidly came to offer a linchpin of coherence. This expectation of leadership long antedated appeals to biblical texts such as the Petrine commission of Matt. 16: 16–18, which first appear in the middle of the third century in sharp exchanges between Cyprian of Carthage and Stephen of Rome.

The erection of memorials to Peter in the necropolis on the *mons Vaticanus*, to Paul on the road to Ostia, on the sites where their basilicas now stand, that for Peter constructed in or about the year 165, strengthened the consciousness of the Roman community: their leadership in an empire-wide Church depended not upon the secular dignity of their great city so much as on the religious treasury of their heroes' tombs.

In the third century Cyprian's flat rejection of Stephen's judgement, that baptism given outside the Catholic Church in water and in the name of the holy Trinity should not be repeated when those so baptized seek reconciliation with the one Catholic Church, received support from the Greek east. Firmilian bishop of Caesarea, metropolis of Cappadocia, could assure Cyprian that since Rome's liturgical customs differed from those found at Jerusalem, they could not be imposed as the one and only apostolic tradition. The Donatist schism in fourth-century north Africa gave Rome in 313 the opening to make it a condition of communion with the Catholic congregations at Carthage and Roman Africa that Cyprian's theology of baptism was abandoned. So it came about that the eventual victory of the Roman view bequeathed the crucial legacy that, unlike the churches of the Greek east, western tradition has found it easier to acknowledge, if not all sacraments, at least the baptism of Christians given in true faith in separated ecclesial communities.

There is here a latent connection with the observation that the Orthodox east thinks instinctively and naturally of the Church on earth as a mirror of an unchanging worship of the Lord in heaven, whereas the western Church contains within its bloodstream a strong sense of movement and change in the struggle, under divine grace, to realize the unity of the people of God.

Divergences between east and west may go deep without being divisive. No other division has seemed easier to heal and yet has been in experience more recalcitrant to all attempts at reconciliation. In part the divergence between east and west has pre-Christian roots. Romans and Greeks in antiquity were conscious of tensions, Romans feeling inferior to the Greek classical philosophers in the clarification of ethical questions, but vastly superior in war, government, and law.

Romans despised the people of Egypt and Syria for effeminacy and excessive luxury. In battle the legionaries were assured by their generals that they were superior to 'Cilicians, Syrians, Jews, and Egyptians' (Dio Cassius 71. 25. 1). In the late fourth century the *Historia Augusta* enjoyed snide disparagements of Syrians and Jews. It was a long tradition reproduced by the crusaders (William of Tyre 22. 15).[1]

[1] A demonstration of this background has been made by Professor Benjamin Isaac, *The Near East under Roman Rule* (Leiden, 1998), ch. 18.

Some Romans thought Greeks, especially if trained philosophers, too clever by half; echoes of such ancient prejudices surface as late as the letters of Pope Gregory the Great (590–604).[2] Gregory on returning to Rome after his time as apocrisiary or nuncio to the emperor at Constantinople found himself criticized by laity for using the Greek 'Kyrie eleison, Christe eleison, Kyrie eleison'. He defended this by the argument that Greek custom was not to mention Christ in the second petition.[3]

In the ninth century the patriarch Photius, who endured much from western barbs, commented in one letter (85) that the old pagan west worshipped gluttony and sex, not intelligence and technical achievement. He was suggesting that this still contained truth.

An additional factor contributing to the divergence between Greek east and Latin west was memory of the past. To Latins the history of the Roman Republic with its great soldiers and writers was constitutive of their identity. For the Greeks the classical past was located in stories told by Homer, Herodotus and Thucydides—authors who, as Josephus once astringently observed (*c. Apion.* 1. 66), never mention Rome. Greeks did not forget that they had invented philosophy with Plato, Aristotle, Stoics, Sceptics, and Epicureans, whom Latins could merely echo, and that the same held for epic poetry, tragedy, and comedy. For Greek-speakers in the eastern Mediterranean provinces, strong Roman power arrived with Pompey, Julius Caesar, and Augustus' empire imposing bureaucracy and law.

In the sixth century AD under Justinian the civil servant John Lydus at Constantinople could take it for granted that the empire which he served began with Aeneas, while the Antiochene Greek chronicler Malalas looked back to Romulus and Remus. But by the sixth century the Roman empire's centre of gravity was in the east, and the people called themselves *Rhomaioi*, their territory Romania. The titles of almost all important officers of state were transliterations of Latin words. John Lydus even knew an oracle predicting that if ever the east Roman capital of New Rome lost the knowledge and use of Latin, the empire would fall (*De magistratibus* 2. 12, repeated 3. 42). The west, though in law and administration Latin-speaking, consisted in Lydus' time of separate barbarian kingdoms formed by Germanic invaders. They did not think of themselves as Romans unless they happened to live in Rome. Wherever they lived in the empire, Jews did not think of themselves as Romans.

---

[2] S. Jeffrey Richards, *Consul of God* (1980), following E. Caspar, *Geschichte des Papsttums* (Tübingen, 1933), ii. 347–8.

[3] *Reg.* 9. 26 to John bishop of Syracuse.

Beards

Curiously a social difference between some Greeks and some Romans would survive from the age of the Roman Republic to provide abrasions between the Greek and Latin churches. In the first century before Christ Cicero (*Pro Caelio* 33) regarded beards as indicating Greek culture; philosophical tutors had beards (Epictetus 3. 1. 24). Early in the second century in the Greek orator Dio of Prusa (36. 17) and in Apollonius of Tyana (*ep.* 63), to be clean-shaven was effeminate. The philosopher-emperor Marcus Aurelius could have an impressive beard, reported by Herodian (5. 2. 3–4) and Julian (317 c), but Caracalla appearing clean-shaven at Antioch was thought less than heroic (Dio Cassius 78. 20). Late in the fourth century Jerome (*in Isai.* 3. 7. 21–2, p. 115 Vallarsi) felt it worthy of note that the Gothic tribesmen invading the Balkans were clean-shaven; not what he expected. Beards were a sign of virility. But unkempt beards could provoke comment, and at Antioch the emperor Julian's provoked mockery answered in his embarrassing *Misopogon* (the Beard-Hater).

Jerome's attack on Jovinian, a monk and priest, declared that the only difference between Jovinian and a goat was that he shaved off his beard (2. 21). This is the earliest evidence for the custom with western clergy. Those who felt that a beard added dignity and authority wanted priests to keep their beards, and this was included among the rulings in the *Statuta Ecclesiae Antiqua* produced by a fifth-century canonist in southern Gaul, repeated by a synod at Barcelona in 540. These rulings, however, imply that shaving had become normal in the Latin Church.

In the Greek east the sixth and seventh centuries appear to have been the period after which clergy and monks became expected to be bearded, and by the tenth century the custom had become a painful issue in disputes between the Greek and Latin churches. In the eleventh century Sardinian clergy failing to remove their beards were threatened by Pope Gregory VII with confiscation of property (*ep.* 8. 10). He was perhaps a pope for whom what was not forbidden was compulsory; such a matter could not be left to personal discretion. Early in the thirteenth century in Calabria, where Greek and Latin clergy existed side by side, Joachim of Fiore suggested that their difference was prefigured in scripture by hairy Esau and smooth Jacob.[4]

---

[4] On beards in the Middle Ages see Giles Constable and R. B. C. Huygens in *Apologiae duae* (Corpus Christianorum, Cont. Med. 62). See also the article 'Barbe' in *Dict. d'arch. chr. et de liturgie*, ii/1 (Paris, 1910), 478–93 and P. Hofmeister, 'Der Streit um des Priesters Bart', *Zeitschrift für Kirchengeschichte*, 62 (1943–4), 72–94.

4

DIFFERENCES IN THEOLOGY

There soon developed causes of distrust which were more theological and technical, evident in the letters of Bishop Ignatius of Antioch.

After the churches of the west became predominantly Latin-speaking there began to be difficulties about establishing equivalent terms. Tertullian first created the vocabulary for the Latin theologians, e.g. terms such as *Trinitas*, or 'three persons in one substance'. He derived the word *persona* from interpretation of biblical texts such as Psalm 2, allocating different verses of the psalm to the Father and the Son respectively. At the same time Tertullian was concerned to insist that the Son is one with but not identical with the Father, and thereby bequeathed a nest of problems about identity and difference which were also discussed by Platonic philosophers expounding the *Parmenides* of Plato.

The doctrine that Father, Son, and Holy Spirit are different adjectives for describing aspects of the one God was advocated in the third century, especially by a Roman presbyter named Sabellius who, despite his obscurity, gave his name to this interpretation of trinitarian language. He was opposing the more pluralistic language of writers such as Justin Martyr or Hippolytus who spoke of the Word and Son of God as distinct from the Father—Justin said 'numerically distinct'. In the third century Origen wrote of the Father and Son as one in power but 'two in hypostasis'. The bishops at the Council of Nicaea in 325 were made apprehensive by such expressions, and to their creed appended an anathema on the notion that the Son is of 'a different *ousia* or hypostasis' from the Father. For admirers of Origen such as Eusebius of Caesarea (in his letter to his church cited by Athanasius) this anathema required careful and subtle exegesis to make it acceptable. Throughout the Arian controversy of the fourth century many Greek bishops suspected the west, especially Rome, of being either Sabellian or defenceless against that view; the 'one substance' of Tertullian came into Greek as 'one hypostasis'. On the other hand, the plurality of hypostases of many Greek theologians sounded to Latins like rank tritheism. Distrust was bred and lasted long.

Nevertheless the contrast cannot be made simply into an antithesis between east and west in the ancient period. Marcellus of Ankyra (Ankara) was a Greek with deep reservations about the doctrine of Origen and his pluralistic way of thinking about Father, Son, and Spirit. And Marcellus received a degree of sympathy from Athanasius, though he was not an avowed critic of Origen in the way that Marcellus was.

First Council of Nicaea (325)

Episcopal congratulations to Constantine on the accession of a Christian emperor together with disagreements about the calculation of the date of Easter and the conflagration caused by opinions of the Alexandrian presbyter Arius led to the calling of a large, multi-provincial synod in the early summer of 325, which was transferred by Constantine from Ankyra to the beautiful lakeside city of Nicaea. Representatives attending from the west were few but influential. They included the bishop of Carthage and two presbyters sent by Pope Silvester, who had been kept in touch with the doctrinal quarrel by Alexander bishop of Alexandria, and by Ossius (or Hosios) bishop of Corduba, already used by the emperor as a trouble-shooter in the Alexandrian dispute and its sharp repercussions at Antioch in Syria. Arius eased the task of the council's steering committee by a declaration that the alternative to his theology ended in the (to him) absurd notion that the Son of God is of one being with the Father, *homoousios*, 'of one substance'. The drafters of the council's creed seized on this term to express orthodoxy; the term had precedents in orthodox writers. The affirmation of identity of being in Father and Son, with an anathema censuring differentiation of *ousia* or hypostasis in God, was hard for theologians who admired Origen. It proved more congenial to west than to east. In 325 urgent questions about the Holy Spirit had not yet been raised; so the third article of the Nicene creed simply affirmed belief 'in the Holy Spirit', with no words about 'proceeding from the Father'. The creed, adapted with anti-Arian words, originated in the baptismal confession of the Church in Jerusalem.

Although the Nicene creed enjoyed so little currency in the Latin west that Hilary of Poitiers could be bishop for some years before hearing about it, it was sympathetically received in Rome. 'Of one substance' was in Tertullian.[1] Defenders of the Nicene creed against supporters of Arius, notably Marcellus of Ankyra, were welcomed there. The Greek east, more sophisticated than the west in intricate theological questions, saw with some reason that the creed of 325 provided no defences against the modalist or Sabellian view that Father, Son, and Spirit are adjectival terms to the substantive term God.[2] Distrust between east and west was rapidly engendered,

---

[1] Tertullian, *Adversus Praxean* 4 (the Son is 'de substantia patris'), and 13 ('unius substantiae'). Against the view that this inspired the Nicene creed see J. Ulrich, *Die Anfänge der abendländischen Rezeption des Nizänums* (Berlin, 1994).

[2] The point is conceded by Hilary of Poitiers, *De synodis* 68.

and was exacerbated when Athanasius of Alexandria, exiled to Trier by Constantine in 335 (for no doctrinal cause), was able to exploit Rome's distrust of the Greek east, identifying his own cause with opposition to the supporters and friends of Arius.

The Arian Controversy. Serdica

In the fourth century the controversy provoked by the Alexandrian presbyter Arius (d. 336) made his bishop Athanasius (328–73) central to the events. Constantine's decision to exile Athanasius to Trier, where he found a sympathetic reception, transformed a Greek controversy into a conflict between east and west. In 340 Pope Julius I (336–52) received to communion, apparently on the confession of the simple Roman baptismal creed (parent of the so-called Apostles' Creed), not only Athanasius, against whom no charge of unorthodoxy was raised, but also Marcellus bishop of Ankyra, whose trinitarian theology seemed unitarian to Greek churches. After Constantine's death (22 May 337) his eldest son Constantine II sent Athanasius back to Alexandria, but riots in the city (notorious in antiquity for its disorderly mob) made him flee to Rome.

Julius took it for granted that the see of Rome had the right to be consulted about both Athanasius and Marcellus, whatever Greek synods might have decreed. Athanasius could argue that his accusers at the council of Tyre in 335 had been heretical Arians and therefore disqualified from sitting in judgement. Julius' claim to be judge of his appeal precipitated dispute with Greek bishops, who held their synodical judgement to be binding and not subject to review by a western bishop, even of so distinguished a city, asserting (they complained) a dictatorial primatial authority over the whole Church, not the old tradition.

The threat of schism between Greek east and Latin west led the emperors Constans, governing the western provinces, and his elder brother Constantius, governing the east, to summon a synod at Serdica (modern Sofia) in 342 or 343. Constans had eliminated the eldest of Constantine's three sons in 340, and was putting pressure on Constantius, whom he was coming to think superfluous in government. Constans was going to support Julius and Athanasius.

At Serdica the emperors got the fiasco they intended to avert. West and east cursed one another. A major issue was Rome's appellate jurisdiction. Canon 5 of Nicaea (325) ruled that, if an individual bishop were accused by a brother bishop, a provincial synod should decide, without any bishop from outside the province. The exclusion of an external bishop was soon modified in a canon of Antioch, but from a unanimous decision there could be no further appeal. At Serdica the Greek bishops expressly set aside the apparently

Roman notion of a tyrannical dictatorship over the Church (*principatus eccle-siae*), abhorrent to the 'old custom of the Church' in usurping conciliar authority (CSEL 65. 65).

Western bishops, led by Ossius of Corduba, instinctively looked to Rome as an arbiter in disputes. 'To honour the memory of the most holy apostle Peter', they ruled that if a censured bishop appeals, those who judged him are to refer the case to the bishop of Rome, who, if he thinks reconsideration needed, shall refer the matter to bishops from a nearby province. The west-ern canon did not expect Rome to exercise a monarchical or imperial power, but maintained the understanding that an appeal from a synodical decision should be referred to another synod.

Nicene and Serdican Canons: A Sharp Contention

The sixth canon of the Council of Nicaea in 325 affirmed the jurisdiction of the see of Alexandria over all provinces of Egypt and Libya, which Libyan bishops disliked. The canon cited the analogy of Rome and Antioch having jurisdiction over several provinces. Rome, Alexandria, Antioch was the cus-tomary order of precedence of great cities of the empire. In the fifth century and later canonists in the Roman chancery did not want the implication that papal ecclesiastical authority was bestowed by conciliar canon law rather than by succession from St Peter, and altered the opening sentence to say that 'Rome has always had the primacy.'

In the Roman chancery the Serdican canons were added to the twenty canons of Nicaea without indicating a distinct source. Whether this was an accident in transmission or deliberate to meet the view held by e.g. Innocent I that the papacy recognizes the authority only of Nicene canons is undecid-able. Difficulties arose between Carthage and Rome in 419 when Pope Zosimus cited two Serdican canons as possessing Nicene authority. Consequent exchanges of information between Carthage and Alexandria enabled the African bishops, anxious to affirm their autonomy in relation to the Roman see, to correct Zosimus, and also provided the Alexandrian patri-archate with Serdican material. The Serdican canons in Greek did not enter Greek collections until the sixth century.

The mistake of the Roman chancery in attributing Nicene authority to canons coming from less august assemblies is explicable. Some manuscripts of early western canons actually attest the Nicene and Serdican canons together without a break. In one letter (*ep. extra coll.* 14 ed. Zelzer, CSEL 82. 263 = M63. 64)[3] Ambrose cites as 'Nicene' a canon of the Council of

---

[3] Ambrose's letters are cited from Zelzer, CSEL 82–5, with M the old number as in PL.

Neocaesarea (canon 7); the context being controversy whether or not a married man (incidentally rich) could be a bishop.

The eastern bishops at Serdica resented the charge of heresy. The following year an eastern synod sent a long statement of faith to the west, disowning the accusation of teaching a tritheism implicit in their affirmation of 'three hypostases' in God. Disagreement about the Trinity and Roman primacy foreshadowed coming splits. In the east the western canons about Roman appellate jurisdiction were understood to refer to the Latin patriarchate, not to the east.

Pope Damasus

At Rome Pope Damasus (366–84) inherited a church divided by faction. During Liberius' exile Rome had had a bishop Felix, and on Liberius' return some of his followers were not easily reconciled. Damasus faced a rival bishop Ursinus consecrated a few days before him, and Ursinus' supporters accused Damasus of being 'successor to Felix' as a source of dissension. Fighting caused over a hundred and thirty deaths when Damasus' supporters attacked those of Ursinus. The city prefect expelled Ursinus, but there remained those who held Damasus responsible for the massacre. Moreover a Reform anti-Arian group did not forgive him for maintaining Liberius' conciliatory policy towards bishops who at Ariminum in 359 had signed away adherence to the Nicene creed.

Pope Damasus was aware that the sovereign jurisdiction over the western churches associated with his see by the west was not immediately acknowledged in the east. The schism at Antioch, especially the tension between Paulinus, recognized at Rome and Alexandria, and Meletius, recognized by the Cappadocians, created explosive difficulties in the correspondence between Basil of Caesarea and Damasus. Damasus' consciousness of the sacredness of the Roman Church and see was reflected in the adornment and verse inscriptions which he placed at the shrines of Rome's martyrs. At the shrine of both Peter and Paul by the third milestone on the Via Appia (now San Sebastiano) he acknowledged that the apostles had come from the Greek world, but Rome's possession of their bones now imparted superior authority to the capital. His letter to the bishops in Gaul stressed his opposition to *diversitates* whether in faith or in practice. Unity of faith for him required uniformity of expression. This public face of consistency was for him a sign of the holiness of his Church. He was 'episcopus ecclesiae sanctae' presiding over a 'plebs sancta' with a primacy assured by the very presence of St Peter as patron and guardian.

Damasus was well supported from Milan by Ambrose, and returned this loyalty. Ambrose's family had an emotional attachment to Pope Liberius, whose surrender of communion with Athanasius and softness towards signatories at the Council of Ariminum would not have taught Ambrose to be a hardliner. Damasus probably taught him that opposing Auxentius and then his friends required a less tolerant stand for the Nicene position.

Constans' death in 350 made possible the rise to sole power of Constantius, whose advisers in church matters regarded the Nicene creed and Athanasius of Alexandria with distrust. His distrust of Athanasius was enhanced by the belief that he had had treasonable correspondence with the western usurper Magnentius. Constantius was persuaded that in the creed 'identity of essence' was dangerous and that 'the same' should be replaced by 'like'. To demonstrate the unity of Greek east and Latin west he called two parallel complementary synods in 359 to meet at Ariminum (Rimini) and Seleucia in Isauria (Silifke). By skilful operations the support for the Nicene creed was sidelined, and the universal confession of faith to be accepted by both Latins and Greeks said no more than that the Son is like the Father. The story would later provoke Ambrose of Milan to the comment that in this controversy the true faith had been more faithfully preserved by the laity than by bishops (*in Ps. 118*, 17. 18). John Henry Newman famously echoed this.

Pope Liberius (352–66) had yielded ground to the emperor Constantius, assenting to the condemnation of Athanasius and even to a less than Nicene confession of faith. He accepted communion with Auxentius of Milan, no friend to the Nicene creed. His successor Damasus, elected in 366 after a passionate and bloody dispute between rival factions, reaffirmed the authority of the Nicene creed, but faced the difficulty that the bishop of Milan, Auxentius, close to the emperor's residence, tenaciously upheld the formula of Ariminum to his death in 374 when he was astonishingly succeeded by Ambrose, the provincial governor who came to keep order between rival factions for and against the Nicene creed. Gradually Ambrose succeeded in getting anti-Nicene bishops marginalized in north Italy and Illyricum, and insisted that, without any adopting of Roman liturgical customs by other churches, communion with Peter's see was a hallmark of catholicity. In a sermon on Ps. 40 (CSEL 64. 250. 19) he followed the text of Matt. 16: 18 with the words 'Where Peter is, there is the Church.' The Apostles' Creed had been faithfully guarded by the Roman Church (*Ep. ex. coll.* 15 = M42, CSEL 82/3. 305. 51). By eschewing all additions to this creed, it could be a formula of reconciliation between contending factions at Milan, since its content was pre-controversial.

At Milan the creed learnt by catechumens before baptism was a simple western formula, identical with that used at Rome. Terms from the Nicene creed entered only as glosses in the bishop's preparatory homilies in the time of Ambrose. No doubt his predecessor Auxentius, no admirer of Athanasius and upholding the Likeness formula of the Council of Ariminum, followed the same method but with different glosses. However, at Milan Auxentius was confronted by a vehement Nicene group refusing communion at his hands, and this group enjoyed external encouragement especially from Bishop Filastrius at nearby Brescia. Riots occurred. Gallic synods and Pope Damasus supported this minority. When the see fell vacant by death, and factional disorder broke out at the cathedral, the choice of the governor Ambrose seemed divine. The *plebs*, inspired (some said) by a child whose voice, as often for ancient people, was an oracle, shouted for Ambrose himself to be their bishop. Hitherto unbaptized, he reluctantly yielded with the permission of the prefect and the emperor Valentinian I, who notoriously refused to take sides in church disputes. Ambrose could represent a similar neutrality, and probably to the horror of ultra-Nicenes recognized the clergy ordained and formed by his predecessor provided that they held communion with him. This averted hostility from a majority group. Gradually, however, Ambrose's pro-Nicene sympathies could become more evident, especially after Valentinian I's death a year later. The new western emperor Gratian was cautiously and at first hesitantly sympathetic to him. Naturally the more open Ambrose became in his hostility to the Likeness formula, the sharper became the antagonism in Milan of those who preferred the more 'broad church' term, supported at the palace by Justina, Valentinian I's widow, and soon by a rival bishop in the city.

5

EMPEROR THEODOSIUS:
COUNCIL OF CONSTANTINOPLE (381)

Imperial authority played a major role in the course and the outcome of the Arian controversy. The catastrophic defeat of the Roman army by the Goths at Adrianople in August 378, with the death of the emperor Valens, made possible the advent to power of Theodosius from the west, determined to bring order and Nicene orthodoxy as upheld by the Roman see. Gratian accepted him as partner, probably reluctantly. At least they saw eye to eye on the Church. An edict of 28 February 380, *Cunctos populos*, commanded all to practise 'that religion which the divine Peter the apostle transmitted to the Romans' and which was now taught by Damasus bishop of Rome and Peter bishop of Alexandria.

The policy announced was essentially western, particularly in its implication that among the competing bishops of Antioch the rightful incumbent was Paulinus, recognized by Rome and Alexandria and intransigent for one hypostasis and the Nicene 'consubstantial'. Theodosius soon learnt that the majority of Greek bishops regarded Paulinus' language (a single hypostasis) as dangerous and heretical, and that if he was to get support for a council to affirm the Nicene faith, he must give the presidency to Meletius of Antioch, with whom the great Cappadocians (Basil, Gregory of Nyssa, and Gregory of Nazianzos) were in alliance. In 379 Meletius had presided over a council at Antioch at which a confession of faith was approved with clauses from the old Roman creed inserted in a slightly modified form of the creed of Nicaea (325) and with assertions of the equality of the Holy Spirit with Father and Son. This was probably the document that became the creed of the Council of Constantinople in 381, perhaps used at Nectarius' baptism before consecration as bishop.

Theodosius' support for the pro-Nicene cause strengthened the hand of Ambrose, who moved decisively to the position that the Council of Nicaea was sanctified by being attended by the sacred number of 318 bishops, the number of Abraham's servants and in Greek numerals symbolizing the cross of Jesus (*TIH*). So it ranked above all other councils such as Ariminum. Therefore its anti-Arian decisions were not open to free discussion but must be accepted by all who did not wish to be labelled Arian; the Nicene creed was an irreversible confession of faith. In 380 Ambrose presented Gratian with an intellectually unimpressive defence of the Nicene position (*De Fide*), designed to assure the emperor of the link between orthodoxy and military victory against the invading Goths and to prevent him making concessions to anti-Nicene opponents in Illyricum whose geographical location put them in the front line of barbarian attack after the disintegration of the Danube frontier defences. Gratian needed support from these Goths to repel Huns.

The Councils of Constantinople and Aquileia (381)

With both emperors, Gratian and Theodosius, reasonably sympathetic to the Nicene cause (neither being intransigent for hard-line interpretations), it seemed desirable to reassert its authority by some general council. Gratian decided to hold one at Aquileia to which both western and eastern bishops would be summoned; but independently Theodosius decided to call one for the Greek bishops at Constantinople, and the latter met a few months before the assembly at Aquileia in 381. Probably there was some rivalry between the two emperors in this matter.

Because of Theodosius' action the original plan for Aquileia was abandoned. Gratian had to relax his summons by inviting bishops to attend at Aquileia without any being required to come. One notable attendant at Aquileia was Evagrius, Paulinus' supporter at Antioch. Ambrose was able to mobilize sufficient Nicene support to use the Council at Aquileia to exclude from communion bishops in the Balkans tenacious in their adherence to the Likeness formula of Ariminum. The Balkan bishops resented Ambrose's autocratic style in managing the council and probably ignored the dictatorial decisions of Aquileia. For them the anti-Nicene Gothic missionary bishop Ulfila was their hero, and he had been explicit in regarding the Nicene creed's *homoousios* as guilty of fatally confusing the Father and the Son. For Ambrose the Nicene orthodoxy which he associated with the Roman see was vindicated by the evident fact that the barbarian Goths had poured into the Arian Balkans but not into mainly Nicene Italy.

The Balkan bishops roughly handled at Aquileia by Ambrose expressed confidence that their position would get support in the east. The claim is strange when one recalls that in May–June of the same year Theodosius' policy of requiring communion with Rome and Alexandria was silently modified at his Council of Constantinople only to require assent to the Nicene formula, expelling those who could not sign. About 377 Damasus had issued a list of censured doctrines, prominently condemning Apollinaris' denial that Christ possessed a human mind, a censure probably made at the request of Paulinus of Antioch. That could have announced a greater intolerance than Theodosius wanted. Damasus is not known to have been invited to send legates to Constantinople for the council and was not officially represented, though Gregory of Nazianzos vainly pleaded with the council to risk no breach with Rome and the west. The council's anti-Arian creed could be signed by Apollinarians and other dissidents Theodosius wished to reconcile. Its target was either Arians rejecting 'identical in being with the Father' or those who denied the deity of the Holy Spirit. Athanasius had affirmed the sufficiency of the Nicene creed to exclude all heresies. Basil of Caesarea (d. probably 379) thought a supplementary expansion of its third article was necessary to make clear that the Spirit is not a creature. Gregory of Nyssa and Gregory of Nazianzos went further: the Holy Spirit is one being with the Father and the Son and 'proceeds from the Father' (John 15: 26).

Theodosius' Council of Constantinople irritated the west and Egypt by canonical decisions, especially when it affirmed the prerogatives of the see of Constantinople 'because it is New Rome', a title not new in 381 since it is commonly found in pagan writers under Constantius and Julian (e.g. his *orat.* 1. 8 C and Libanius, *orat.* 20. 4, 59. 94). Ambrose was offended by a creed which ignored Damasus' condemnation of Apollinarians—though a censure of Apollinarius was agreed—and by the presumption of a council ignoring the west. In 382 Damasus in council at Rome with Paulinus of Antioch, Epiphanius of Salamis (Cyprus), Jerome, and Acholius of Thessalonica (papal agent in Illyricum, briefly present at Theodosius' council the previous year), issued a vigorous counterblast: all precedence in the universal Church depended on the three Petrine sees, Rome, Alexandria founded by St Mark Peter's disciple, and Antioch.

That this order of precedence was derived from their normal secular ranking was set aside. Bishops of Rome hated the implication that Roman leadership depended on the secular dignity of their city rather than on the shrines and relics of Peter and (in a subordinate clause) Paul, whose apostleship to all nations, Jews and Gentiles, had apostolic and biblical sanction (Gal. 2: 1–10). Even more dangerous was the notion that Roman authority hung on the decisions of canon law in Church Councils (Serdica?) or even the rescripts of emperors who could easily suppose their rulings to possess no less binding power than canon law. The canon of Constantinople's honour was equally resented at Alexandria, long reckoned second city of the empire and, by the sixth canon of Nicaea, second see in the hierarchy after Rome. (The Council of Aquileia stressed Alexandrian dignity, marking western support.) Resentment was to affect relations between the sees of Alexandria and Constantinople for decades to come, as in the quarrel between John Chrysostom and Theophilus of Alexandria in and after 402. Pope Innocent I would support John against Theophilus in a manner which hastened his killing. Theophilus' successor, his nephew Cyril, skilfully mobilized Roman support to make possible the fall of Nestorius at Constantinople in 431 after this bishop of New Rome, an over-excitable person, had tactlessly granted audience to some Alexandrian dissidents censured by Cyril and to Pelagian sympathizers unacceptable to Rome.

In 381 there were other sources of distrust between east and west. In 379–80 Constantinople retained a bishop, Demophilus, who could not accept the Nicene creed and quietly retired when Theodosius required his assent to it. Meanwhile a dissident pro-Nicene group in the capital had been unofficially cared for by Gregory of Nazianzos, whose masterly oratory expounded a coequal consubstantial Trinity. Naturally he faced problems. Critics in the city mocked this Cappadocian outsider with a provincial accent. (Twenty years later the bishop of Gabala, a pleasant town in Syria, acquired large sums for his homilies, but was mocked for his Syrian accent.) Worse for Gregory was a split within his own little congregation. He was scorned for political ineptitude, and then failed to endear himself by discovering financial maladministration.

Meanwhile the division at Antioch between the old pro-Nicene believer Paulinus and the more recent recruit to Nicene language Meletius entailed hostility to Gregory from the Nicene bishop of Alexandria Peter, who, with Rome, recognized Paulinus not Meletius supported by Gregory. Egyptian bishops sent by Peter (who at Alexandria faced a rival Arian bishop Lucius) arrived in Constantinople to consecrate an adventurer and in Gregory's eyes charlatan, named Maximus or Hero.[1] Maximus claimed to be a Cynic philosopher (not a much-loved type, as the emperor Julian makes clear), and had written an anti-Arian tract. The rival consecration was done 'privately in Maximus' own house'.

The emperor Theodosius refused to recognize Maximus. This was not enough to help Gregory. To support his friend Basil of Caesarea he had once accepted consecration to be bishop of a wretched dusty hamlet and post-station in Cappadocia, Sasima. He had not visited the place and took no services there, but now fell foul of the canonical disapproval of episcopal translations. He could not preside over Theodosius' council to settle the Nicene question. He retired to compose a verse lament by way of auto-biography, sad that no good came from any synod.

By special inspiration, it was believed, Theodosius selected Meletius of Antioch to preside over his council designed to rally hesitant Greek bishops to Nicene orthodoxy. Meletius would posthumously enter the Roman calendar of saints, but during his lifetime was never in communion with the Roman see. He spoke of three hypostases in the one being or nature of the

---

[1] See Justin Mossay, 'Note sur Héron-Maxime', *Anal. Boll.* 100 (1982), 229–36.

one God, and that would carry many bishops who feared Paulinus' term of a single divine hypostasis. The choice implied rejection of Paulinus even though he was the Antiochene bishop in communion with Rome and Alexandria. But Meletius died during the council. Gregory of Nazianzos urged recognition of Paulinus to please the west. To the great majority of Greek bishops that seemed dangerous and impossible. They preferred for Antioch the presbyter Flavian. To Ambrose of Milan that seemed an insult to papal authority.

Hardly less problematic was a decision to ordain for Constantinople a lay officer of state, the city praetor Nectarius. He was baptized and promptly ordained bishop. He had the merit of no ecclesiastical past. It was understood that he would uphold the Nicene creed. Many laity at the capital remained averse to Nicene terminology, and there was a riot in which Nectarius' house was torched (Socrates 5. 13; Ambrose, *ep.* 74 = M40. 13).

The second canon of Nicaea in 325 had forbidden the practice of ordaining a person virtually immediately after baptism. That canon was ignored in Nectarius' case. No complaint on this score came from the west; the position of Ambrose at Milan was equally incompatible with the canon. But Ambrose did not keep silence about his opinion that the synod should have chosen Maximus the Cynic supported by the Egyptians. Saying not a word about Milanese disputes concerning his own ordination, he wrote angrily to Theodosius that, if Nectarius failed to stand down, he saw no way of maintaining communion between east and west. That was a huge threat of actual schism, which indicates the passion and seriousness with which he reacted. Ambrose continued repeatedly to urge Maximus' claims over those of Nectarius. Evidently he had not been told when he wrote that Pope Damasus, briefed no doubt from Thessalonica, had already withdrawn all support for Maximus.

Ambrose had been educated in the liberal arts in the city of Rome during the 340s and early 350s. The family held in veneration the memory of Pope Liberius, who had given the virgin's veil to his sister Marcellina. When Damasus emerged victor in the ferocious conflict with the rival Pope Ursinus, Ambrose was clear that Damasus had been 'elected by God's verdict', an opinion strikingly confirmed when in the 370s Ursinus bid for support at Milan and the court by making common cause with Ambrose's Milanese opponents. Ambrose wrote to the emperor Gratian begging him not to allow the Roman Church, 'head of the entire Roman world and the sacrosanct faith of the apostles', to be overthrown, when this Church 'is the source of authentic communion' (*iura communionis*) to all.

When Ambrose was accused of insufficiently respecting the Greek churches, he replied that he deeply admired Athanasius because he had referred problems to the authority of the Roman see.

No Acts of the Council of Constantinople in 381 survive,[2] but the story in summary is in Gregory of Nazianzos' verse autobiography, Ambrose's letters, and the fifth-century historians Socrates and (better) Sozomen. Theodoret preserved a prickly letter from a second synod at Constantinople in 382 replying to the western barrage of criticism. This makes it certain that the council (381) claimed the title ecumenical and insisted on 'three hypostases'. The creed first attributed to the Council of 381 (probably correctly) by the bishops at Chalcedon in 451 is marked by reserve, hoping perhaps to reconcile bishops who accepted the Nicene creed but felt unable to say that the Holy Spirit is equal to the Father and the Son. Ambrose (*ep. extra coll.* 8 = M14. 4) was shocked that Apollinarians could sign the creed; and Gregory of Nazianzos thought it not free of ambiguity.

Among Greek bishops there was astonishment when Damasus summoned them to a further revising council in Rome 'as if we belonged to him'. They were of course glad to know that the doctrine of the creed was welcome in the west. But for Damasus that meant that the decisions of Nicaea enjoyed authority not merely because a consensus in the west accepted it but because and insofar as the Roman see had ratified it with Petrine authority, not because the conciliar decision had weight on its own.

Paulinus of Antioch versus Meletius

The question of recognition for Paulinus of Antioch was a crux. Pope Damasus could not be anything but cold when Theodosius had appointed the rival Nicene bishop Meletius, only lately come to orthodoxy, to preside over his great council rather than the confessor bishop long in communion with Rome and Alexandria. That decision of the emperor was imposed by the deep lack of confidence that Paulinus inspired. Disastrously he had been on cosy terms with Marcellus of Ankyra (who died about 374), who for the Origenist tradition in the east was a bogey. The Cappadocians led by Basil had deeply opposed his adherence to the doctrine of a single hypostasis in the Trinity, and interpreted the Nicene anathema very differently.

Paulinus' association with Italian bishops was strengthened by Evagrius, an ex-civil-servant who had lived for ten years with Eusebius bishop of Vercelli, exiled by Constantius for his intransigent adherence to the Nicene creed. About 370 Evagrius translated Athanasius' *Life of Antony* into Latin. In the contested papal election he supported Damasus against Ursinus and about

[2] See A. M. Ritter, *Das Konzil von Konstantinopel und sein Symbol* (Göttingen, 1965). There is historical matter in the symposium of the Orthodox Centre, Chambésy, on *La Signification et l'actualité du IIᵉ concile œcuménique pour le monde chrétien d'aujourd'hui* (Geneva, 1982). For recent controversy about the creed see R. Staats, *Das Glaubensbekenntnis von Nizäa-Konstantinopel* (Darmstadt, 1996).

373 was sent by Damasus on an unwelcome embassy to Basil of Caesarea. He was to succeed Paulinus as bishop on his death in or about 388, and would have nothing to do with Meletius' successor at Antioch, Flavian.

In 400 Theophilus bishop of Alexandria wrote to Flavian urging him to acknowledge as valid the clergy of Evagrius' little congregation: their orders had been recognized by Pope Anastasius (399–401), and there was good precedent in Ambrose's liberal decision at Milan to recognize as valid the orders conferred by his anti-Nicene predecessor Auxentius. Theophilus saw that the schism would be perpetuated by the rejection of validity in the separated group. His letter survives because early in the sixth century this in turn provided precedent for the Monophysite patriarch of Antioch Severus in his surprising opposition to hard-line members of his party wanting to insist that orders conferred by Chalcedonians were null and void.

The Revised Creed

At the Council of Constantinople in 381 the momentous revision of the creed (assuming the attribution to this council in 451 is correct) combined some of the terms of the Nicene creed of 325, especially 'of one substance', with phrases more familiar in the Roman baptismal creed, a fact which suggests a certain concern to please Rome where it did not cost much. Since the previous twenty years had seen a fairly bitter controversy in the Greek churches about the full deity of the Holy Spirit, the creed's third article set out to deny that the Holy Spirit belongs to the creaturely order, as some were saying. The Spirit 'proceeds from the Father', said the Lord (John 15: 26); the liturgical doxology, the trinitarian baptismal formula, and the inspiration of scripture all vindicated the equality of the three hypostases in the divine Trinity.

The autobiography of Gregory of Nazianzos attests a debate at the council whether the creed of Nicaea 325 was sufficiently clear and unambiguous. A reason for thinking it very possible that the Constantinopolitan creed was at least favoured, if not formally enacted, by the bishops is simply that it does not explicitly affirm the equality of the Holy Spirit in the Godhead and adopts a cautious approach, such as Basil of Caesarea would have approved had he lived to be present. The emperor Theodosius' policy was inclusive.

With Theodosius the Christian counter-culture conquered society. Originally felt to be alien in the empire, mad, bad, and dangerous to know, the Church had now merged its aspirations with *Romanitas*, Greek and Latin alike. It was no doubt sad for Theodosius that the Arian controversy was brought to an end in an atmosphere of high tension between east and west.

6

AUGUSTINE: *FILIOQUE?*

Dislike of the Nicene 'consubstantial' was not confined to parts of the Greek east. Hostility to the Nicene formula was widespread especially in Illyricum and a few places in northern Italy. Towards the end of Augustine's life (he died in 430) Christians of Arian persuasion arrived in North Africa, and he engaged in polemic against their doctrine. He had already written one of the principal western critiques of Arianism in his large work *On the Trinity*, in which he was concerned to refute snide pagan critics who thought it absurd nonsense to speak of One being also Three. Augustine knew nothing about Theodosius' Council at Constantinople in 381, and it is unlikely that anyone in the west knew much about the creed associated with that assembly (resented and in most of its canonical decisions rejected at Rome and hated at Alexandria) until it was prominently disinterred and reaffirmed by the Council of Chalcedon in 451, which needed it to prove that one could gloss the Nicene creed without 'adding' to it (which the Council of Ephesus in 431 had forbidden).[1] Augustine therefore knew of no recent authoritative formula, stamped with the majesty of an ecumenical council recognized in the west, to which someone in the east might expect him to conform when he set out to state a doctrine of the Trinity which excluded the possibility of Arian exegesis. To maintain the equality of Father, Son, and Spirit, he judged it wise to affirm that the Son participated in the Spirit's 'proceeding' from the Father. This was suggested by the Son's gift of the Holy Spirit to the apostles (John 20: 22). Augustine thought the Arians could drive a coach and horses through a doctrine of the Trinity which excluded the Son from the coming forth of the Spirit from the Father. We should therefore say that the Spirit proceeds from the Father and the Son—'from both'. Such language was not unprecedented in Greek theology. In the 330s Marcellus bishop of Ankyra (quoted by Eusebius, *Eccl. Theol.* 3. 4) had argued that Father and Son are one

---

[1] In 429–30 Cyril of Alexandria could write in a way presupposing ignorance of the creed's existence. Theodore of Mopsuestia (d. 428), however, knew a form of it (*Catech.* 9). Bishops of Alexandria regretted most of the decisions of the Council of 381 (e.g. on the see of Antioch, and on the elevation of the see of Constantinople to be second to Rome), and would not have been predisposed to acknowledge authority in anything the Council had done. The Epitome of Theodoros Anagnostes (348, p. 99 ed. Hansen) records the 'hatred' felt at Alexandria for the Council of 381; this explains why Dioscorus and the second Council of Ephesus (449) never mention it.

God because the Spirit comes from the Word as well as proceeding from the Father. The *Filioque* theme expressed the unity of the Trinity.

Augustine's *Filioque* would in time encourage among Greek theologians a keen distrust of Augustinian theology generally. The interpretation of salvation as 'deification', or the elevation of redeemed humanity to actual participation in the divine life by grace, became characteristic of Greek language. It was no less so of Augustine's. Greeks, it is true, were not comfortable with what seemed to them an excessive disparagement of fallen human nature and of 'original sin', though there again one can find in Cyril of Alexandria an estimate of human nature remarkably akin to that of Augustine.

An edge was imparted to Augustine's language by his observation that the Arian thesis of an ineradicable difference or dissimilarity between Father and Son had rested for its plausibility and power on being to all appearances a fair deduction from the language used by orthodox apologists of the Catholic tradition. To leave open the question of the Son's participation in the Spirit's procession within the Trinity therefore seemed to his mind dangerous to a degree. Moreover, there was good precedent for his language in the work on the Trinity written by the passionately anti-Arian writer, Hilary of Poitiers, for whom he had well-deserved respect.

In *De Trinitate* 15. 26. 47 Augustine concedes that the Father alone is the originating source of both the Son and the Holy Spirit. In other words, his *Filioque* is no prejudice to the monarchy of the Father. The Son is not causal of the being of the Spirit in the sense that the Father is. In Gregory Nazianzen 'procession' (*ekpóreusis*) is the given term for the coming of the Spirit from the Father, but this procession is shared by both Son and Spirit (*or.* 39. 12)

Augustine's great work on the Trinity shows his awareness of differences between Greek and Latin theology. He is the earliest writer to speak of the 'eastern church', not as a separate church but at least as a distinct entity with its own language and customs.

Augustine did not suppose the *Filioque* objectionable to Greek theologians. In the Greek churches similar language is also found in Epiphanius of Salamis and especially Cyril of Alexandria,[2] in whose writings there were as many pages devoted to anti-Arian polemic as to the Christological controversy with Nestorius and the Antiochene school of Theodore of Mopsuestia.

---

[2] Epiphanius, *Panarion* 62. 4: Cyril, *in Ev. Joh.* 2, p. 126 (PG 74. 443 B); *De ador.* 1 (PG 68. 148 A), cf. *Thesaurus* 34 (PG 75. 585 A). The formulation offensive to Theodoret is in Cyril's ninth Anathema (Theodoret, *ep.* 151, PG 83. 1417 D, accusing Cyril of holding the Spirit to be created by the Son, which Cyril certainly did not hold). However, he made no concession to his critic— though Theodoret (*ep.* 171, 1484 C) claimed that he did so; and this claim became a weapon at the council of Florence for Mark Eugenikos to ward off powerful citations of Cyril by John de Montenero OP (*Acta Latina* 220–2).

Cyril's affirmation that the Son participates in the procession of the Spirit from the Father was attacked by Theodoret, and the exchanges seem like a preview of later dissension. Cyril's language was welcome to later Greek defenders of the western *Filioque*, notably Maximus Confessor in the seventh century or patriarch John Bekkos in the thirteenth century.[3] In medieval disputes about the western *Filioque* it would be a godsend of a weapon to the Latins that Theodoret, to whom the Eastern theologians appealed, had been censured (for entirely different reasons) at the Council of Constantinople, 553.

Naturally it would be one-sided to imply that theological considerations were central to the gradual sense of alienation between east and west. 'Alienation' is too strong a term. Mutual irritation would be more accurate. Both east and west, Greek and Latin, lived within a single Mediterranean social and economic order deeply conscious of its shared high culture in contrast with the barbaric life north of the Danube or the Crimea and south of the Nile Valley or the High Atlas mountains. There was profound awareness of contrast with the un-Roman nomadic peoples of far north and deep south. But along the shipping lanes of the Mediterranean it was with interruption from Vandals a single society until the Arabs conquered north Africa and much of Spain. Throughout late antiquity and the early medieval period Rome retained a substantial Greek-speaking population.

The citizens of Constantinople felt themselves to be fully as 'Roman' as any inhabitant of the old Italian city. Modern writers for convenience call them 'Byzantines'. They called themselves 'Romans', *Rhomaioi*, and that consciousness was much enhanced by Justinian's decision to undertake a military conquest of as much as possible of the territory of the old Roman empire before the west split into different barbarian kingdoms, reinforced by the happy and much used title of Constantinople as 'New Rome'. In practice by the time of Justinian, Procopius (*Wars* 3. 4. 29) was speaking naturally of 'both empires'.

The fifth-century historian Priscus records that the east had a treaty with the Vandals which precluded any help to the west under Vandal attack (fr. 39, p. 342 Blockley).

Because of rivalry the division of the empire in 395 between Theodosius I's two sons, Arcadius in the east, Honorius in the west, had unfortunate results. Tensions developed between the emperors and the barbarian army commanders who controlled major decisions. The prefecture of Illyricum

[3] Max. Conf. PG 91. 135 A; Bekkos, PG 141. 184–484. See A. de Halleux, *Patrologie et œcuménisme* (Leuven, 1990), 367–95; Marie-Odile Boulnois, *Le Paradoxe trinitaire chez Cyrille d'Alexandrie* (Paris, 1994), 482–529; G. C. Berthold, 'Cyril of Alexandria and the *Filioque*', *Studia Patristica*, 19 (1989), 143–7, 'Maximus Confessor and the *Filioque*', *Studia Patristica*, 18/1 (1985), 113–17.

was the source of good fighting men. Under Theodosius I Greece and the Balkans as far west as Belgrade had been ruled from Constantinople. The great general Stilicho in the west (hated in the east) wanted Illyricum returned to Milan and would have succeeded if Alaric the Goth had not interfered.

In 395, the eastern provinces of Illyricum were transferred to Constantinople; although ecclesiastical jurisdiction remained with Rome, in practice it amounted to less and less as time went on. The popes preserved a façade of authority by using bishops of Thessalonica as their 'vicars' or deputies in relation to the east generally. The Council of Chalcedon in 451 took it for granted that Thrace fell under the authority of the see of Constantinople. The frontier between east and west was gradually moving nearer to the Adriatic.

During the sixth century the influx of Avars and Slavs into the Balkan region ended the life of many famous cities and disrupted ordered church structures; many bishops became refugees in Italy together with their flocks. Gregory the Great tried to restore Roman authority, conferring a pallium on the primate in the region of Iustiniana Prima (Skopje), warning him against simony and conferring of holy orders for bribes (*Reg.* 5. 16 of 594). The emperor Heraclius (610–41) invited Croats and Serbs to settle and check the Avars and Slavs. In time Croats would look to Rome for their faith, Serbs to Constantinople, Bosnians to Muslim Istanbul.

The controversy in the seventh century whether Christ had one (divine) will or two (human and divine) offered reconciliation in the Greek world between Chalcedonians and moderate Monophysites, but at the price of introducing additional estrangement between east and west. In 649 the wretched Pope Martin I attempted to assert Roman authority in the Greek realm, but suffered for his pains. The Sixth Ecumenical Council of 680–1 represented a great change in east Roman policy, the emperor needing western support to hold off Arabs to the south and Bulgarians to the north. At that council the bishop of Thessalonica signed as the Pope's representative. But little more than a decade later the so-called 'Quinisext' canons of about 692 read as an assertion of Byzantine authority; the signatories include the bishops of eastern Illyricum.

The establishment in 395 of distinct and equipollent centres of government with two uncooperating emperors in north Italy (Milan, then Ravenna) and at Constantinople had led some to think of the bishops of Old Rome and New Rome as having distinct spheres of influence, perhaps presiding over two churches which, in the aftermath of the affair over John Chrysostom, were engaged in a verbal dissension with each other. But was there more than one Catholic Church? The question underlies some remarks found in the writings of Augustine of Hippo. He observed with a polemical edge that even if there were many (local) churches, the Catholic Church, prior to all individual adherents, could not be other than one. It was a point against the Donatist schismatics of north Africa that their majority in Numidia was merely regional: Augustine's minority church was in communion with the great Church worldwide, 'the communion of the emperor' (Augustine, *En. in Ps.* 57. 15), as they were not. The authentic Church spread through the entire world was not transformed into two churches by the secular divisions of imperial governments. Nor was language a real source of division. The one Church spoke many languages beside Latin and Greek, and linguistic diversity was no ground for breach of communion.[4]

The Donatists defended their position partly by asserting the holiness that is a necessary note of the authentic Church, contrasting that with the Catholic community polluted by contagion with bishops who, during the Great Persecution of 303, surrendered to the authorities Bibles and sacred vessels, but partly also by their maintenance of the orthodox doctrinal tradition and especially their careful preservation of the episcopal succession. Parmenian, Donatist bishop of Carthage, even claimed that the bishop in the true (Donatist) succession stands as the authorized mediator between God and the laity—language which Augustine regarded as 'intolerable to Christian ears', indeed 'the voice of Antichrist'. For Augustine, the voice of Christ is heard whenever the preacher proclaims the truth (*sermo* 17. 1).

Substantial elements of Augustine's argument against the Donatists were already set out by Optatus bishop of Mileu about 370 in reply to Parmenian, Donatist bishop of Carthage. Optatus already put the point that Donatists cannot be the universal Church because they are almost confined to Africa and lack communion both with the apostolic foundations of the Greek east and with the apostolic see of Peter at Rome, which possesses the *memoriae* or shrines of both Peter and Paul. Optatus is the first western writer to assert that 'Peter was superior to the other apostles and alone received the keys of the kingdom, which were distributed by him to the rest' (7. 3). Optatus owed much to Cyprian's *De Unitate*, but here used language going beyond Cyprian.

More than once Augustine used what had evidently become everyday idiom and cliché, speaking loosely of the 'eastern church' in contrast with the 'western'.[5] He even reflected a self-consciousness of the superiority of Latin Christianity when, during the Pelagian controversy, he deplored the Pelagian appeal to Greek theologians such as John Chrysostom. 'In many

---

[4] Augustine, *Conf.* 6. 4. 5 (*ecclesia unica corpus tui*); *c. ep. Parmeniani* 1. 1. 1; *ep. ad Catholicos* 13. 33; *c. Julianum* 1. 4. 14; *En. in Pss.* 147. 19, 44. 24; *Tr. in ev. Joh.* 6. 3, 32. 7; *s. Denis* 19. 11.

[5] *S.* 202. 2; *c. du. epp. Pelag.* 4. 20; *ep. Divjak* 4.

cases Greek exegetes were heretical', and so he preferred the authority of Ambrose or Cyprian.[6]

In north Africa there were people, probably found among the officers of government, who spoke and wrote of two churches side by side. Augustine absolutely rejected the notion that a plurality of authentic churches could exist not sharing a common eucharist and not recognizing each other's ministry and sacraments, as if there could be 'as many churches as there are schisms'.[7] The Donatists wholly rejected the validity of all Catholic sacraments; the issue was sharp and painful, and the opposition to mixed marriages affected families directly at a point where it hurt. Defenders of a pluralistic ecclesiology argued that the apostle Paul had written letters to several different churches. To this contention Augustine ingeniously answered that, if one counted the region of Galatia as a single church, the total number of churches receiving epistles from Paul added up to the highly symbolic number of seven, signifying completeness.[8]

Yet Augustine never understood the Church's unity to need uniformity of rites. Liturgical differences did not disturb him unless they affected the observance of high festivals.[9] (Donatists kept no feast on 6 January, and thereby illustrated the point that they were out of communion with the Church of Jerusalem.)[10] Clergy were expressly instructed not to confuse their people by introducing liturgical ceremonies which they had witnessed abroad.[11] Characteristically Augustine discerned a symbol of unity and diversity in the one Church when the Psalmist described the queen's golden robe as wrought with a variety of colours.[12] One faith was wholly compatible with diversity of expression. Augustine could also grant that 'there can be something Catholic outside the Catholic Church'.[13]

Augustine's conviction that to repel Arianism one must affirm the Son's participation in the 'procession' of the Spirit achieved a following, first in southern Gaul and Spain, where it was part of the catechism by the second half of the fifth century, and entered the Arlesian *Quicunque Vult* or 'Athanasian Creed'. At Toledo in 589, in a Spain ridding itself of an Arian past held by the Visigoths, the *Filioque* was prominent in the confession of faith accepted by the king Reccared and the Visigoth aristocracy. The Visigoth bishops all renounced Arianism.

In the Pelagian controversy the acquittal of Pelagius at the Palestinian synod of Diospolis and the appeal of his critics to Greek authorities could not have increased Augustine's admiration for the eastern churches. Jerome at Bethlehem did not convey to the west a friendly portrait of the bishop of

---

[6] *Ep.* 82. 23–4.   [7] *De baptismo* 1. 11. 15.
[8] *S. Mainz* 62. 51, ed. F. Dolbeau. The theme is already in the Muratorian Canon.
[9] *Ep.* 36. 9. 22; 54. 20; 55. 34–5.   [10] *S.* 202. 1; cf. *Ep.* 87. 1; *c. litt. Petiliani* 2. 51. 118.
[11] *Ep.* 54. 3.   [12] *En. in Ps.* 44.   [13] *De baptismo* 7. 39. 77.

Jerusalem and, in correspondence with Pope Damasus, had spoken scornfully of Greek trinitarian theology with its three hypostases. It offended
Jerome that the east did not (in his time) keep feast on 25 December.

Augustine was capable of understanding more Greek than he would admit
in controversy with Numidian Donatists. Rome remained for him the symbolic centre of the one empire. The capture of the eternal city by Alaric in
August 410 provoked deep questions about divine providence in human history, which he sought to answer in the *City of God*, and Greek theologians
never produced a comparable theodicy. But (as Walter Kaegi demonstrated
in 1968 in his book *Byzantium and the Decline of Rome*), the east was not
unmoved by barbarian kingdoms' taking over the western empire. There
was a gradual decline in the amount of Greek understood in the west and the
amount of Latin known in the east except by lawyers, who needed it profes-
sionally. In the fifth century it became customary for the pope to keep permanent envoys or nuncios, called apocrisiaries, at Constantinople, accredited
at least as much to the imperial court as to the patriarchate, and the diplomatic experience was often thought to qualify them to become pope. From
the eighth century the popes found it desirable to have similar nuncios at the
Frankish court in Aachen. At Constantinople the Roman delegates were
integrated into the hierarchy of officials attending the emperor on his prescribed routine of ceremonies and church visits, described by Constantine
Porphyrogenitus. These official links helped to maintain understanding and
some degree of mutual cooperation, but at the same time Roman delegates
such as Gregory the Great remained firmly critical of what appeared in Latin
eyes excessive claims by the patriarch of New Rome.

The difference of government and power between the eastern and western emperors was not the only way in which the structures of the Church
were affected. Procedures at episcopal councils naturally tended to follow
those familiar in secular contexts, where the rules were well understood. The
letters of Ambrose and Augustine illustrate that a bishop needed to know
something of Roman law, especially after Constantine had invested bishops
with the power of magistrates, and in the second half of the fourth century
and in north Africa early in the fifth there first appears evidence of laymen or
clergy with legal training acting as advisers to bishops who were called upon
to arbitrate in property disputes and other domestic quarrels in families.
There were also questions about asylum in churches for runaway slaves or
even criminals where a bishop ignorant of the law could end in trouble.
Bishops inevitably came to be expected to exercise social or secular functions
on behalf of their people, and it could be an important factor affecting the
choice of a bishop that the person selected was more likely than other candidates to intercede effectively with taxmen or magistrates.

7

CONSTANTINOPLE'S GROWING POWER: SOCRATES THE HISTORIAN

Great cities like Rome, Alexandria, and Antioch in Syria were centres of civil administration for several provinces grouped together. If an individual bishop appealed against a negative decision by his provincial synod, he naturally looked to the bishop of a great city to rehear his case—if he did not directly appeal to the emperor, a procedure which fourth-century synods deplored[1] but which was encouraged by the assumption, explicit in St Jerome, that synodical decisions could be overturned by imperial authority. Constantine's new capital at Constantinople, New Rome, gave its bishop an importance that rapidly grew to be decisive. The large Greek Council there in 381 not only ended the influence of bishops unsympathetic to the creed of Nicaea (325) but also, by the canon on the privileges of Constantinople as New Rome, offended Alexandria and Antioch. Further tensions followed from the mere proximity of the bishop to the imperial palace, and already in John Chrysostom's time a visiting bishop seeking audience with the emperor had to be presented by the local bishop,[2] who, during the early decades of the fifth century, came to be entitled 'patriarch'. Bishops of Rome and Alexandria were already being addressed as 'papa'.

The resentment felt at Alexandria towards the upstart see of Constantinople surfaced with force when John Chrysostom received Origenist monks who had exchanged hard words with Theophilus of Alexandria. John thereby mobilized against himself the impassioned heresy-hunter and anti-Origenist Epiphanius bishop of Salamis in Cyprus. He vexed the empress Eudoxia by preaching against feminine frailties, such as less than modest clothing, and his support of the rights of the poor irritated powerful

---

[1] e.g. canon 11 of the Council of Antioch (mistakenly ascribed to the council of 341). Text in F. Lauchert, *Die Kanones der wichtigsten altkirchlichen Concilien* (Freiburg, 1896; repr. Frankfurt a. M., 1961), 46. Jerome on the emperor's authority to supersede synodical decisions is in *ep. adv. Rufinum* (= *Apol.* 3) 18.

[2] John Chrysostom, *Hom. in Act. Apost.* 3. 4–5. That the patriarchate derived its mystique of authority from the city of Constantine, not from the proximity of the emperor (Constantius II did not reside there anyway), is stressed by P. Karlin-Hayter in *Kathegetria for Joan Hussey* (Camberley, 1988), 179–210.

senators. Synodically deposed at the Synod of the Oak he appealed to Pope Innocent I and other western bishops asking for an 'ecumenical council'. Innocent supported him, holding no communion with his (virtuous) successors for some time. The affair did nothing to allay Roman distrust towards the Greek east. At Constantinople anger at Pope Innocent's intervention was a cause of John's death.

At Rome the assertiveness of Constantinople aroused misgiving. An epigram of Pope Damasus told pilgrims to the apostolic shrines that while the apostles came from the east, yet Rome possessed their graves and had a superior title to their authority. At Alexandria anger was reinforced when in 451, at the Fourth Ecumenical Council in Chalcedon, the privileges of Constantinople were reaffirmed, which reinforced Egyptian reservations towards the council's Christological definition that Christ, one person, one hypostasis, is 'known in two natures'. In the west Pope Leo I, who had instructed his legates at Chalcedon to withhold consent from any claims on behalf of New Rome, risked undermining the acceptance of the Christological definition in the east by his anger and consequent delay in confirming acceptance of the council's Christology.

Soon a patriarch of Alexandria, of pro-Chalcedonian sympathy, had to tell the emperor at Constantinople that he could not hope to gain the support of the Egyptian churches for Chalcedonian doctrine because of the council's slight to the dignity of Alexandria.[3]

Socrates

Written a few years before Theodosius II's death (450), a notable church history in continuation of Eusebius was compiled by Socrates of Constantinople. From two anti-Christian tutors he had a classical education but was certainly a Christian and had overt sympathies with the followers of Novatian. His motive was to foster the peace and unity so little apparent in the controversies of the previous century and a half, and in his time threatened by a major thunderstorm in the Christological controversy. His story is this: Constantine gave the Church peace, but the end of persecution at once precipitated civil war in the Church (1. 4. 5–6). The Arian controversy engendered a 'Labyrinth' of divergent creeds (2. 41. 17). Individuals and groups sought to impose their own favoured interpretation as if it were the binding creed of the universal Church (2. 40. 21). Faction had become endemic, and in some dreadful cases powerful bishops had resorted to violence to impose their will, physically forcing dissenters to receive the

---

[3] Zacharias of Mitylene, *Chron.* 4. 10. The epigram of Damasus is no. 20 in A. Ferrua's edition (Rome, 1942), 26 in Ihm's. Discussion in e.g. my article in *JTS*, NS 8 (1957), reprinted in my *History and Thought of the Early Church* (Aldershot, 1981), no. II, pp. 34–5.

eucharistic host at their hand. Bishop Macedonius of Constantinople brought shame on the Church by this kind of action; his 'virtuous acts on behalf of Christianity' included murders (2. 38. 33).

Socrates considered that in at least the majority of issues disagreements were not rooted at the level of essential faith (5. 22. 31). Theophilus of Alexandria used the dispute about the orthodoxy of Origen to declare war on John Chrysostom of Constantinople (6. 10. 8). The real issues producing mutual excommunications were not the pretended questions of faith (I. 24. 1–2; 2. 42. 2 ff.; 4. 29. 5; 5. 9. 5; 5. 23. 10). Unanimity was rare enough to be deemed a divine sign (4. 30. 5, 8). One source of trouble lay in confusions about the precise meaning of terms like *ousia* and especially 'hypostasis' (of which he gives a superficial exposition, 3. 7. 11 ff.), with excessive confidence that human language is capable of formulating truth about God in adequate terms (3. 7. 21 cites a warning of Evagrius Ponticus, a writer Socrates admired). It is not only that sects differ from one another; 'there is dissension among members of the same group' (5. 10. 19). Meetings held to resolve disputes 'fail to heal schisms and can make divisions more contentious than before' (5. 10. 10).

In a long and famous chapter (5. 22), motivated by an internal dispute in the Novatianist community about the date of Easter which had led to a painful split, Socrates recorded differences of liturgical and other custom between different places in the Church, starting from divergences in the observance of Holy Week and Easter. 'It would be hard to find two churches with an absolutely identical ritual' (57). The Roman Saturday fast is not the custom elsewhere (58), and in the east it is not a requirement that the clergy be celibate, which is a matter for their personal decision (50). Socrates was not aware in his time of tension between east and west arising from this difference in custom and canon law, though the tension of east and west was a factor in the conflict at the Council of Serdica and the credal exchanges of the 340s. He was content to make the point that mutual agreement in communion did not depend on uniformity. Yet differences could easily become contentious.

Socrates had no doubt that the *homoousios* of Nicaea was sufficient, right, and necessary, but also that it allowed diversity of interpretation. For the radical Arian Eunomius he had no time at all. But that was not merely an opposition based on a judgement that he was a heretic. It was also reaction against a man who seemed to think that one could talk about God as if one were reading a news bulletin.

At the end of his story Socrates remarks that controversy and conflict are the very stuff of church history, and that if the Church were suddenly to be at peace, there would be nothing for his successors to record (7. 48, cf. 1. 18). Ironically he wrote on the eve of one of the most painful and lasting splits in

Christendom within a few months of the second council of Ephesus in 449, named by Pope Leo I a council of brigands, *latrocinium*, and curtain-raiser for centuries of conflict about the unity of the person of the divine and human Redeemer.

The finer points of the Nicene–Arian debate were not interesting to him. They were merely a figleaf to cover the ambitions of power-hungry bishops engaged in a 'night-battle' (1. 23. 6; cf. 7. 32. 5 of the Nestorian controversy). The grand controversy of his own time concerning Cyril and Nestorius led him to read some of his patriarch's writings, which convinced him how untrue it was to malign him as teaching Christ to be mere man. On the other hand he was also persuaded that Nestorius was uneducated in his subject, and could have kept out of trouble if he had read Origen and Eusebius of Caesarea, both theologians for whom the term *Theotókos* or Mother of God occasioned no problems. Eusebius was in Socrates' view also maligned by those who charged him with Arianism (an accusation important 300 years later at the time of the iconoclastic debate). The polemic against Marcellus of Ankyra was surely correct (2. 20–1). Socrates liked theologians who stood in the tradition of Origen, not only Eusebius but Didymus the Blind, Gregory Thaumaturgus, and Evagrius. They were all imbued with high culture as well as being competent divines.

The austere discipline of Novatian had retained a considerable following in Asia Minor and especially in the city of Constantinople, where it had a succession of devout and cultivated bishops whom Socrates found congenial society. Moreover, Greek Novatianists were strict upholders of the Nicene creed and had no sympathy for Arians of any colour. Socrates makes no secret of his affinities with the Novatianist community. The account of Novatian's separation in Rome 200 years earlier carries no suggestion that he was mistaken in his judgement. Socrates' criterion for his evaluations of prominent Orthodox bishops lies in their degree of toleration for the Novatianists. He is repeatedly insistent that the Novatianist body is strict in adhering to the Nicene creed and has no truck with Arians. He is deeply critical of the weak attitude of Orthodox bishops towards penitential discipline, notably Nectarius, who abolished the office of penitentiary presbyter at Constantinople on the political ground that public confession of grave sins brought the Church community into disrepute. It is hard to resist the conclusion that his allegiance with the Novatianists was not a thing of the past from which he had turned away. If in old age he had decided to be reconciled with the Orthodox community, he gives not the slightest indication of inward tension. That, however, may be a slippery argument. Not all converts hate the body they have abandoned, common as that may be throughout history whenever conversion is a critical manifesto of anger or disappointment. There are also converts who leave the ecclesial body of their baptism with sadness, and seek to build a bridge for others to follow their example. Sharp criticism of bishops does not mean that Socrates was cynical about Orthodox Catholic clergy as belonging to a community in rivalry to his own.

Socrates does not regard the Novatianist community as having left the Church. Their disagreement with the Orthodox tradition (not that Socrates uses this formula) is a controversy within the one Church. Hence his contention in the chapter on differences of custom (5. 22) that divergences are local and matters of indifference. If the Nicene creed is a matter of fundamental consensus, and the episcopal order is equally maintained, what is needed is mutual recognition, not submission. More than once Socrates looks to 'the old' writers (5. 10. 11; 7. 32. 14) to provide a standard for consensus and the end of controversy; for they were 'teachers before the Church became divided' (5. 10. 15).

When one recalls Socrates' emphatic attitude to the causes of division in the Church as being non-theological, it is evident that he was writing with an aspiration to facilitate reconciliation, at least to the point of mutual toleration and courtesy, among all who could accept the Nicene creed. He would like the Great Church and the Novatianists to regard their mutual differences as *adiaphora*.[4]

Closely following Socrates, Sozomen copied much of his work, including passages about the Novatianists. But it is impossible to discern in Sozomen any apparent motivation to correct Socrates' too benevolent attitude towards the separated body. Sozomen differs rather in the number of original documents and *acta* which he includes and in his greater sympathy with monasticism.

Socrates judged bishops responsible if liturgical differences between churches caused tensions. But his attitude to power in the churches turns out to be ambivalent. On the one hand he had no reservations about the moving of high officers of state into the episcopate, such as Ambrose (4. 30. 8) or Nectarius (5. 8. 12). He thought it in the interest of the Church when Thalassius, on the eve of being gazetted as praetorian prefect, was suddenly consecrated metropolitan of Cappadocian Caesarea (7. 48. 6). On the other hand he saw no reason to deplore the supra-provincial jurisdiction of the five patriarchates, Rome, Alexandria, Antioch, Jerusalem, and (always last in his lists) Constantinople. Once he frankly censures the bishops of Rome and Alexandria for having become agents of secularized power (7. 11). By that he meant intolerant coercion of dissenting believers such as the Novatianists, among whom he counted many friends.

---

[4] Beside G. C. Hansen's critical edition of Socrates (Berlin, 1995), see monographs by Theresa Urbainczyk (New Haven, 1997), Hartmut Leppin (Stuttgart, 1996) and especially Martin Wallraff (Göttingen, 1997). The early Armenian version has been translated by Professor Robert Thomson in Hebrew University Armenian Studies, 3 (Leuven, 2001). It has important variants.

The great legal collection of the Theodosian Code was produced in 438. Socrates has no reference to this, though it has an important source for church law in book 16. Apart from one or two references to matters of canon law, e.g. on episcopal translations, unlike Sozomen he is not interested in legal questions or rulings. Nevertheless the emperors are never marginal to the vicissitudes of the churches, and the seven books of Socrates' *History* are articulated round the reigns of successive emperors, which enables him to devote the whole of book 3 to debate with Libanius' idealization of a pagan hero, Julian, and the whole of book 6 to John Chrysostom (for whom his admiration was qualified).

8

THE UNITY OF CHRIST:
DEVOTION TO MARY

The Christological controversy created huge problems in ecumenism. Holding together in one communion both the followers of Cyril of Alexandria and the disciples of Theodore of Mospuestia seemed massively difficult. For Cyril and the Alexandrians the power of Christ to redeem is grounded in the complete and real presence of God in the incarnation. Finite, ignorant, sordid, rebellious creatures, in whom the image and likeness of the Creator have been deeply marred, cannot be rescued by one who embodies the highest and best of humanity's capacities but no more. Therefore the humanity born of Mary is a divine humanity constituted to be a single person, a single being, 'one nature, one hypostasis', and Mary herself is *Theotókos*, 'Mother of God'. To be cool about this devotional acclamation (current since at least the middle of the third century) was in Cyril's eyes to confess to doubts about the truth of the incarnation, and therefore to strike at the lifeline of salvation.

For Theodore of Mopsuestia (d. 427) and his pupils, especially Nestorius, archbishop of Constantinople 428–31, and Theodoret bishop of Cyrrhus, a remote town in Syria (d. 466), redemption is made possible by the perfect self-offering of Jesus, pioneer and head of the Church, in whose sacrifice and intercession before the Father baptized believers participate by the making of the eucharistic memorial. Were the humanity of Jesus to be submerged and lost in the union of the incarnation, redemption would be affected. The Antiochene Christology of Theodore might have difficulty in explaining why the Virginal Conception was needed for the incarnation, but could see the Resurrection as the crowning reward for perfect obedience (rather than a divine intervention in the created order). For Theodore it seemed Apollinarian language to affirm Christ to be one hypostasis constituted from two natures. On Cyril's interpretation of St John's gospel Theodore's Christology was a threat to salvation. Each regarded the other as a dangerous perversion making it impossible to be Christian.

One bishop of the time, Firmus of Cappadocian Caesarea, drily observed that the task of reconciliation was like that of Sisyphos in Homer's Hades, condemned for ever to push a heavy boulder up a steep hill, and always finding that it slipped from his grasp just as he was reaching the top.

Debate crystallized round the term *Theotókos* (Mother of God) in monastic devotion. Nestorius at Constantinople offended monks by adding 'mother of man', and by warning against treating the Virgin Mary as a goddess. This controversy was already lively when four Alexandrians disciplined by Cyril appealed to Theodosius II, who naturally referred the hearing to Nestorius. It was intolerable to Cyril that the upstart see of Constantinople should judge. He mobilized support at Rome from Pope Celestine, with whom it rankled that Nestorius had received Pelagians censured at Old Rome. A theological split was soured by the rivalry of great cities. Cyril could disqualify Nestorius by an accusation of heresy. The emperor called a council at Ephesus. Cyril's party and the Syrians sat separately and cursed one another. At court Cyril won in the outcome. The catalogue of his bribes to high officials survives. The see was much impoverished thereby to the distress of his clergy.

The Alexandrian victory at the Council of Ephesus in 431 appalled Syrian bishops, who deemed Nestorius a good pastor maligned. Under imperial pressure in 433 Cyril of Alexandria agreed that, provided Nestorius was censured and deposed, he would accept a union formula drafted by Theodoret, which affirmed Mary *Theotókos* and safeguarded Antiochene Christology by a clause that Christ, perfect God and perfect man, 'is of one substance with us in his humanity'. Cyril's act amazed zealot supporters. Many Antiochenes who were turned out of their sees resented jettisoning Nestorius and accused Theodoret of being a traitor to an old friend.

Cyril sought to placate critics by attacking Theodore of Mopsuestia's memory. Cyril died in 444 to be succeeded by Dioscorus, leader among malcontents resenting Cyril's concessions of 433. Theodoret found himself isolated and under Alexandrian attack. Dioscorus formed an alliance with a Constantinople archimandrite Eutyches who was close to the omnipotent court chamberlain Chrysaphius and who detested Theodoret's 'two natures' Christology. Patriarch Flavian of Constantinople was confronted by Eutyches challenging the Union of 433 and the orthodoxy of his patriarch. Intrigue produced an imperial calling of a council at Ephesus (449), controlled by Dioscorus but attended by legates of Pope Leo I, one being a deacon Hilarus who protested against Dioscorus and had to take refuge from violence in St John's shrine. A contemporary inscription in the Lateran Baptistery records how St John rescued him. Leo, initially unfriendly to Flavian, came to realize that if Eutyches could not affirm the real humanity of Christ as having redemptive value, he was a heretic. He had written a formal letter ('Tome'; *ep.* 28) to Flavian setting out a two-nature Christology, the divine performing the miracles, the human showing weaknesses, tears, even ignorance. Dioscorus would not have this read at Ephesus. Leo was outraged. Patriarch Flavian appealed to Rome, was roughly handled and died on the road to exile, surely a martyr.

The imminent breach was temporarily averted when in 450 Theodosius II died by falling off his horse, and power was assumed by his virgin sister Pulcheria, who took as consort Marcian (a soldier), eliminated Chrysaphius the eunuch, and correctly saw that a breach with Rome was politically damaging to imperial as well as ecclesiastical interests. In 451 a corrective council was summoned to meet at Nicaea, then moved to Chalcedon across the water from the palace. Dioscorus of Alexandria attempted a pre-emptive strike by declaring that Leo's Tome rendered him excommunicate. A large assembly of bishops was directed to bring peace amid dissension. An initial draft formula affirmed Christ to be 'of (*ek*) two natures', but Dioscorus of Alexandria unwisely declared this acceptable to him. Anything that Dioscorus could sign was sure to displease Pope Leo. A revised formula replaced 'of' by 'in', the one point in the final Definition where Leo's Tome had influence. Otherwise the Chalcedonian Definition exploited concessive clauses found in Cyril, juxtaposed with the very 'one nature' proposition that Christ is 'one *prosopon*, one hypostasis'. Antiochenes could growl at 'one hypostasis' but otherwise won protection for their rights of citizenship in the Church. The Fourth Ecumenical Council, as it was later to be called, prevented a legitimate option from being closed. Nestorius in exile thought his position vindicated by Leo. Egypt was scandalized to think that true and was also furious at a resolution of the council (the Roman legates abstaining) in effect giving the bishop of Constantinople jurisdiction over many eastern churches.

Devotion to Mary

In the fourth-century churches one aspect which did not become a source of tension between Latin west and Greek east was devotion to the Virgin Mary. The ascetic movement throughout the empire wanted to affirm her perpetual virginity. Hilary's commentary on Matthew was sure that she remained a virgin even in the birth of Jesus (PL. 9. 921–2). That she remained virginal in the act of bringing forth her divine son seemed certain to Zeno of Verona (PL 11. 414–15). Contemporary with Zeno in the Greek world, Basil of Caesarea thought the question belonged in the realm of devotion; one should not upset devout people and that is ground for affirming perpetual virginity (PG 31. 1457–67, especially 1458 B).

Epiphanius knew of critics of Marian devotion whom he calls Opponents of Mary (*Panarion* 78). Her role as a spiritual mother was important to Epiphanius himself, and he was interested in her end on earth.

In the west Augustine knew something of Epiphanius' work against heretics, which he used in his own treatise on the subject. In Augustine Mary is the model for all religious sisters in community. Her life was so holy as to be free of any sinful action.

Nevertheless it would be very difficult to find a text in Augustine which could securely support a doctrine of Immaculate Conception, i.e. that she inherited no original sin. The silence of the sixth book of the incomplete work against Julian (6. 22) tells against Augustine having considered this possibility. 'Mary died because of Adam's sin in the flesh of the Lord' (*En. in Ps.* 34. 3). A striking feature in Augustine's language about saints and martyrs is his natural belief that the saints and martyrs are received in heaven at death and therefore remain an active part of the universal Church interceding for the church militant. One would expect him to write of the intercessions of Mary for the faithful on earth. This is remarkably absent. He did not wish to say that Mary is mother of Christ's divine nature (*Tract. in ev. Joh.* 8. 8). She is model for the Church. He may have remembered a warning in St Ambrose (*De spiritu sancto* 3. 80) that Mary was God's temple, not God of the temple; that is, held in high honour but not worshipped as divine.

In the century after the Council of Chalcedon, among Palestinian monks there appears coupling of the *Theotókos* title with a careful and not unsubtle concern to stress Mary's human place in the succession of the kingship of David, as in the gospel genealogy of Matthew 1.

In Egypt and Syria, and especially at Jerusalem, many thought the Chalcedonian formula failed to protect the unity of the person of Christ against the language of Nestorius, whose reservations about the title *Theotókos* seemed offensive to numerous monks. Nestorius and his mentor Theodore of Mopsuestia used troublesome language about a 'juxtaposition' of divine and human in Christ, anxious to safeguard the humanity of the Lord from being swallowed up. Estrangement of these major provinces from Constantinople led the emperors to a succession of attempts to restate and qualify Chalcedonian Christology in a way that would reconcile the critics. The division was socially disruptive, capable of engendering urban riots; and confidence in the maintenance of authentic orthodoxy and unity was necessary for the preservation of divine favour towards the Roman empire. Nevertheless the Latin west, especially the Roman see, had deep misgivings about successive compromises.

The fact that the pro-Chalcedonians had the support of the emperors helps to explain the feeling of being embattled found among the anti-Chalcedonians of Egypt and Syria. At Alexandria they competed for possession of the patriarchal throne, and in time there came to be two rival patriarchs, though before the Arab conquests it was not always possible for the Monophysite patriarch to live in the city of his diocese.

At Antioch in Syria there were successive competitors for the patriarchate, for and against Chalcedon. One of them, Peter the Fuller, in the 480s, asserted the orthodoxy of those who disliked Chalcedon by a momentous move: he was the first bishop to insert the creed into the eucharistic liturgy. Its primary place was the baptismal catechism. These liturgical contexts not only made the text of the creed well known to the laity, but also imparted to the text a quality of being sacrosanct. In time the operation of consecrating a Monophysite patriarch became dangerous. (One dissenting patriarch from Alexandria attempting to provide a colleague for Antioch was detected in the act and had to escape through a stinking sewer.) In Severus of Antioch, patriarch for a short six years, 512–18, the Monophysites had the most important Greek theologian of the age. His letters attest the passionate divisions, leading Monophysites to be unwilling to recognize the sacraments of Chalcedonians (Severus thought the validity of a sacrament was independent of the minister's moral worthiness, but not of his orthodoxy), yet in particular situations allowing recognition.

The terms of the formula approved at Chalcedon had unhappy consequences for the unity of the churches in the Orient. In Syria, Armenia, the Nile Valley, and neighbouring Ethiopia, reservations about the words 'in two natures', admittedly when misrepresented by critics as 'Nestorian' implying a mere juxtaposition of divine and human without an integrated or 'hypostatic' unity of being, led to a separation lasting for many centuries and unhealed to the present day.

For many East Syrian Christians the catechetical lectures and biblical commentaries of Theodore of Mopsuestia were felt to be the very charter of their understanding of faith. For Theodore, as for his influential pupil Theodoret, it was of the very essence of the gospel of redemption to affirm the pioneer achievement of the humanity of Jesus. For other Syrians the truth was never so incisively proclaimed as by the arch-critic of Theodore and Theodoret, Cyril of Alexandria, but they were confident that Cyril himself would not have accepted Chalcedon's language, had he lived to hear it. Their leader and master of anti-Chalcedonian polemic was Severus of Antioch, reinforced by the native Syriac-speaker Philoxenos (d. 523), bishop of Hierapolis (Mabbug). In Egypt the large majority of Christians held the same view of Chalcedon's infidelity to Cyril. Their opponents disparagingly labelled them Monophysites, or 'one-nature' people, but exaggerated their criticism by identifying the Monophysite position with that of the ultra-zealot archimandrite Eutyches whose denial that Christ fully shared in our common humanity they strenuously disowned.

The divisive consequences inherent in the potential of ecumenical assemblies was thereby strikingly exemplified. In the Syriac-speaking churches the separation from the Chalcedonian churches in communion with Constantinople and Rome, so far from being negative in effect, had the result of stimulating a vigorously independent theology and spirituality and, in addition, a broad cultural life enriched by translations of Greek philosophical texts and of major pre-Chalcedonian theologians, Basil, Gregory of Nyssa, and Gregory of Nazianzos.

In Syria and points east there were many bishops who thought Nestorius had been misrepresented and unjustly condemned at Ephesus in 431. Gradually a separate 'Nestorian' Church formed beyond the frontier of the Roman empire in Persia, and at Edessa until expelled in 489, the school there being moved to Persian Nisibis. The patriarchal see of the primate or Catholicos was at Seleucia-Ctesiphon on the Tigris. Nestorian missionaries travelled along the trade-route to China. A Nestorian community survived in eastern Turkey until 1917 when they suffered severe Muslim repression. Survivors were moved, with the help of American Presbyterians, to San Francisco in 1934.

The Christological definition of the Council of Chalcedon provoked impassioned dissension and created social and political problems for the emperors' government, at least in the Greek east. In the west the transformation of the empire into a loose gathering of barbarian kingdoms and the increasing weakness of any central imperial authority brought about the ending of the line of western emperors in 476 or 480—a change which not many at the time noticed as making serious difference to life. Yet the west retained at Rome a bishop who was felt to be the special guardian of a now Christian Roman tradition, presiding over a city which looked to St Peter and St Paul rather than to Romulus and Remus as its founders and protectors.[1] In the barbarian kingdoms education was in decline. Early in the sixth century in Ostrogothic Italy the Roman aristocrat Boethius commented on Aristotle's confident statement that in future the human mind would solve some problems which in his time had not found their solution, remarking that his own fear now was that matters which had hitherto been well understood would soon not be comprehended by anyone, so serious was the barbarizing of society.[2]

At Rome the prime significance of the Council of Chalcedon was located in the east's acknowledgement of the authoritative 'Tome' issued in 449 by Pope Leo I, recognized by the Greek bishops at Chalcedon as an authentically orthodox and Petrine utterance. It was a correct judgement that Leo's intervention had decisive influence on the course of events, and the story would have been very different if he had refused to confirm the council's

---

[1] Augustine, *En. in Ps.* 44. 23.
[2] Boethius, *in Categ.* 2 (PL 64. 230). On education in late antiquity and the early medieval period in the west see the studies by P. Riché, especially *Education and Culture in the Barbarian West, Sixth through Eighth Centuries*, trans. J. Contreni (Columbia, 1976).

definition because of his explicit anger at the council's resolution (not strictly a canon and not assented to by the Roman legates) reaffirming 'in line with the decisions of the Fathers' that they had been right 'to grant primatial privileges to Old Rome as the imperial city', but also to give 'equal privileges' to the see of New Rome, the city honoured with the imperial power and the senate, in the second place after Old Rome. The resolution added that the see of Constantinople was to have rights of consecrating bishops in the Pontic, Asian, and Thracian dioceses as well as bishops for the barbarians. At Rome there would have been qualms about the allocation of Thrace, but more at the notion of Old Rome's primacy being granted by a decision of the Church through a conciliar canon.

From this it followed that all attempts by eastern emperors and patriarchs to heal the wounds of controversy in a highly intricate area and, by clarification or concession, to pacify the oriental Monophysite critics of Chalcedon, appeared to papal authority to be an insulting challenge to a juridical decision which Pope Leo I had made once for all. A struggle which in the Greek east produced dialectical disputes of mind-boggling complexity was treated at Rome almost exclusively in simplistic terms of Roman supremacy in the universal Church. In 513 a disillusioned Greek metropolitan had written a *cri de cœur* to Pope Symmachus asking Rome for an authoritative untangling of the Christological problem, to show the Christian world the coherence of the 'middle way' between Nestorius and Eutyches, the heretics who alone seemed to offer logically consistent positions. Boethius records the consternation which this request produced in Rome, where both will and ability to discuss the problems were lacking. Authority was all, and in Roman eyes the one and only issue was to obtain Greek submission to papal supremacy. In 518 Pope Hormisdas successfully ended thirty-four years of painful division not by a carefully balanced Christological statement calculated to win the assent of all orthodox persons but by a blunt assertion of St Peter's primacy.[3] His formula was to enjoy later echoes and to be restated by the first Vatican Council in 1870.

The enforcing of Chalcedonian 'two-nature' Christology on eastern Christians convinced that it was heretical and Nestorian provoked riots in which lives were lost. In Syria and other eastern provinces some bishops tried to impose coercion. Travelling merchants would carry in a little pyx the host consecrated by a priest of their own communion. Each side claimed to be vindicated by miraculous signs, while at the intellectual level the logicians

---

[3] Hormisdas, *epp.* 7, 61 (ed. Thiel, pp. 754–5, 853). On the Greek metropolitan's letter see my *Boethius* (Oxford 1981), 181–3. The uncomprehending discussion precipitated in Rome is described by Boethius, *Contra Eutychen et Nestorium*. Most of Hormisdas' letters are in the Avellana collection (CSEL 35). See also C. Nole (ed.), *Atti del convegno su Papa Ormisda* (Frosinone, 1993).

took the argument to extremes of sophistication. The gulf between the two sides was small. Several cases of switching allegiance are attested.

Those in Egypt and Syria who either doubted or rejected the Christological definition of Chalcedon and the Tome of Pope Leo experienced mounting difficulties in keeping a united front among themselves. In Egypt the Monophysites were the dominant majority, but had their own splits; there was dissension whether Eutyches, the ally of Dioscorus of Alexandria at the time of the council of Chalcedon, was right to deny that the humanity of Christ was identical in being with ours, or whether the more moderate position of Cyril of Alexandria was correct in conceding this. In 482 the ingeniously worded Edict of Union or 'Henotikon' of the emperor Zeno and patriarch Acacius had a clause disparaging the orthodoxy of some at Chalcedon (below, p. 50). Peter Mongos (i.e. 'Hoarse'), patriarch of Alexandria (477, then 482–9), who accepted the Henotikon but disliked Chalcedon, found that to hold his own supporters he was forced to declare that he understood the Henotikon to be a censure of Chalcedon and Leo; but he still faced a secession of large proportions, led by the bishop of Antinoe, because he had not excommunicated those who did not so interpret it. To explain the Henotikon as a rejection of Chalcedon was to destroy its value as a formula of reconciliation. Early in the sixth century in the last years of the emperor Anastasius (491–518), for whom the Henotikon was an official norm, Severus, an ex-lawyer who had become a monk in anti-Chalcedonian company, became prominent especially in defending the critics of Chalcedon's 'two natures' from accusations of Eutychianism. In 512 he became patriarch of Antioch for six years, and leader of the ingenious approach to the Henotikon, insisting that it rejected Chalcedon and, if so interpreted, could be accepted. (This position was strong under the emperor Anastasius, but unacceptable from 519 under Justin.) He issued a detailed attack on the Chalcedonians' claim that Cyril of Alexandria himself would have supported the council's definition. The definition used so many of Cyril's concessive clauses that there was a strong case to answer. Severus was sure that Cyril agreed with his interpretation, and had no sympathy for Theodore of Mopsuestia, Theodoret of Cyrrhus, and Ibas of Edessa, patrons of two-nature Christology.

Severus' letters illustrate the problems of a partisan patriarch. Zealous anti-Chalcedonians thought him too concessive and gradualist. Could a patriarch avowedly denouncing Chalcedon as Nestorian attend the deathbed of one of his suffragans who did not share this opinion? The case against Chalcedon seemed to him confirmed by that council's rejection of Nestorius, which he thought disingenuous. Moreover he discovered that at Tarsus in Cilicia (in his patriarchate), the name of Nestorius was being included among the saints with whom that church was in communion.

Severus' most serious critics were among those who shared his view of Chalcedon. A faithful disciple of Cyril of Alexandria, he was attacked by Julian of Halicarnassus, who maintained that Christ's humanity shared in divine incorruptibility even before the resurrection, and therefore suffered human frailties by choice of will, not as part of his natural human condition. The quarrel produced a split in Alexandria, with two rival Monophysite bishops, Theodosius siding with Severus, Gaianos with Julian (whose views persuaded some eminent Chalcedonians, including at the end of his life the emperor Justinian). A further split arose from the advocacy, by an exceptionally intelligent group of Monophysites, of a frankly tritheistic doctrine of God. Monophysite and even Chalcedonian Christology affirmed one hypostasis in Christ. 'One of the Trinity was crucified for us', they cried in a liturgical acclamation. ('One of the Trinity became incarnate' stood in the Henotikon.) Orthodoxy proclaims three hypostases in God, and for a Monophysite 'hypostasis' is an interchangeable term with *physis*, nature. In Cilicia in the 560s 'tritheist' doctrine acquired a following, but was condemned by the Monophysite majority. Nevertheless the doctrine gained the adherence of John Philoponos of Alexandria, commentator on Aristotle. John was one of the sharpest minds of the sixth century (he was to anticipate a high proportion of the discoveries of Galileo—as Galileo himself willingly conceded). His defence declared that the oneness of the Godhead was an intellectual abstraction, and that the actuality is three Gods, three natures or substances. In the 580s two Monophysite bishops of Alexandria (Damian) and Antioch (Peter of Callinicus) parted company on the correct answer to the tritheist contention, Peter thinking Damian too concessive.

For the Chalcedonians these dissensions and quarrels were a godsend. In the monasteries on both sides of the divide there was a strong tendency to find refuge from the debates in a spirituality of prayer and wonder, relying on miracle and authority to vindicate their separate points of view. Among the trained philosophers such as Leontius of Jerusalem on the Chalcedonian side and Philoponus on the Monophysite side, the disagreements were ideal matter for intricate dialectical disputations.

The records of the Council of Chalcedon show how a difference between eastern and western understandings of authority were coming to the surface as a result of the debate. Pope Leo I had achieved much for the power of the Roman see by the Council of Chalcedon's recognition of his Christological statement the 'Tome', abrasively ignored by Dioscorus of Alexandria dominating the Council of Ephesus in 449. In Leo's judgement, however, the function of the Greek council was to manifest its own orthodoxy by submissively indicating its assent to the ruling already given by himself, the legitimate juridical successor of Peter the prince of the apostles. It was axiomatic for Leo that the Roman see has received and guards the true apostolic tradition, is predestined by God for this service to the entire Church, is therefore protected from leading the Church astray, and in jurisdiction possesses a universal responsibility inherent in being Peter's successor; synods whether of east or west did not have an independent power to define and safeguard Christian faith in a reliable way.

The Greek east did not instinctively think in this kind of idiom. Authority to safeguard truth resided for the east in the eucharistic communion of all the local dioceses led by their bishops and especially metropolitans, who, since the sixth canon of Nicaea (325), exercised power of veto over episcopal elections in their provinces. Since the early decades of the fifth century eastern bishops came to look to the principal sees, especially Constantinople, Alexandria, and Antioch, joined in the course of the Council of Chalcedon by Jerusalem. Together with Rome these were named patriarchates, and in Justinian's ecclesiastical legislation the five together formed a 'Pentarchy' of leaders at ecumenical councils. The presupposition was that the five retained an independence of judgement, and that the eastern patriarchs did not owe to Rome the duty of obedience but retained a right to be consulted and had as much right as Rome to participate in dogmatic decisions.

At Rome the authority of the western patriarch was largely, not entirely, absorbed in the more universal primacy. Nevertheless the pope's residence at the Lateran was regularly called the *patriarchium* in the *Liber Pontificalis* at least from the time of Sergius I (687–701).[4] Not before commentaries on Gratian's *Decretum* would canonists mark a distinction between papal and Roman patriarchal jurisdiction, important later in debates about Gallicanism.

[4] See Adriano Garuti, *Il Papa Patriarca d'Occidente?* (Bologna, 1990).

9

ZENO'S HENOTIKON, ROME'S FURY, AND THE ACACIAN SCHISM: DIONYSIUS EXIGUUS

Each major attempt to reconcile to the 'two-nature' formula of Chalcedon those who held it in abhorrence as Nestorian and insisted on 'one nature, not two, after the union' saw the peace process doomed to failure, enhanced tension, and was productive of schisms. The Egyptian Churches were particularly alienated.[1] To reconcile them the emperor Zeno in 482 issued an edict popularly known as the Union or Henotikon, drafted by the patriarch of Constantinople Acacius.[2] It affirmed the supreme authority of the Nicene creed of 325 confirmed at Constantinople (381) and followed by the Council of Ephesus (431); pronounced anathema on both Nestorius and Eutyches at either extreme; accepted the twelve anathemas attached to the third letter of Cyril of Alexandria to Nestorius; insisted on the unqualified unity of the person of Christ incarnate of the Holy Spirit and Mary the mother of God (*Theotókos*); and finally anathematized any who had held or now holds a different doctrine, 'whether at Chalcedon or any other synod'. Alexandria had just acquired a new patriarch Peter, who shared the reservations about Chalcedon held by many of his flock. The Union formula was put to him, his signature being the price required for imperial recognition. He signed, and Acacius of Constantinople held communion with him. Rome was not consulted and was offended. The Henotikon's unenthusiastic reference to Chalcedon seemed insulting to papal authority. Acacius and the eastern patriarchs were excommunicated by Rome and for thirty-four years east and west were not in communion.

At one point Acacius assumed, perhaps asserted, that he possessed the jurisdiction to decide an issue in the Greek churches. This was not language

---

[1] See the classic account by E. Schwartz, *Publizistische Sammlungen zum acacianischen Schisma* (Abhandlungen der Bayerischen Akademie, phil.-hist. Kl., NF 10; Munich, 1934). Thereon P. Peeters, *Anal. Boll.* 54 (1936), 143–59; W. H. C. Frend, *The Rise of the Monophysite Movement* (Cambridge, 1972). Felix II on Acacius' claim to be 'head of the whole Church': *ep.* 2. 8, pp. 237–8 Thiel; on Nicaea needing Roman ratification, *ep.* 11. 4, p. 255.

[2] Evagrius, *HE* 3. 14.

calculated to pacify irate bishops of Rome, who took him to be claiming to be 'head of the entire Church'. In a sharp correspondence successive popes stressed that Peter's see was the sole locus of decision. Felix II held a Roman synod (5 October 485) which insisted that even the decisions of the Council of Nicaea (325) lacked ecumenical authority until the holy Roman Church had confirmed them. Against a Byzantine conciliar ecclesiology Pope Gelasius I (492–6) countered that St Peter's successors at Rome needed no synods to ratify their decisions.[3]

The Acacian schism between east and west raised thorny questions about canon law. Soon after Pope Gelasius died (496) there came to Rome a bilingual monk of Scythian ancestry (i.e. from the Dobrudja or Danube delta) named Dionysius. He regularly signed himself Dionysius 'exiguus', a common epithet for an ascetic at this time. Dionysius saw that east and west were at odds in part because they did not have a common system of canonical rules. He therefore set out to provide good translations of major Greek texts such as Cyril of Alexandria's principal letter to Nestorius and the less able Tome for the Armenians composed by Proclus of Constantinople concerning the Christological controversy. Above all, Dionysius took an existing corpus of Greek canon law in which the councils were arranged in order, normally chronological, the canons being numbered consecutively in series, and produced a Latin version of the decisions of Nicaea, Ancyra, Neocaesarea, Gangra, Antioch, Laodicea, Constantinople (381), Ephesus (431), and Chalcedon. A revised edition included fifty of the eighty-five Apostolic Canons, the canons of western Serdica, north African canon law, and then an important collection of papal decretals from Siricius to Anastasius II (496–8). This last item was distinctively western and marked a major difference between the Latin list and the Greek corpus. However, the Roman decretals are largely concerned with the western patriarchate other than Innocent I's intervention on behalf of John Chrysostom, his letter to patriarch Alexander of Antioch on the mutual bond of Petrine primacy, and Leo on the vicariate of Thessalonica. The selection of Gelasius' decretals surprises by including none of his bellicose pieces on the schism with Constantinople.

The emperor Justinian (527–65) did not doubt his exalted responsibilities for governing the Church throughout the Roman empire, including the west. A considerable body of imperial legislation illustrated his control of church organization and finance.[4] It was self-evident for him that the authority of Old Rome, 'caput orbis terrarum', was fully shared with New Rome

---

[3] Gelasius, *ep.* 10. 4, p. 343 Thiel (cf. p. 393).

[4] On Justinian's ecclesiastical policy see Evangelos K. Chrysos, Ἡ ἐκκλησιαστικὴ πολιτεία τοῦ Ἰουστινιανοῦ (Analekta Vlatadon, 3; Thessaloniki, 1969).

(*CJ* 1. 17. 1. 10), and that the highest authority in the Church was the consensus of the five patriarchs, among whom Old Rome was acknowledged leader with Constantinople in the second place of honour (*Novel* 123. 3, 131. 2). 'Any difference between *sacerdotium* and *imperium* is small' (*Novel* 7. 2. 1), and therefore responsibility for protecting orthodoxy lay with the emperor (*Novel* 6, preface), a principle exemplified in Justinian's actions to condemn Origenism and the Three Chapters. His council at Constantinople in 553 was to confirm these censures, ultimately with the reluctant assent of Pope Vigilius.

Justinian was not the first and far from being the last emperor to legislate on ecclesiastical matters overlapping with canon law. At Byzantium in the mid-seventh century an anonymous canonist produced the earliest 'Nomocanon' fusing imperial laws with conciliar canons. In 883 a revision of this was made which, though not compiled by Photius, was published under his patriarchal patronage.[5]

Imperial legislation on faith and order in the Church did not find its way into Greek collections of canons until after Justinian's death. A canonical collection classified under sixty titles had been produced by an unknown compiler. This was critically revised with a classification under fifty titles by John the Scholastic, a native of Antioch, whose labours were rewarded when Justinian, shortly before his death in 565, controversially appointed him to be patriarch of Constantinople. To a second edition of his canonical collection John added a selection of Justinian's Novels bearing on church matters. The collection under fifty titles included the Apostolic Canons (from the eighth book of the *Apostolic Constitutions*), the canons of Serdica including that on Rome's appellate jurisdiction, and numerous canons from the canonical letters of Basil. The inclusion of Serdica implied no recognition of ecumenical authority.[6]

John the Scholastic had a colleague and kindred spirit, Athanasius of Emesa, who compiled a handbook of the Novels of Justinian, classified under twenty-two titles, the first being concerned with ecclesiastical rulings. His second edition survives. The preface claims the friendship and support of John the jurist of Antioch.[7]

---

[5] R. Schieffer, 'Das V. oekumenische Konzil in kanonistischer Überlieferung', *ZSSR*, Kan. Abt. 59 (1973), 1–34. Add to his survey the evidence that in 1054 some summary of the Acts of the Fifth Council was being read customarily on 20 July each year: C. Will, *Acta et scripta quae de controversiis ecclesiae Graecae et Latinae saeculo undecimo composita extant* (Leipzig and Marburg, 1861; repr. Frankfurt a. M., 1963), 167ª30.

[6] Text of the Nomocanon of Photius in RP i.

[7] John the Scholastic is edited by V. Beneševič (Abhandlungen der Bayerischen Akademie, phil.-hist. Kl., NF 14; Munich, 1937).

The Christological controversy was too intricate and too passionate to be susceptible of resolution by canonists, though their concern for coherence and unity was obviously not marginal to the debate.

In a painful and angry split hard words were used. Yet it was throughout taken for granted by all parties that there is and can be one and one only Catholic Orthodox Church. Suspension of communion could not be more than merely temporary while the issues were sorted out.

In 518, after discourteous exchanges between the Pope and the emperor Anastasius, who at one point was writing in irritation to Rome that he did dislike being personally insulted, the accession of the new emperor Justin, advised by his nephew Justinian, opened the way for restored communion. The then Pope Hormisdas (514–23) made it a condition that Greek bishops submit to papal authority with signatures to a formula destined to have a long future at Florence (1439) and Vatican I (1870):

Christ built his Church on St Peter, and so in the apostolic see the Catholic faith has always been kept without stain. There is one communion defined by the Roman see, and in that I hope to be, following the apostolic see in everything and affirming everything decided thereby.

The patriarch of Constantinople cannily subscribed his agreement to 'everything orthodox defined by Rome', and this sufficed. By this act communion between Old and New Rome was reinstated. From the imperial palace pressure on the patriarch was overwhelming. For the move was indispensable to Justinian's future political programme (announced on 18 March 536) restoring the old Roman empire in both west and east, crushing independent barbarian kingdoms (Goths in Italy, Vandals in North Africa; his armies were less successful against the Visigoths in Spain), and so using the maximum of force to make Constantinople the controlling centre of power throughout the Mediterranean world. The programme was motivated by the conviction that the Christian empire was 'sacred', *sanctum imperium*, and he had a duty to unite the inhabited world under one Christian and Roman law. For popes and the western churches that programme would create discomfort mainly because they saw the pope rather than the emperor as its proper instrument. The east Roman policy was indeed to restore the old empire, but with New rather than Old Rome as its capital.

In 519 Pope Hormisdas seemingly triumphed over Greek ambitions for autonomous decisions in the east. He soon found that Justinian's determination to restore social coherence to the empire required concessions to Monophysite critics of Chalcedon's 'in two natures'. The emperor was impressed by the ecumenical potential of a formula adapted from the Henotikon, 'one of the Trinity suffered in the flesh', advocated by Scythian monks from the Danube delta. Hormisdas disliked any such move. Tension between Italy and Constantinople at the political level was enhanced by Justinian's determination to take back control of Italy from king Theoderic the Ostrogoth at Ravenna and his successors. Pope Silverius (536–7), Hormisdas' son, was nominated by the then Gothic king Theodahad, and this became a lever for his expulsion engineered by his archdeacon Vigilius, ambitious to succeed him. Vigilius received private assurance of support from the empress Theodora at Constantinople, a fervent Monophysite; she intrigued with Vigilius to help him to become pope and provided a huge bribe of gold if he would hold communion with Monophysite friends of hers as patriarchs of Constantinople, Alexandria, and Antioch. He secretly agreed.

10

THREE CHAPTERS:
THE FIFTH COUNCIL (553)

Justinian was sure Constantine the Great had intervened in church affairs, and produced texts to demonstrate the point. In 543 and 544 Justinian issued edicts condemning speculations associated with Origen's name supported by Palestinian monks and then, more formidably, the three fifth-century advocates of 'two-nature' Christology, Theodore of Mopsuestia, Theodoret of Cyrrhus, and Ibas of Edessa, held in abhorrence by Monophysites. Theodore died in 427, but at Chalcedon Theodoret had been finally accepted by the bishops and a letter from Ibas, critical of Cyril of Alexandria, had been expressly declared to be orthodox. To reject these three clearly meant large concessions to Monophysite critics of Chalcedon, and in the case of Ibas this conclusion could be evaded only by inventing the subtle and certainly false story that the letter approved by Chalcedon was distinct from that hated by critics of the council and now damned by Justinian.

Pope Vigilius (537–55) was brought to Constantinople by Justinian's order early in 547 in the hope that, like the (reluctant) Greek patriarchs, he could be persuaded to add his signature to the imperial edicts. With a background of intrigue with Theodora the pope could be expected to cooperate, but he had become aware of strong opposition to the censure of the 'Three Chapters' in Africa and the Latin west. Confidentially he wrote to Justinian that his sole reason for delaying assent was to preserve Rome's prerogatives, but he now anathematized Ibas' letter, Theodoret's teachings where erroneous, and the person of Theodore. He confessed one *subsistentia*, i.e. one person, one operation. The document became public on Holy Saturday, Easter Eve, 548, and provoked strong Latin opposition, leading Vigilius to withdraw it as negative reactions were reported from western metropolitans.

Justinian realized that a papal assent disowned by western churches was of small value. His edicts needed the seal of an ecumenical council with coercive power. The Latin bishops were conciliar in their thinking about the nature of the Church, and (following Augustine) understood the authority of the Roman bishop to be that of executant of synodal decisions.

To his wrath Vigilius at Constantinople was subjected to violence. While the largely Greek council met, he reserved his position and stayed away, sending a judgement uncongenial to Justinian's aspirations. The emperor's rough handling of the Pope moved him (14 May 553) briefly to stand against censure of the Three Chapters.

Vigilius' absence from the conciliar proceedings raised awkward questions (which long reverberated in the east) about ecumenicity. Since the western patriarch's assent was essential, Justinian's council was declared to retain communion with Peter's see while excommunicating the temporary incumbent, i.e. with the *sedes*, not the *sedens*, a formula later important to Gallicanism. The council's condemnation of the Three Chapters provided authority for coercing dissidents, especially in Africa (where Facundus of Hermiane, a leading opponent, survived by hiding). On 23 February 554 Vigilius capitulated: had not Augustine written *Retractations*? Even popes could honourably change their minds. In spring 555 he left for Rome but died at Syracuse (7 June), bequeathing angry schisms in Africa and Italy, except at Ravenna where Justinian's viceroy (exarch) left the bishop with no choice.[1]

The intricacy of the Three Chapters controversy baffled western observers. How could one condemn three prominent defenders of 'two natures' Christology and simultaneously deny that this affected the authority of Chalcedon's definition and Pope Leo's Tome? It left the west with the term 'Byzantine' as synonym for intricate, deficient in transparency, even underhand and devious.

It could be subtly argued that only the first six sessions of the Council of Chalcedon with the definition of faith were binding, not the later approval of Theodoret and Ibas. Such arguments were not likely to appease irate bishops in Africa and north Italy convinced that the Pope had bought his own survival at the price of surrendering true faith. Dying on the return journey saved Vigilius from fearful problems. His successor Pelagius I had as deacon opposed the censure of the Three Chapters; but Justinian discerned that he would think it worth changing his mind to obtain the papal throne. Pelagius could find only two bishops willing to consecrate, assisted by a presbyter from Ostia. (By tradition, first attested in Augustine, the bishop of Ostia was principal consecrator for popes.) In Rome Pelagius gradually asserted authority though against vocal criticism, and appealed to the Petrine inheritance located in 'the apostolic sees'—a plural which in the eleventh century helped the canonist Deusdedit to mitigate Roman claims to absolute autocracy and so to reconcile east and west.

---

[1] D. Athanasius, *Novellensyntagma*, edited by Dieter Simon and Spyros Troianos (Frankfurt a. M., 1989).

A shortened edition of the Acts of the Council of 553 was produced to conceal Vigilius' refusal to participate, thereby obscuring his opposition to Justinian and his absence, which called in question the ecumenicity of the assembly. This did nothing to placate north Italy and Africa, where bishops thought the Pope had sold Chalcedon and Pope Leo down the river. Vigilius in conciliatory mode had twice declared that while there are two natures in Christ, there is only one activity, *enérgeia*. In the next century this was monothelete and heretical; in consequence the Roman legates at the Sixth Council of 680 declared these places heretical corruptions of the original Acts, and the Acts of 553 were transmitted only in a small part in Greek. They survive as a whole only in Latin, a surprising fact for a council reckoned in Greek Orthodox tradition as one of the sacred Seven Councils. The council was significantly ignored by the Greek canonist John Scholasticus, but was discovered in the west by Ivo of Chartres (*Decr.* 14. 49. 62–3). It was known to Mark Eugenicus of Ephesus at the Council of Florence.

In answer to the hostility of so many western churches to the condemnation of three bishops who had died in peace in communion with the universal Church, the Fifth Council (*Acta* 5. 56) appealed to 'letters of Augustine' to the effect that it was a duty to anathematize heretics even after their death. The letters in question are those in which Augustine says that, if the Donatists could succeed in proving Caecilian of Carthage guilty of the crimes attributed to him, he would willingly anathematize him even after death. This reference was to prove useful to Aquinas (*Summa contra Gentiles* 4. 24) and to the Latins at Florence. It showed that Greek tradition could acknowledge Augustine's authority.

A factor whose consequences can only be guessed was the devastating epidemic which ravaged the empire from 542 onwards. It is likely to have produced extreme feelings of insecurity when so many were being carried off; it could readily be interpreted as the manifestation of divine wrath.

Justinian spared no effort in his ecumenism, but it failed. The closer the parties were brought together in words, the more alarmed the hawks on either side became. The passionately anti-Chalcedonian bishop of Edessa Jacob Baradai created an underground Monophysite episcopate, making reconciliation far harder. Group rivalry and loyalty resulted, and any step to achieve peace seemed treachery. In practice there continued a two-way traffic of conversions from one party to the other. In Egypt an impassioned critic of Chalcedonian Christology, Nephalius, changed to being an equally zealous defender of the council; Severus of Antioch had had to engage him in controversy.

The continuing refusal of the churches in north Italy to recognize the Fifth Council's condemnation of the Three Chapters, to which Pope Vigilius finally assented, was a problem not only for the Byzantine exarch at Ravenna but also for the Roman see. It became necessary to stress authority and to give no reasons. Pope Pelagius I, Vigilius' successor, found a text under Augustine's name saying that anyone separating from communion with the apostolic see defines himself as schismatic. Pelagius was suspect in the west for condemning the Three Chapters but protested that he accepted the first four ecumenical councils. Papal supremacy and Rome's unswerving adherence to Chalcedonian faith became principal arguments against north Italian dissidence, used by successive popes until and including Gregory the Great (590–604).

In Gregory the Great's letters a legacy of distrust towards eastern patriarchs and sometimes even emperors is visible. Himself a papal envoy at Constantinople for some years, he found on his return that at Rome this brought distrust. For he accepted the Fifth Council of 553 while retaining primacy for the first four 'like the four gospels'. His letters to north Italy were worded with caution. Gregory hated the eastern title 'ecumenical patriarch', to which his predecessor Pelagius II had taken exception as if it must imply universal jurisdiction and had an anti-papal motivation.[2] But he did not think of Latin west and Greek east as different entities and in one letter (*Reg.* 10. 14) insisted that the old Greek and Latin Fathers were unanimous, a view which became invaluable in much later ecumenical exchanges.

Pope Boniface III (606–7), angered when the church of Constantinople described it itself as 'first of all churches', won a ruling from the emperor Phocas that Old Rome had that position (*Liber Pontificalis* 68).

---

[2] Gregory the Great, *Reg.* 5. 41 (MGH Epp. i. 332. 6). In correspondence with north Italy Gregory found it expedient not to mention the Fifth Council: *Reg.* 4. 37. A good discussion in Robert Markus, *Gregory the Great and his World* (Cambridge, 1997). On the wish among Ravenna clergy to be independent of both Rome and Constantinople see T. S. Brown, *Settimane Spoleto*, 34/1 ('1986' [1988]), 127–60.

II

ONE ENERGY, ONE WILL

During the seventh century the emperors and patriarchs of Constantinople made a last, valiant attempt to reconcile moderate Monophysites to the legitimacy of the Chalcedonian 'in two natures'. Even if 'two natures' was accepted, one could qualify that by saying there is only one centre of activity (*enérgeia*) or one will.[1] The 'one will' formula had difficulty with the gospel narrative of the agony in the garden of Gethsemane ('not my will but yours be done'). But 'one energy' had been language used by Pope Vigilius at the time of the Fifth Council (553).[2] 'One will' was smiled on by Pope Honorius[3] in 633–4 when at Alexandria the clever Chalcedonian bishop Cyrus succeeded in reconciling the majority group of moderate Monophysites on the basis of 'one theandric energy'—a formula from Dionysius the Areopagite, by 633 generally accepted as authentic.[4] Cyrus persecuted Copts unwilling to cooperate.

The body of writings put out under the name of Paul's convert at Athens was composed about AD 500, after the time of Proclus, head of the pagan school at Athens who died in 485, but before a citation at a colloquy in 532 and before Severus, patriarch of Antioch 512–18, in whose works (undatable) references to Dionysius are found. The unknown author was therefore writing at a time when Zeno's non-committal Henotikon ruled imperial

---

[1] The principal documents of the monothelete controversy are cited in the Acts either of Pope Martin I's Lateran Council (649) or of the Sixth Council at Constantinople (680–1). The Acts of these two Councils are edited by R. Riedinger in the second series of *Acta Conciliorum Oecumenicorum*. Most of the works of Maximus Confessor are in PG 90–1. There is a good English translation of important texts of Maximus by G. C. Berthold (Classics of Western Spirituality, 1985); and by Andrew Louth (1996); an introduction to recent work by Aidan Nichols, *Byzantine Gospel: Maximus Confessor in Modern Scholarship* (Edinburgh, 1993).

[2] *ACO* IV i. 187. 32 and 188. 14. The authenticity of this utterance was anxiously denied by the Roman legates at the Sixth Council in the fourteenth session (*ACO*² II 638 ff., especially 646–7, 652–3).

[3] *ACO*² II 550. 15. Honorius judged either one energy or two to be no proper matter for dispute (555. 5).

[4] *ACO*² II 594–600. Dionysius Areopagita, *ep.* 4, PG 3. 1072 C. Sophronius of Jerusalem objected to 'one theandric energy' in Cyrus' monothelete text, but accepted the authenticity of Dionysius the Areopagite; see his florilegium in Photius, *Bibliotheca* 231. On Sophronius' role see C. von Schönborn, *Sophrone de Jérusalem* (Paris, 1972); thereon A. de Halleux, *Rev. théol. de Louvain*, 5 (1974), 481–3.

government policy in regard to the sharp controversy about the Christology of the Council of Chalcedon. While Dionysius' primary motive in writing was to domesticate within the Church the mystical Neoplatonic terminology of Proclus, he could hardly avoid saying something about Christology and on the Trinity. His language about the nature or natures of Christ was capable of being interpreted by either party in a manner which satisfied the demands of the rival orthodoxies. Competing groups therefore devoted much attention to arguing either that when correctly interpreted Dionysius supported their party's position, or that, if his text supported the other side, then his works were not authentic products of the apostolic age, a scepticism which could be supported by observing that these writings were never mentioned by Origen or by Eusebius of Caesarea and that they described ceremonies and church customs first established long after the first century. The high probability is that 'Dionysius' was the mouthpiece of a reconciler seeking to express himself in terms that would help the warring factions towards a 'cease-fire'. For the Chalcedonian bishop Cyrus of Alexandria needing rapprochement with moderate Monophysites in Egypt, Dionysius offered an open door. His position in regard to Christology could look either way, much as he did also on the principle governing icons, to which he might be as strongly averse as favourable.

Unhappily it is the destiny of many proposals for reconciliation that they in turn become the subject of disputes. The Alexandrian union of 633 produced deep division among the Chalcedonians, and in the autumn of 638 the emperor Heraclius had become so alarmed by the rising temperature of debate that he issued an edict or *Ekthesis* forbidding talk of either one or two energies but concluding for one will. This was erected in the narthex of Hagia Sophia at Constantinople, and was endorsed by patriarchal synod.[5]

During his tenure of the papacy Honorius was held in respect. His ecumenical intention in supporting the Alexandrian agreement was high-minded, and his letters indicating approval were cautiously worded. Nevertheless after his death in 638 the higher Roman clergy received reports of consternation at Jerusalem from the newly elected patriarch Sophronius, and of distress in a prodigiously learned Greek monk and ex-civil servant Maximus. It would become a grave question whether Honorius' successors could approve of Heraclius' *Ekthesis*.

Maximus' profound misgivings about monothelete language led him to retire from the emperor's service and to retreat to a monastery. His mind was

<hr/>

[5] The *Ekthesis* is cited in full at the third session of the Lateran Council, 649: *ACO*² I 156. 20–162. 9. Near the end of his life Heraclius disowned responsibility for it, a fact reported in the Acts of Maximus Confessor's trial (PG 90. 125). A new fragment (from a florilegium in Marcianus gr. 573, s. ix–x) is printed by S. Rizou-Couroupos in Jürgen Dummer (ed.), *Texte und Textkritik, eine Aufsatzsammlung* (TU 133; Berlin, 1987), 531–2.

trained in logic and philosophy, but the strong inclination of his religion being towards mystical theology, he found the writings of Dionysius the Areopagite congenial. He was also much disinclined to welcome originality and innovation, above all in theology, and was a well-read master of the great patristic authors of the past. The monk in him profoundly valued the teaching of his spiritual director and in him more than one stream of ascetic theology found its confluence. The Chalcedonian definition safeguarded the integrity of the humanity of the Redeemer, and to Maximus that was of the greatest importance for his understanding of salvation and of the ascetic path. Anxieties about the ambiguities inherent in talk about 'activity' and 'will' led him to a considerable and in large part original analysis of these terms. The monothelete proposal prejudiced the spontaneity and self-determination distinctive of being human, though Maximus granted that in Christ the divine will forms the human will and in the Garden of Gethsemane there is no question of double-mindedness.

A tenth-century Studite Life of Maximus, which used some earlier material, reports a dream or vision in which Maximus heard two angelic choirs singing, one in the east, the other in the west. He reported that the singing of the western choir was clearer and better.[6]

Maximus saw the only hope for orthodoxy in stirring up the popes to oppose a false irenicism which in his eyes was treachery and compromise of the truth. Surprisingly, he defended Honorius, but with embarrassment. With the support of Greek monks in Rome he organized the opposition to the 'one will' or monothelete formula, culminating in Pope Martin I's Lateran Council (649), for which Maximus asserted that it had the status of the Sixth Council. The patriarch of Constantinople certainly commissioned no legate to represent his see there. Maximus evidently regarded the presence of himself and other Greek monks as sufficiently imparting ecumenical status to an otherwise largely Latin assembly of Italian and Sicilian bishops, whose contribution to the discussions was almost zero.

Discussion was absent at the Lateran Council anyway. The sessions were dominated by a florilegium of citations in support of two wills in Christ presented by Maximus and the Greek monks in Rome, together with an anthology of monothelete citations in illustration of the heresy. No comment other than simple assent was needed or expected from the bishops present. To this generalization the Acts of the Council offer one exception, namely Pope Martin himself, whose interventions were fairly numerous—perhaps composed for him by Maximus since the Pope's familiarity with Greek would have been small. Before Martin consented to affix his signature to the Acts, he required that they should first be read to the assembly in a Latin translation.

---

[6] PG 90. 89 c. See W. Lackner, *Anal. Boll.* 85 (1967), 185–316.

In reaction to pressure from emperors and patriarchs at Constantinople to allow the 'one energy, one will' formula to be free of heresy and therefore at least a legitimate option, Maximus' only recourse was the supreme authority of St Peter's see. That was, he felt, for all truly orthodox minds the ultimate source of judgement and the criterion of catholic communion.[7] He thought it monstrous of people at Byzantium to deny authority to Pope Martin's Lateran Council on the legalistic ground that it did not enjoy the emperor's assent and ratification. As for Honorius' embarrassing letter supporting 'one will', the drafter, still living, had assured him it meant only Christ's human will. To critics at Constantinople Maximus' defence of Pope Honorius must necessarily have seemed astonishing and gratifying. To the emperor and patriarch Honorius' approval of their wise ecumenism, which is what monotheletism was, seemed a godsend. At the Sixth Council in 680 citations from Honorius were embarrassing. Yet Maximus had defended him. His defence was known to Anastasius the Roman librarian (MGH Epp. vii. 425. 14–15) who also reports that Pope John VIII composed an apology for Honorius, needed at a time when supporters of Photius at the Council of 869 were contending that popes were not incapable of grave mistakes. Pope John's apologia implied a rebuke for his predecessor Hadrian II who, to the council of 869–70 at Constantinople, had conceded that heresy was the one ground on which a charge could legitimately be brought against a pope.

Photius was aware of the Sixth Council's condemnation of Honorius (*ep.* 1. 330, i. 12 LW). When Nicolas I claimed infallibility, he mentioned Honorius as a counter-instance. In a list of 'Ten Questions and Answers' (PG 104. 1219–32) Photius mentioned Liberius and Honorius as instances of popes in error; and Felix II was 'impudent' to claim that the Council of Nicaea had given the Roman see the supreme power of ratifying or not any synod whatsoever.

It is worth noting that Maximus' reference to the drafter of Honorius' letters shows that, even before Anastasius the Librarian, popes were using curial officials in this sensible way.

The 'one will' formula split the Chalcedonians. By enlisting support from Honorius' successors with the argument that authentic Chalcedonian Christology was thereby prejudiced since the Monophysites were gleefully claiming to have been vindicated, Maximus made the issue one between east

---

[7] On Pope Martin see the conference papers of 1991 in *Martino I papa e il suo tempo* (Spoleto, 1992). The Acts of the Lateran Council, 649, are edited in *ACO²* I by Riedinger, who also showed the Latin text to be translated from Greek. Greek monks in Rome had influence and enabled the council to be ranked 'ecumenical': see P. Conte, *Il sinodo lateranense dell'ottobre 649* (Vatican City, 1989). A main text for Maximus on authority is PG 91. 137–40: 'To anathematize the Roman see is to condemn the Catholic Church.' See J. M. Garrigues, *Istina*, 21 (1976), 6–24. On Honorius see G. Kreuzer, *Die Honoriusfrage im Mittelalter und in der Neuzeit* (Stuttgart, 1975), 116.

and west. The patriarchs of Alexandria and Antioch were for a time in favour of the reconciliation; and in Syria monothelete support was strong enough to ensure that one group, the Maronites, remained loyal to this position until pressure from the crusaders brought them, in 1182 and ever since, to accept communion with Rome.

From 542 and periodically until the mid-eighth century, the east Roman empire was ravaged by bubonic plague, removing up to a third of the population. That drastically weakened its power, and the seventh century brought a serious crisis of successive hammer-blows. At huge cost the eastern armies managed to repel a formidable attack from the Persian empire. But restive Arabs were already carrying out successful raids in Palestine and Syria, and suddenly discovered that they could pour forces into the vacuum created by the exhaustion and collapse of the contending powers of Persia and Constantinople. The new militant religion of Islam imparted zeal. By 638 they had captured Jerusalem, by 641 Alexandria and Egypt. By the end of the century the north African provinces had fallen to them. The *Didascalia Jacobi* (a defence of Jesus' Messiahship by a compulsorily baptized Jew under Heraclius at Carthage in 640) notes the vastness of Roman power from Scotland to Persia; 'but today we see Romania brought low'.

The effect of military defeat on the empire was to make many fear that the protection of heaven had been lost, perhaps because of heresy or the divisions between rival ecclesiastical factions. The emotional power behind Pope Martin I's Lateran Council in 649 was to stem the overwhelming pressure from Constantinople in favour of the monothelete compromise, which might reconcile the alienated population in Syria and especially Egypt. In the outcome Maximus was arraigned for challenging imperial authority, causing Arab success. Pope Martin was arrested, taken under guard to Constantinople, and put on trial for treasonable rebellion against the sovereignty of the emperor. He had failed to oppose a usurper Olympius in Italy and, irrespective of his theology, was politically guilty. He subsequently suffered to the point of death. A successor at Rome was consecrated and apparently accepted even while Martin was still alive.

Nevertheless, the events fostered awareness that the strength of Rome, as protector of the western interest in relation to the east, lay in the establishment of new churches in the Anglo-Saxon and Germanic regions. This awareness is to be seen in the sending of Theodore of Tarsus to be archbishop of Canterbury and to establish a school there with serious study of Greek, and in the formal letter of Pope Agatho at the time of the Sixth Council of 680, where, in rebutting the monothelete claim to provide a reconciling and universal faith, the Pope catalogued the many barbarian churches of the west which regarded the claim as offensive. The Christological controversy was ending with distrust between east and west.

12

THE SIXTH COUNCIL (680–1)
COUNCIL *IN TRULLO* (692)

Pope Martin's predecessor was Theodore I (642–9), a Greek who had come to Rome from Jerusalem, where the patriarch Sophronius' opinion of the monothelete controversy was well known. In correspondence with Constantinople Pope Theodore expressed orthodox belief in terms that explicitly included the Augustinian affirmation that the Son participates in the 'proceeding' of the Holy Spirit from the Father. That was to hand the eastern defenders of 'one will' a momentous counter-argument: to affirm that the Spirit proceeds not only from the Father but also from the Son was to add to the ecumenical creed of the Council of Constantinople (381), a creed which contained the crucial term *homoousios* and was therefore often (incorrectly) called 'Nicene'. Was not this addition irreverence to a general council? If the popes were teaching the *Filioque* as true catechetical doctrine (after all, it was in the so-called Athanasian Creed), that for the Greeks invalidated Roman claims to have a universal teaching authority able to correct eastern patriarchs. Greek monotheletes appealed to Pope Honorius against Pope Martin. Maximus tried to reconcile the two popes.[1]

The west had no intuitive understanding of the critical position of the east Roman empire, where the split over the correctness of Chalcedon vastly weakened the emperor's power to maintain the frontiers against Persian and then Arab attacks. Eight years before Pope Martin's Lateran Council, Alexandria fell to Muslim forces. The invasions, however, made the emperors conscious of their need for western aid. At the Sixth Council at

---

[1] Maximus Confessor (PG 91. 135 A) defended the Roman *Filioque*. It had precedent in Cyril of Alexandria's commentary on St John. Maximus would himself say the Spirit proceeds from the Father through the Son (PG 90. 672 C; 814 B). At Rome he had inquired about the meaning of maintainers of the *Filioque* and had been satisfied that, though their idiom was different, the sense was not unorthodox. This defence of the *Filioque* was known to Anastasius the Librarian (MGH Epp. vii. 425, 20). Discussion by G. C. Berthold, 'Maximus Confessor and the *Filioque*', *Studia Patristica*, 18/1 (1986), 113–17. For 'six councils' see PG 91. 137 D. The Lateran Council of 649 is numbered 'Sixth Council' in a source used by the Antiochene revision of the tenth-century Melkite chronicler Eutychius patriarch of Alexandria or Saʿīd ibn Baṭrīq; PG 111. 749 reprints E. Pococke's translation of a Bodleian text (Oxford, 1659). See M. Breydy, *Études sur Saʿīd ibn Baṭrīq et ses sources* (CSCO 450, Subsidia 69; Leuven, 1983).

Constantinople (680–1) the emperor, who faced a military pincer of attacks from Arabs in the south-east and Bulgarians in the north, brought his bishops, except Patriarch Macarius of Antioch, to agree with the west and to reject the 'one will' formula.

By personal intervention the emperor directed the patriarch of Constantinople to ensure that the monothelete patriarch of Antioch was deposed to meet the expectations of Pope Agatho. The patriarch of Antioch appealed to the letters of Honorius. If the patriarch of Antioch fell, so did that pope. Much conciliar debate turned on the authenticity of patristic texts. Those in the florilegium of the patriarch of Antioch were rejected.

The bishops at the Sixth Council were confronted by an intricate task. The emperor needed unreserved support from the west. Therefore the Petrine authority of the pope had to be trumpeted loud, yet not so loud as to make it impossible to censure Honorius with named patriarchs. The price exacted by the Greek bishops was the inclusion of Honorius in the list of condemned heretics. The Roman legates had to agree, and Pope Agatho had to ratify. At the council his legates twice rejected a proposal that it would suffice to condemn the doctrine while mentioning no particular names. They had no preconception that it was inherently impossible for a bishop of Rome to maintain a heresy.

The record of the condemnations subtly placed the name of Honorius in the middle of a list of patriarchs of Constantinople, in such a way as to make it easy for uninformed persons later to imagine that this Honorius was not bishop of Rome but one more of the patriarchs of Constantinople whose orthodoxy was suspect in the west. Nevertheless Honorius' condemnation was hard for Rome to swallow. Agatho died on 10 January 681. His successor Leo II was not installed until 17 August 682. The long gap would be explicable if Leo was trying to persuade the emperor not to make unreserved assent to Honorius' condemnation a condition of imperial ratification necessary for his own appointment. Might it suffice that Macarius of Antioch and his main supporters were exiled and incarcerated in Roman monasteries? The emperor did not yield.

In the seventies of the ninth century the Sixth Council's inclusion of Pope Honorius among the heretics censured, with papal ratification, would become a factor in the tensions of that time between Constantinople and Rome. The case of Pope Honorius was used to demonstrate that a successor of St Peter could err. To Photius both Nicolas I and his successor Hadrian II were in error. So a lively interest in the Honorius question was shown by Pope John VIII and Anastasius the papal librarian. To defend Honorius, just possible for Maximus Confessor, was difficult after the Sixth Council's condemnation. Nevertheless it is not easy to think that Honorius was sympathetically or justly treated. He suffered a fate common to ecumenists.

The Sixth Council of 680 enacted no disciplinary canons. Nor had the Fifth done so in 553. But in 691–2 a supplementary synod, under the emperor Justinian II with Roman apocrisiaries, met in the domed hall or *Trullos* of the imperial palace at Constantinople.[2] A miscellany of canons corrected laxities in the Greek churches: fees not to be charged for celebrating the eucharist, clerical dress, simony, prohibited degrees of affinity in marriage, the honour of Mary; canon 79 forbids the practice of offering her fine bread on the day after the celebration of Christ's Nativity on the ground that this is inappropriate for a mother who was a virgin—presumably it was good custom for mothers who bore children by the normal process. Sexy icons are forbidden (100). One canon (82) directs that icons must represent Christ as human, not as a lamb. (A possible echo of this canon is the decision of Pope Sergius to insert *Agnus Dei* in the mass.) The council also asked for corrections beyond the Greek region. The Roman demands that other churches keep a Saturday fast and expect celibacy of inferior clergy were expressly censured (canons 13, 30, 55). Armenian churches were told not to eat cheese and eggs on Saturdays and Sundays in Lent, not to boil meat in church buildings (56 and 99), and not to treat clerical office as hereditary (33). The bishops were also anxious to stop pagan rites among students of the civil law (71). such superstitious survivals as jumping on bonfires at new moon (65), and other rustic customs.

Rulings forbade clergy to attend race-meetings (24) or theatrical shows and dances (51). Resort to soothsayers, elderly fortune-tellers called 'centurions', or to travelling entertainers with she-bears, and magicians (61), is forbidden; likewise special fires on 1 March, and dances in which the men wear female clothing and the women male, or masks are worn and Dionysus is invoked for the vintage (62). Oaths invoking pagan gods are censured (94). Clergy trading as pimps are to be degraded (86). Nor may they have taverns (9). Abortion is murder (91). Clergy and monks may not go to the baths when women are washing (77). Church music is not to be noisy or secular (75). A surprising canon (63) forbids reading in Church stories of martyrs of

---

[2] On the council *in Trullo* see H. Ohme, *Das Concilium Quinisextum und seine Bischofsliste* (Berlin, 1990); critical edition by G. Nedungatt and F. Featherstone, *The Council in Trullo Revisited* (Kanonika, 6; Rome, Pontifical Oriental Institute, 1995) including M. Van Esbroeck's translation of the Armenian Catholicos's discourse. The canons have attracted detailed studies, e.g. Judith Herrin, 'Femina Byzantina: The Council in Trullo on Women', *Dumbarton Oaks Papers*, 46 (1992), 97–105; J. Williams, 'Use of Sources in the Canons of the Council *in Trullo*', *Byzantion*, 66 (1996), 470–88. F. Trombley discusses the canons about paganism, heresy, etc. in *Comitatus*, 9 (1978), 1–18. The Quinisext canon 82 also appears cited in a letter, of hotly contested genuineness, to the patriarch Germanus from Pope Gregory II cited at the fourth session of Nicaea II. That Gregory II was against iconoclasm is not in doubt, but the case for thinking the letter at least to be heavily interpolated, perhaps entirely spurious, is weighty.

such extravagant nature as to induce unbelief, composed by enemies of the truth.[3]

There is another reference to the embarrassment caused by Lives of Saints in Leo Choirosphaktes (PG 107. 660–1), an admirer of Julian the Apostate on the Galileans (below, p. 127 n.11). Leo was Secretary to the emperor Leo VI (the Wise).

A canon (70) forbidding women to speak (presumably meaning to teach or preach) during the divine liturgy evoked a later sad canonist's scholion: 'Probably at that time there were women able to do what now even bishops are incapable of doing' (*XIV Titles*, ed. Beněsevič, St Petersburg, 1905).

For some centuries to come voices from Rome repeatedly asked the Greek churches to keep the custom, believed at Rome to be of apostolic origin, whereby Saturday was a fast day. At Rome no one could recall its introduction, and it was probably correct that the custom was of very high antiquity, originating in a wish to mark a difference from the synagogue where sabbaths are feasts (Jubilees 2: 31) and fasting altogether forbidden. The ancient Didache (8: 1) records a concern that Christians fast on Wednesday and Friday, not with the synagogue on Monday and Thursday.

Churches outside Rome did not have this custom of a Saturday fast. In recording dissent the Quinisext Council, 'Fifth–Sixth' or Penthekte as it was later called, was asserting the east Roman sense of independence. The Saturday fast was valued at Rome as integral to the inherited deposit of faith. Disparagement was offensive. But for the west the supremely painful canon (36) of the Quinisext council reaffirmed the ruling of the Council of Chalcedon (not accepted by Leo I) that the see of Constantinople's privileges are equal to Old Rome's, to which it is second in honour. Pope Sergius I refused to ratify the canons, though his legates had accepted them. Nevertheless the Trullan canons became basic to Greek canon law. Nothing was enacted at the council in regard to the western *Filioque*.

That Quinisext canons were cold towards Roman autocracy was obvious to Nicetas of Nicaea about 1100, who knew that the then pope had not assented to them (PG 120. 717 A). This was evident also to Balsamon (RP ii. 300).

A discourse by the Armenian Catholicos survives, given to the Council of 692 to answer criticisms of Armenian customs. Among other things, it stresses Armenian use of unleavened bread in the eucharist, not mentioned in Quinisext canons but perhaps the subject of critical discussions at the council. Controversy between Greek and Armenian surfaces much later, but the *Chronicle* of pseudo-Dionysius of Tel-Mahre, reproducing the

---

[3] I. Rochow, 'Zu heidnischen Bräuchen bei der Bevölkerung des byzantinischen Reiches im 7. Jhdt. vor allem auf Grund des Trullanum', *Klio*, 60 (1978), 483–97, illustrates the Trullan canons forbidding peasant customs and old rituals from texts such as the seventh-century *Passio S. Dasii* or Justinian's *Digest* (*C. Omnem* 9, p. 12 Krueger), forbidding games of new law students, or later evidence of Balkan folklore attested in the fourteenth century by Joseph Bryennios.

sixth-century historian John of Ephesus, seems to imply disputes among the Syrian Orthodox (i.e. Jacobites), where both leavened and unleavened bread were thought sufficient, but the latter preferred. Dionysius bar Salibi (d. 1171) shows the Syrian Orthodox of his day using leavened bread and in controversy with Armenians.

In the west there remained lack of unanimity about the status of the canons of 692. In the east they were cited as possessing the authority of the Sixth Council. A number of the canons were included by Ivo of Chartres and from his collection passed to Gratian, thence to be cited as authoritative by Pope Innocent III and by several bishops and theologians at the Council of Trent. However, in the acrimonious onslaught on patriarch Michael Cerularius by Cardinal Humbert in 1054, the Roman legate did not conceal his objection to the Quinisext affirmation of the dignity of Constantinople.

The Quinisext canons provide the earliest evidence for tension between east and west on the subject of priestly celibacy. Late fourth-century monks could be scornfully censorious of town clergy who had wives and therefore were concerned for the prosperity of their children and other worldly anxieties. Greek and Latin classical texts treat sexuality as a fit subject for low comedy on stage but a barrier to high aspirations of the mind and soul. In the Church it was no different. If a Christian priest was celebrating the eucharist, the laity expected his mind and heart to be pure, and undistracted by erotic thoughts. From the third-century sermons of Origen onwards there came to be mounting pressure on those responsible for ministering holy things to the people of God. This was especially felt once the celebration of the eucharist became daily. The Gallic Council of Tours in 567 (canon 19) classified presbyters, deacons, and subdeacons who had conjugal relations with wives as 'Nicolaitans', that is, followers of the licentious sect of Apoc. 2: 15. In eighth-century Ravenna a bishop who continued to live with his wife found his Latin clergy and laity refusing to take communion at his hands. Such refusal was censured at the Council of Gangra (c.355?).

In the Greek east the rule came to be that celibacy was expected of bishops and monks, but not of presbyters and deacons in towns and rural villages. Deep offence was caused when western travellers to the east applied to the local clergy the same kind of moral pressure to which western clergy were subjected. The tension directly affected the laity. In time, e.g. in the drive to enforce priestly celibacy in the Gregorian reform of the eleventh century, there came to be cases where the laity grossly insulted priests living with female partners and trampled under foot consecrated hosts sanctified by married presbyters. In 1074 the monk Sigebert of Gembloux published a protest against this attitude and action.[4]

    [4] Sigebert's protest is in MGH Libelli de lite ii. 437–48, discussed by A. Fliche, *La Réforme grégorienne*, iii (Louvain, 1937), 39–48.

At the Sixth Council of 680–1 and in 692 the *Filioque* played no part in debate. Pope Agatho's letters to Byzantium carefully omitted the issue.[5] Conscious perhaps that his jurisdiction was in practice less universal than popes liked to claim, he was delighted to inform the Greek emperor that in the west he had the unqualified support of a long catalogue of barbarian kingdoms and bishops, including Theodore of Canterbury 'the philosopher'. What the Pope could not do was to send on the English synod's statement of faith agreed under Theodore's presidency at Hatfield (near Doncaster), since this not only affirmed the five ecumenical councils but strongly emphasized adherence to the *Filioque*.[6] Bede saw Theodore's synod as reassuring Rome of English orthodoxy. Perhaps Bishop Wilfrid of York, who in 679 went to Rome complaining of Theodore's autocratic ways, had insinuated that this learned Greek monk originating from Tarsus and Rome was unsound, and Theodore was rebutting the charge. In the Acts of the Sixth Council there is one approximation to the issue when Macarius, monothelete patriarch of Antioch, submitting his faith at the eighth session, included belief that 'the Holy Spirit proceeds from the Father and is revealed through the Son'.[7] This formula had been favoured by the anti-monothelete Maximus Confessor, and would reappear at the iconophile second Council of Nicaea in 787 when, during the third session, the presiding patriarch Tarasius laid before the bishops his Synodika on assuming office (an elevation causing controversy since he was previously a lay civil servant). In the Frankish empire, where the iconophile decisions of the second Council of Nicaea were most unwelcome, Tarasius' words attracted adverse comment, but Pope Hadrian I (772–95) defended them as compatible with western orthodoxy.[8]

During the three decades following the Sixth Council, mountingly dangerous Bulgarian and Arab attacks, at one point reinforced by the Armenians, produced profound anxiety and insecurity at Constantinople, and the fearful

[5] Agatho's letter to the emperor for the Sixth Council, together with the record of his Italian Synod, is in the fourth session of the Sixth Council: *ACO*² II 53–123, 123–59. On the date of Agatho's council to investigate the complaints of Wilfrid of York, and on his conception of papal authority, see Stephan Kuttner in *Studia in honorem . . . A. M. Stickler* (Rome, 1992), 215–24.

[6] Bede, *HE* 4. 17. H. Chadwick, 'Theodore of Tarsus and Monotheletism', in *Logos: Festschrift für Luise Abramowski* (Berlin, 1993), 534–44. In a richly learned discussion, Michael Lapidge has observed that Theodore of Tarsus was among the Greek monks in Rome who together with Maximus Confessor formed the Acts of the Lateran Council 649. 'Through the Son' was accepted doctrine for Maximus, probably therefore for the Greek monks associated with him and Pope Martin. See M. Lapidge, *Biblical Commentaries from the Canterbury School of Theodore and Hadrian* (Cambridge, 1994), 139–46. Dr Alan Thacker, 'Memorializing Gregory the Great: The Origin and Transmission of a Papal Cult in the Seventh and Early Eighth Centuries', *Early Medieval Europe*, 7 (1998), 58–84, shows Theodore fostering veneration of the papal founder of his see and therefore his loyalty to Rome.

[7] *ACO*² II 220. 1.

[8] Tarasius is attacked for this formula by the Libri Carolini, 3. 2–3 (MGH Concilia ii supp. i. 345 ff.); Hadrian's defence in his letter to Charlemagne: MGH Epp. v. 7. 21 ff.

question was asked whether the doctrine of two wills was in fact correct. The emperor Philippikos Bardanes (December 711–June 713) declared for the monotheletes, sending a letter for information to the Pope Constantine I (708–15). His successor Anastasius II had to rectify that.

13

ICONS

Western iconoclasm had been suppressed by Gregory the Great, saying pictures are a Bible for the illiterate. But western devotion seldom regarded icons as quasi-sacramental sharing in the sanctity portrayed. Hence questions: Are they to be honoured and venerated as real presences of Christ, the Blessed Virgin Mary, and the saints, deriving their holiness from the holy person they bring before the eye? Or at the opposite extreme does their popular veneration pass into attitudes indistinguishable from idolatry, that is the worship of the creaturely in place of the Creator? Or is there a middle way in which they are valued as visual aids, just as the architecture of a church building is a help towards the spirit of awe and worship, analogous to the way in which the words of scripture or the musical chanting of psalms can move the mind to a realization of the presence of God? In this middle way, it is an important consideration that in a society where a fairly high proportion of people either cannot read or find it more natural to cope with a picture than to unravel the meaning of sentences, icons are a Bible for non-readers.

A derivative question concerns the manner in which sacred pictures may properly be venerated. A kiss was a normal greeting of deep respect, whether to an emperor or a bishop. That was equally natural for a holy picture. One would also expect to show one's respect for the person depicted by lighting a candle, or on special occasions using incense as a symbol of ascending prayer, the saint's intercession being invoked. A candle and incense were media also used by polytheistic idolaters to honour their domestic gods and heroes. So the question arose whether this form of showing honour was transformed into a Christian act by the holy person being honoured, or whether the mental attitude was so close to pagan cult as to mean that Christ or Mary or the saints were being used for the ends of 'natural religion'—i.e. to obtain not moral and spiritual strength but success in this world's affairs in love, commerce, health.

Asia Minor, Egypt, Syria, and Palestine bore the brunt of Arab attacks in the seventh century. The Byzantine empire lost much territory by defeats, and the anxious question was being asked if God, the giver of victory, was offended by the veneration of icons as being idolatrous, especially seeing that the successful Muslims had no such pictures. On the other hand, iconophiles liked to argue that iconoclasm was at home in the Jewish synagogue. When John of Damascus wrote in defence of icons, he included critical passages on Judaism.

In 725 or 726, after a huge eruption of the volcano at Thera (Santorini), and dangerous Arab incursions into Asia Minor with the capture of Cappadocian Caesarea and Nicaea, the emperor Leo III at Constantinople issued a decree forbidding icons. Was Arab military success caused by their rule against pictures of human beings?

The tangles and wrangles of the Christological controversy were bewildering to many of the laity. Holy icons had the merit of not being doctrines, and therefore had the capacity to bring together believers sundered by disputes about natures. Those who felt debarred from sharing the eucharist together could nevertheless venerate the same icon, especially in the quest for healing. Icons, however, became during the eighth and early ninth centuries as divisive between east and west as the *Filioque* had begun to be since the dissension about 'one will'.

Icons were not the only matter for tension between Rome and Constantinople. The emperor Leo III was faced with high military costs in resisting the Arabs who besieged Constantinople at this time (717–18). Leo III demanded that the Italians pay more for their own defence against the Lombards and not expect him to provide everything needed. High tax on church lands angered Pope Gregory II (715–31), who, according to his biography in the *Liber Pontificalis*, survived both assassination plots and an attempt by imperial officers to remove him. Gregory was supported by the Italian population in resisting both the new taxes and the emperor's decision that churches in his empire should have no pictures of angels, saints, and martyrs, not even of Christ and his virgin mother. A Roman synod in 731 supported icons with a substantial florilegium (part of which survives in a letter to Charlemagne from Pope Hadrian I). Nevertheless, the breach between Italy and an iconoclast Constantinople was only gradual, and did not become serious until the 750s. The fall of Ravenna to the Lombards in 751 would have sounded many alarm-bells. The Arabs' military successes had deprived the empire of rich provinces in Syria, Egypt, and north Africa, and the treasury at Constantinople was deprived of a huge proportion of its revenues in land tax. The emperor looked to Italy to help out.

When the iconoclasts under the emperor Constantine V held a council at Hiereia on the Marmara coast south of Constantinople in the year 754, the 338 bishops assembled claimed ecumenicity on the ground of the orthodoxy of their doctrine and the authority of the emperor who was lord of all the world. That claim raised questions. There were no representatives present from the patriarchates of Rome, Alexandria, Antioch, and Jerusalem. In any event the bishop of Rome was in opposition to the iconoclast doctrine. But the popes were already inclined to look to the Frankish court for support. It would prove a source of uncertainty that the Frankish attitude to iconoclasm was less negative. The Franks' relation to Byzantium was a mixture of desire for cooperation to combat the Arabs and an ambition to challenge the east Roman empire in its claim to control the west. The latter aspiration was going to be more influential on their attitude, and would affect church relations.

A confrontation over icons was not long in coming. At Pippin's court in 764–6 papal legates and imperial ambassadors from iconoclast Constantinople were in sharp contention (recorded in Codex Carolinus 36, MGH Epp. III). At a synod in Rome in 769 a florilegium of citations from approved authors was compiled, defending the use of icons as well as the western *Filioque*. The double thrust of this defence must imply that the Roman refusal to support the iconoclasm of the emperors since 725 had precipitated a renewal of eastern attacks on the right and authority of the papacy, i.e. the western patriarch, to define orthodoxy for the universal Church, as had been claimed long before by Popes Gelasius and Vigilius. The florilegium survived to be useful in preparing for the troubled encounter between east and west at the Council of Lyon in 1274.[1]

The iconoclast Council of Hiereia was abhorrent in the mind and memory of the contemporary papacy. Pope Stephen III's Council in 769 anathematized the iconoclast Council of 754, and reaffirmed the traditional papal opposition to the destruction of valued aids to devotion. It cannot have been acceptable to Rome that the east Roman emperor could think his council possessed ecumenical standing when there had been no participation by any Roman legates in the council's proceedings. For Constantine V it was made ecumenical by his authority.

The eighth-century controversies raised the question of the authority and constitutive elements that made a council 'ecumenical'. The epithet meant 'worldwide' and very early had been applied to the Council of Nicaea in 325; it had been borrowed from secular usage, where it was applied to a world-wide association of professional actors who were allowed tax-exemption.[2] But for Christian bishops the word carried the aura of catholicity. All the ancient ecumenical councils were called and ratified by emperors, who in

---

[1] See A. Alexakis, *Codex Parisinus Graecus 1115 and its Archetype* (Dumbarton Oaks Studies, 34: Washington, DC, 1996), 39–40, especially on the reuse of the florilegium of 731 in the Roman council of 769. On the iconoclast emperor Constantine V, see Ilse Rochow, *Kaiser Konstanin V. (741–775): Materialien zu einem Leben* (Berliner byzantinistische Studien, 1; Frankfurt a. M., 1994). The wider context of the iconoclastic controversy is well treated by Judith Herrin, *The Formation of Christendom* (Oxford, 1987). The Codex Carolinus is edited in MGH Epp. iii (1893), also PL 98.

[2] 'The Origin of the Title Ecumenical Council', *JTS*, NS 23 (1972), 132–5, reprinted in my collected studies, *History and Thought of the Early Church* (Aldershot, 1981), no. XI.

each case except in 381 had the cooperation of Rome and the great sees of the east. From Damasus in 371 popes began to hold that papal ratification was constitutive of a council's universal authority. In the east most Greek bishops took it for granted that the emperor's approval was the crucial necessity. The ruler of the *oikoumene* decided such things.

Eusebius of Caesarea's *Life of Constantine* presented the emperor as God's viceroy on earth, in his sole monarchy representing the divine Monarch.[3] It was to become a principle of east Christian political theory that 'nothing should be done in the Church contrary to the will of the emperor'.[4] The decisions of the Fourth Ecumenical Council at Chalcedon received their ratification from the emperor Marcian.[5] The Henotikon was promulgated with the authority of Zeno.[6] The emperor exercised a priestly function, acknowledged even by western figures such as Pope Leo the Great.[7] The emperor Leo III justified his iconoclast edict with the declaration 'I am emperor and priest.'[8] Ecumenical councils were called by emperors; since they embodied sovereignty over the whole empire, over all persons and in all causes within their dominions they were supreme, the sole source of law, and therefore 'not bound by canon law'.[9] Crowning and anointing by the patriarch were not legally indispensable to imperial authority.[10]

Emperors usually took much trouble, as Marcian and Pulcheria did in 451–2, or Justinian in 553, to persuade a reluctant pope to assent to their ecumenical synods. However, this theory of ratification placed the criterion of ecumenicity in juridical and external factors. In the eighth century the Greek bishops experienced two incompatible councils both claiming the title 'ecumenical', one iconoclast and the other iconodule. Each had the ratification of the then emperor. The iconodule council at Nicaea in 787 was to have a

---

[3] The theme is treated in a famous paper by N. H. Baynes, 'Eusebius and the Christian Empire' (1933) reprinted in his *Byzantine Studies and Other Essays* (London, 1955), 168–72, and in F. Dvornik, *Early Christian and Byzantine Political Philosophy: Origins and Background* (Dumbarton Oaks Studies, 9; Washington, DC, 1966); thereon Oswyn Murray in *JTS*, NS 19 (1968), 673.

[4] So the patriarch Menas arguing with rebellious monks, *ACO* III 181. 35.

[5] *ACO* II i. 478 (Mansi vii. 477–8) of 13 Mar. 452. At the first session at Chalcedon, an acclamation salutes the emperor as 'high priest-emperor' (*ACO* II i. 138. 28, *actio I*, §469; Mansi vi. 733). Pope Simplicius told the emperor Zeno that he should have a priestly mind (Avellana 66, CSEL 35). Cf. G. Dagron, *Empereur et prêtre* (Paris, 1996).

[6] Evagrius, *HE* 3. 14.   [7] Pope Leo I, *ep.* 134 (78).

[8] Pope Gregory II (?), *ep.* 13, PL 89. 521 C, remonstrates with the emperor Leo the Isaurian that the emperors rightly able to claim priestliness were those who upheld orthodoxy. J. Gouillard, *Travaux et mémoires*, 3 (1968), 243–307, argued Gregory's letters to the emperor Leo to be spurious, probably forged about 800. See also P. Speck, *Ich bin's nicht: Kaiser Konstantin ist es gewesen* (Bonn, 1990), 638–95. Gouillard did not convince H. Grotz, *Archivum Historiae Pontificiae*, 18 (1980), 9–40, a paper in turn criticized by H. Michels in *Zeitschrift für Kirchengeschichte*, 99 (1988), 376–91. See further Alexakis (above, n. 1), 108–9, 119 ff.

[9] e.g. Leo VI's *Novels* 46–8 (PG 108).

[10] Byzantine emperors wore crowns on accession.

smile of welcome from Pope Hadrian but less than a formal declaration of juridical assent, while among the Frankish bishops it was greeted with anger and horror as a 'pseudo-synod', failing not for lack of canonical correctness but for the uncatholic character of its encouragement of the superstitious abuse of icons. For the Franks what made a council 'ecumenical' was the content of its decrees. They reserved their position to consider whether or not decrees were in line with scripture and sacred tradition.[11] To them this was not manifestly the case with the second Council of Nicaea.

The arguments about which councils did or did not have the rank of being 'ecumenical' during the late eighth and the ninth centuries gave an impetus to the development of an older theme, already presupposed in the pro-Chalcedonian thesis that the first four general councils had a status corresponding to that of the four canonical gospels. In other words, there was a canonical number of such assemblies enjoying superior authority. The theme contributed to the difficulty in ascribing ecumenical authority to the Fifth Council of 553, the decisions of which were most unwelcome in north Italy and Africa, and for some centuries to come the inclusion of the Fifth, Sixth, and Seventh Councils in the ecumenical list did not imply their equality of rank or importance with the first four. In the Greek east there was less of a tendency to think post-Chalcedonian Councils not quite equal to the first four. Liturgical readings from the Acts of the Fifth and Sixth Councils were assigned to particular days in the Calendar—the Fifth Council on 20 July, the Sixth on the Sunday following the feast of the Exaltation of the Cross on 14 September.

Evidently problems would result from elevating certain councils to a rank not enjoyed by other assemblies with no less weighty agenda, especially after the seven councils became a kind of canon to which additions could not be made, since that inevitably reduced the authority of bishops in synod to cope with new controversies.

Iconoclasm was not new in the eighth century. John Moschos' *Pratum*, compiled before 634, treated iconoclasm as worse than fornication (45). About 684 a Gallic pilgrim to the East was told of the horrendous fate of those who damaged icons of St George and of the Virgin Mary, recorded in Adomnán (*De locis sanctis* 3. 4–5). Bede's exposition of Solomon's temple (2. 19. 10), written 729–31, has polemic against those who think Exod. 20: 4 forbids carving or painting in churches.

During the eighth century the popes, with the support of Roman aristocrats, came to dream of having greater independence both from Byzantium with its exarch at Ravenna (until 751), and from the Lombard kings at Pavia.

---

[11] The point would be emphatically made by Hincmar of Reims; below, p. 105.

Lombard government spread to take over tracts of Italy hitherto under
Byzantine control from Ravenna, and Byzantine arms were not strong
enough to protect the popes from Lombard interference. The emperor in
722–3 alienated the papacy by taxing Roman estates.[12] At the time nothing
was said about papal jurisdiction in the Balkans, but that was eroded as control from Constantinople was gradually extended. Three years later harmony
was further endangered by the Pope's rejection of the imperial edict forbidding icons other than the cross.[13] In the Latin west images as vehicles of the
sacred did not enjoy the intensity of devotion that they came to have in the
east at least outside Asia Minor. But to western catholic ears the notion of a
prohibition on artistic aids to devotion was offensive. The emperor retorted
by removing Illyricum, Calabria, and Sicily from Rome's ecclesiastical jurisdiction and transferring them to Constantinople.[14] That was to remove from
papal control valuable estates which had long been part of the Roman
Church's *patrimonium*, the extent and importance of which in Sicily is richly
attested in the letters of Pope Gregory the Great. Admittedly Arab incursions
would have made much of this income precarious. The emperor's decision
was no doubt primarily military. Arab attacks on south Italy and Sicily and
Bulgar attacks in Illyricum made direct control from east Rome necessary.

Nevertheless, it could become difficult for the east Roman army to maintain a hold on Sicily and Italy at the same time as fighting wars on the eastern
front. From the sixth century the Lombards were threatening much of Italy.
As early as 577, when the eastern army was engaged in a Persian war, the
question was being raised whether the Franks could be persuaded to check
the Lombard advance if the Lombards could not be bribed to leave the land
alone. Menander the Guardsman records that the emperor sent a large
amount of gold in lieu of an army to be used for either of these purposes
(fr. 22, p. 196 Blockley).

[12] *Liber Pontificalis* 91. 16 (i. 403. 23 Duchesne); Theophanes AM 6217. The gradual emergence
of an independent papal state is traced by T. F. X. Noble, *The Republic of St Peter* (Philadelphia,
1984).

[13] That the emperor Leo put pressure on the Pope seems certain from *Liber Pontificalis* 91. 17 (i.
404. 9 Duchesne). Cf. Theophanes AM 6218.

[14] The emperor Leo also removed the papal revenues from South Italian and Sicilian estates:
Theophanes AM 6224. See M. V. Anastos, 'The Transfer of Illyricum, Calabria and Sicily to the
Jurisdiction of the Patriarchate of Constantinople', *Studi bizantini e neoellenici*, 9 (1957), 14–31.

14

THE PAPACY AND THE FRANKS

Bishops of Rome at this period were subjects of the emperor at Constantinople, but were not sorry if Byzantine attention was distracted by need to repel Arab and Lombard invaders in Italy or Sicily. However, in Italy the Lombards became increasingly aggressive and successful. The emperor looked to the pope, often rightly, to give a lead in checking the invaders. Gold bought the Frankish armies to maintain imperial power in Italy. But in 751 the Merovingian king Hilderich was ejected, tonsured, and confined to a monastery (an early example of a monastery used as a prison). At Soissons Pippin was elected king according to Frankish customs. In the same year, however, Lombards had captured Ravenna and ended the control of Italy by the viceroy or exarch.

Pope Stephen II perhaps had the emperor's good will in negotiating with Pippin to restore the exarchate. He went to Pippin to beg protection for St Peter's lands, which meant financial support important for the Roman see. Pippin recaptured the lost territories but, not wishing to be the emperor's tool, decided that the Pope would best govern them, not a Greek official. Thereby he created the Papal State, to last over a thousand years. Stephen's cooperation did not please the emperor. When in 756 the Lombard king at Pavia reopened hostilities and the Pope took the initiative in calling for Frankish aid, the emperor was not consulted and was offended. Constantinople began to nurse fear that Latin princes would take over the western remnants of the Roman empire. One day they might cross the Adriatic. Pippin protested that his sole motives in invading Italy had been 'love of St Peter and the forgiveness of his sins' (*Liber Pontificalis* 94. 251, i. 453 Duchesne). The emperor found that hard to believe. The strong Frankish military presence in Italy was not good for imperial control, and the consequence was alliance between the empire and the Lombards.

The Ravenna exarch had had supreme power not only over military, political, and financial matters but also over the Church. If, for example, a schismatic bishop wished to rejoin the Church, his initial request was addressed to the exarch, among whose duties was the reconciliation of dissidents—by force if necessary. Gregory the Great found that his bishops looked down on their pope because his authority was inferior to the exarch's.

Bishops appealed from his verdicts to secular judges (*Reg.* 5. 39). In that situation popes would have few regrets if Greek exarchs ceased to exist.

In 791 Charlemagne commissioned a collection of papal letters to Frankish princes from the time of Charles Martel to his own, among which those to Stephen II and his brother and successor Paul I gave evidence of intimate friendship and also to the independence of the Latin west over against the Greeks and the eastern empire. A copy survives in a Vienna manuscript written late in the ninth century for an archbishop of Cologne Willibert (870–89) and is edited under the title Codex Carolinus (MGH Epp. iii. 469–857). Several letters attest anger at Rome with Constantinople and vice versa. Paul I wrote to Pippin of 'the utterly wicked Greeks, enemies of God's holy Church and attackers against the orthodox faith', defects manifested in their intention to recover Ravenna, which reveals 'how great and of what nature is the impious malice of the heretical Greeks' (Codex Carolinus 30, p. 536. 14; 32, p. 539. 8; 38, p. 551. 10). Meanwhile the emperor was complaining to Pippin that his letters to the west were being corrupted by deliberate mistranslations and was offering large subsidies for Frankish help in the imperial recovery of Ravenna and the exarchate. Pippin remained unmoved in his adherence to the papal interest: St Peter's keys and intercessions were more to him than gold.

The emperor's reference to mistranslated letters underlines an important factor of the age in the evident widening of the gulf between east and west, namely the increasing ignorance of Greek in the west and of Latin in the east. Many of the high officials appointed to govern Italy in the time of Gregory the Great (*Reg.* 10. 10) were Greeks, and Gregory was displeased when they wrote to him in Greek. When a Latin was appointed to be military commander (*dux*) at Rome, he had to swear an oath of fidelity to the emperor, attested in the *Liber Pontificalis*.

Soon a further indication of the gulf came when Pope Hadrian I (772–95), though son of a high officer under the exarch, abandoned dating his letters by the emperor's regnal year and substituted dating by his own pontificate and Charlemagne's regnal year. It was a step in a lengthy process moving the centre of gravity of Christendom towards the Latin-speaking world and north-west Europe. The process was encouraged by unhealed memories of bitter controversies in the seventh century over monotheletism and an undercurrent of resentment that 'Greek bishops' had enforced the condemnation of Pope Honorius at the Sixth Council. Alienation was also fostered by the Muslim power in north Africa and Spain, disrupting the common trade and political unity between the north and south sides of the Mediterranean, and also by the irruption of Slavs into the Balkans, making communication between Italy and Constantinople more hazardous.

Meanwhile the fiercely iconoclast Constantine V, emperor 741–75, was vindicating his policy by defeating the Arabs. In 754 his large council of bishops at Hiereia to sanction iconoclasm gave authority for coercing iconophiles, some of whom were shamefully treated. Constantine V was noted for his aversion to the veneration of icons of Mary the Mother of God. The council condemned idolatrous worship of icons as pagan but said nothing against the veneration of relics or the intercession of the saints. The council's final definition (read in full in the Acts of Nicaea II in 787) was agreed in the Church of the Mother of God at Blachernae by the Golden Horn, a shrine sanctified by the robe (*maphorion*) of Mary, as if enforcing the point that the honour of icons was rejected by the Mother of God herself: she at least was not offended by iconoclasm.

There was a paradoxical source of tension in the fact that while the Franks, now becoming the principal political and military defence of the papacy's rights and property, were not sympathetic to the iconoclasm of Hiereia, neither were they in any serious rapport with the iconophiles. The Frankish Annals record that in 767 at Gentilly near Paris, a conference was held between 'Romans' and Greeks concerning the two topics of the doctrine of the Trinity and the veneration of icons. At that date the Greeks who met with the Franks will have been delegates of an iconoclast emperor and patriarch. It is not recorded that on the matter of icons they had a quarrel, but there may well have been Greek expressions of reserve about the *Filioque* if by that date Frankish churches had begun to use it liturgically. In the background was a political need for Greeks and Franks to cooperate in opposing the threat presented by Arabs.

Frankish power was steadily rising and it had been prudent of the popes to assure these potent princes that, if they protected St Peter's properties, 'all would be well with them both in this world and hereafter'.[1] There was the problem of suspicion at Constantinople on political grounds. And among Greek iconophiles it came to be feared that the popes and the Franks could be in agreement in failing to share the right standpoint about the almost sacramental significance of holy pictures. The Roman tradition needed reasserting. In 769 Pope Stephen III's council at Rome pronounced anathema on the

---

[1] Pope Gregory III (731–41) in Codex Carolinus 1 (MGH Epp. iii. 477. 13–14), cf. ibid. 2 (478. 30); Stephen II (752–7), ibid. 4 (487. 16–17), 6 (490. 21–3); Hadrian I to Charlemagne, MGH Epp. v. 6. 30 ff. (protection of the Roman Church will ensure victory over barbarians now and the kingdom of heaven later). Charlemagne would tell Pope Leo III that his royal duty was to protect Christ's Church from external attack by pagans and infidels, and within to defend the catholic faith; 'yours is to help my efforts by lifting your hands like Moses in prayer to God' (MGH Epp. iv. 137). On the Gentilly meeting Michael McCormick has important remarks in *Settimane Spoleto*, 41 (1994), 95–162 at 113 ff. with the suggestion that the papal letter preserved in Codex Carolinus 37 (MGH Epp. iii. 547–50), containing a reference to Greek envoys at Rome and at the Frankish court, refers to this same occasion.

emperor's iconoclast council at Hiereia, and no doubt iconophiles were pleased. Nevertheless Greek venerators of icons found it hard to remember Roman hostility to imperial iconoclasm. Only a few decades later it was easier at Constantinople to think of all western churches as adopting moderately critical attitudes to icons and to forget moderately supportive utterances from incumbents of the Roman see with its memories of Gregory the Great teaching that pictures are the Bible for the illiterate.

Although the seventh century had seen debate about the propriety of venerating icons, the subject was kept off the agenda of the Sixth Council in 680–1, and at the supplementary Quinisext Council in 692 holy pictures remained marginal. Canon 82 (p. 66 above) was not concerned with disagreements between east and west. Nevertheless the Greek critics of icons and the devotional practice of kissing them were coming to be encouraged by western reservations towards the Quinisext canons. On the other side, iconophiles were grateful for canon 82 as clear evidence in conciliar canonical material that a council could approve of icons subject to certain qualifications.

The empress Irene, wife of the emperor Leo IV (d. 780), valued icons as her husband did not, and after his death, acting as regent, she planned a reversal of iconoclastic policy. She was assisted by the troubled conscience of her patriarch Paul, for whom it undermined the authority of the pentarchy of patriarchs to be out of communion with the Petrine sees of Rome and Antioch. In 784 he died, and Irene succeeded in persuading a high-ranking lay civil servant, Tarasius, to succeed him.[2] He protested his unworthiness as a mere layman, but assented to be consecrated on condition there should be an ecumenical council, to which Pope Hadrian would be invited to send legates, as also the patriarchs of Alexandria and Antioch. Peace with the Arabs would make it possible for the latter to attend. The forthcoming council would have the authority to overthrow the iconoclast decisions of Hiereia (754).

The council met initially at Constantinople but army units of iconoclast sympathy threatened the bishops, and Irene halted the proceedings while bishops of iconoclast sympathy cried out 'We have won!' The following year, the army units having been discharged, the council was reconvened at Nicaea (787), moving back to Constantinople for the final definition in the Magnaura palace.

Pope Hadrian's support was a delicate matter. He disapproved of the promotion of a layman to be patriarch. He wanted to make the restitution of Roman jurisdiction in Illyricum a condition of his good will. Perhaps in his

---

[2] The *Life of the Patriarch Tarasius* by Ignatius the Deacon is edited with translation and commentary by Stephanos Efthymiadis (Aldershot, 1998).

time if not in that of Nicolas I, the Roman chancery gathered a collection of papal decretals of the time of Siricius and Innocent I showing that at least in Siricius' time Thessalonica in eastern Illyricum had belonged to Roman ecclesiastical jurisdiction (Collectio Thessalonicensis). However, on icons Hadrian was gentler. In 785 in reply to the formal letter from Tarasius, Hadrian (in a letter not all of which was read at the second session of the second Council of Nicaea in October 787) followed the patriarch in citing Quinisext canon 82 as authoritative. This marked a shift in the Roman position and a move towards an accommodation with the east.[3]

At Nicaea II the patriarch Tarasius took pains to vindicate the authenticity of the Quinisext canons and their secure attribution to the bishops of the Sixth Council. His language betrays evident awareness of coolness both at Rome and among Greek iconoclasts. He was glad to have the reading at the council of Hadrian's letter accepting the canons of all six ecumenical councils, and to arrange the omission from that reading of the Pope's too explicit regret at his own elevation from layman to patriarch. So whatever tensions were occasioned in 692, they had subsided in 787. Celibacy and Saturday fasts remained in the background to be brought out when tensions revived in the next century. Tarasius managed the council brilliantly, protecting the honour of Irene's dynasty by allowing penitent iconoclasts to be reinstated.

Tarasius' toleration of penitent reinstated bishops was disapproved by zealous Studite monks, whose hostility became stronger after the patriarch allowed a priest to conduct the wedding ceremony when the emperor Constantine VI, already married, decided to marry his mistress. The so-called Moechian controversy (i.e. concerning adultery) ensued.

Tarasius even arranged for the decisions of the Council of 754 to be read by one of the bishops present at that assembly who was among the reconciled penitents, now rescued by the Holy Spirit.

The two Roman legates, one being bilingual, occupied a presiding position at Nicaea II. Pope Hadrian told Charlemagne that he approved the council's sanction of icons.[4] He was not yet willing (he told Constantinople) to confirm the council's decisions and to give full and formal ratification until Rome had regained jurisdiction in Illyricum and the lost patrimony in Sicily. Nicaea II was a local Greek synod making decisions for the eastern churches, not binding on the Franks.

[3] The Quinisext canon 82 also appears cited in a letter, of hotly contested genuineness, to the patriarch Germanus from Pope Gregory II cited at the fourth session of Nicaea II. That Gregory II was against iconoclasm is not in doubt, but the case for thinking the letter at least to be heavily interpolated, perhaps entirely spurious, is weighty.

[4] MGH Epp. v. 56. 36. On Hadrian's relation to Nicaea II see M. Maccarrone, *Annuarium Historiae Conciliorum*, 20 (1988), 53–149. On the council's recognition of Roman primacy see his paper in *Il Primato del vescovo di Roma nel primo millennio: Ricerche e testimonianze* (Vatican City, 1991), 357–60.

The second Council of Nicaea was only slowly acknowledged to have the rank of an 'ecumenical council', not merely in the west because of Frankish opposition and papal caution, but also because of the reservations of iconophile monks like Theodore of Studios. Theodore knew of justified iconoclast criticisms to the effect that the representatives of the patriarchs of Alexandria, Antioch, and Jerusalem at Nicaea in 787 had simply been refugees from the Arabs who were now living in the capital. The palace and the patriarch Tarasius had solved a juridical problem by a disturbing short cut, and Theodore thought the iconoclasts were right to point an accusing finger. Rome had sent legates, but Hadrian's insistence that Rome's restored jurisdiction must be a condition of full recognition looked like reserve towards the Greek iconophiles as well. Iconophiles repeated the appeal to the 82nd canon of the Quinisext Council of 692 directing that Christ should be represented in icons as human, not as a lamb; this canon gave conciliar vindication to the use of holy pictures. It was not lost on iconoclasts that in 692 the papacy had painfully and sharply rejected the authority of the Quinisext canons without distinction. When at the second Council of Nicaea Tarasius had felt it necessary to make his elaborate statement asserting the binding authority of the Quinisext decisions, no objection was offered by Roman legates. Nevertheless, the impression had been conveyed that the popes were in sympathy with at least the more moderate iconoclasts. Theodore of Studios underlined the fact that in the eyes of the Roman see the second Council of Nicaea was accepted merely as a local Greek synod without ecumenical standing (*ep.* 1. 38, PG 99. 1043 CD = *ep.* 38, i. 110. 63–5 Fatouros).

Studite hostility to Tarasius underwent a sea-change when the emperor Leo V reinstated iconoclasm with a campaign against the authority of Nicaea II. The compromising patriarch, who had been mild to former iconoclasts and to unnumbered bishops who obtained their sees by simony, was suddenly reckoned among the saints (*ep.* 475), and his deposed successor Nikephoros received generous letters (286 and 426). After Patriarch Methodios restored icons in 843 the Studites renewed their campaign against Tarasius and his successor and provoked Methodios' anger. In Photius' time Tarasius' portrait in mosaic was granted a place in the room above the southwest vestibule of St Sophia.[5]

---

[5] A. R. Cormack and E. J. W. Hawkins, 'The Mosaics of St Sophia at Istanbul: The Rooms above the South-West Vestibule and Ramp', *Dumbarton Oaks Papers*, 31 (1977) 226–7, fig. 40.

15

AACHEN AS A THIRD ROME: CAROLINE
BOOKS; *FILIOQUE*; ERIUGENA

The Franks held in veneration that principal Church which guarded the bones and the tradition of St Peter himself. King Pippin gave order that the old Gallican chants were to be replaced by those customary at Rome 'ob unanimitatem apostolicae sedis' and for the sake of peaceful concord in the Church. This ruling was a consequence of Pope Stephen II's visit to the court of Pippin early in 754, during which the Pope also negotiated support for temporal power over some part of Italian territory, thereby initiating the Papal State.[1] In Roman rhetoric the Frankish king would be hailed as a 'New Constantine'. Enthusiasm for things Roman led to the gradual sidelining of Gallican liturgical forms, Romanization varying from diocese to diocese with Aachen in the lead.

Legend declared that Constantine the Great had been baptized by Pope Silvester rather than by the embarrassingly Arian Eusebius of Constantinople, formerly of Nicomedia.[2] The age witnessed a rise in the veneration of Silvester, and this drew attention to important forgeries associated with his name, created soon after 500 to reinforce the claims of Pope Symmachus against his anti-pope rival Laurence and to protect Symmachus from any superior jurisdiction being claimed or exercised by a Roman council summoned to scrutinize his worthiness to be bishop, a matter which numerous people thought very uncertain. The language of the Silvester

---

[1] Libri Carolini 1. 6 (MGH Concilia ii, supp. i. 136); Ansegis, *Capitularia* (ed. MGH Legum sectio II, NS i, 1996), 1. 74, p. 471. On the Romanizing of liturgy in the Frankish empire see R. McKitterick, *The Frankish Church and the Carolingian Reforms* (London, 1977), 124 ff.

[2] The legend is accepted by, for example, Pope Nicolas I, *ep.* 88 (MGH Epp. vi. 465. 14 = PL 119. 938 D). It goes back to the *Vita Silvestri* (fifth century), which provided the background for the Donation of Constantine, and also contained an iconophile text gratefully cited at the second Council of Nicaea (787) See a richly documented paper by W. Levison, 'Konstantinische Schenkung und Silvesterlegende', originally in *Miscellanea F. Ehrle*, ii: *Per la storia da Roma e dei papi* (Studi e Testi: 38; Rome 1924), 159–247, enlarged in his *Aus rheinischer und fränkischer Frühzeit* (Düsseldorf, 1948), 390–465; H. Fuhrmann, 'Konstantinische Schenkung und Silvesterlegende in neuer Sicht', *Deutsches Archiv*, 15 (1959), 523–40; 'Konstantinische Schenkung und abendländisches Kaisertum', *Deutsches Archiv*, 22 (1966), 63–178. The twelfth-century patriarch of Antioch, Theodore Balsamon, interpreted the Donation of Constantine as empowering the patriarch of New Rome (RP iv. 539–42).

legends would become congenial to those who wanted to bring more law and order to the western churches by magnifying the office of the incumbent of the see of St Peter and St Paul, notably to the author of the Donation of Constantine (below, pp. 99 f.).

Texts forged in Symmachus' cause in 500 laid down that 'the primatial see cannot be judged by anyone'.[3]

The Franks' merging of their interests with those of Peter's see corresponded to an ambition to make their kingdom into a western empire as Roman as possible. The bishop of Rome's blessing could make their empire holy and Roman. After the crowning of Charlemagne in 800 the rite of coronation was like the consecration of a bishop. In art the kings could be represented as uniquely invested with divine power (so much so as to make an investiture controversy almost inevitable sooner or later). The old Roman empire based on Constantinople was a problem. The chronicler Theophanes (AM 6293) records that, after his coronation as Roman emperor by Pope Leo III, Charlemagne sent an embassy with papal legates to propose marriage to the empress Irene, uniting east and west. But Irene fell from power. Writing in 1148 Anna Comnena would see the Frankish wars with the Byzantine army as continuing evidence of an aspiration to take over the east Roman empire as well as the west.[4]

A major step towards this end was achieved by Charlemagne with his astonishing success in creating a western empire at least equipollent with the east Roman empire. His sense of the western Church being actually superior to the Greek Church was enhanced by the shock he experienced on reading a bad translation, which he thought official, of the Acts of the second Council of Nicaea (787). That council's defence of the veneration of images was cast in terms which were heard by the Franks to imply worship of icons on a level with that of Christ himself. In fact the Council of Nicaea II sharply distinguished the honour to icons of Christ and the saints from the worship (*latreia*) of the holy Trinity. A catastrophic mistranslation in the Latin version of the Acts had the Cypriot bishop Constantine of Constantia declaring that he gave the same adoration to images as to the Trinity, the opposite of his words at the first session of the council. This indefensible proposition horrified Charlemagne; according to Hincmar of Reims (PL 126. 360), he had received the translation from Pope Hadrian. If so he had no duty to question its authority.

Hadrian kept Charlemagne supplied with important Roman documents. In 774 he was presenting the king with Dionysius Exiguus' translation of the

---

[3] PL 8. 839 C.

[4] Wars: Theophanes AM 6293, p. 475 de Boor; Anna Comnena 16. 4. In 787 Frankish–Byzantine political relations were tense. Theophanes AM 6281 reports that immediately after the second Council of Nicaea hostilities broke out over Italian territories.

Greek canon collection together with papal decretals in an edition revised in the Roman chancery. In 784 or soon thereafter a copy was sent of the Gregorian Sacramentary to be supplemented and edited by Alcuin. Hadrian's successor Leo III was to continue this process, providing Charles with the *Liber Pontificalis*. Numerous Latin manuscripts of this period reflect the Frankish interest in the Roman empire, e.g. the so-called *Scriptores Historiae Augustae* and the parent of the surviving copies of the *Notitia Dignitatum*.[5] The papal letters in the Codex Carolinus, where each Frankish prince is 'patricius Romanorum', reflect the same consciousness. Those describing Greeks as heretics would be congenial.

Under the Frankish king's aegis, in implementation of his convictions, bishop Theodulf of Orleans, a Visigothic refugee from Islamic Spain, compiled the 'Caroline Books' (the original title was 'Opus Caroli regis contra synodum') condemning both iconoclast and iconophile councils, and denying all spiritual value to images except to recall past events or to provide decoration.[6] Exception was taken to an iconophile contention that icons are no more material than scripture—paradoxically citing a sentence of Pope Hadrian I gratefully used at Nicaea II. At one point in Theodulf's argument in the third book (3.17) the utterance attributed to Bishop Constantine was pilloried, and in 794 at the Frankish Council of Frankfurt, attended by two Roman legates, the notion was condemned and treated as typical of a most dangerous assembly. Even Pope Hadrian's defence of the council in reply to Charlemagne's attack showed no awareness that what Frankfurt condemned was the opposite of what the good bishop Constantine said.[7]

Charlemagne followed Gregory the Great in holding icons a good substitute for scripture for the illiterate. He did not think their veneration a matter of obligation, and feared superstition. Pressure was put on Pope Hadrian to censure eighty-five errors found in the Nicene Acts; the Pope quietly and courteously stood his ground, claiming his undisputed primatial authority to

[5] Charlemagne received more books from Pope Leo III including the *Liber Pontificalis*, Clement of Alexandria on the Catholic Epistles, and Didymus the Blind. See B. Bischoff, *Manuscripts and Libraries in the Age of Charlemagne*, ed. M. Gorman (Cambridge, 1994), 58–60.

[6] The Libri Carolini have been given a magistral edition by Ann Freeman with Paul Meyvaert (MGH Concilia ii, supp. i, 1998) and an important introduction and bibliography. Authorship: Meyvaert, *Revue bénédictine*, 89 (1979), 29–57; Freeman, *Speculum*, 32 (1957), 663–705; ead., *Settimane Spoleto*, 41 (1994), 163–95; cf. ead., 'Carolingian Orthodoxy and the Fate of the Libri Carolini', *Viator*, 16 (1985), 65–108. On difficulty in achieving ecumenical status for Nicaea II see H. J. Sieben, *Die Konzilsidee der alten Kirche* (Paderborn, 1979), 306–43. On the Frankish Council of 794 see R. Berndt (ed.), *Das Frankfurter Konzil von 794 im Spannungsfeld von Kirche, Politik und Theologie* (Mainz, 1995).

[7] The bad translation of Nicaea II was replaced by Anastasius Bibliothecarius, implementing Pope John VIII's relaxation of tension. On Gregory the Great's influence on the Franks' view of icons see Celia Chazelle in J. C. Cavadini (ed.), *Gregory the Great* (Notre Dame, 1995). On the Church Fathers in Carolingian theology see W. Otten in Irena Backus (ed.), *The Reception of the Church Fathers in the West* (Leiden, 1997).

decide the matter. But Hadrian was anxious not to displease the Greek empress Irene for financial reasons. He wanted Charlemagne to press for the restitution of Roman Church estates confiscated by the emperor Leo III more than half a century earlier; he declared himself ready to excommunicate Irene if she did not agree.[8] So his approval of the second Council of Nicaea remained conditional and provisional.

The 'Caroline Books' embodying Charlemagne's horror at the risks of superstition in the decisions of the Council of Nicaea in 787 were also intended to trumpet loudly the overwhelming supremacy enjoyed by the Roman see in a worldwide Church. Early in the first book it was laid down that in the light of Matt. 16: 18 the Roman Church has not been entrusted with authority over other churches merely by the decision of synods, but holds the primacy by the authority of the Lord himself (1. 6, PL 98. 1020 A). The language of this statement reacts to a sophisticated Greek argument, viz. that the apologists for papal primatial authority wish both to appeal to the western Council of Serdica to vindicate Rome's appellate jurisdiction, and at the same time to devalue synods and canon law as in no way providing the source of Petrine primacy. The two arguments are not obviously consistent. There is a sharp insistence on the procession of the Spirit from both Father and Son (3. 4).

For Pope Hadrian the delicate and embarrassing problem was how to steer a middle course between the positive estimate of holy icons conveyed in his letter of 785 to Irene and her son and consort Constantine, crucial for harmony with an east turning iconophile, and the political necessity of good terms with the Frankish king. The Caroline Books reflected Frankish distaste and were a frontal challenge to Hadrian's policy on icons, but had taken for granted that the Pope's support would be for the position of Gregory the Great, and even affirmed (1. 6) the sole authority of the Pope to decide. Charlemagne had to change his plan to diffuse the Caroline Books as warning against superstitious idolatry and against pressure to add Nicaea II to the six ecumenical councils. He preserved the working manuscript (Vatic. lat. 7207) in case Hadrian's successor thought differently. He did not change his mind. The pope's duty was to pray for the emperor. The emperor's was not merely to defend the Church from external attack but also to defend Catholic faith within it.

Pope Hadrian depended for his own survival too much on Frankish support to risk confrontation. Charlemagne treated him well and wept on learning of his death on 25 December 795.[9] However, at Constantinople and among iconophiles in Greek monasteries an indelible impression was being received that the west was in sneaking sympathy with iconoclasts, that the

[8] MGH Epp. v. 57. 20 = PL 98. 1292 B.   [9] Einhard, *Life of Charlemagne* 19.

papacy was painfully half-hearted about correcting the Franks' reserve towards Nicaea II, and moreover that even if the Roman see was not in favour of iconoclasm it was becoming as dangerous about icons as about the *Filioque*. Militarily Greeks were not a little afraid of Franks.

Pope Leo III

In a controversial election in which passions ran high, Hadrian was succeeded by Leo III (795–816), a Roman presbyter without his predecessor's noble birth to commend him.[10] Leo's tenure of the papacy was made precarious by intimidation with unpleasant charges and physical assault organized by opponents led by Hadrian's nephew. Leo fled to Charlemagne at Paderborn, and as the king came out to meet him he chanted *Gloria in excelsis*. The meeting had vast consequences for Europe's future. Charles set up an inquiry before which Leo vindicated himself on oath. Alcuin commented that the accusers were insufficiently innocent to be casting the first stone, and in any case he was content to rest on the principle, affirmed for Pope Symmachus in 501, that none may sit in judgement on the Pope.[11] Charles showed his support by coming to Rome; he was devoted to St Peter and in the apostle's basilica on Christmas Day 800 he went to mass. Leo was declared innocent and replied by crowning the king as 'Roman emperor and Augustus'. He would then drop his previous title 'patricius Romanorum'. Probably Leo anointed him, as Theophanes says, since that ceremony was Frankish custom for kings (Codex Carolinus 7, MGH Epp. iii. 493. 11). Coronation was followed (not preceded) by acclamations and by the Pope's 'adoration' of the emperor—on the Byzantine model. Charles accepted the new title, impressed by the argument that the Greeks now had 'only a woman', but, from fear of vexing the emperor at Constantinople, disowned responsibility for Leo's surprising action. Before 800 Alcuin had already been writing of his 'imperium christianum' (see the index to MGH epp. iv for several references).

---

[10] The primary source is the life of Leo III in *Liber Pontificalis*, with the Frankish Annals s. aa. 799–801. On Leo III and *Filioque* see V. Peri, *Rivista di storia della Chiesa in Italia*, 41 (1987), 3–58, id., *Rivista di storia e letteratura religiosa*, 6 (1970), 268–97. Leo was a social outsider without upper-class background: H. Beck, *Frühmittelalterliche Studien*, 3 (1969), 131–7. His energy and sense of theatre in the coronation: P. Llewellyn, *Le Moyen Âge*, 96 (1990), 209–25, That Leo and Charlemagne both needed the coronation, Charles to bolster his authority over the Saxons, is persuasively argued by H. Mayr-Harting, 'Charlemagne, the Saxons, and the Imperial Coronation of 800', *English Historical Review*, 111 (1996), 1112–33. In Justinian's time John Lydus (*De magistratibus* 1. 6) says 'Caesar is a superior title to King'. On the ceremonies of 800 see P. E. Schramm, 'Die Anerkennung Karls des Großen', *Historische Zeitschrift*, 172 (1951), 449 ff. and R. Folz, *The Coronation of Charlemagne* (London, 1979).

[11] MGH epp. v. 63–4; Alcuin, *ep*. 179 (MGH Epp. v. 297. 24).

There may have been a problem in the fact that, although he understood Latin, and honoured the great educator Alcuin from York, Charlemagne ordinarily wore Frankish clothes and the language he normally spoke was Frankish. His appearance was strongly barbarian. Significantly both Pope Hadrian and Pope Leo persuaded him to dress in a more Roman way when in Rome (Einhard, *Vita Caroli* 23).

'Emperor' was a title superior to 'king', and Charlemagne's conquests had subdued tribes, especially the Saxons, for whom the majesty of empire could be greater than that of a kingdom. Saxons did not even possess kings.

The conferring of the imperial title by the bishop of Rome did much for Pope Leo's prestige in his struggles against a hostile Roman aristocracy and probably many of the populace. Notker Balbulus (1. 26) would comment that 'the people of Rome are always hostile to every pope'. Leo needed the ceremony, which manifested his intimate bond to Charlemagne.

The story in Einhard's *Life* of Charlemagne that the title 'emperor of the Romans' had been conferred upon an unwilling and astonished recipient was good propaganda to answer the consternation felt by the east Roman emperor at Constantinople, who was certainly understood to be the only Roman emperor in due line of succession. At Constantinople—New Rome people were unlikely to feel serene if they heard about the Frankish poet who wrote a panegyric on Charlemagne and pronounced Aachen to be a second Rome with Charlemagne as a new Aeneas, second founder of the western empire, indeed a new Justin, implying sovereignty over the eastern empire as well as the west.[12] The Greek east was unlikely to hear nothing of the rumours with which the west was agog that Charlemagne's masterly territorial conquests in western Europe were going to culminate in his taking over the Roman empire of the Greek east (Notker Balbulus 1. 27). His known ambition was to restore the pride and splendour which Old Rome had lost. He could achieve that end through the Church and bestowed great wealth on the endowment of St Peter's (Einhard, *Vita Caroli* 3. 27).

Although eastern emperors were going to be unhappy when the Franks spoke of merely 'the emperor of the Greeks' (as often in the Libri Carolini, so unfriendly to the Greek Churches and their veneration of icons), in practice the emperors needed amicable relations with Aachen's power. Einhard records that successive emperors of the ninth century sought Charlemagne's friendship, and their envoys to Aachen were instructed to greet Charlemagne as 'emperor' (Frankish Annals, s.a. 812). Anything less would have seemed insulting and counterproductive.

---

[12] See Christine Ratkowitsch, *Karolus Magnus—alter Aeneas, alter Martinus, alter Justinus* (Wiener Studien, Beiheft 24; Vienna, 1997). Agnellus, *Liber Pontificalis* of Ravenna (94), remarkably records Charlemagne's receiving 'imperium Romanorum' without reference to the negative view at Constantinople.

There were, however, further causes of tension. Iconodules in the east were in the main emphatic in regarding the second Council of Nicaea as the seventh ecumenical synod, and were distinctly ruffled to discover that popes and Frankish bishops were willing to speak of only six general councils, with the pointed implication that the second Council of Nicaea was a merely local assembly, despite its summons under the authority of the empress Irene. Was she empowered to make decisions binding on the universal Church of both east and west? The buzz of debate about the *Filioque* was not silenced.

At what precise moment the *Filioque* became generally current in the liturgical use of churches in Charlemagne's empire is not known. (It was not part of the Romanizing process in liturgy.) In the sacramentary of Angoulême in Aquitaine, written probably between 768 and 781 (Paris BNF lat. 816), the delivery of the creed to candidates for baptism, which the deacon had to give in both Latin and Greek, included no *Filioque*, though at that date this city was in Charlemagne's kingdom. But it was soon being included in the singing of the liturgical creed in the royal chapel at Aachen. This was bound to provoke rumbles which became an explosion far from Rome and Aachen.[13]

Devout Frankish Christians thought it good to go on pilgrimage to the Holy Land.[14] They had a monastery on the Mount of Olives providing a hospice for pilgrims, and this brought them into direct contact with the local Greek monks and clergy. As in St Jerome's time when he lived at Bethlehem, relations were prickly.[15] In 808 a Greek monk from the famous house of St Sabas in the Kidron ravine accused the Franks of heresy in their trinitarian beliefs. He received the retort that by implication he was bringing an accusation of heresy against the apostolic see of Rome, the bishopric of St Peter himself, and therefore thinking what was for Franks the unthinkable. The Franks further answered their Greek critics by claiming that the *Filioque*, which they included in the liturgical creed having heard it so sung at Aachen, was only one of a long list of accepted and non-controversial liturgical differences between the Greek and Latin churches. For example, in the *Gloria Patri*,

[13] See M. Borgolte, 'Papst Leo III., Karl der Große und der Filioque-Streit von Jerusalem', *Byzantina*, 10 (1980), 403–27. The sacramentary of Angoulême is edited in CCSL 159C (Turnhout, 1987).

[14] Frankish interest in the holy places at Jerusalem was fostered by the patriarch, who in 799 sent Charlemagne a blessing and relics (*Annales Francorum* s.a. 799).

[15] For the documents in this story see MGH Epp. v. 64–6; Concilia ii. 240–4, ed. A. Werminghoff. The letter of the Olivet monks to Leo III is also in PL 129. 1257–60; Leo's reply, PL 102. 1030–2. See Richard Haugh, *Photius and the Carolingians* (Belmont, Mass., 1975). D. Callahan, *Revue Bénédictine*, 102 (1993), 75–134, thinks the monks' letter to Leo III and Charlemagne a forgery by Ademar of Chabannes motivated by hostility to Greeks and devotion to papal authority. On this lifelong forger see Richard Landes, *Relics, Apocalypse and the Deceits of History* (Cambridge, Mass., 1995).

Greeks would not append 'As it was in the beginning . . .'. In the *Gloria in excelsis* they did not have (and disapproved) 'You alone are holy . . . most high in the glory of God the Father.' Their wording for the Lord's Prayer differed slightly from the Latin form.[16] Why then should there be a fuss about the *Filioque*? Evidently to the Franks the singing of the creed at mass was felt as an acclamation rather than a catalogue of credenda. A defence on the ground of variant liturgical custom, congenial to later western theologians such as Anselm of Canterbury, generated uproar in Jerusalem: to Greeks dogma was no proper matter for regional diversity.

The Franks on the mount of Olives accordingly wrote to Pope Leo III asking if they could be provided with a florilegium of quotations from the Greek and Latin Fathers to vindicate the orthodoxy of the *Filioque*, of which (they added) 'the Greeks think badly'. Pope Leo also received an account of the controversy from Thomas, patriarch of Jerusalem, and sent on the entire dossier to Charlemagne for his comments.[17] Charlemagne commissioned Alcuin to gather proof texts from the approved Fathers of the ancient Church, and told Theodulf of Orléans to write on the Holy Spirit. Theodulf's book received formal endorsement in 809 at a council in Aachen. Meanwhile Leo III replied to the Frankish monks in the Holy Land, giving support to the extent of affirming the double procession of the Spirit as true catechetical doctrine. But it had not in Leo's time become Roman custom to include the *Filioque* in the creed affirmed by candidates for baptism. The creed was probably not yet in all Latin eucharistic liturgies.

To insert the *Filioque* into the liturgical recitation of the creed in the context of the sacraments was, in Roman eyes, an indiscretion and an insensitive mistake. It asserted a particular church to be prior to the universal. Charlemagne's Aachen synod thought otherwise. Probably they were the first to sing *Veni Creator Spiritus* with the final stanza praying for acceptance of the truth of the *Filioque*: 'Teach us to know the Father, Son, and thee of both to be but one.' They reasserted the doctrine of the procession of the Spirit from the Father and the Son, and conveyed a decision on the point to

---

[16] The reference is perhaps to the Greek inclusion of 'the Father and the Son and the Holy Spirit' in the concluding doxology said by the priest: F. E. Brightman, *Liturgies Eastern and Western* (Oxford, 1896), i. 392. 6. The condemnation of 'Tu solus sanctus. . .' in the *Gloria in excelsis* would be repeated by Patriarch Michael Cerularius (PG 120. 792 A). In the west Berno abbot of Reichenau (d. 1049) confronted dissenters who refused to chant *Gloria in excelsis* after the initial biblical sentence; they disliked hymns with unscriptural words. In Gaul and Spain such dissenters were excommunicated: *De officio missae*, PL 142. 1059. See Gregory of Tours, *HF* 6. 40 on tense differences between Gallic and Spanish churches concerning the *Gloria Patri*.

[17] MGH epp. v. 66–7 (PL 129. 1259). Patriarchs of Jerusalem, surrounded by unfriendly neighbours, liked contact with the west. Late in the ninth century King Alfred of England was visited by a delegation from Patriarch Elias: Asser, *Life of Alfred* 91, p. 77 ed. Stevenson, a story needlessly doubted by Alfred P. Smyth, *King Alfred the Great* (Oxford, 1995), 208. The Royal Frankish Annals record several visits to north-west Europe from a Jerusalem anxious to encourage pilgrimage.

Pope Leo III sent by the hands and voices of Bernard, bishop of Worms, and Adalhard, abbot of Korvey. The Frankish bishops requested the Church at Rome to come into line with the model of Charlemagne's great Church at Aachen and to include the *Filioque* in the creed at baptism (and perhaps eucharist), not merely as a truth to be mentioned in catechetical instruction. The protocol of the meeting in Rome astonishingly survives.[18] The Pope unreservedly supported the truth of the *Filioque*, underpinned by such major western authorities as St Augustine, but was wholly opposed to its introduction into the Roman liturgy. Indeed he asked the Frankish envoys to have it removed from the text sung at Aachen, gradually perhaps, to avoid upsetting people averse to liturgical changes. If the omission were to make difficulty for the chanters in the choir, the papal solution was to stop singing the creed and to say it without music.

That the *Filioque* was a truth necessary to salvation was a proposition found in the so-called 'Athanasian' Creed, *Quicunque Vult*; so the question arose whether a truth so necessary should not find its place in the creed in the context of the two great sacraments in which all believers share. Leo III no doubt could recall Hadrian his predecessor standing up to Charlemagne on icons. Against Aachen he was unwilling to concede that the creed must include all the mysteries of the faith. He persuaded the reluctant Franks to concede that not all truths of the faith are of equal weight and importance: *Non aeque omnia necessaria sunt*. Some truths are too profound for public recitation.

Although the outcome of the consultation was to treat the *Filioque* as a secondary truth to which the highest importance could hardly be attached, Leo III evidently regarded the exchanges at this debate as being matters of high public importance to the community at large. In protest against the Franks, perhaps to reassure the many Greeks in Rome, he caused to be erected on either side of St Peter's Confessio two silver shields inscribed with the creed of Constantinople (381) in Greek and Latin, in both cases with no *Filioque*.[19] (The shields were there 300 years later for Abelard to see and comment on.) The eighth-century Gelasian sacramentary shows that the form of creed used at Rome in catechism during the eighth century had no *Filioque*,[20] so that Leo

---

[18] MGH Concilia ii. 240–4, ed. Werminghoff (= PL 102. 971). For the placing of the hymn in the context of the Aachen synod see Heinrich Lausberg, *Der Hymnus Veni Creator Spiritus* (Abhandlungen der Rheinisch-Westfälischen Akademie der Wissenschaften, 64; Opladen, 1979). The earliest witness to the text is a Fulda manuscript of the tenth century.

[19] *Liber Pontificalis* 98. 84 (Leo III; ii. 26 Duchesne); Photius, *ep.* 291. 80–3 LW; Anastasius Bibliothecarius, PL 128. 1238; Peter Lombard PL 192. 552; Peter Abelard, PL 178. 629, 1075, 1375. Discussion by V. Peri, *Rivista arch. crist.* 45 (1969), 191–221.

[20] Ed. L. C. Mohlberg (Rome, 1960), 312, H. A. Wilson (Oxford, 1894), 54–5. The Latin Constantinopolitan creed in the late eighth-century Stowe Missal in the Royal Irish Academy at Dublin originally lacked the *Filioque*, later added (interlinearly) by a subsequent hand, probably under Carolingian influence. See Aidan Breen, *Proceedings of the Royal Irish Academy*, 90 C 4 (1990), 107–21.

was affirming existing Roman tradition, even if there can only have been a conscious statement of dissent from Aachen. That at Aachen there was any serious intention of following Pope Leo's wish that the *Filioque* be dropped is most unlikely. Two centuries later the *Filioque* had become so universal throughout the Latin west that apparently even Rome could yield on the point of liturgical use under pressure from the Saxon Ottos.

Leo III's refusal to give way to Frankish pressure in 810 is remarkable when one recalls how profoundly he was dependent on Charlemagne's support if he was going to hold his own against powerful critics still living in Rome. The Frankish Annals record that when the news of Charlemagne's death reached Rome (814), there was a revived conspiracy against Pope Leo which was suppressed with discreditable ferocity unfitting in the vicar of St Peter. The most vehement of Leo's opponents had been exiled in 800, and were brought back to Rome only after his death. There is no evidence that the *Filioque* was an issue in the factions at Rome for and against Leo. (Alcuin knew only charges of adultery and perjury.) But his courageous disagreement with the Council of Aachen on this neuralgic point could obviously have provided critics with additional weaponry.

Pope Leo's actions show him determined not to allow disagreement about the *Filioque* to become a source of suspended communion between east and west. But Greeks were upset and the questions rumbled on. According to the life of Michael,[21] *synkellos* of Patriarch Thomas of Jerusalem, Michael, together with two monks from the Lavra of St Sabas, travelled to Constantinople with the intention of going on to Rome to convey their negative opinion of the *Filioque*. They may have had difficulty in obtaining support from Patriarch Thomas, who, on the evidence of his letter to the Armenians commending Chalcedon, was deeply respectful of Roman authority and therefore likely to be slow to attack a western usage tolerated by the popes. However, the three could have gone to consult the ecumenical patriarch on his advice. Their iconophile sympathies could not have pleased the authorities, from 815 converted to iconoclasm once again. Their

[21] The *Life of Michael the Synkellos* is edited with translation and commentary by Mary B. Cunningham (Belfast Byzantine Texts and Translations, 1, 1991). His panegyric on Dionysius Areopagita stressed that the Spirit 'proceeds from the Father alone and comes forth through the Son' (PG 4. 640 B), a reference I owe to Professor A. Louth. Michael's iconophilism detained him at Constantinople (no doubt in a monastery used for detention purposes) between 815 and 843 (cf. 668 C). Doubts about the reliability of Michael's *Life* are strongly expressed by M. F. Auzépy, 'De la Palestine à Constantinople (VIIIᵉ–IXᵉ siècle): Étienne le Sabaïte et Jean Damascène', *Travaux et mémoires*, 12 (1994), 183–218 at 209–12. She suggests Michael left Jerusalem because of conflict with Patriarch Thomas, not as his legate, perhaps because of Thomas's too ultramontane view of papal authority and of his disinclination to question the Frankish *Filioque*. Patriarch Thomas's letter to the Armenians, urging that Chalcedon had Petrine authority, is in PG 97. 1504–21. Sent in Arabic composed by Theodore Abu Qurrah of the Lavra of St Sabas, the letter was put into Greek by Michael Synkellos (1504 D).

leader Michael became abbot of the monastery of the Chora and *synkellos* to the new patriarch, Methodios, in 843. Nothing happened to change his mind on western trinitarian speculations. The issue of the *Filioque* was temporarily quiescent, but was sure to revive.

In the meanwhile the Frankish Church remained adamant in rejecting the second Council of Nicaea (787). At a council at Paris in 825 the bishops were outspoken in criticizing Pope Hadrian I: right to condemn iconoclasm, but how unwise to sanction the adoration of images. It was out of character for the successor of St Peter to fail to instruct the faithful correctly. The Franks were determined to use their alliance with the papacy to erect a fortress against the Greek east, even if that had to be achieved at the price of digging a chasm between the two main halves of the Church. However, the bishops at Paris in 825 were saying only what was at the time the prevalent opinion at Constantinople, where iconoclasm (and the harassment of zealous iconophiles) remained public policy from 815 until 843. The synod in 825 was happy to learn from the Greek emperor Michael that his judgement coincided with that of Charlemagne.[22] It would seem an acknowledgement that Charlemagne and the Council of Frankfurt had been right all along when the Greeks were wrong.

Exchanges over the *Filioque* between Franks and Greeks at Gentilly in 767, or at Jerusalem early in the ninth century and then in the circles close to Charlemagne, made western theologians conscious of the existence of a yawning divergence on the point between east and west. Earlier writers such as Gregory the Great or Boethius simply assumed that the Augustinian pattern of trinitarian doctrine was true beyond cavil. Confrontation with the Greek tradition caused anxiety. Awareness of this is apparent in the great work by the Irish theologian at the court of Charles the Bald, *Periphyseon* or *De divisione naturae* by John the Scot or Eriugena. Writing about 860–2 he devoted some pages of his second book to the *Filioque*. He had been much influenced by Neoplatonic elements in the thinking of Dionysius the Areopagite and Maximus Confessor. Maximus' use of the conciliatory formula that the Holy Spirit proceeds from the Father 'through the Son' seemed to Eriugena to offer a way of affirming the compatibility of the eastern and western traditions. The formula had the merit of being anticipated in Gregory of Nyssa. John of Damascus used it, and it is among the paradoxes of the story that the 'Caroline Books', attacking Patriarch Tarasius' use of the 'per Filium' formula, were to be found in agreement on this point with such zealous iconodules as John of Damascus and Photius. The Franks wanted 'and' not 'through'; Eriugena however, regarded both as satisfactory alternatives. He was in complete agreement with his contemporary Photius that

[22] Mansi. xii. 421, MGH Concilia iv/2. 478–9.

there could be no question of two first principles or prime causes. The generation of the Son and the procession of the Spirit are of the Father's being alone (a proposition that Greeks would like). The silence of Greek theology on the Son's participation in the procession of the Spirit expresses reverence for the divine mystery.

16

POPE NICOLAS I

During the ninth century tension between Rome and Constantinople mounted. Frankish backing gave popes more confidence in claiming the right to consecrate the archbishop of Syracuse (though Sicily was mainly Greek-speaking), and old anger still smouldered over rivalry for jurisdiction in Illyricum—i.e. the Balkan peninsula into which from 600 Slav and Turkic tribes had been pouring. In the rather distant past these regions of the old Roman empire had looked more to the Church at Rome than to Constantinople, and the papacy had used bishops of Thessalonica as papal vicars in relation to the east Roman world. Popes of the ninth century had not forgotten the action of the emperor Leo III in removing Illyricum from Roman jurisdiction when his iconoclastic policy failed to gain papal support. It was not unnoticed when, at the second Council of Nicaea in 787, Pope Hadrian's request for restoration of Roman authority was not included in the reading of his letter to the council.[1] Under Nicolas I (858–67), with strong Frankish support, interest was vigorously revived in the reassertion of Roman authority over this region, and Christian missions to the Slavs soon became competitive. The decision of the Croats to look towards Rome, while the Serbs eventually sought authority in the east, bequeathed a legacy of religious tension that was to persist through the period of Ottoman domination, and would contribute to conflicts of painful inhumanity in the twentieth and twenty-first centuries.

Pope Nicolas I ensured from the start of his pontificate that the alliance of papacy and Frankish empire was closely cemented. The emperor Louis II

---

[1] Hadrian's letter to Irene and Constantine was read at the second session of the second Council of Nicaea. His complaints about jurisdiction in Illyricum, of loss of revenue from Roman estates, about the elevation of Tarasius from lay status to be patriarch, and about the title 'ecumenical patriarch', are lacking in the Greek Acts. These sections, however, were known to Anastasius Bibliothecarius, who used the point to accuse the Greeks of rewriting conciliar Acts after councils ended and those present had gone home: MGH Epp. vii. 415. 2 ff. The excisions were made in 787, not in the 860s during Photius' controversy with Rome; the latter opinion is urged by L. Wallach, *Diplomatic Studies in Latin and Greek Documents from the Carolingian Age* (Ithaca, NY, 1977), 3–26. Wallach's argument is treated with reserve by Patrick Henry, 'Images of the Church in the Second Nicene Council and in the Libri Carolini', in *Law, Church and Society: Essays in Honor of Stephan Kuttner* (Philadelphia, 1977), 237–52 at 248–49. Roman suspicion of Greek falsification of conciliar Acts appears in Gregory the Great, *Reg.* 6. 14 (September 594).

was present in Rome for the consecration, ensuring Nicolas' prayers for his
military success, assuring the Pope of Frankish partnership in the assertion of
Roman authority. The nine and a half years of Nicolas' tenure of the papacy
were marked by the strongest affirmations of his Petrine authority to govern
all churches in the universal body: Rome is 'magistra, mater, et caput' of all
churches—teacher, mother, and head.[2] The bishop of Rome is Peter's
deputy (*vicarius*).[3] The Petrine privileges of the Roman see are directly
derived from the prince of the apostles, and are utterly independent of all
conciliar decisions.[4] The sixth canon of the Council of Nicaea therefore
should not be reckoned to be making any increase in an already recognized
leadership; that canon of the Council of 325 was concerned only to justify the
bishop of Alexandria's jurisdiction beyond the Egyptian provinces into
Libya, and that of the bishop of Antioch more widely than Syria.[5]
Nevertheless Nicolas had to concede that papal authority was at least made
visible through reception, to which conciliar canons bore witness. He frequently appealed to the western Council of Serdica (342), which was taken
to accord to Rome the status of final court of appeal when a bishop felt that
he had not received justice from his provincial synod. However, as soon as
there was controversy about the 'small print' of primatial jurisdiction, the
authority of this western council would be put in question, since its canons
were not acknowledged in the Greek east as having binding authority for the
eastern church. In addition to his arsenal of canon law and papal decretals,
Nicolas owed much to language about the universal and supra-conciliar
authority of his see employed during the schism between Rome and
Constantinople from 484 to 518, especially to the terms employed by Pope
Gelasius I (494–6) and to the ultramontane defence of Pope Symmachus in
the writings of Ennodius of Pavia.[6]

[2] MGH Epp. vi. 398, 11 (PL 119. 905 D). Similar terms in Pope Stephen II in 753 to Pippin (PL
97. 127 A 'mater et caput omnium ecclesiarum Dei'). Rome has been *caput* since Pope Boniface I
(PL 20. 777 B), *mater* since the seventh century. On Nicolas there is a good summary by J. Fried in
Theologische Realenzyklopädie, xxiv (Berlin, 1994), 535–40. For his letters see E. Perels's edition in
MGH Epp. vi; many are printed in *Acta Romanorum Pontificum*, i (Vatican, 1943), 599–691. A summary of papal ideology in Nicolas in W. Ullmann, *The Growth of Papal Government in the Middle Ages*
(London, 1962).
[3] MGH Epp. vi. 471. 16, 528. 13 (PL 119. 945 A, 1084 A).
[4] Ibid. 475 (PL 119. 948 D).   [5] Ibid. 476. 4 ff. (PL 119. 949 D).
[6] Beside the many marked citations, numerous passages echo Gelasius without naming the
source. Nicolas' letters contain so many citations and reminiscences of earlier popes that they offer
good evidence for the quality of papal record-keeping. In composing his letters he received material help from Anastasius, later to be librarian under Hadrian II. On the papal archive at this period see
T. F. X. Noble, 'Literacy and Papal Government in Late Antiquity and the Early Middle Ages', in
R. McKitterick (ed.), *The Uses of Literacy in Early Medieval Europe* (Cambridge, 1990). See also Noble,
The Republic of St Peter (Philadelphia, 1984). Nicolas' dependence on Ennodius, noted in F. Vogel's
edn. (MGH Auct. Ant. 7, p. xxvii), is discussed briefly by A. Lumpe in *Annuarium Historiae
Conciliorum*, 1 (1969), 15–36. The synod of 502 ruled that it had no power to sit in judgement on the
incumbent of the first see—a victory for the curial/papal ideology over the conciliar/episcopalist.

Nicolas knew, and accepted as wholly authentic, documents forged about 500 in the defence of Pope Symmachus troubled by charges of unfitting conduct with old flames of his unregenerate youth. The forged texts claimed that no council was valid without papal ratification, and that Peter's see was above the judgement of any episcopal synod.[7] In time Nicolas also came to know and use the False Decretals,[8] a brilliantly constructed corpus of canon law, inextricably mingling authentic conciliar canons and papal decretals with spurious texts, especially decretals given to pre-Constantinian bishops of Rome. The creative editor was concerned to restrict the power of metropolitans to depose their suffragans without papal sanction. Individual bishops needed Roman protection against their own provincial synods. Naturally the collection was welcome at Rome. Probably it was produced in the Frankish world in the interest of Ebbo, deposed bishop of Reims, and those he ordained who were hostile to Ebbo's replacement, the formidable Hincmar.[9]

The False Decretals bore on a question already disputed among the Franks: had the Roman see power to overturn a synodical decision? Agobard, archbishop of Lyon 816–40, opposed an opinion that Gallican canons lacked validity unless legates from pope or emperor were present at the meeting. Many Frankish bishops felt that papal autocracy had been superimposed on an originally conciliar Church. By creating decretals ascribed to early popes the compiler implicitly answered that argument. Initially surprised, Nicolas accepted the new collection's authenticity, and

---

[7] For the background see my *Boethius* (Oxford, 1981), ch. 1. For the history of the primatial formula forged in Symmachus' interest see S. Vacca, *Prima sedes a nemine iudicatur: Genesi e sviluppo storico dell'assioma fino al decreto di Graziano* (Miscellanea Hist. Pontif. 61; Rome, 1993). On the Symmachian forgeries see Duchesne, *Liber Pontificalis*, i, pp. cxxxiii–cxli, *Clavis*, 1679–82. A clear summary in E. Caspar, *Geschichte des Papsttums*, ii. 107–10. Vacca, op. cit. explains their role in the defence of Pope Symmachus (pp. 33–78), and catalogues the writers who invoke the principle that the first see cannot be judged. Alcuin, *ep.* 174 (MGH Epp. iv. 297. 21), takes for granted the authenticity of the 'canons of Pope Silvester'. Constant's 1721 text of almost all the documents is reprinted in PL 6. 11–20; 8. 822–40, 1388–93; PL Suppl. 3. 1249–55. A recent critical edition in E. Wirbelauer, *Zwei Päpste in Rom: Der Konflikt zwischen Laurentius und Symmachus* (Munich, 1993).

[8] Edited by P. Hinschius, *Decretales pseudo-Isidorianae et Capitula Angilramni* (Leipzig, 1863). For a masterly examination of the character and origin of the collection see Horst Fuhrmann, *Einfluß und Verbreitung der pseudoisidorischen Fälschungen*, 3 vols. (MGH Schriften xxiv/1–3; Stuttgart, 1972–4). The forged canons were not produced at Rome. When in 858 Lupus of Ferrières asked Pope Nicolas to confirm the authenticity of a canon ascribed to Melchiades, pope early in the fourth century (MGH Epp. vi. 114), Nicolas was baffled and unable to confirm or deny. So he had not encountered pseudo-Isidore by that time. The centralizing ecclesiology centred on the papacy in Gregory VII, though not created by pseudo-Isidore, derived from the collection its justification. Pope Urban II's canonist Deusdedit drew much upon it, as also Gratian.

[9] On the story of Ebbo see Jean Devisse, *Hincmar, archevêque de Reims* (Geneva, 1975–6), i. 71–96. In controversy with his nephew, namesake, and suffragan Hincmar of Laon, who appealed to the Isidorian decretals, Hincmar of Reims expressed doubts about their authority: *Opusculum LV Capitulorum*, 20 ff. (PL 126. 282–3).

soon was being short with Frankish bishops raising doubts about the authenticity of the very early decretals on the ground that they were absent from
their hitherto standard canon-collections.[10]

Although not directly produced in the papal or Roman curial interest, the
False Decretals were obviously going to be congenial to the centralizing
instincts of Pope Nicolas I. The Decretals offered a solution to a problem
which had long caused difficulty to the papacy, namely that canon law
had been originally made not by primatial authority but by provincial
councils, which the bishops of primatial sees such as Rome or Carthage or
Constantinople were expected to enforce. The Decretals were to undermine
the older conciliar theory of Church authority. At the same time they offered
a hedge against secular and royal dominance of the Church. They specify that
the secular power may not interfere in matters which belong to the proper
decision of the bishops. There is no demand that bishops be invested with
political power. Even Pope Gelasius I at the end of the fifth century, when in
sharp controversy with the Byzantine emperor Anastasius, had conceded
that in matters of imperial law bishops are subordinate and obliged to obey.
But in spiritual matters the emperor's duty is to follow the counsel and precepts of the pope.[11] The doctrine that the Church possesses both swords is
not met until the twelfth century in the justifiably famous treatise of Bernard
of Clairvaux, *De consideratione* (4. 3. 7). Nevertheless the Decretals reflect the
desire of Frankish bishops to be more independent of secular monarchs in the
powerful nation-states emerging from the dominant barbarian kingdoms of
the west, and it would not have been natural to them to share in the submis-
siveness of Pope Gregory the Great when he assured the Byzantine emperor
Maurice that he was the emperor's most loyal subject (*Reg.* 3. 61, 5. 37).
Under the rules in the Decretals it became almost impossible to accuse a
bishop successfully.

So the Decretals were to provide a store of canons which elevated the
Roman see far above provincial councils and protected individual bishops
from harassment by national episcopal conferences. A generation after Pope
Nicolas' time, the chronicler Regino of Prüm could comment (s.a. 868) that
'from the time of Gregory the Great to the present, no pope equalled Nicolas
in honour; for he issued commands to emperors and tyrants, and exercised
authority as lord of the world.' The False Decretals were in effect providing
a blueprint for the kind of papal monarchy associated with Gregory VII or
Innocent III.

[10] MGH Epp. vi. 392 ff. (PL 119. 899 ff.). Agobard, *De dispensatione ecclesiasticarum rerum* 20 (PL
104. 241–2)

[11] Gelasius, *ep.* 12. 2, p. 35 ed. Thiel, p. 20 ed. Schwartz (ch. 9 n. 1): 'quantum ad ordinem per-
tinent publicae disciplinae . . . legibus tuis ipsi quoque parent religionis antistes.' Elsewhere (Tract.
iv, p. 568 Thiel) Gelasius says that bishops 'use' secular laws.

At Rome a similarly sublime view of the papal office was held by a dark background figure, Anastasius called 'the librarian' (Bibliothecarius) after Nicolas' successor Hadrian II put him in charge of archives. He was drafter of letters for both Nicolas and Hadrian, and continued in this role under Pope John VIII. With a good knowledge of Greek he made himself indispensable as a translator. He addressed Nicolas as 'God's vicar' with the keys of heaven and the keys of knowledge. His letters are edited in MGH Epp. vii.

In a world threatened by anarchy, there can be considerable attractions in turning towards autocracy.

The False Decretals enjoyed immense success, mainly because, in an age when mastery of canon law had become crucial to good order in the Church surrounded by social and political disorder, the Decretals offered texts which a large body of people wanted to believe. Any suggestion that autocratic papal authority had been a comparatively recent accretion which the ancient Church was not blessed to have (an opinion certainly held by some Frankish bishops) was refuted by providing numerous rulings ascribed to early popes of the second century, their names being taken from the *Liber Pontificalis*. These texts purported to show that what popes like Nicolas were asserting in the ninth century was consistent with a continuous line, a veritable arsenal of canons going back to Clement of Rome who succeeded St Peter. The papacy was not sorry to have such reinforcement. At the same time it was congenial to have texts making it clear that metropolitans had no authority to depose difficult or recalcitrant suffragans without the agreement of the Roman see, and that a similar power to remove bishops from office was not possessed by kings and princes.

An important and influential proposition in the False Decretals laid down that no councils were to be held binding unless ratified by 'apostolic authority' (pseudo-Damasus in Hinschius 503). An approximation to this occurs in Pope Gelasius at the end of the fifth century (*ep*. 26. 3, p. 395 Thiel = CSEL 35. 372. 14–15).

Donation of Constantine

A major text which became widely known with the diffusion of the pseudo-Isidorian Decretals was the Donation of Constantine, *Constitutum Constantini*.[12] By this the great emperor Constantine bestowed on Pope

---

[12] The critical edition of the Donation of Constantine in MGH is by Horst Fuhrmann (Fontes iuris, 10; 1968). The clearest account of its origin is by him in *Settimane Spoleto*, 20/1 (1973), i. 257–92. There is no clear evidence of an eighth-century pope using it. It could have been produced at Rome by private enterprise to assert Roman authority over Ravenna and other Byzantine land. An origin late in the eighth century is probable. E. D. Hehl, '798, eine erstes Zitat aus der konstantinischen Schenkung', *Deutsches Archiv*, 47 (1991), 1–17 argues that the Roman synod of 798, quoted by the Roman synod of 964, used the same trinitarian invocation as the Donation, and is the earliest citation of it.

Silvester and on all his successors in blessed Peter's see until the end of the world authority superior to the four eastern patriarchs, jurisdiction to decide on all matters affecting Christian faith and worship, and the right to permanent residence in the Lateran Palace, so that the Pope's dignity would be the equal of the emperor's at Constantinople. There in the east Constantine would now make his residence so as to avoid all rivalry to the Pope in the west.

The Donation built on the forgeries associated with the name of Silvester created in 499–501 to serve the interest of the beleaguered Pope Symmachus. Its origin is shrouded in mist. No pope of the eighth or ninth century appealed to the Donation to justify primatial jurisdiction. The Silvester fictions, generally accepted as authentic, provided sufficient material for that. Pope Hadrian I writing to Charlemagne in 778 declared that 'By Constantine's largess the Roman Church was raised and given dominion in these parts of the west', a sentence which is as likely to have inspired the making of the Donation as to reflect knowledge of its text. Hadrian's language at least illustrates the point that in the second half of the eighth century senior Roman clergy were thinking the kind of thoughts which the Donation would articulate. In the eighth and ninth centuries the Donation did not influence events or what popes said and did. Its effect in that regard came much later, in 1054 at the time of abrasive exchanges between Rome and Constantinople, or in later medieval centuries when papal jurisdiction was being asserted to be universal.

The Donation sounded good for papal authority until it came to be realized that the document made the Pope's claim to universal ordinary jurisdiction, even over eastern patriarchs and all bishops everywhere, a matter dependent on a secular emperor, not on the dominical commission to St Peter. Its spuriousness was seen by Pecock in England, Nicolas of Cusa in Germany, and Valla in Italy in the fifteenth century. The papacy was better off without it.

The names of Constantine and Silvester were enjoying high authority in the eighth and ninth centuries. The regular name for the Lateran basilica was the Constantiniana or the Caesareum. And the veneration of Pope Silvester was actively promoted, especially in the time of Pope Paul I (757–67).

In time the False Decretals would reinforce an interpretation of Church authority in strongly juridical terms. If all power, indeed the very possibility of being Christian at all, must be derived through the mediation of the Pope, that must simplify the system of canon law by concentrating in one person or institution the power to make the rules. Yet it would be hard to assert that the Decretals implanted in Nicolas grander notions of his authority than he already possessed, mainly by inheritance from his predecessors since the time of Leo I and especially Gelasius I and the popes of the age of the Acacian schism (484–518), whose letters he studied carefully. His convictions were amplified by the language of Anastasius, his learned archivist, for whom Nicolas was simply God's deputy. To be out of communion with the see of Rome was to be outside the ark of salvation, and as universal bishop he had to give account for all believers at the Last Judgement. He had inherited the power to bind and loose entrusted by Christ to St Peter, and therefore determined both doctrine and discipline, being entirely within his rights in deposing disobedient bishops. With the authority of a 'superinspector'[13] he had power to inquire into every church, and could take initiatives in regulating whatever might be amiss.

Just as the authority of officers of the empire is derived from the emperor, so for Nicolas metropolitans derive authority from Peter's see.[14] Other patriarchs derive their jurisdiction from no other source than St Peter, a qualification which simultaneously subordinates the Petrine sees of Alexandria and Antioch to Rome and disqualifies Jerusalem and Constantinople (below, pp. 265 f.). It offended him when Gallic bishops imagined that by provincial decision they could depose a colleague without reference to Rome (*ep.* 71). He held in abhorrence the notion current in the east that the primatial jurisdiction of Rome depended on canon law enacted by episcopal councils rather than being directly inherited from St Peter. And regional provincial synods depended for their authority not merely on manifesting the consensus of a large body of bishops drawn from a wide or at least substantial geographical area ensuring doctrine in line with scripture and sacred tradition, but also and above all on Rome's ratification. In 485 Pope Felix II had asserted precisely such powers of papal assent or veto even in relation to an assembly as august as the Council of Nicaea in 325, at which no pope was present personally and Constantine the Great had exercised crucial influence.

Even the sword entrusted to the emperor at his coronation is power delegated from St Peter through his heir the pope, to be used against infidels (Nicolas, *ep.* 34). The emperor at Constantinople, Michael III, was admonished for the deposition of Patriarch Ignatius without reference to St Peter's vicar. He is to acknowledge that the Roman Church is his 'mother' and not to be ungrateful for the pope's parental remonstrance.

It would be illusion to suppose that Nicolas always had his way. He needed to be assertive because relatively little was happening as he wished. In Church history the most trumpet-tongued statements of Roman authority have come at times when papal power felt weak or ignored. Anastasius discloses that in the city of Rome itself there was a powerful faction opposed to him. Trouble did not come only from Constantinople.

[13] MGH Epp. vi. 316. 17 (PL 119. 973 A).   [14] Ibid. 475 (PL 119. 949 B–C).

Nicolas found that in western provinces he had critics. A letter of 858 to Bishop Guenilo of Sens darkly refers to some like scorpions who scorn St Peter's see.[15] Evidently they are in Francia. He had serious problems with the bishop of Ravenna's aspirations to independence.[16] Among his western critics, some conveyed their feelings against his autocratic style to ready ears at Constantinople. The more vocal and tiresome the critics, the more determined Nicolas became to stress the supremacy of Peter's see not only over other bishops but over synods. Indeed even the first Council of Nicaea did not possess that full authority which the Roman Church is privileged to inherit from Peter. In the *Liber Pontificalis* Nicolas is acclaimed as 'a new Peter'.[17]

Instinctively Nicolas felt distrust of the conciliar process. He knew, correctly enough, that regional synods are capable of making mistakes especially when they consider only the limited and limiting factors of their own pastoral and cultural situation, and disregard wider and more universal considerations. In any case both in relation to the Frankish churches and even more in his dealings with the Greek east, he found difficulty in understanding the conciliar concept of authority. When Photius contended that east and west had different customs which deserved to be respected, Nicolas was wholly unimpressed (*ep.* 86, MGH Epp. vi. 51. 1–7).

---

[15] Ibid. 611. 32 (PL 119. 769 B).

[16] The desire of archbishops of Ravenna for independence from Rome was linked with the fact that the city was the residence of the Byzantine exarch, and had a strong consciousness of belonging to the east Roman world. On Nicolas' dispute with bishop John see the long account in the life of Nicolas in *Liber Pontificalis* 107. 21–35 (ii. 155–9 Duchesne), with K. Herbers, 'Der Konflikt Papst Nikolaus' I. mit Erzbischof Johannes VII. von Ravenna (861)', in P. J. Heinig (ed.), *Diplomatische und chronologische Studien aus Arbeiten an den Regesta Imperii* (Cologne, 1991), 166 ff., and the paper by H. Fuhrmann, *ZSSR*, Kan. Abt. 75 (1958), 353–8. About 666 Pope Vitalian (657–72) demanded submission from Maurus the then archbishop of Ravenna on pain of excommunication. Maurus ceased to commemorate Vitalian at mass. The emperor Constans 'liberated his Church from the yoke of servitude to the Romans' (Agnellus, *Liber Pontificalis Ecclesiae Ravennatis* 112–15, ed. O. Holder-Egger, MGH Scriptores rerum Langobardicarum et Italicarum vi–ix. 350–3).

[17] *Liber Pontificalis* 108. 28 (ii. 179 ed. Duchesne).

17

HINCMAR OF REIMS[1]

Not all western bishops of Nicolas' age thought about the nature of the Church in exactly the same way as their pope did. The eloquent and coherent voice for collegiality in the western Church of the ninth century was that of Hincmar, archbishop of Reims from 845 to his death in 882. In the disorder of society and of the churches in his generation Hincmar was prominent among those who stressed the value of canon law providing rules of procedure for clergy and laity, and was familiar with the principal texts of Roman law. Zeal for metropolitan rights did not inhibit him from acknowledging that the holy catholic apostolic Church of Rome, whose missions founded the churches throughout the west, is 'mother of all'.[2] He expected popes to support him, not to interfere. He could be emphatic on the importance of Roman primacy as a bond of unity and order and, although from time to time he found himself protesting against what he thought to be ill-judged interferences on the part of the Roman see in local pastoral problems of the *collegium* of Frankish churches, he disowned the least intention of being disobedient to the commanding authority of the see of St Peter, the great defender of local bishops against dominant secular lords.

There was difficulty for Hincmar when Nicolas insisted on reinstating Rothad bishop of Soissons, whom Hincmar in Synod had judged unworthy of office. He frankly declared Nicolas' action 'uncanonical, and an act of

---

[1] Hincmar is subject of a three-volume monograph by Jean Devisse (Geneva, 1975–6). On his ecclesiology see Y. M. J. Congar, *L'Ecclésiologie du haut moyen-âge* (Paris, 1968), 166–77; G. H. Tavard, 'Episcopacy and Apostolic Succession according to Hincmar of Reims', *Theological Studies*, 34 (1973), 594–623; G. Schmitz, 'Concilium perfectum: Überlegungen zum Konzilsverständnis Hinkmars von Reims', *ZSSR*, Kan. Abt. 65 (1979), 27–54. Hincmar's work on Lotharius' divorce begins by laying down that in matters of doubt the Roman see is judge. See further Janet Nelson, 'Kingship Law and Liturgy in the Political Thought of Hincmar of Reims', *English Historical Review*, 92 (1977), 241–79; the article on him in *Theologische Realenzyklopädie*, xv (Berlin, 1986), 355–60 by R. Schieffer; J. M. Wallace-Hadrill, 'History in the Mind of Archbishop Hincmar', in *The Writing of History in the Middle Ages: Essays Presented to Richard William Southern* (Oxford, 1981). On Hincmar's thesis e.g. that conciliar canons have more authority than papal decretals: H. J. Sieben, *Die Konzilsidee des lateinischen Mittelalters (847–1378)* (Paderborn, 1984), 75–112. Flodoard of Reims (30. 11–18) describes Hincmar's relation with the Roman see; M. Sot, *Un historien et son église au Xe siècle: Flodoard de Reims* (Paris, 1993), 559.

[2] PL 125. 213–14. Hincmar is echoing Innocent I, *ep.* 25. 2 (PL 20. 552 B).

mere power'. It is very possible that Rothad provided Nicolas with the False Decretals or excerpts from them. In 870 Hincmar defended the rights of metropolitans in a special work, *De iure metropolitanorum* (PL 126. 282–494). which provoked opponents to charge him with thinking the pope's powers were no greater than a metropolitan's. Flodoard reports that such accusations were brought up at a synod at Troyes in 878. So the papacy had supporters in the powers being claimed. Papal sovereignty over metropolitans came to be symbolized by the conferring of the pallium.

Hincmar shared Pope Nicolas' alarm when the archbishops of Cologne and Trier supported the determination of their king Lotharius to divorce his childless wife Theutberga and to give legitimacy to the son of his concubine Waldrada by formal marriage with her.[3] That would preserve his kingdom, which was an object of hungry covetousness in Charles the Bald and Louis the German. To exclude interference from Nicolas the two archbishops proposed an independent territorial Church in communion with the see of Peter but not subject to papal jurisdiction (a striking anticipation of Febronianism nine centuries later). Nicolas and Hincmar used powerful rhetoric, but the defeat of Lotharius' ambition was no doubt largely due to the secular pressure from Charles the Bald and Louis.

Hincmar had learnt from his reading in early church history that bishops should be unhesitant and courageous in pointing out the moral faults of royal persons. The humility of the emperor Theodosius I before Ambrose of Milan after the massacre at Thessalonica seemed to him a model for Frankish princes.

Lotharius' brother the emperor Louis II descended on Rome to intimidate Pope Nicolas and his flock; Nicolas had to seek asylum by St Peter's shrine. The two archbishops supporting the divorce appealed for wide support with an encyclical letter accusing Nicolas of making himself an apostle and indeed 'emperor of the entire world'. Nicolas was intransigent against both them and the king. The material interests of the Church in Germany were no reason for compromise. In the struggle Nicolas won the day, so that when Lotharius died in 869, his natural son could not inherit the kingdom, which

---

[3] Annals of St Bertin for 862 and 864 (translated and annotated by Janet Nelson, Manchester, 1991). Hincmar on the divorce of King Lotharius and Queen Theutberga is edited, with rich commentary, by Letha Böhringer, MGH Concilia iv, Supplementum ii (Hannover, 1992). To facilitate divorce proceedings an adolescent confession of Theutberga was used that she and her brother had had an incestuous relationship of mutual masturbation. The British Museum has an exquisitely cut rock crystal depicting Susanna cleared of adultery, inscribed 'Lotharius rex Francorum fieri iussit', its occasion being less probably reconciliation with Theutberga than a vindication of Waldrada— but either interpretation is possible. Illustration: Peter Lasko, *Ars Sacra 800–1200²* (New Haven, 1994), 41 pl. 54. See J. L. Nelson, *Charles the Bald* (London, 1992), 199–200. Pope Nicolas' correspondence about the divorce is in MGH Epp. vi. 209–40. See also T. Bauer, 'Rechtliche Implikationen des Ehestreites Lothars II.', ZSSR, Kan. Abt. 80 (1994), 41–87.

was divided between Charles the Bald and Louis. The morally right was politically disastrous.

Both the Franks and perhaps to a lesser degree Pope Nicolas regarded with misgiving the more iconophile enthusiasms of Byzantine monks. Neither the Frankish bishops nor the pope would admit the second Council of Nicaea to their catalogue of ecumenical councils with universal authority. The *Liber Diurnus*, containing formularies of the papal chancellery compiled at the end of the eighth century, allows for six general councils. For Hincmar the necessary qualification for a council to be ranked as ecumenical was not merely that it enjoyed the magisterial sanction of emperor and pope but also that its decisions were generally received (*receptissima*) and therefore accepted as manifestly correct guidance for the whole Church.[4] That could not be affirmed of the second Council of Nicaea, which for Hincmar was a 'pseudo-synod' lacking western ratification, the errors revealed in the Acts being providentially corrected by the certainly general Council of Frankfurt in 794.[5] Like Charlemagne, Hincmar thought icon-smashers and icon-adorers were equally wrong. He discovered the anti-Greek Libri Carolini, his copy of which survives in the codex Paris Arsenal 663 (the only complete text).

Pope Nicolas' correspondence with the Greeks did not conceal his reservations about iconophile anxieties to include Nicaea II among the general councils. He therefore had fairly frequent occasion to give space in his letters to explanations that the Roman see was not actually in favour of iconoclasm. Roman past reservations about the Council *in Trullo* of 692 as well as about the authority of Nicaea II conveyed an impression of lukewarm interest in the struggle.

Photius' letters make it evident that iconoclast sympathizers in the east, who after 843 were far from defunct, could make capital out of western reservations, which proved Nicaea II to be no more than a local assembly with merely limited recognition.[6] As late as 864–5 Photius had to write to refute a subtle iconoclast argument rejecting the very possibility of any universally valid estimate of icons, on the ground that Romans, Indians, Greeks, and Egyptians have differing ways of representing Christ, none of which can be called authentic, all being the product of limited iconographical traditions.[7]

---

[4] PL.126. 359 B. The *Liber Diurnus* has been edited by Hans Foerster (Bern, 1958).

[5] PL 126. 360 A.

[6] Explicit in *ep*. 2. 378 ff. LW. The Greek canonist Balsamon, commenting on Trullanum, canon 2 (RP ii. 311), comments that decisions by local synods, not ratified by the emperor, are regarded by some as lacking authority and binding force.

[7] *Ep*. 65 LW. Augustine (*De Trinitate* 8. 4. 7–8. 5. 8) felt no discomfort in the observation that all believers have different mental pictures of the physical appearance of Jesus and Mary. F. Dvornik, 'The Patriarch Photius and Iconoclasm', *Dumbarton Oaks Papers*, 7 (1953), 69–87.

18

JURISDICTION: ILLYRICUM, BULGARS. PAULICIANS

There were those at Constantinople to whom Nicolas' claims to universal jurisdiction in the Church were incomprehensible. Some weighty Greek voices took it for a self-evident truth that when the emperors from Constantine onwards left Rome for the Bosporos ecclesiastical authority accompanied the transfer, and that primacy throughout the Church now belonged to the bishop of the 'queen city', 'Constantinople-Rome' as it was in law entitled. (It was an inverted form of the Donation of Constantine.) In one letter Nicolas I explicitly ascribed this view to the Byzantine leaders, and that he was correct in this is illustrated both by Pope Felix II's report in 485 that the patriarch Acacius was claiming to be head of the whole Church, and especially by a passage in the *Alexiad* of Anna Comnena (1. 13). Anna wrote scornfully of Pope Gregory VII's allegedly inhuman treatment of the German emperor's ambassadors:

acts of one whom the Latins imagine to be first high priest and president of the entire empire (*oikoumène*). This is their arrogance; for when the emperor's authority was transferred thence to our royal city, with the senate and the entire government, the order of the high priests' sees was moved also. The Council of Chalcedon put the see of Constantinople in the highest place and placed all dioceses of the empire under its jurisdiction.

Anna was incorrect on both Gregory VII and Chalcedon; but her judgement of the situation would appear almost justified when one recalls that the Latin provinces of the old Roman empire were in her time barbarian kingdoms. For Anna it was a self-evident assumption, which no reasonable person could contest, that with its living heritage of classical culture in Greek literature and philosophy the civilization of Byzantium was immeasurably superior to the west. Moreover, it was a general presupposition in the east Roman world not merely that New Rome with its senate and seven hills had received all the authority lost by Old Rome but also that Constantine the Great had been God's chosen agent in founding this Christian city and making the east Roman empire into an instrument for the worldwide extension of the Christian faith. Anna could be mistaken in detail. But in any event her sentiments evidently expressed what had long been a general opinion on the Golden Horn. Theophylact Simocatta, the historian of the emperor Maurice, who owed his teaching post to patriarch Sergius I (607–38), writing early in the seventh century, included in his preface a salute to Sergius as 'the great high priest of the entire empire (*oikouméne*)'. Of this 'Roman empire' Church, he was obviously head.

At the Roman *patriarchium* the archives were carefully kept and filed. Among the documents of the past the Roman see had a collection of letters concerning the commission entrusted to the bishops of Thessalonica to act as representative of the Roman see in the Balkan peninsula. Nicolas I knew this file in his archive, and thought it clear evidence of the fact that at one time in the past Peter's see had exercised jurisdiction in the region loosely called Illyricum, and therefore that there had been an erosion of papal authority by the see of New Rome at Constantinople.

The question of Roman jurisdiction in Illyricum had a long history in the past. Damasus' successor Siricius had evidently felt some kind of threat with the powers implicit in the honour decreed for Constantinople in 381. In correspondence with Anysius bishop of Thessalonica Siricius appointed him papal vicar with power of veto over episcopal ordinations in Illyricum. This was to set up competition with Sirmium. At the Council of Aquileia in 381 bishop Anemius claimed his see to be 'caput Illyrici'. Pope Innocent I followed Siricius in telling Anysius that his vicariate covered eleven provinces, including Thessaly and even Crete, and Nicolas repeated most of this list in his letter to the emperor Michael III in 869.

The extent of jurisdiction attaching to Constantinople was an issue both political and ecclesiastical in the tension between Old Rome and New Rome about the bilingual region of Illyricum. Eastern Illyricum (Dacia and Macedonia) had had its civil administration transferred to Constantinople in 395 and constituted a praetorian prefecture. In July 421 an imperial constitution told the prefect that conciliar canons were to be enforced by his authority, and cases of doubt were to be referred to the see of Constantinople 'which enjoys the prerogatives of old Rome'. The law was objectionable to the then Pope Boniface. Nevertheless it evidently mirrored the assumptions of authority at the eastern capital.[1] The decision of the iconoclast emperors in the eighth century to reject all papal jurisdiction in any part of Illyricum was not negotiated and left smouldering resentment. At least it was not thunder out of a clear sky when, at the pro-Photian Council of 880, the

---

[1] Nicolas I, *ep.* 101 (MGH Epp. vi. 605. 19–24 = PL 119. 1157 B). On Pope Felix II see Ch. 9 n. 1. Anna Comnena 1. 13 (pp. 45–6 Reifferscheid). The imperial edict is Cod. Theod. 16. 4. 45. Pope Boniface I, epp. 4–5 (PL 20. 760–3). Socrates, *HE* 2. 16. 6 says that Illyricum is not part of the eastern empire.

ecumenical patriarch was acclaimed as the Church's chief pastor with universal jurisdiction.

On the western side Pope Nicolas consistently wrote about the Greek churches with an undercurrent of distrust, inherited from an all too sedulous reading in the exchanges at the time of the Acacian schism. Apart from differences over authority and the aftermath of Chalcedon, more recent questions about the *Filioque* and about icons did nothing to foster peace.

The latent volcano erupted from a chance factor that had little to do with past tensions, namely the appearance at Constantinople of two rival parties supporting different patriarchs. To a pope anxious to assert old Roman authority in Illyricum, the instinctive course of action was to support whichever of the two rivals would be willing and able to surrender to Roman jurisdiction the new churches coming into being from 864 among the Bulgars. Admittedly the Bulgars had not occupied more than a relatively small part of the region belonging to the old provinces of Illyricum. In any event by the ninth century 'Illyricum' had become an imprecise term which could be used in a vague sense much as 'the Balkans' might be spoken of today.

In a sermon on Ps. 45 (*En. in Ps.* 44. 17) St Augustine hit a rare mood of triumphalism, seeing in the universality of the episcopal order in the Catholic Church a divinely given principle of government extending through the Christian community to society at large, so that bishops (he foresaw) would become 'princes over all the earth'. The passage did not pass unnoticed by Pope Nicolas I.[2] From Gelasius I he had learnt that in matters both of faith and of ethics, indeed in any matter in which the Church had a proper concern, the Pope had a right and a duty to be the voice summoning even secular rulers to submit to God's will.

The Bulgars

Nicolas' decision to launch a rival Latin mission to the neophyte Bulgars, already evangelized by Greek missionaries, presupposed not only that he was claiming the restoration of Roman rights in Illyricum but also that in his judgement east Christian belief and practice must be deemed insufficient and even erroneous in comparison with the strict discipline of the west, where St Peter's see could guarantee truth as no other see could. Nicolas did not shrink from aggressive language in addressing the Byzantine emperor and patriarch. Just as Virgil's Anchises in the sixth book of the *Aeneid* (851–3) exhorted the Romans to remember that ruling an empire was their manifest destiny, using generosity to the submissive and tough measures against people of proud and

---

[2] Augustine, *En. in Ps.* 44. 17; Nicolas, *ep.* 88 (MGH Epp. vi. 475. 33 = PL 119. 949 c).

independent spirit, so also Nicolas' pattern of dominance appears as a Christianized version of centralized imperial power, and without that, he felt, the unity and universality of the one universal and apostolic Church could never be realized in the mess of human history.

For several decades from the fifth century onwards, the Bulgars had been a threatening presence on the Danube frontier with the military capacity to inflict serious defeats on the east Roman army. In time this would be felt at Constantinople to be so uncomfortable that the emperors would come to think it more important to crush the Bulgars than to recover lands lost to the Arabs—a decision with momentous consequences for the empire, making defence of the capital central. In 680 they moved south of the Danube to take possession of the plain and to create a citadel at Pliska. Their victory over the Byzantine army at the time of the Sixth Council (680–1) was taken by the losing monotheletes to be a sign of celestial displeasure at the council's acceptance of Pope Agatho's doctrine of two wills in Christ. This is reflected in the Acts of the Sixth Council. The Bulgars, Turkic nomads, dominated the Slav tribes settled in the Balkans and, while ambitious to share in the power and gold of Byzantine glory and to rival Frankish power, were also anxious to retain political independence. Catastrophe befell Byzantine expeditions, the emperor Nicephorus being killed in battle (811) and his skull made a drinking-cup. Michael I (811–13) lost his throne after grave defeat. With the Franks the Bulgars began to cultivate peaceful relations, and negotiated a frontier, according to the Frankish Annals in the year 826, which may have prepared the way for further conflicts with Byzantine forces in the 830s (attested in the Life of St Peter of Atroa). In 862/3 Khan Boris met King Louis to plan a joint onslaught on the Moravians squeezed between them.

Frankish bishops invited them to conversion. From Frankish sources the information reached Pope Nicolas that the Bulgars were contemplating the possibility of accepting Christian baptism and tribal conversion.[3] Very probably the same information was reaching Constantinople from Greek prisoners of war resident in the territories now under Bulgar control. The last thing the Byzantine empire needed was a hostile warrior force on its immediate

---

[3] Nicolas, *ep.* 26 (MGH Epp. vi. 293. 1 ff. = PL 119. 875 C). For a good discussion of the missionary competition for the soul of Bulgaria see J. M. Sansterre, 'Les missionaires latins, grecs et orientaux en Bulgarie dans la seconde moitié du ixe siècle', *Byzantion*, 52 (1982), 375–88. There were some churches in this region before the conversion of Khan Boris; see Peter Schreiner, 'Das Christentum in Bulgarien vor 864', in V. Gjuselev and R. Pillinger (eds.), *Das Christentum in Bulgarien und auf der übrigen Balkanhalbinsel in der Spätantike: II. Internationales Symposion Haskovo (Bulgarien), 10–13. Juni 1986* (Miscellanea Bulgarica, 5; Vienna, 1987), 51–61. Nicolas' interest in the Bulgarians may have been aroused by the existence of a Bulgarian colony in south Italy close to Beneventum, where the immigrants became bilingual: Paul the Deacon, *History of the Lombards* 5. 29. Bulgarian–Byzantine tensions are described by F. Dvornik, *Byzantine Missions among the Slavs* (New Brunswick, 1970), 42 ff.

northern flank, and the prospect that this bellicose race might end in alliance with grasping and ambitious Franks was alarming. In 863 a substantial show of Byzantine military strength proved decisive. The Khan Boris (853–89, d. 907) adopted as his baptismal name that of the Greek emperor Michael, and members of the ruling class were also baptized. The Khan acknowledged the sovereignty of the east Roman emperor—an act which was to cause pain to Pope Nicolas.

In Byzantine eyes to accept Christian baptism at the hands of Greek clergy from Constantinople was to bring oneself within the political world of the most Christian Roman emperor. For the emperor Justinian this proposition had been a self-evident axiom: missionary work and foreign policy went hand in hand. The Antiochene chronicler of Justinian's reign, John Malalas, records several instances where the influence of New Rome and its empire in providing protection for lesser principalities and tribes led on to baptism. Or indeed vice versa: to accept baptism at the hands of priests from Byzantium was also to become a constituent of the Roman empire. This could presuppose peace. In his *Tactica*, or handbook on military science, the emperor Leo the Wise (886–912) is emphatic:

Since the Bulgars have accepted peace in Christ and share the same faith as the Romans, we do not think it right to arm ourselves against them. Defence against them lies in God's hand. We have therefore decided not to describe their armaments against us nor ours against them, since we are dealing with brothers in Christ.[4]

Other texts of this age illustrate the axiom that to accept baptism from subjects of the east Roman emperor was understood by the converts as being an acknowledgement of the emperor's sovereignty over them. At the fourth session of the Council of Constantinople in 879 a speech by Basil of Martyropolis was explicit: 'Arabs were asking for baptism wishing to be subjects of the most holy emperor.' Nicolas I (Mysticus), patriarch of Constantinople (901–7 and 912–25), writing to Symeon the Bulgarian Khan put it directly: 'By baptism you become Romans' (*ep.* 17).

The Bulgarian desire to retain independence was far from dead, and their acceptance of Greek missionaries in no way put a brake on further negotiations both with the Franks based on Regensburg and with Pope Nicolas at Rome. For the Pope the conversion of the Bulgarians provided an acid test

---

[4] Nicolas, *ep.* 100 (MGH Epp. vii. 801 = PL 119. 1153 B). Leo, *Tactica* 44 (PG 107. 958 AB); cf. §61 (960 D): 'Turks differ from Bulgars only in that the latter have adopted the Christians' faith and changed to Roman ways, abandoning their wild and nomad customs together with unbelief.' Patriarch Nicolas Mysticus, *ep.* 31 (p. 208 ed. Jenkins–Westerink) tells the Bulgarian Khan Symeon that since the Bulgarians are God's people too, they should not attack the Christian emperor, Christ's vicar. Christian armies had special prayers and masses before going into battle, e.g. the emperor Leo VI, *Tactica* 14. 1 (PG 107. 848 D), or the Mozarabic prayers in Toledo cathedral 'when the Visigothic king goes to war', printed in M. Férotin, *Le Liber Ordinum* (Paris, 1904), 149.

of papal universal jurisdiction and raised the question whether he could demonstrate Roman authority by imposing western canonical discipline on the infant Bulgarian churches. At the same time the new Moravian churches, converted through Cyril and Methodius, missionaries sent by Photius from Constantinople, were already looking to Rome for further guidance rather than to Constantinople. In Bulgaria the Greek missionaries soon found themselves competing with Latin clergy who were not shy about telling the new converts that in essential respects the western version of Christianity was superior to the eastern.

The political complications did not modify Khan Boris's determination to be and to remain Christian. A dangerous pagan reaction was suppressed with embarrassing ferocity.[5] His aspiration to assert independence took the form of a request, initially put to Constantinople, that the new Bulgarian Church be headed by a bishop enjoying the title and powers of a 'patriarch'. The Byzantine emperor and the patriarch Photius already had enough trouble in affirming the patriarchal status of Constantinople in relation to western criticism, and did not wish the title to be devalued. Refusal stimulated the desire of Boris to discover if he could negotiate a better bid from the venerable see of St Peter. The proceedings came to resemble an auction with the Bulgarians suggesting that they would be guided by whichever of the two Romes was willing to give them what they wanted.

Paulicians[6]

Other competitors for the Bulgar soul were Armenians, probably including Paulician heretics resettled in Thrace by Constantine V to be a barrier to Bulgar attacks. They were keen missionaries averse to icons, priests, and Marian cult. In their eyes the Orthodox were those in the gospel parables who expected a place in the Kingdom but were excluded. Under their leader Sergius their citadel was at Tefrik in eastern Asia Minor. They derived their name from admiration for St Paul, and leaders took the name of the apostle's companions. The disparaging remarks about Paul's obscurity in 2 Pet. 3: 16 led them to drop the Petrine letters from their scriptures. Their story was written in 869 by Peter of Sicily to provide the Greek archbishop of Bulgaria with an arsenal against them.[7] Peter had been sent to Tefrik by Basil I for exchange of prisoners.

---

[5] Nicolas, *ep.* 99. 17 (MGH, Epp. vi. 577. 3) in his *Responsa* to the Bulgarians.

[6] Ibid., §§103, 106 (MGH Epp. vi. 599). See Nina Garsoian, *The Paulician Heresy* (The Hague. 1967); article by W. Klein in *Theologische Realenzyklopädie*, xxvi (Berlin, 1996), 127–9.

[7] Ed. P. Lemerle, *Travaux et mémoires*, 4 (1970), 3–67; see also id., *Travaux et mémoires*, 5 (1973), 1–144.

Emperors from Michael I (811–13) onwards decreed death for these 'Manichees'. But executions at Neocaesarea led to revenge, killing bishop and exarch with Saracen help. In 871 Basil I led a campaign against Tefrik. In what was perhaps a bid to recover Basil's favour Photius justified the attack, which attracted criticism, writing a book 'Against the Manichees' (PG 102. 15–264), mainly plagiarizing Peter of Sicily but adding details about their harassment. There was debate whether churchmen could properly support the death penalty (Theophanes AM 6304), Studite monks being opposed.

The Armenian (non-Paulician) Church retained a Catholicos resident at Philippopolis (Plovdiv) who about 1170 disputed Chalcedonian Christology with Theorianus (PG 133. 119–298). Photius' efforts to reconcile Armenians to Chalcedon provoked Pope Nicolas to warn the Armenian prince against him (*ep.* 87, MGH Epp. vi. 451–4; not in Migne).

The Bulgars also received Arab books of Muslim propaganda. All the competitors will have imparted urgency to the Orthodox task in hope of converting warlike tribesmen to Christian peace.

One of Pope Nicolas' arguments to persuade the converted Bulgars to acknowledge the primacy of Rome was that rival Greeks and Armenians and other variants were already pouring into their land, and in this Babel of different voices the great Church represented by St Peter's see must be best (*ep.* 99. 106, MGH Epp. vi. 599).

19

POPE NICOLAS' ADVICE TO THE BULGAR
KHAN. ROME'S SATURDAY FAST

The Bulgar Khan sent a series of questions to Rome, together with the request to provide a bishop with patriarchal standing. Pope Nicolas' answers, the 'Consulta Bulgarorum',[1] provide a mine of information about the problems of Christianization for a warlike race deeply attached to old customs, particularly to special rituals practised before and on the field of battle. In summary form it is clear from the 'Consulta' that the Pope felt it necessary to come to terms with a warrior ethic; he judged it necessary to replace the heathen pre-battle rites with liturgies such as Christian armies used. The horse's tail, which the Bulgarians used as their military standard, should be replaced by the victory sign of the Cross. So far as Church practice was concerned, Nicolas' canonistic mind appears at many points in his document and is revealed, for example, in his concern about the correct observance of prohibited degrees of kinship for matrimony. Nicolas claimed to be following the precedents set by Gregory the Great, notably in his answers sent to Augustine of Canterbury. By the eighth and ninth centuries, however, the text of Gregory's answers had been purged of a dangerous liberalism that allowed marriage in the third degree, and Nicolas adopted a line of unrelenting rigidity.

Many of the questions about canonical correctness are likely to have been more in the mind of Nicolas than of the Bulgarian Khan or the missionaries to his people. But the majority of his instructions show this pope to have been a wise and prudent pastor, concerned to bring the new converts a

---

[1] One can feel only regret that the text of the Responsa makes it impossible to accept the argument that Nicolas' answers to the Bulgarians betray no trace of anti-Greek animus, presented by G. T. Dennis, 'The Anti-Greek Character of the Responsa ad Bulgaros of Nicolas I?', *Orientalia Christiana Periodica*, 24 (1958), 165–74. More moderate and almost acceptable is the minimizing view of L. Heiser, *Die Responsa ad consulta Bulgarorum des Papstes Nikolaus I.* (Trierer Theologische Studien, 36; 1979). A judicious summary is in D. Obolensky, *The Byzantine Commonwealth* (London, 1971), 87–91. Striking analogies between Bulgarian and Anglo-Saxon conversion are shown by Henry Mayr-Harting, *Two Conversions to Christianity: The Bulgarians and Anglo-Saxons* (Stenton Lecture, University of Reading, 1994). An analysis of the text is in Ivan Dujčev, *Medioevo bizantino-slavo*, i (Rome, 1965), 125–48; cf. iii (1971), 143–7. The survival of Nicolas' text owed much to the canonist Ivo of Chartres.

civilized framework of law as well as the gospel. He sent not only missals and liturgical books but also standard textbooks of Roman law and canon law and, together with Roman catechists, two bishops, one being Formosus, later to become pope (891–6). The bishops were to be a resource for settling any doubtful points that might arise. Meanwhile, it was important for the new converts to keep rules of abstinence especially from meat and sex during Lent, and to observe saints' days by allowing no court cases to be heard on them. While they must be right to grant burial to suicides, so that the stink of the corpse would not molest the living, they should allow no requiem or prayers for them at the funeral.[2]

In regard to prohibited degrees of matrimony, Nicolas (*ep.* 99. 39) cited Justinian's *Institutiones*, where the section 'De nuptiis' (1. 10) lists, from Gaius, degrees of affinity forbidden under civil law, and, to take care of the prohibited degree set up by the relation of godparent to baptizand, referred without detail to the *Decreta* of Pope Zacharias (745–52), 'which we leave to your bishop to explain'. Nicolas was evidently conscious that the austere rigidity of Zacharias' ruling might cause the Bulgarian Khan a shock if set down in lucid prose. There was no important disagreement on this question between western canon law and the rulings of Greek canon law, attested in e.g. the 53rd canon of the Council *in Trullo*. Nor was there disagreement between east and west in the prohibition of bigamy. There were, however, issues where Nicolas felt bound to warn the Bulgarians against Greek customs.

The Greek missionaries had provided married presbyters to be pastors in accordance with the general custom of the eastern churches. The Bulgarians were aware that in the Latin west all presbyters and deacons as well as bishops were expected to be celibate, and inquired of Nicolas whether these married clergy were to be ejected from office. Surprisingly the Pope coupled a condemnation of their married state ('reprehensible') with a prohibition on action, at least by lay authority, to deprive and degrade them.

One Greek missionary, claiming presbyteral orders, had been minister of baptism to a large number of Bulgarians. It was then discovered that his orders were at the least questionable. Nevertheless Nicolas insisted that the baptisms of which he had been minister, given in water in the name of the Trinity, were valid.

In several respects the requirements proposed by Greek missionaries were more rigorous than those proposed by the Latins. Neither party questioned the validity of the other's sacraments. Even Nicolas, however, prohibited hunting in Lent. The Pope wisely said not a word about the *Filioque*, on which the Greeks had critical things to tell the Bulgarian converts.

---

[2] See Alexander Murray, *Suicide in the Middle Ages*, ii (Oxford, 2000), 267–9.

Nicolas found it hard to treat of some Greek customs without allowing a hint of mockery to come into his language. It was hard to be quite brotherly. The Greeks were so different. The Bulgarians had been puzzled by some of the ceremonial prescriptions given by Greek missionaries. Was it right to deduce from the gospel saying 'Let your loins be girded about . . .' that at the eucharist belts should be worn? That at prayer in church the hands ought to be folded on the chest—this being in the Byzantine world a gesture of submission and obedience? That baths be not taken on Wednesdays and Fridays? Nicolas was happy to support the Greeks in condemning polygamy. In contrast with relatively trivial matters, the Bulgarians were disturbed about the effect of Christianity on war (an art in which they had considerable and terrifying skill), on all resort to violence, on the proper restraint of criminals, on the legitimacy of torture to obtain confessions of guilt, on coercion of hardline pagans, on alliances with pagan nations. They also had traditional ethnic customs such as religious incantations, jokes, and war-dances before battle, oaths taken on a sword.[3] And could they pray for deceased ancestors? Nicolas said, only if they were believers in Christ. The Pope, unlike the Greek missionaries, did not object if they ate animals without removing the blood (cf. Acts 15: 20). The Greek canonist Balsamon, commenting on Apostolic Canon 63 and the Council *in Trullo*, canon 67, observed the eccentricity of the Latins in ignoring the Apostolic Decree. He evidently thought this a typical disregard of inspired authority.

It is unnecessary and mistaken to read Nicolas' responses as substantially dominated by anti-Byzantine motives. At least, if such motives were strong within him, he might have put it all rather differently. Nevertheless, he writes as one with authority to correct what Greek missionaries have said and, on the subject of patriarchs, an all too frank disparagement of the standing of Constantinople was not calculated to be conciliatory. Towards New Rome the Pope was scornful.

Nicolas told the Bulgarians that, although they could not have a patriarch, soon, if all went well, they would have an archbishop, which was not far short of what they wanted; but in any event patriarchs were less important than the Greeks might have told them. Only Rome, Alexandria, and Antioch had the status of real patriarchates.[4] Constantinople had no apostolic foundation (i.e.

---

[3] In the emperor Maurice's *Strategicon*, soldiers in the emperor's army shouted 'Kyrie eleison' and 'Dominus nobiscum' as battle began, though with the qualification that the latter cry could make cowards more afraid than before. Corippus (Ioh. 8) in Justinian's time describes the Christian dedication of armour to the service of God.

[4] Nicolas, *ep.* 99. 92 (MGH Epp. vi. 596–97 = PL 119. 1012). Recognition of the patriarchal dignity of Constantinople by Rome comes with the creation of a Latin patriarchate under Innocent III (cn. 5 of Lateran Council 1215).

Nicolas set aside claims to St Andrew and to St John the evangelist);[5] there
'patriarch' was no more than a courtesy title conferred on the bishop by the
emperors. Jerusalem had no greater claim.[6] There was nothing Christian
about the emperor Hadrian's garrison city founded under the very pagan
name of Aelia Capitolina; Jerusalem was formally still called Aelia in late
antiquity and early medieval times.[7] For true believers the authentic
Jerusalem is in heaven, not an earthly city at all. That the earthly city was for
believers an inherently numinous place was disproved for Nicolas by the
observation that, though the hill of Golgotha was now found within the
walls, the original line of the walls before Hadrian's time placed it outside
the city—a fact significant of the city's comparative unimportance as a holy
place.

Not since Eusebius of Caesarea had such negative language about 'the
holy city' (Matt. 27: 53) been heard.[8] Whether the Frankish monks on the
Mount of Olives would easily have agreed with the Pope must be doubtful.

In the east this language about the status of the patriarch of Constantinople
could hardly be construed as other than insulting. An angry Pope Gelasius

[5] These claims had been boldly put forward by the patriarch Ignatius in 861, as recorded by
Deusdedit 603: 'I have the throne of John the apostle and of Andrew, the Lord's first disciple.' See
F. Dvornik, *The Idea of Apostolicity in Byzantium and the Legend of the Apostle Andrew* (Dumbarton
Oaks Studies 4; Washington, DC, 1958). In disparaging Constantinople, Nicolas follows earlier
popes, e.g. Boniface I, *ep.* 15. 5 (PL 20. 782); Leo I, *ep.* 104. 3 (PL 54. 995); especially Gelasius I, *ep.*
10. 6, p. 345 Thiel. The Arab conquest of both Syria and Egypt deprived the patriarchs of
Alexandria and Antioch of their previous influence.

[6] Hincmar, PL 126. 343–4, and 125. 212 A, similarly rules out Jerusalem—on ground of the
ancient city's disbelief. Pope Nicolas' *ep.* 100 to Hincmar, 23 Oct. 867, admits a Jerusalem patriarch.
Contrariwise, Theodore of Studios writes to the (congenial) patriarch of Jerusalem that, though
ranking fifth, he is really first among the pentarchy: *ep.* 2. 15 (PG 99. 1161 AB) = *ep.* 276 ed.
G. Fatouros (Berlin, 1992), ii. 410. 26–32. On the Pentarchy see V. Peri, *Settimane Spoleto*, 34/1
(1988), 209–318, and the monograph by F. R. Gahbauer, *Die Pentarchie-Theorie* (Frankfurter
Theologische Studien; Frankfurt, 1993). The pentarchy concept stems from Justinian, *Novel* 109 of
541. In the twelfth century the canonist Balsamon had to explain that the exit of the Roman see into
heresy in no way diminished the authority of the pentarchy (PG 138. 1015 B). The doctrine that the
universal Church is led and governed by the consensus of five patriarchs was convenient to
Byzantine emperors, since its effect was to enhance their power. It was never congenial at Rome,
though its intention was not to level down and to emasculate Roman primacy. Deusdedit held that
in dogma the see of Rome is supreme over all, but in matters of discipline the Pope operates with
the consensus of the pentarchy.

[7] *ACO* IV iii/3. 178, index. The name Aelia still appears in medieval lists: see J. Darrouzès,
Notitiae episcopatuum ecclesiae Constantinopolitanae (Paris, 1981), Notitia IV, p. 248.

[8] For the contrast between Christians who believed the holy places of the gospels had become
sacred by association and those who thought no place more holy than any other, see P. W. L.
Walker, *Holy City, Holy Places? Christian Attitudes to Jerusalem and the Holy Land in the Fourth Century*
(Oxford, 1990). Eusebius of Caesarea inherited from Origen (e.g. *Homilies on Joshua* 6. 3) the judgement that for a Christian no place is inherently holy. Pope Gregory the Great thought a place could
become holy because of the acts there of holy people (*Reg.* 7. 29, 11. 56a. 2 = MGH Epp. i. 476. 7,
ii. 334, 10). His view is echoed in Ruotger's Life of Bruno of Cologne, written c.967–9 (cap. 34 ed.
Ott, MGH SRG, NS x. 34. 31).

had said much the same four centuries earlier. The Bulgarians had been deeply impressed by the dignity of that office, and had received from the patriarch Photius a polished letter composed in high style describing the shape of orthodoxy in terms which perhaps they found hard to understand.[9] It was natural for the new converts, with strong ethnic pride, to want a similarly authoritative figure in their Church. They were understandably anxious not to be second-class citizens in the Christian society of churches. They were concerned that their conversion, catechism, and baptism should be the best, and would incorporate them in whichever body, among the evidently competing rivals in Constantinople, Rome, and Francia, could be described as being 'without spot or blemish'. Pope Nicolas was able to assure them that in the holy Roman Church, St Peter was alive in his successor to preside over all and to provide an absolute guarantee of flawless faith to those who were seeking for truth.

The Roman intervention was offensive to the emperor at Constantinople. The Byzantine army had been fighting off Bulgarians for 350 years. East Romans necessarily regarded Bulgaria as their sphere; it was in their back yard, and Nicolas' attempt to claim the new Church for his own was stamped with political unreality. Soon it was conveyed to the Bulgarian converts that Roman missionaries were wrong to include *Filioque* in the catechism. They were also wrong in making celibacy a requirement for parish priests and in forbidding them to give chrism at baptism; in failing to require clergy to keep beards unshaven; in promoting deacons to the episcopate without passing through the presbyterate—as was common custom at Rome, including Nicolas himself; in requiring fasting on Saturdays as obligatory for all churches.

Rome's Saturday Fast

Based on the authority of Pope Silvester, Nicolas' demand for fasting on Saturdays appears in *ep*. 100 (October 867), and corresponds to a theme long heard from Roman voices. The custom of a fast on Saturday prolonging that on Friday was so ancient as to be regarded at Rome as apostolic tradition received from none other than St Peter himself. Early in the fifth century Pope Innocent I could tell his nearby suffragan Decentius of Gubbio that Saturday fasts were of universal obligation. At Hippo in north Africa Augustine was once sent by an African priest a particularly intolerant and hot-tempered treatise by a Roman writer (unnamed) peremptorily demanding that the Saturday fast must be observed by all churches in east and west alike. Although a few churches in north Africa had adopted the Roman

---

[9] Photius, *ep*. 1.

custom, it was not normal there. Augustine thought 'most of the west and all of the east' would find such language offensive. Such an argument did not come well from a Church where the normal Friday fast was not taken seriously; St Peter may indeed have given the custom to Rome, but for the east 'where the gospel was first preached' the other apostles left different traditions. In Psalm 44 (45) the king's daughter can be all glorious within and still have a variegated pattern on her robe. So the one Church can have the same faith, though particular churches have different customs. Therefore it sufficed if visitors to Rome, or to the handful of African churches following the Roman custom, kept the local observance, and for that judgement no less a personage than Ambrose 'who baptized me' provided authority.

In spite of Augustine's view that local usages should be treated as a matter of ultimate indifference (qualified by his ready concession that pastoral needs imposed limits on diversity), Innocent's verdict that all Christians should do as Rome was doing long remained the firm papal position, and was vehemently objected to at the Quinisext Council (692) canon 55. As Augustine expressly feared, the issue long remained contentious.[10] That was bound to be the case when one party to the debate regarded as indispensable what others regarded as less than fundamental and a matter of free choice.

[10] Nicolas, *ep.* 100 (MGH Epp. vi. 603, 17–18 = PL 119. 1155). Innocent, *ep.* 25. 7 (PL 20. 555). Augustine, *ep.* 36 to Casulanus. The fifth-century historian Socrates included a famous chapter on variety of customs (5. 22). Augustine states the case for liturgical variety in *ep.* 54. 2, *City of God* 19. 17, and for limits to diversity in *ep.* 55. 35. Gregory the Great's instruction to Augustine of Canterbury exhorted him to be tolerant of non-Roman usages, such as those that the Queen from Merovingian Gaul was accustomed to have (*Reg.* 11. 56a).

20

PROBLEMS AT CONSTANTINOPLE:
PATRIARCH IGNATIUS

Rivalry for possession of the Bulgarian soul was sharply exacerbated by the coincidence of a painful internal squabble in the Church at Constantinople originating in causes wholly unconnected with missions to northern tribes or with past disagreements between east and west.

During the first half of the ninth century the east Roman Empire suffered grave losses of territory to the Arabs, who had already taken north Africa from the empire by the early years of the eighth century. Arab attacks moved on to take most of Sicily, south Italy, and Crete, which passed out of effective Byzantine control. Impassioned debate about holy pictures during the eighth century had been bound up with fear that celestial disapproval of what might be idolatry was causing military failures. At the time of the second Council of Nicaea (787) the empress Irene had to deploy considerable skill to avert the army preventing the bishops from reversing the iconoclastic policy of the previous sixty years. When early in the ninth century iconoclasm revived at the palace, there remained smouldering division. Embarrassing Arab victories were sure to qualify army enthusiasm for iconoclasm, but iconophile zealots continued to suffer persecution. A synodical letter purporting to be addressed from the safety of Arab-controlled Jerusalem in 836 sent the emperor an iconophile manifesto under the authority of the three patriarchs of Antioch, Alexandria, and Jerusalem. It must be unlikely that circumstances would have allowed them to meet, but perhaps not impossible. The letter warned the emperor of the bad experiences of past supporters of heresy, praised the empress Irene and her council at Nicaea, and suggested that the defeat of the Bulgarians depended on abandoning iconoclasm. Special stress is placed on the power of icons of the Blessed Virgin. The drafter was familiar with John of Damascus' homilies on icons.[1]

In 843 the widowed empress Theodora, with the carefully planned support of a small group of officers of state together with monks anxious to see icons restored, decided to phase out the iconoclast patriarch John. His place

---

[1] The *Letter of the Three Patriarchs* is now edited with important commentaries by J. A. Munitiz, J. Chrysostomides, E. Harvalia-Crook, and Ch. Dendrinos (Camberley, Porphyrogenitus, 1997).

was taken by Methodius, an iconophile from Sicily who had found protection from iconoclasts at Rome (Nicolas I, *ep.* 88, MGH Epp. vi. 473. 3). His
task was to bring healing to a deeply divided Church and was in effect
'mission impossible'. On one side was a mass of unreconstructed iconoclast
clergy upon whom the palace and the patriarchal synod required the imposition of a change in discipline. On the other flank the Studite monks both in
the capital and on Mount Olympus in Bithynia regarded the least concession
towards penitent clergymen as treachery.

As a symptom of his skilled diplomacy, Methodius granted to the iconoclasts that, as commanded in Deuteronomy 4, statuary should be avoided
while icons were allowed. Actual practical steps to restore icons where they
had been destroyed were gradual. Naturally that left zealous iconophiles ill
content, already vexed by Methodius' compromising willingness to keep in
post bishops who had supported iconoclasm and now said how sorry they
were. In zealot eyes one could not have a spoon long enough to sup with
such people. To satisfy this anger Methodius removed some as scapegoats.
The hagiographer responsible for writing Methodius' *Life* made the most of
this and, no doubt grossly exaggerating, reported that twenty thousand
clergy were removed from office.[2] The empress Theodora was determined
to avoid a synodical condemnation of her late husband, and that put out of
the question a rigorist harassment of all former iconoclasts.

Methodius' synod in 843 is probably rightly associated with the origins of
the 'Synodicon of Orthodoxy', celebrating the restoration of icons on the
first Sunday in Lent, and annually repeated. The liturgical reading was
accompanied by the singing of a 'canon' (printed in the Triodion), chanted
in procession from Blachernae to Hagia Sophia. The synod formally declared
that the second Council of Nicaea of 787 possessed 'ecumenical' status.

Tension between bishops and ascetics is virtually conterminous with the
history of the Church. But the iconoclastic controversy sharpened distrust
between the mainly iconophile monks and successive patriarchs who wanted
peace and unity even at the price of compromise. After 843 iconophile
houses like Studios no longer had the same cause to fight for, unless it were
to censure keeping in office bishops who had collaborated with the imperial
iconoclast policy. Monks from Sicily were unwelcome at Studios anyway.
Methodius' struggles brought him to severe disciplinary measures to check
Studite vehemence. After a disturbed four years in the patriarchate he died.
The choice of his successor was marked by a reaction against the previous
policies of reconciliation and moderation. The man selected to succeed was

---

[2] See D. E. Afinogenev in *Λειμών: Studies Presented to Lannert Rydén on his Sixty-Fifth Birthday*
(Uppsala, 1996), 79–91.

Ignatius, younger son of the emperor Michael I (811–13).[3] In the year 813 he had been castrated to ensure he had no descendants to aspire to the imperial purple, and was then sent to live imprisoned as a monk at Terebinthos on the Princes Islands.[4] He can hardly have refused communion with the iconoclasts in power, but this was no issue.

Normal procedure at Constantinople for nominating a new patriarch was for a decision to be made by the local clergy and senators, acting in collaboration with an assembly of bishops and metropolitans, who then had to ascertain that their proposal would be acceptable to the ruling power at the imperial palace.[5] It was not dissimilar at Rome: the biography of Pope Leo IV (847–55) in the *Liber Pontificalis* records that no one would dare to consecrate a pontiff who did not enjoy the emperor's assent.[6] At Constantinople in 847 the ruling power lay with the regent, the empress Theodora. Her religious affinities had come to be with the more enthusiastic iconophile monks, and were now cool towards any suggestion of a patriarch who would continue Methodius' policy of avoiding confrontations at a time when iconoclast feeling was far from moribund. Fear that icons might be idolatrous did not die overnight in 843. Ignatius owed his appointment to Theodora's autocratic nomination without consultation with or recommendation from bishops and metropolitans. A devout ascetic known for strenuous mortifications,[7] Ignatius was inexperienced in political skills and suspicious of moderation that could be labelled compromise. At least he had the merit of not provoking Studite opposition. There were crypto-iconoclasts now keeping their heads down but unreconstructed in their opinions. Before long some acute problems came to bedevil Ignatius' discharge of his patriarchal duties. He did

---

[3] Most of the sources for Ignatius' biography are bitterly hostile to Photius, notably the *Synodicon Vetus*, edited by John Duffy and John Parker (Dumbarton Oaks Texts, 5; Washington, DC, 1979). and above all the *Vita Ignatii* compiled out of Ignatian party pamphlets by Nicetas David (PG 105. 489 ff.), motivated in part by his horror at yet another case of lax morals in the royal house with the four marriages of Leo VI. See R. J. H. Jenkins's paper in *Dumbarton Oaks Papers*, 19 (1965), 241–7. reprinted in his *Studies in Byzantine History of the 9th and 10th Centuries* (Aldershot, 1970). On Methodius and Studite monks, see E. von Dobschütz, *Byzantinische Zeitschrift*, 18 (1909), 41–105: J. Darrouzès, *Revue des études byzantines*, 45 (1987), 15–57.

[4] *Vita Ignatii*, PG 105. 496. Critical discussion of the sources in P. Karlin-Hayter, *Studies in Byzantine Political History* (Aldershot, 1981), no. IV, pp. 475–84. On Terebinthos see R. Janin, *Les Églises et les monastères des grands centres byzantins* (Paris, 1975) 61–2.

[5] Cf. Photius, *ep.* 288. 46–50 LW, and especially Cardinal Deusdedit's record of the synod of 861 (Ch. 19 n. 5). The Canons of Photius' Council of 861 are printed in RP ii. 437–743.

[6] *Liber Pontificalis* 105. 8 (Leo IV), ed. Duchesne ii. 107. 20 '. . . sine imperiali non audebant auctoritate futurum consecrare pontificem' (the motive being stated as fear that the Romans might need imperial power to protect them against enemy attack). Other instances are gathered by H. Leclercq in *Dict. d'arch. chr. et de liturgie*, ix (Paris, 1930), 258–9. San Clemente, Rome, has a surviving portrait of Leo IV: ibid. iii/2 (1914), 1889; J. Osborne, *Proceedings of the British School at Rome*, 47 (1979), 58–65.

[7] *Vita Ignatii*, PG 105. 496 A. Cardinal Deusdedit's record shows that Ignatius did not deny that he owed his elevation to Theodora without any synod of bishops.

not lack courage but his confrontational ways brought trouble. His nomination by the palace offended those in the tradition of Theodore of Studios who did not think the emperor above canon law and cared for the Church's independence from the State.

At the time of Ignatius' consecration there was at Constantinople a bishop of Syracuse in Sicily, Gregory Asbestas, probably asking the emperor for help to keep invading Arabs at bay. He was an iconophile friend of Methodius, whose biography he wrote. He publicly regretted the uncanonical unelected eunuch being consecrated to succeed Methodius, 'nominated by a woman'. At the consecration ceremony there was a dramatic scene in which Gregory and his friends were ejected from the church. Ignatius went on to a formal sentence deposing him and a group of bishops supporting his cause. Gregory decided to appeal from New Rome to Old, and submitted a plea to Pope Leo IV (847–55) complaining of Ignatius' possession of the see without proper election and of his own ejection from the see of Syracuse. The appeal was well received at Rome. It was another matter to get Ignatius to alter his view.[8]

Ignatius was not of a mind to kowtow to the see of Old Rome. Granted that that venerable see had the honour of being Peter's, had not his own see been that of Peter's brother Andrew? Was not the patriarch of Constantinople inheritor of the apostolic mantle of John the evangelist, author of the Apocalypse? As a manifestation of his equal status to that of his Roman brother, he made bold to send Leo IV a pallium.[9] It was returned with a polite note that a pallium was an honour conferred by and not on a pope.[10] When Leo requested copies of papers about Gregory Asbestas, Ignatius briefly answered that it was simply for the Roman see to confirm his

---

[8] *Vita Ignatii*, PG 105. 512 B; Anastasius Bibl. in Mansi xvi. 3; Photius, *ep.* 112 LW. Nicolas I regretted that bishops of Syracuse were consecrated at Constantinople and that Sicily was part of the Byzantine patriarchate (MGH Epp. vi. 439. 10). Syracuse did not fall to the Arab invaders until 878. At that point Photius, back in office as patriarch, translated Gregory to Nicaea (*Vita Ign.* 573 A). Gregory wrote a short extant treatise opposing the emperor Basil's coercive pressure on Jews to be baptized: ed. G. Dagron, *Travaux et mémoires*, 11 (1991), 313–57. See also P. Karlin-Hayter in *Iconoclasm*, 141–6. Anastasius Bibliothecarius (MGH Epp. vii. 404. 32) and Symeon Magister (PG 109. 732 D) say Gregory was deposed before Ignatius' elevation to be patriarch. If so, this may have been in the iconoclast period. But Methodius may have placed him under censure for his consecration of Zacharias to be bishop of Taormina, when he was the patriarch's legate to Rome.

[9] A letter from Pope Leo IV of about 853 to the patriarch Ignatius rebukes him for having deposed bishops without consulting the Roman see. The reference is probably to Gregory Asbestas of Syracuse: MGH Epp. v. 589. Gregory's appeal to Rome implied a question-mark against Byzantine jurisdiction in Sicily. Nicolas expressly asked for the right to consecrate bishops of Syracuse: MGH Epp. vi. 439. 10. At Byzantium the allocation of Sicily to the east was justified no doubt by the fact that the inhabitants were Greek-speaking. It was also contended that Rome was under barbarian (i.e. Frankish) control and therefore disqualified. (So a note in a medieval Notitia edited by Darrouzès, *Notitiae*, 249.) There was competition for Syracuse between Rome and Constantinople in Gregory the Great's time: *Reg.* 9. 26.

[10] MGH Epp. v. 607.

negative decision without further examination.[11] Gregory repeated his petition to Leo's successor Benedict III (855–8), who again wrote to Ignatius asking for the file of documents in the case. Ignatius ignored the new Pope's letter altogether.[12] He evidently did not foresee the possibility that one day he himself might be glad of support from the west. In the background there will have been an awareness that popes had long resented Sicily being in Byzantine jurisdiction, and that, if the ecumenical patriarch was to retain his rights, he must on no account concede that Syracusan church matters could be properly considered at Rome.

[11] Ibid. 436. 31 (PL 119. 776 D).
[12] Hadrian II, ibid. vi. 753. 12–15 (PL 122. 1285 A); Deusdedit 604. 606.

21

PHOTIUS

Ignatius remained strong with the support of the empress who had appointed him. In 856 popular rumour in the city alleged that Theodora's brother and rival for power, Bardas, living in the same house as his bereaved daughter-in-law, enjoyed an incestuous relationship with the young widow.[1] Ignatius judged it his moral duty to join the voices of hostility to Bardas and publicly denounced the Caesar repelling him from communion. Evidently he felt Bardas to be some threat since, unwisely, he defended the character of a man found guilty of conspiracy to murder Bardas. Not unnaturally Bardas reacted. He decided it was time to oust Theodora from power and consign her to a nunnery, to install her adolescent son Michael as sole emperor, to take into his own hands the reins of government, and to rid Church and capital of an illiberal monkish patriarch who had publicly insulted him.

The fall of Theodora removed Ignatius' patron and left him defenceless. A synod was held at which charges were brought against him, above all that, in defiance of Apostolic Canon 30 (31) which decreed deposition and excommunication upon any bishop who obtained his appointment to the see by the help of the secular power, he had been appointed patriarch by Theodora without an assembly of bishops and clergy to hold a proper election. The best defence Ignatius could make was the precedent of Tarasius, also appointed patriarch by a woman (the empress Irene was felt to have an authority no sound iconophile could question). After being in office as patriarch for eleven years he had a body of supporters but also numerous critics. His removal was bound to be controversial, and more than that if one believed it was revenge for his denunciation of incest in high places. Under pressure he abdicated. His supporters believed that frightful methods were employed to get him to sign away his office. Photius understood him to have retired voluntarily, and one source sympathetic to Photius (the *Life of St Euthymius the Younger* by Basil archbishop of Thessalonica early in the tenth century) records that Ignatius declared himself much more content to live a quiet life

---

[1] *Vita Ignatii*, PG 105. 503 A; Theophanes Continuatus 4. 30; Anastasius Bibl., Mansi xvi. 30. See F. Dvornik, 'Patriarch Ignatius and Caesar Bardas', *Byzantinoslavica*, 27 (1966), 7–22.

of prayer in his monastery than with the hubbub of the city and political affairs.[2]

With Bardas in power the pendulum swung yet again in the choice of the replacement for Ignatius. This time the election was carried out in proper formality with the customary assembly of bishops and metropolitans. Ignatius had been notoriously hostile to liberal learning[3] and to the study of classical pagan literature, at that period enjoying some resurgence in Byzantine intellectual circles. He was packed off to exile, eventually moving to his old monastery on Terebinthos in the Princes Islands.[4] His duly chosen successor was Photius, the most learned man not only of his own generation but of Byzantine history generally. He was, however, ignorant of Latin. His culture was entirely Greek. Though his career had been in the civil service, he was well read in theology and biblical exegesis. By a series of coincidences his career came to focus the long existing ecclesiological differences between east and west to such an extent that in the retrospect of posterity his tenure of the patriarchate seemed a hinge-point in the relations between Constantinople and Rome. Eventually strong advocates of Roman universal jurisdiction who resented as dissident and schismatic the eastern Orthodox stand for canonical independence and against the western *Filioque* would sum up their description of this stance by the single word 'Photianism'.

Later estimates of the tension between Greek east and Latin west would make Photius so central a figure in the story that the detail of his problems with the west needs to be looked at carefully.

From the start the new patriarch met difficulties. A number of bishops and probably laity in the capital admired Ignatius, not least for his antipathy to the high culture represented by Photius but also for his courage in repelling Bardas from communion and in supporting the story that the Caesar's relationship with the widowed daughter-in-law in his palace was incestuous. Ignatius had indeed signed resignation from office; even his most strident supporters conceded that. Their view was that before resigning Ignatius had issued an instruction to the metropolitans called to elect a successor that they must be sure to elect a patriarch 'of his communion', which in a word meant not Gregory Asbestas. This instruction could be interpreted as a condition attaching to his deed of resignation. Perhaps he may have hoped for one of the Studite monks who had been loyal to him as they had not been to Methodius.

---

[2] Text edited by Louis Petit, *Revue de l'Orient chrétien*, 8 (1903), 178.

[3] Expressly stated by Anastasius Bibliothecarius in his preface to the Latin translation of the Acts of the Council of 869. On the cultural tension between Ignatius and Photius and their supporters see Dvornik, 'Photius et la réorganisation de l'Académie patriarcale', *Anal. Boll.* 68 (1950), 108–25.

[4] *Vita Ignatii*, PG 105. 506 B.

But Photius sympathized with Gregory Asbestas, who was highly cultured and had once been his teacher (Nicetas, *Vita Ignatii*, PG 105. 512 B). When Asbestas was invited to share in Photius' consecration, the Ignatian party could argue that, as he had been excommunicated by Ignatius, this broke the condition on which Ignatius had resigned, namely that his successor be of his communion. In the subsequent contentions Photius did not strongly insist on Ignatius' having signed a deed of resignation, though by the emperor Michael this was regarded as *res judicata* not open to renegotiation (so Pope Nicolas, *ep.* 88, MGH Epp. vi. 460. 17). Moreover, the signed paper was reinforced by a synod declaring him deposed. The anti-Photian *Life of Ignatius* (521 D) claims that under pressure Ignatius had signed a paper confessing that his occupation of the patriarchal throne had been contrary to customary law. His opponents were citing the 30th Apostolic Canon forbidding a bishop from being installed by secular authority, as Ignatius certainly had been.

One supporter of Ignatius, a monk named Theognostos, escaped from Constantinople in secular dress and reached Rome. Ignatius appointed him abbot general to supervise the many Greek monks there.[5] He became the principal Ignatian agent at the Lateran supplying horrific accounts of Bardas' suppression of dissidents.[6] In all probability Theognostos had begun work well before Photius' letter announcing his consecration had reached the desk

---

[5] Greek monasteries in Rome had a long history: J. M. Sansterre, *Les Moines grecs et orientaux à Rome aux époques byzantine et carolingienne* (Brussels, 1980). They were still flourishing in 1054: Leo IX to Michael Cerularius, PL 143. 764 A.

[6] Theognostos: Nicolas rejected the view at Constantinople that his portrait of the situation was prejudiced. MGH Epp. vi. 477. 21, 478. 26. Pope Hadrian II commended him to Ignatius: ibid. 749 (1 Aug. 868). On Photius a fundamental study remains F. Dvornik, *The Photian Schism* (Cambridge, 1948); a different estimate by P. Stephanou, *Dictionnaire de spiritualité*, xii/1 (Paris, 1984), 1397–1408. For his career before becoming patriarch see C. Mango, in *Iconoclasm*, 133–40. A good outline by G. Dagron in *Histoire du christianisme*, iv (Paris, 1993). Photius' homilies are translated by C. Mango with learned notes (Dumbarton Oaks Studies, 3; 1958). His letters were edited in 3 vols. for Teubner by B. Laourdas and L. G. Westerink (cited as L–W). The Acts of a symposium on Gregory Nazianzen and Photius at the University of Thessaloniki in October 1993 contain sixteen papers on aspects of Photius. There is a bibliography of Photius studies by G. D. Dragas in the Greek journal, Ἐκκλησία καὶ Θεολογία, 10 (1989–91), 531–669. On ideological tension over papal jurisdiction, see D. Stiernon in M. Maccarrone (ed.), *Il primato del vescovo di Roma nel primo millennio: Ricerche e testimonianze* (Vatican City, 1991), 661–705; also Klaus Herbers, 'Papst Nikolaus I. und Patriarch Photios: das Bild des byzantinischen Gegners in lateinischen Quellen', in O. Engels and P. Schreiner, *Die Begegnung des Westens mit dem Osten* (Sigmaringen, 1993), 51–74. The old 3-vol. biography of Photius by J. Hergenröther (Regensburg, 1867–9, repr. Darmstadt, 1966), though the main thesis needs to be corrected by Grumel and Dvornik, remains a mine of illumination in detail. See also E. Amann's article on Photius in *Dict. de théologie catholique*, xii/1 (Paris, 1933), 1536–1604, and papers by V. Grumel in *Échos d'Orient*, 29 (1930), 33 (1934), 39 (1940). J. Darrouzès's revision of fasc. 2–3 of the *Regestes du patriarcat de Constantinople* (Paris, 1989) has weighty matter. Problems in the *Bibliotheca* are clarified by Jacques Schamp, *Photios historien des lettres* (Bibliothèque de la faculté de philosophie et lettres de l'Université de Liège, fasc. 248; Paris, 1987). The subject has clear treatment in Joan Hussey, *The Orthodox Church in the Byzantine Empire* (Oxford, 1986), and F. Tinnefeld, *Theologische Realenzyklopädie*, xxvi (Berlin, 1996), 586–9.

of Pope Nicolas I. Theognostos was careful never to speak slightingly of the
emperor Michael (Nicolas, *ep*. 88, MGH *Epp*. vi. 477. 30).

At the time of his election Photius was a highly placed layman. His uncle
Sergius had married a sister of the powerful Caesar Bardas. A great-nephew
of the patriarch Tarasius, he and his parents had suffered under the iconoclasts, his father and (Armenian) mother losing their property and dying in
exile.[7] A successful career in the central administration brought him to
become head of the imperial chancellery (*protoasecretis*), and he had served as
ambassador to the Arabs.[8] His love of icons was linked with devotion to
Christ and His Mother evident in many of his homilies. A cultivated urbane
academic, he loved books and was inventor of the book-review. Of 279
codices which he had read he wrote a descriptive account (*Bibliotheca*), which
survives to be important for classical studies[9] and, in the more numerous
patristic entries, demonstrates his mastery of intricate issues in theology at
and after the Council of Chalcedon (451)—issues far from dead in his time.[10]
The most recent work reviewed in his *Bibliotheca* was a history of iconoclast
persecution (741–828) perhaps composed by his father Sergius (codex 67).

Contemporary revival of interest in classical culture and intellectual
paganism moved him to compose a (lost) refutation of the emperor Julian's
attack on the Galilaeans, a work evidently enjoying some vogue.[11] Photius
himself preserves one fragment of this lost work (*Qu. ad Amphiloch.* 101). He
had no time for philosophical intellectuals who disparaged the popular use of
icons as superstitious.[12] He was directly critical of those (some among them

[7] Photius, *ep*. 114 LW.

[8] So the preface to the *Bibliotheca*, dedicated to his brother.

[9] The title 'Bibliotheca' is not that given by Photius, but that of his editors. The most recent
edition by R. Henry, replacing Bekker in 9 vols, including index, has an annotated French version
marred by errors. A selection is presented in an excellent English version by N. G. Wilson (London,
1994). J. H. Freese produced an English translation of codd. 1–165 (London, SPCK 1920). Which
of the books reviewed was in his own private library is not known. For the theological works he no
doubt drew on the library at the patriarchate. See C. Mango in the symposium from Dumbarton
Oaks, *Byzantine Books and Bookmen* (Washington, DC, 1971), 43.

[10] Photius devoted himself not only to missionary work among the Bulgarians and Slavs but also
to the labour of ecumenical reconciliation with Armenians who remained reserved towards the
decisions of the Council of Chalcedon. He claimed some success in this: *epp*. 284–5 LW, esp. *ep*. 2.
38 (encyclical of 867); above Ch. 18 n. 6.

[11] Photius, *ep*. 187 LW. That Julian enjoyed a revival is also evident from the writings of Arethas,
archbishop of Caesarea from 902, on whom see P. Lemerle, *Byzantine Humanism* (Eng. tr.
Canberra, 1986) 237–80. Arethas' writings are in PG 106; some are edited by L. G. Westerink
(Leipzig, 1968–72). Julian's writings were openly admired by Leo Choirosphaktes, who rose to be
the emperor Basil's private secretary, and served his son Leo as ambassador to Bulgarians and to
Arabs at Baghdad. Cf. p. 67. PG 107, 660 F prints pieces by him.

[12] In the eleventh century at Constantinople one of the causes of offence in the philosopher John
Italos was his scorn of icons: Anna Comnena 5. 9 end. On trial in 1082, Italos was accused of deny-
ing the Virgin Birth and any possibility of 'miracle': Synodicon of Orthodoxy, ed. J. Gouillard,
Travaux et mémoires, 2 (1967), 59.

being bishops) who censured biblical authors for barbarisms of style or who questioned the compatibility of the virginal conception of Jesus with natural laws given by the Creator.[13] He was unmarried, and therefore not disqualified to be a bishop. Critics complained that he was not a monk,[14] which was customary but not a canonical requirement in the making of a bishop in the Greek Orthodox churches until considerably later. But he did what he could to gain the confidence of the monasteries. As patriarch he restored, at his own personal expense, the monastery of Manuel damaged by earthquakes at Constantinople during 866.[15] His remains were eventually to lie there.

It is safe to assume that the monks would have liked Photius' sustained hostility to iconoclasm. Examination of the illustrations in ninth-century Byzantine psalters led Kathleen Corrigan to the plausible view that Photius fostered a veiled polemic against the enemies of icons through this medium.[16]

Greek churches liked their patriarchs to be monks. Balsamon's comment on the sixth canon of Carthage remarks how it would be with reluctance, if at all, that anyone would disclose private temptations to a bishop or priest who was not a monk (RP iii. 312). This reflected a general attitude bound to create difficulty for Photius. In Byzantine society where monks could enjoy a popular respect not commonly granted to bishops, a patriarch might find his task difficult if many monasteries were intransigently opposed.[17] He soon found it desirable to write formal letters, evidently intended for publication, in which he declared his warm inner sympathy for the monastic ideal: monasteries were not to find in him a source of harassment or negativity. He and his parents before him had an impeccable record for their opposition to iconoclasm. He liked to stress this credential.

In the west there was an old tradition of opposition to the not uncommon practice of electing to the episcopate a rich or highly influential layman—a

---

[13] Photius, *epp.* 156, 208 LW. Cf. C. Mango, *The Homilies of Photius* (Cambridge, Mass., 1958), 163.

[14] Nicolas mentions this several times in his letters, e.g. MGH Epp. vi. 535. 28 (PL 119. 1048 B), evidently briefed by Theognostos and the Ignatian faction. *Vita Ignatii* 509 c: 'Photius did not choose the way of humility or try to enter the kingdom of God as a child.'

[15] RP ii. 675; R. Janin, *La Géographie ecclésiastique de l'empire byzantin*, i/3 (Paris, 1953), 331.

[16] Kathleen Corrigan, *Visual Polemics in the Ninth-Century Byzantine Psalters* (Cambridge, 1992), 130–1.

[17] The monks of Mount Olympos in the diocese of Nicomedia were solid for the patriarch Ignatius (Photius, *ep.* 17); also the monks of the house of Philippikos on the Bosporos (*ep.* 78). For recent studies of the authority of monks see V. Deroche, 'L'autorité des moines à Byzance du VIIIe au xe siècle', *Revue bénédictine*, 103 (1993), 241–54; R. Morris, 'Spiritual Fathers and Temporal Patrons: Byzantine Monasticism in the Tenth Century', ibid. 273–88, and her monograph, *Monks and Laymen in Byzantium 843–1118* (Cambridge, 1995). Lives of Saints (e.g. Peter of Atroa, ed. Laurent) record bishops seeking a holy man's blessing, or living under his direction. Augustine found himself expected to work healing wonders (*En. in Ps.* 130. 6). He was both bishop and monk.

practice arising directly from the need of the congregation to have a bishop who could intercede for any of them who might be in trouble with the law-courts or the tax-gatherers. To the *plebs* it seemed more important and urgent in the short term to have a bishop of the class and standing to defend them now in this world than a bishop whose holy intercessions might defend them in the life to come.[18] At the western Council of Serdica Ossius, bishop of Corduba, moved for the approval of the bishops the proposal that anyone proposed for consecration to the episcopate should not be a wealthy man or a lawyer taken from the forum (*agora*) but should be chosen from the inferior orders of reader, deacon, and presbyter and should serve in these lower ministries for sufficient time to prove his worthiness and quality of faith, gravity, and modesty; moreover, one chosen for the episcopate should not be a neophyte, as scripture declares in 1 Tim. 3: 6. The canon was approved, but was evidently an act of resistance to the general tendency, and in practice was likely to have had difficulty in being strictly and in all circumstances observed. A century before Photius, a passionately disputed election to the papacy had turned on the point. Pope Nicolas claimed to be shocked by the frequency of elevating laymen in the east.[19] But the practice was not uncommon in the west. Augustine's descriptions of enforced consecrations in north Africa shows that there it was virtually normal.

Not long before Nicolas' time the Church in Rome had become acutely conscious of the question about the promotion of laymen to episcopal orders *per saltum* (without prior service as deacon or presbyter). The Life of Pope Stephen III (768–72) in the *Liber Pontificalis* 96. 18 shows that, in competition with his rival Constantine consecrated before him, he argued that the rival had been a layman until consecration to the see and was disqualified. Constantine replied by invoking actual precedents: a bishop of Ravenna had been made bishop without having been deacon or presbyter, and Stephen himself had consecrated a layman bishop of Naples. A Roman precedent could not be found. But Greeks had precedents (Theophanes AM 6298).

In 769 Stephen's council ruled against promoting laymen directly to be bishops (*Liber Pontificalis* 96. 20). But in the Frankish churches elevating laity to the episcopate *per saltum* was common though not uncontroversial

---

[18] Sidonius Apollinaris, *ep.* 7. 9. 9.

[19] MGH Epp. vi. 540. 10. Disapproval of electing high officials to be bishops is expressed by Pope Siricius (*ep.* 6. 3, PL 13. 1165 A); cf. Innocent I, *ep.* 37. 5 (PL 20. 604 B); In 1024 John XIX passed from being layman to pope in one day: Rodulfus Glaber, *Hist.* 4. 1. 4, p. 176 ed. John France (Oxford, 1989). His successor Benedict IX was a dissolute young man prior to being made pope in 1032. In a letter of August 595 to the Frankish king Childebert II, Gregory the Great (*Reg.* 5. 60) tells him that the bishop of Arles is appointed papal vicar and has received a pallium; but he goes on to deplore the elevation of laymen to be bishops *per saltum* without training so that in effect 'they speak and act as laymen; how can such people intercede for the sins of their people?' Simony is no less of a problem.

(Gregory of Tours, *HF* 8. 22). There would be awkwardness if the layman elected did not put his wife into a convent; in that event his clergy might refuse to receive the eucharist at his hand as happened to Sergius of Ravenna *c.*750.[20] Probably he was the bishop to whom Constantine appealed.

The western pressure against presbyters retaining their wives would have been awkward at Ravenna, which with its close links to the east could well have had married Greek clergy if only as visitors. Canon 19 of the Council of Tours of 567 described the cohabitation of clergy with their wives as the Nicolaitan heresy of Rev. 2: 15, language repeated in 1054 by Cardinal Humbert (below, p. 211). Not unnaturally there were clergy wives who deeply resented being exiled to a convent. Gregory of Tours (*HF* 1. 44) sadly records how the wife of Urbicus bishop of Clermont-Ferrand banged on his door in the middle of the night, obtained access to his room and bed, and nine months later presented him with a baby daughter.

Nicetas' *Life of Ignatius* (PG 105. 512 A) says that on day 1 the layman Photius was made a monk, on day 2 a reader, on day 3 subdeacon, then deacon, then presbyter, finally on the sixth day being the Nativity of Christ he was advanced to the 'hieratic throne' and pronounced a blessing on the people, though 'in his mind there was no true peace'. So the consecration of Photius was on 25 December 858. In the spring of 860 he wrote to Rome to inform Pope Nicolas of his installation. Such delays were not abnormal, and could be explained by violent raids in the Mediterranean or on the great Roman road from Constantinople to Durazzo on the Adriatic coast. Patriarch Nicephorus I, consecrated on 12 April 806, first informed Pope Leo III late in 811 with apology for tardiness.

Nicolas objected to Photius' elevation on the ground that he was a 'neophyte', i.e. newly baptized. There is no ground for supposing him to have been correct on this point; it might imply he was identifying the church with the clergy. It was perhaps in Roman memory that Nectarius, made bishop of Constantinople in 381 with the authority of a council (much later than 381) acknowledged to be ecumenical but at the time detested in the west, had first been baptized before consecration.

Nectarius' elevation to be patriarch anticipated that of Photius in that he was a competent civil servant and a layman. When the emperor called him to ecclesiastical duty, he immediately submitted to baptism and in one jump was consecrated bishop. This and other non-theological proceedings at the Council of 381 were not welcome in the west or at Alexandria. But since the council eliminated 'Arians' and Apollinarians, the orthodox west could not totally reject the conciliar decisions.[21]

---

[20] Agnellus, *Liber Pontif. Ravenn.* 154 (MGH Scr. rer. Lang. 377–810); new edn. by Claudia Nauerth (Fontes Christiani 21; Freiburg im Breisgau, 1996).

[21] A. M. Ritter, *Das Konzil von Konstantinopel und sein Symbol* (Göttingen, 1965).

A similar pattern occurred when the empress Irene ended iconoclasm. By her influence in 784 a new patriarch was chosen, Tarasius being an experienced bureaucrat. As patriarch until 806 he managed the second Council of Nicaea (787), struggling to restrain the hostility of Theodore of Studios and his monks, who thought it insufferable that the council allowed former iconoclasts to apologize as penitents and then remain in their sees.[22] Tarasius' successor Nicephorus, patriarch until exiled in 815, also came from the civil service as a layman.[23]

Misgivings of western churchmen had to be muffled when they were reminded of the elevation of Ambrose, provincial governor, to be bishop of Milan in 374.[24] A detailed account of that election would have been familiar to Greeks from Socrates' *Church History* (4. 30). Whether or not, like Photius,[25] Ambrose passed through the inferior orders on his path to becoming bishop is unclear in the nearly contemporary biography by Paulinus, and since there was contention about the canonical status of the consecration, the ambiguity may suggest that he did not.[26] Probably in the interest of justifying Photius' ordination in argument with the west, a Greek version of Paulinus' biography was made in the ninth century (edited by Papadopoulos-Kerameus, 1891).[27] In 787 Pope Hadrian I expressed regrets

---

[22] A survey of prickly relations between the Studites and the patriarchs is given by E. Patlagean, 'Les Stoudites, l'empereur et Rome: figure byzantine d'un monachisme reformateur', *Settimane Spoleto* 34/1 (1988), 429–65. See also P. Henry, 'Initial Assessments of the Seventh Ecumenical Council', *JTS*, NS 25 (1974), 75–92; M. F. Auzépy, 'La place des moines à Nicée II', *Byzantion*, 58 (1988), 5–21. On Tarasius' installation, Theophanes AM 6277. Theodore of Studios opposed Tarasius' elevation, defending his refusal of communion with the patriarch: *ep.* 1. 53 (PG 99. 1101 C–1104 A) = *ep.* 53, i. 156. 1–31 Fatouros. The Studites seem to have felt hurt at being marginalized in and after 787; they had borne the heat of the struggle.

[23] Paul Alexander, *The Patriarch Nicephorus of Constantinople* (Oxford, 1958). Studite opposition to Nicephorus was as strong as that to Tarasius, because a priest Joseph had sanctioned the adulterous remarriage of the emperor Constantine VI, and Nicephorus had synodically absolved Joseph: R. Devreesse, *Anal. Boll.* 68 (1950), 44–57. The emperor was not above God's law.

[24] Photius, *ep.* 290. 301 (iii. 133 LW). Cf. *Vita Ignatii*, PG. 105 512 A.

[25] Photius' letter of self-defence to Nicolas explains his reluctance to be made a bishop; but 'we agreed to be nominated through the synodical procedure on condition of passing through the hieratic steps': *ep.* 290. 322–3 LW. In 1255 the monk Arsenius, by command of the emperor, passed through the orders of deacon, priest, and bishop (patriarch) on a single day (Georgios Akropolites, *Chron.* 53, p. 107. 13 Heisenberg).

[26] Nicolas interpreted Paulinus to mean that Ambrose was promoted 'per continuos gradus' (MGH Epp. vi. 449. 6). Paulinus might have intended this, but is not at all explicit. Ambrose's ordination in 374 at Milan had been controversial, and the 'Homoean' faction was not reluctant to question the propriety of elevating a provincial governor to be a bishop with such rapidity. In a letter he defended it by the example of Nectarius at Constantinople (*ep. extra coll.* 14 = M63. 65), though he had serious doubts about Nectarius' ordination.

[27] There is a study of this Greek translation's language and accuracy by R. McClure in *Sacris Erudiri*, 21 (1972), 57–70.

at Tarasius' elevation,[28] and Charlemagne deployed the argument as an additional objection to the iconophile second Council of Nicaea.[29]

In short, though there was a tradition of criticism, Photius' elevation had precedents in both east and west.

Roman sensitivities about the promotion of laymen to the episcopate were naturally much enhanced by the row in the time of Pope Stephen III (above, p. 129).

In controversy with Pope Nicolas I Photius made only modest use of the abdication of Ignatius (above, p. 124), which one would have thought to be crucial to his argument since it answered the Ignatian story being fed to Nicolas that Photius had been uncanonically intruded. But he was also remarkably reticent to Rome about the Ignatian charge that his consecration was invalidated by the participation of Gregory Asbestas, excommunicated and deposed by Ignatius. Perhaps he left the answering of such charges to the emperor Michael.

When the emperor Michael asked Nicolas I to explain what were his objections to Gregory Asbestas, the Pope's answer was oracular and gave no detail (Nicolas, *ep*. 88, MGH Epp. vi. 484. 1 ff.).

Photius gave written, sworn assurances that he did not question the legitimacy of Ignatius' patriarchate, and therefore that he would recognize ordinations deriving from him. He was evidently conscious of needing a wider degree of support. However, this conciliatory policy was taken further in that the bishops chosen to consecrate Photius were not from one party. They were selected from different factions. One of them was Gregory Asbestas of Syracuse, the leader in 847 in expressing aversion to the zealot policies of Ignatius. His standing had been restored by emperor and bishops. Nevertheless Gregory's inclusion among the consecrating team of bishops offered a weapon to the pro-Ignatian opposition, which was reinforced by the political critics of Bardas at the palace.

The Supporters of Ignatius

Opposition to Photius, though 'a small and tiny party, perhaps not even a party' (Photius, *hom*. 6. 9), was noisy. A little group of intransigent bishops devoted to Ignatius and owing to him their ordination was displeased with the change of patriarch, and many monks supported them. No one suggested that Ignatius was not a man of righteous life, though evidently he lacked diplomacy and discretion. To the regret of his party Ignatius sent no appeal

---

[28] This was in that part of Hadrian I's letter to the second Council of Nicaea which Tarasius suppressed.

[29] Libri Carolini 1. 20, 3. 2 (MGH Concilia ii supp. i. 196. 1–12, 342. 1–4; also PL 98. 1049 B, 1115 D).

to Rome to beg for Nicolas' intervention on his behalf,[30] but although he had undoubtedly resigned, his friends found defeat hard to accept. A group of metropolitans gathered in the Church of St Irene to plan action and to draft an appeal to Rome in Ignatius' name. Ignatius himself remained detached from this action. But the metropolitans were bound to move Photius against their faction. At a synod of 170 bishops assembled in the Church of the Holy Apostles Ignatius was formally declared deposed and indeed anathematized together with his leading supporters Metrophanes of Smyrna and Antony of Cyzicus, the latter being replaced by Photius' close friend Amphilochius, to whom he dedicated many scholia on biblical interpretation.

The inevitable conclusion was that if the Ignatian party felt unable to recognize Photius as legitimate patriarch, the synod would return the compliment and refuse to acknowledge Ignatius and all those ordained by him. That was to produce a long civil war in the Greek churches. Meanwhile Photius' authority in the city was enhanced when he processed with the Virgin's robe from Blachernae successfully invoking her protection during a merciless surprise attack by Russians, a hitherto unknown race, who 'like a thunderbolt' sacked the suburbs in June 860.[31] The Ignatians fought back with generous alms for the poor.[32] An earthquake in August following Photius' consecration was taken by the Ignatian party as a manifestation of celestial displeasure (Nicetas, *Vita Ignatii*, PG 105. 525 A). They similarly read a quake on Ascension Day 861 which brought down a statue of the emperor Justin (529 CD).

[30] Ignatius is emphatic on this, according to Deusdedit's record (pp. 606–7). Nicolas' letter to the emperor Michael (*ep.* 88, MGH Epp. vi. 482, 4–8; PL 119. 956 AB) names the group of Ignatius' determined supporters, among whom Lazarus turns up in Deusdedit 608, where for 'R(omanum)' read 'P(resbyterum)'.

[31] Photius, *hom.* 4, p. 102 tr. Mango.   [32] Ibid. 6, p. 135 tr. Mango.

22

POPE NICOLAS I SUPPORTS IGNATIUS

Appeals to Roman jurisdiction to settle disputes were the route by which papal influence had steadily increased. Nicolas shrewdly perceived that, in a situation where two rival patriarchs at Constantinople were bidding for his suffrage, he had some leverage by which he could further the long endeavour of the papacy (unsuccessfully attempted by Hadrian I when asked to support the second Council of Nicaea in 787)[1] to recover former Roman jurisdiction in Illyricum, removed by an angry emperor Leo III when Rome would not support iconoclasm. The power of the palace in getting rid of Ignatius naturally predisposed the Pope to think Ignatius likely to be the proper person to support: 'The secular power has no authority to judge bishops. . . . Are laity to be allowed to do what they like without clergy rebuking them?[2] Nicolas knew he was backing the weaker man. Nevertheless his legates could encourage whichever was going to have the power and the will to concede Roman control in the Balkans.

In the first instance, his approach to both men was distinctly cool and cautious. At the same time as writing to the emperor asking for jurisdiction in Illyricum and restored revenues in Sicily and Calabria,[3] he sent a letter welcoming the *synodika* in which (without a request for consent or ratification) Photius had announced his succession in the office of patriarch and had set out the orthodoxy of his faith as defined by the seven ecumenical councils.[4] But while glad to be assured of Photius' orthodoxy, Nicolas suspended any decision on recognition in view of the bar in the canon of the western Council of Serdica against elevating laity to be bishop without having been presbyter or deacon. The fact that (on successive days) Photius had been given the orders of deacon and presbyter was not known to him. The Pope wished to await the report of his legates on the moral character of the new patriarch. The letter's tone was cool, courteous, not overtly hostile, and was careful to offer no comment on the number of general councils.[5] Neither Photius nor Nicolas expressed doubts about the other's faith.

[1] MGH Epp. v. 57. 5 ff. [2] Ibid. 531. 22–9.
[3] Nicolas, *ep.* 82 (ibid. 439 = PL 119. 773 ff.).
[4] Photius, *ep.* 288 LW. In writing to Nicolas Photius made no allusion to any hesitations he might feel about the western *Filioque*.
[5] Nicolas, *ep.* 83 (MGH Epp. vi. 440 = PL 119. 780).

The Council of Serdica was an awkward precedent to invoke.[6] Intended by the sons of Constantine the Great as an urgent bid to avert schism between east and west, the council had in fact split into two synods sitting separately and roundly cursing one another. It was still entitled 'ecumenical' by the fifth-century historian Socrates (2. 20. 3). The canons of the western group, which accorded some degree of appellate jurisdiction to the Roman see, were current in both Greek and Latin, in differing versions. Some Serdican canons had echoes in the Trullan canons of 692: the Serdican canon 11 (14 Latin version) is reproduced in Trullan canon 80; and the 2nd canon of 692 gives a blanket approval of the Greek canons of Serdica as a whole.

Pope Nicolas took it for granted that in the Greek east not only the canons of Serdica but also the body of papal decretals preserved in Roman archives were generally accepted as binding in both Greek and Latin churches. In this opinion he was probably echoing Pope Siricius (385–98), who could assume from his directive that his rulings sent to one metropolitan would then be circulated widely. Admittedly there was an awkwardness: Innocent I had been insistent that only the canons of Nicaea were accepted by the Roman see and that the canons of Serdica were not regarded as valid (*ep.* 7. 3) Presumably that was a reflection of the view that the actual Serdican canon on appeals to Rome did not really correspond to what had come to be regarded as proper procedure at Rome. The Serdican establishment of Rome as a court of appeal was highly qualified, and did not allow for an autocratic decision by popes. However, the representative of Gregory Asbestas of Syracuse, sent to Benedict III to appeal against patriarch Ignatius' act deposing him, had invoked this canon. That was to bring out into the open the deep feeling at Rome that Syracuse and Sicily in general ought to be under Roman jurisdiction, not under Constantinople.

Photius astonished Pope Nicolas, answering the charge that his elevation from layman to bishop contravened the Serdican canons by saying that the Greek churches did not acknowledge as binding a canon forbidding such elevations; indeed, he had found the duties of his office so dreadful and unpleasant that he could only wish that such a canon had been recognized as being in force. That the canons of Serdica were known in the east is certain. They found their way into the great canon collection of the Fifty Titles of which one letter of Nicolas (*ep.* 92) shows that Rome possessed a copy.[7]

---

[6] Nicolas, *ep.* 92 (MGH Epp. vi. 537. 34 ff. = PL 119. 1050 D). On the history of appeals to Rome under the Serdican canons, see H. J. Sieben, *Theologie und Philosophie*, 57 (1983), 501–34, and his book *Die Partikularsynode* (Frankfurt a. M., 1990), 193–228.

[7] The collection is edited by Beneševič (Ch. 9 n. 7). The *princeps* is in the great edition of Voel and Justel, *Bibliotheca Iuris Canonici Veteris* (Paris, 1661), ii. Photius' apologia acknowledges the generally binding authority of canons shared by east and west, but not necessarily that of local synods; 'it would be thought burdensome to invoke the canon of Side' (not extant, but apparently concerned with Saturday fasts), *Ep.* 290, 200 ff. LW.

Nevertheless Greek canonists treated Serdica as a regional council of the western churches, with only limited regional application, unless the rulings were re-enacted by the Trullan corpus of 692, which was credited with the full authority of the Sixth Council. The Council *in Trullo* had included no ruling on the subject of not consecrating laymen to be bishop *per saltum*. Moreover, at Constantinople there were potent precedents for such consecrations in Nectarius, Tarasius, and Nicephorus. Past papal decretals were simply not available at Constantinople. And how could Nicolas complain when a notorious instance of a layman so promoted was Ambrose of Milan? Nicolas could defend Ambrose's elevation only by claiming that the act had been done in answer to a divine sign, and had been vindicated by his record in suppressing heresy.[8] Even Nicolas had to allow that where the good of the Church was at stake, exceptions could occur to the most edifying of rulings.

That the Serdican canons were regional with only limited application in the east was urged by Photius' defenders in 869, hoping thereby to ward off the claims of papal power; but to the later Greek canonists, Balsamon, Zonaras, and Aristenus, this interpretation of the canon granting appellate jurisdiction to Rome made possible the ascription of similar authority in the Greek east to the ecumenical patriarch.

That the strict letter of canon law was, in case of pastoral necessity, capable of suspension or dispensation was an accepted principle, enunciated by Augustine among others.[9] When Ivo of Chartres (*c.*1093–5) wrote his famous Prologue, he collected numerous instances to illustrate precisely this point.[10] Ivo found special interest in Nicolas I's letters and decretals.

In facing this barrage from Rome on the question of canonical qualification for consecration to episcopal orders Photius was not unwilling to make concessions to Nicolas. At a synod he arranged for a canon to be enacted for the Greek churches that in future a layman or monk should not be elevated to the episcopate without having passed through the diaconate and presbyterate. Naturally he could not compromise on matters where the emperor had a veto (no doubt an allusion to the question of jurisdiction in Illyricum).[11]

[8] Nicolas, *epp.* 85–6 (MGH Epp. vi. 444 ff.).

[9] Augustine, *ep. Divjak* 22*; cf. *JTS*, NS 34 (1983), 426 n. 3 reprinted in my *Heresy and Orthodoxy in the Early Church* (Aldershot, 1991).

[10] PL 161. 47 ff. For the text of Ivo one still depends on Migne. But serious investigation of the manuscripts is advanced; see *Proceedings of the 8th International Congress of Medieval Canon Law*, ed. P. Linehan (Vatican City, 1992), for papers by M. Brett, B. Brasington, and G. Fransen; also R. Deutinger, 'Neue Handschriftenfragmente zum Dekret Ivos von Chartres', *Deutsches Archiv für Erforschung des Mittelalters*, 51 (1995), 539–42. On editions see P. Landau, *ZSSR*, kan. Abt. 70 (1984), 1–44. There is a French translation of Ivo's Prologue by Olivier Échappé and Jean Werckmeister (Paris, 1997).

[11] Photius, *ep.* 290. 319–24 LW; and canon 12 of the council strangely called 'First-Second' (RP ii. 701). Photius had passed through ordination as deacon and presbyter before consecration as

There was a second vulnerable point in Photius' defences, namely the admitted role played by his friend Gregory Asbestas among the bishops consecrating him. Gregory, deposed from the see of Syracuse by Ignatius, appealed to Rome, and this appeal had never been effectively considered—for the reason that Ignatius did nothing to provide the Roman curia with necessary documentation when invited to do so. The emperor and Greek bishops had reinstated Gregory. Could one argue that his Roman appeal still stood undecided, thereby making his canonical status questionable? Gregory had not been censured by papal authority. In 485 Felix II had said that someone deposed by papal authority could not be reinstated by Constantinople without consultation. In 860 Nicolas had a weak case for claiming this principle: Gregory's only utility was to be a rod for beating Photius. No text reveals the precise grounds for his condemnation.

The Retrial of Ignatius

Ignatius, who was to end by gaining Nicolas' support against Photius, cannot have had high hopes of any such conclusion when, in response to Pope Nicolas' reservations about his ejection from the patriarchate, the proceedings for reviewing his case began. Nicolas sent to Constantinople two legates (apocrisiaries), bishops Radoald of Porto and Zacharias of Anagni, both trusted and experienced negotiators. They were briefed with the instruction that their prime objective should be to win back the revenues of papal estates in Sicily and Calabria (which, being now under Arab occupation except for Syracuse, must have been no more than a theoretical question, dependent for its actualization on Byzantine military recovery of these regions), and above all to reclaim for Rome ecclesiastical jurisdiction in Illyricum, where hopes were rising (no doubt through information brought from Frankish frontier contacts) that the Bulgars and some of the Slav tribes could soon be brought to conversion and baptism.[12] (The Royal Frankish Annals record numerous confrontations between Franks and Bulgarians.) The legates were to bring to the patriarchate and the palace a Roman claim to the right to rehear the case against Ignatius. The emperor must be told that a patriarch of Constantinople could not be removed from office without the Roman see being informed and consenting. In reply, the palace justified what had been done by the significant observation that no dogmatic issue was involved, and it had therefore not seemed appropriate or necessary to refer the dispute to the Pope. An important concession to Roman teaching authority was implicit in this

bishop (Nicetas, *Vita Ignatii*, PG 105. 512 A). Nicolas had passed directly from the diaconate to the episcopate without ordination as presbyter.

[12] MGH Epp. vi. 293. 1 ff. (PL 119. 875 C).

answer. This is an early instance of the theme that the authority of the see of Rome is universal in doctrine but not in discipline.

This positive assertion of papal dogmatic authority did not mean for the Byzantine churches that they thought the pope of Old Rome able to decide doctrinal matters without the least consultation. Their estimate of Roman honour was indeed high, but the Petrine see was for them in something of the position of the deanship among the five patriarchates. The patriarch Nicephorus I (806–15) had simply laid it down: 'no doctrinal dispute can be decided without the participation of the Roman Church', and the same *obiter dictum* can be found in the contemporary *Life of Stephen the Younger*.[13] The proposition was not therefore extracted from the emperor in 861 under the pressures of the situation at that time, with the intention of being ingratiating with the two Roman legates. It was an accepted axiom that dogmatic definitions cannot be merely regional.

---

[13] MGH Epp. vi. 469. 24 (PL 119. 943 B): Nicolas tells the emperor 'Sed dicitis fortasse non fuisse in causa Ignatii sedem apostolicam convocare necesse, quia non hunc ullus hereseos error involverat.' Nicephorus, PG 100. 597 A; *Vita Stephani Iunioris* 94, ed. M.-F. Auzépy (Paris, 1997), 242 (PG 100. 1144 BC). Similarly Theodore of Studios, (*ep.* 1. 33, PG 99. 1020 C); 1. 37 (without papal confirmation Nicaea II is not ecumenical). In the fifth century this was axiomatic to Socrates, *HE* 2. 8. 4. Augustine (*c. Cresc.* 3. 34, 38) thought it unimaginable that a Greek council writing to a western church would not write also to Rome.

23

IGNATIUS' RETRIAL:
NICOLAS EXCOMMUNICATES PHOTIUS

The Latin version of the Acts of the retrial of Ignatius contained points of considerable interest for western canonists in the middle ages, and was drawn upon both by Ivo of Chartres and by Cardinal Deusdedit. From the excerpts made by Deusdedit it is possible to derive some picture of the way in which the proceedings went. Deusdedit was particularly interested in a council at Constantinople at which papal primacy was recognized. Canonist to Pope Urban II, a pope much concerned about the restoration of proper relations with Constantinople, Deusdedit's principal motive in compiling his collection of canons was to combat horrid critics 'contemptuous of papal authority as if unsupported by conciliar canons' and to show that the Roman Church is 'mother of all Churches', recognized as such even by the Greeks through the doctrine of the pentarchy of patriarchs of whom the pope is one.

The famous description by Liudprand of Cremona in his *Legatio Constantinopolitana* of his experiences as an unwelcome ambassador to Constantinople in 968 (below, p. 193) may provide some analogy to the hesitant reception initially given to the legates in 861. It was common Byzantine custom to keep embassies waiting for an audience, since by this method the grandeur of the emperor was enhanced. The emperor Michael took his time about gathering the bishops necessary for a synodical investigation. Eventually the papal legates received noble hospitality.

Photius and Bardas met the two Roman legates with courtesy and concessions; Ignatius did not. He reasoned that the examination before the Roman legates implied a cancellation or suspension of the previous synodical action against him, and therefore that he was within his rights by trying to appear before the legates in full patriarchal vestments and insignia.[1] To come before them habited as a simple monk was in principle to concede that he had canonically forfeited office. However, his vestments provoked the emperor

---

[1] *Vita Ignatii*, PG 105. 517. The dispute about Ignatius' vestments also appeared in the appeal addressed to Pope Nicolas in Ignatius' name by the archimandrite and exarch of Greek monasteries in Rome, Theognostos (PG 105. 855–61; Mansi xvi. 293–4). This appeal was evidently composed after the synodical trial which confirmed Ignatius' deprivation.

to require him to appear as a simple monk without insignia. The implication of that was not lost on him: the rehearing before the legates would be an imperially orchestrated action to win western support for a decision already made. After initial refusal of the summons, Ignatius appeared in alb and pallium.[2]

Ignatius therefore manifested high offence that the legates did not assume him to be or to have been the legitimate patriarch or to be entitled to be dressed as one, and moreover that they sat while he as if defendant was required to stand. He helped Photius by adopting a bellicose attitude to the Roman review of the case, and to the legates used language much less than polite towards the see of Peter and Paul. He directly denied the legates' authority to be considering his matter at all, on the technical but important ground that, in disregard of established custom and good practice, they had presented no letter of commission or credit from Pope Nicolas[3] addressed to Ignatius by his full title. Ignatius was reliving the harsh experience of John Chrysostom four and a half centuries earlier, but with no support from Rome as yet. If the legates had brought letters in the manner of those western bishops sent to Constantinople by Pope Innocent I and other Italian bishops, among whom one was Gaudentius of Brescia, in the attempt to rescue John after his synodical condemnation at the Synod of the Oak and his subsequent exile by an offended palace, then Ignatius would have felt bound to recognize their authority. Ignatius' allusions to 'Innocent and Gaudentius' were incomprehensible to the Roman legates, who amazingly claimed to have commendations from these long-deceased authorities.[4] But these western legates coming to attend an apparently genuine rehearing of his case, and then merely giving a Roman rubber stamp to a decision already made, seemed an outrage to Ignatius.

In the west it was commonly thought that the patriarch was no more than an ecclesiastical mouthpiece for the Byzantine emperor, doing and saying whatever the court ruled. From the Byzantine side it could be retorted with an element of plausibility that the then bishop of Rome was hardly more than a puppet of the Frankish king, by whose political support he was personally

---

[2] Deusdedit 610.

[3] This point also appears in Theognostos' draft appeal to Nicolas: PG 105. 857 D. At the anti-Photian Council of 869, the Roman legates were asked for credentials from Pope Hadrian II, and were offended.

[4] Deusdedit 606–7. The Roman legates absurdly reply that they come with the authority of both Pope Nicolas and 'Innocentius and Gaudentius'. It is evident that they did not catch the allusion to Pope Innocent's support for John Chrysostom. This precedent is also in Theognostos' appeal to Nicolas: PG 105. 860 C. Possibly Bardas expressed sympathy for Ignatius' complaint since it implied a challenge to papal authority. Nicolas, *ep.* 100 to Hincmar in October 867, repeatedly execrates any such demand to papal legates as a condition of being received: such demands could be made by but not to popes and their emissaries.

able to sustain his position, as had occurred in the case of Pope Leo III. The chronicler Theophanes observed that 'from that time Rome was under the thumb of the Franks'.[5] Ignatius could insinuate that the two Roman legates sent by Pope Nicolas I could have 'gone native', captivated by Photius' courtesy and the emperor's threats.

Latent in the acts of Ignatius' retrial was a further question. At Constantinople the Roman legates were understood to express the judgement that a negative verdict on Ignatius' claims for reinstatement would entail a decision that all his ordinations were declared invalid.[6] That understanding was naturally of profound concern to all those who owed their orders to the fallen patriarch. It went clean contrary to Photius' initial assurances that he recognized Ignatius' ordinations to be valid. But the Ignatian opposition had been behaving in a manner that had made him doubt the wisdom of his earlier decision; and to remove the leading Ignatian supporters from their sees would reduce, though not eliminate, their power to be a nuisance.

The retrial began by the emperor Michael himself declaring that any rehearing was needless but was being conceded to honour the holy Church of the Romans and the most holy Pope Nicolas in the person of his deputies. The legates invoked the canons of Serdica as justifying Rome's right to hear an appeal. Leading for the Byzantine church, Paul, bishop of Cappadocian Caesarea (who later changed sides to become a supporter of Ignatius) explained again that under Greek canon law there was no ground for the retrial, but the Greeks wished to honour the prince of the apostles and Pope Nicolas. It was *ex gratia*, not a right. That implied that, as Ignatius suspected, in Byzantine eyes the status of the retrial was merely informal courtesy.

Deusdedit's record of the Roman legates' investigation of Ignatius' case shows that with striking tact and sensitivity Photius absented himself from the proceedings. Nevertheless, he obviously had the strongest interest in the argument and the outcome, and it can be assumed that, wherever concessions were made to the legates, Photius was behind the scenes acquiescing in what was being said on behalf of the patriarchate. It would have been damaging to his cause if the two legates, who claimed plenipotentiary powers to represent Nicolas, had taken offence.

In the competition to win the support of the Roman legates, Photius at least gave the impression of suspending his view (common to the Greeks) that the Council of Serdica was a regional western synod not acknowledged as binding in the east. When the legates asked whether or not the patriarch

---

[5] Theophanes AM 6289, p. 472. 29–30 de Boor.
[6] Nicolas, *ep.* 85 (MGH Epp. vi. 445. 23 ff. = PL 122. 793), emphatically disowns the view of his legates on this point.

conceded the authority of the Roman see to rehear the case, they received an unqualified assurance that this was so.[7] Perhaps words which the legates took to be of universal application Photius used in a restrictive sense to apply to the present case of Ignatius but not generally.

When the Greek dignitaries observed that Byzantine customs and proce-dures differed from those of Rome, the Roman legates tersely insisted that they must follow Roman style in such matters. They even invoked the Symmachian forgery, 'the canons of Pope Silvester', which laid down a requirement of seventy-two witnesses for a case against a prelate. The emperor had little trouble in complying with this. Nicetas (*Vita Ignatii*, PG 105. 517 D) says they were seventy-two perjurers.

Ignatius' friends among the bishops and monks in the capital hardly helped his cause. They staged an anti-government demonstration in his favour which was, to say the least, counterproductive. Bardas had the demonstrators roughly handled and bishops exiled, and Photius had to protest at harassment and suppression being carried out in a way which brought obloquy and made his task of reconciliation impossibly difficult.[8] Photius was well content for Ignatius to have the honours and standing of a voluntarily retired patriarch living in peace at his island monastery. But he failed to satisfy zealot monks who correctly saw that their new patriarch was precarious, dependent on the support of the Caesar Bardas who might at any time fall to an assassin's dagger—which in due course turned out to be the case. Though none could complain of Photius' impeccable judgements in matters of orthodoxy and heresy, his prodigious learning in old and classical pagan books did nothing to appease monastic opposition. Nasty malicious gossip reported him to be far more interested in non-Christian books, and even, during Christian prayers, to be repeating *sotto voce* lines from classical Greek poetry.[9] (The account of Christian ethics which he sent to the Bulgarian Khan had con-sisted of a mosaic of quotations from the *Ad Demonicum* ascribed to Isocrates.) Zealot monks could not be expected to like Caesar Bardas or the emperor Michael.

Bardas had been more responsible than anyone for the military pressure on the Bulgars which precipitated their request for baptism. He was unlikely to think it in the political interest of the east Roman empire if Illyricum passed from Byzantine to Frankish control veiled under the ecclesiastical garb of

---

[7] So the record in Deusdedit. At the third session of the pro-Photian Council of Constantinople on 19 Nov. 879, the merely local status of the Council of Serdica was reasserted by Procopius of Cappadocian Caesarea: Mansi xvii. 456 DE.

[8] Photius, *ep.* 6 LW of August 859. *Vita Ignatii*, PG 105. 513 BC. On the rough treatment of Ignatius, Theophanes Continuatus 4. 31–2; Acts of the Council of 869 in Mansi xvi. 39 D.

[9] *Vita Ignatii*, PG 105. 509 A–C. Ps.-Symeon Magister, *De Michaele et Theodora* 672. 8 ed. Bekker. Similar suspicions were entertained about William Ralph Inge when Dean of St Paul's, London, because of his profound classical erudition.

papal jurisdiction. Bardas with Photius had likewise provided the impetus behind the mission of Cyril and Methodius to the Moravians, glad to welcome Greek missionaries to signify a political alliance protecting them against the pincer attacks of Franks and Bulgars. At the same time Bardas was taking the lead in successful campaigns against raiding Arabs, and that task on the south-eastern frontier was made easier if the northern frontier of the empire was at peace.

Photius composed an ultra-diplomatic letter to Pope Nicolas courteously explaining that while, in the cause of brotherly unity, he would be delighted to surrender dioceses for which Rome was asking, decision in such matters rested with the emperor, not the patriarch.[10] Religion and politics were intertwined throughout all aspects of the story. Nicolas was bound to understand this as a rejection of the subtle bargain which his letter to the emperor had offered. Indeed the fact that he first put his demand for jurisdiction over Bulgarian dioceses in a letter to the emperor shows that he recognized where the locus of decision was bound to be.

Pope Nicolas was later to denounce as hypocritical flattery the treacly terms in which, both before and after the visit of his legates, the authorities at Constantinople wrote in praise of St Peter's see and the privileges of the Roman Church. He came to see the flattery as a subtle means of persuasion to obtain his consent (*ep.* 100).

Despite Pope Nicolas' distrust of the Greeks, he had sent legates to the council held at Constantinople in 861, and the presence and assent of those legates enabled Greek canonists to claim that the council enjoyed the status of being 'ecumenical'. The question what constitutes a council as ecumenical rather than merely regional or local had been debated at the sixth session of the second Council of Nicaea in 787, where it was urgent to rebut the claims made on behalf of the iconoclast Council of Hiereia in 754 at which the emperor himself had presided. In 787 the answer given was in terms of representation and assent by all the patriarchs of the pentarchy, each giving ratification on behalf of all churches under his jurisdiction. Hence the painful importance of the fact that Pope Hadrian I approved in general but withheld formal ratification from the second Council of Nicaea. At Rome there was some inclination to think that papal ratification of an eastern assembly where Roman legates had attended sufficed to make the decisions binding on the entire Church. At Constantinople was it the emperor's ratification which could suffice for this high purpose? Theodore of Studios, who disliked the proceedings of Nicaea II and the patriarch Tarasius and who upheld the dignity of Roman primacy, nevertheless thought that the Pope must operate within the pentarchy, not as autocrat above the four Greek patriarchs and

---

[10] Photius, *ep.* 290. 390–2 LW.

apart from them. However, the pentarchy theory gave the popes less authority than they thought (and still think) they had or ought to have. Moreover,
three of the oriental patriarchates were now in Muslim-held lands, so that all
real power in the Greek churches was concentrated in Constantinople and
the ecumenical patriarchate.

The Caroline Books scorned the claim of Nicaea II to be ranked as
ecumenical, but asserted that status for the Council of Frankfurt (794) with
the sharp sentence 'No council can be general unless its teaching is catholic
or universal.' That was hardly a new proposition. Pope Gelasius I, when
pressed to concede that if any part of Chalcedon's decisions were lacking in
universal authority, then the council's Christological definition fell also,
replied that the criterion of authority was consonance with scripture, tradition, the common faith, catholic and apostolic truth, and ratification by the
apostolic see (p. 558 Thiel).

The Constantinople synod under Photius in 861 did more than re-
examine Ignatius' case. At a second session canons were approved against
sudden elevation of neophytes to the episcopate and against the ordination of
castrated persons. This presupposed that Ignatius and Photius were both
equally disqualified if strict canonical procedure was enforced. This balance
of wrongfooting can hardly have been unintended. Paradoxically Ignatius'
elevation to be patriarch despite being a eunuch was later to become, in the
time of Pope Leo IX and patriarch Michael Cerularius, a generalized western allegation that at Constantinople eunuchs were commonly made patriarchs, and indeed that on one occasion a woman had occupied the patriarchal
throne.[11]

The bishops passed on to consider what had been the principal advertised
item on their agenda, the continuing rumbles of iconoclasm. Greek
iconophiles after suffering for their faith were outraged by the west's cold
attitude to Nicaea II. Pope Nicolas had been informed that icons were to be
discussed and sent a letter, content to repeat the censure against the last iconoclast patriarch, John VII (833–42).[12] But when the Acts of the synod of 861
were brought to Rome by a senior civil servant, Nicolas was hurt that only

[11] PL 143. 760 C. The ordination of those who had had themselves castrated, as contrasted with
those castrated for medical reasons or under barbarian attack, had been forbidden under the first
canon of the first Council of Nicaea in 325. Among Christians there were ascetics who were castrated by choice; cf. Sextus, *Sententiae* 13, 273; perhaps Origen (though Epiphanius has a different
account of his chastity). It was a common feature of ancient near eastern cults; A. D. Nock,
'Eunuchs in Ancient Religion', *Archiv f. Religionswiss.* 23 (1925), 27. Hincmar of Reims was baffled
by a priest who castrated himself (Flodoard 3. 23). In royal courts eunuchs guarded the harem (*Real-
Encyclopädie für classische Altertumswissenschaft*, supp. iii. 449–55), and in the Roman empire the imperial chamberlain was normally a eunuch; in the east Eutropius was the first to be consul (Socrates,
HE 6. 5; Sozomen 8. 7) which outraged the west. A broad survey in P. Browe, *Zur Geschichte der
Entmannung* (Breslau, 1936).
[12] MGH Epp. vi. 516, 10 ff. (PL 119. 1071 B).

selections from his letter had been read to the assembly.[13] Details are not given of what was omitted; but it seems a fair deduction that the papal letter had been cautious and had silences interpreted as restating Frankish reservations. If read in full it could have comforted the enemies of images.

Two years later Nicolas had his own synod at Rome reviewing the decisions of Constantinople in 861; he not only rejected Photius, but was also unyielding in recognizing only six general councils.[14] Not only Photius and Ignatius but all iconophile patriarchs since 787 were agreed that the second Council of Nicaea was the seventh general council binding on both east and west, even if Pope Hadrian I had not formally recognized it as such. If Nicolas said or implied some touch of sympathy with the Frankish Council of Frankfurt, it would have been prudent for the reading of his letter to have had omissions. Constantinople would have known that his election as pope owed much to the Franks' pressure, and it would be hard for him to offend them.

Concerning Ignatius, Constantinople regarded Rome as interfering in matters not by custom falling within its responsibilities. Rome thought it a duty to support a patriarch who had bravely denounced alleged immorality in high places. Here was a chance to assert papal care for all churches. The resultant souring of relationships was to have consequences for centuries to come. It was hardly possible, of course, for Nicolas to refuse to be drawn into the partisan local conflict between rival factions at Constantinople. Roman appellate jurisdiction could not be declined if a papal review were invoked, even if Nicolas had not happily succumbed to the temptation to fish in troubled waters and so to recover Roman influence among the now heavily Slav and Bulgar regions of Illyricum. The reality of the matter was that he could not hope to succeed in this respect, least of all with Bardas and Photius. East Roman political power and defence was too closely bound up in the proposal. Even so for a surprisingly long time Nicolas remained cautious and non-committal. Until a late stage, when his correspondence with both palace and patriarchate had become heated and even irate, he could insist that his negative judgement on the canonical claims of Photius to be patriarch remained provisional and entirely open to revision. Indeed, he observed, wise popes do not regard their decisions as irreformable if fresh considerations come to light and circumstances change.[15]

At Constantinople in 861 the two Roman legates gave their support to Photius and entered into communion with him. Bardas and Photius had

---

[13] Photius, *ep.* 214 LW, is an attempt to win over an only half-convinced convert from iconoclasm. The opinion that from 843 onwards iconoclasm was dead is supported by Cyril Mango in *Iconoclasm*, 133–40. This judgement is more likely to be true in political than in religious terms.

[14] MGH Epp. vi. 520. 17 (PL 119. 1075 B).

[15] Nicolas, *ep.* 88, MGH Epp. vi. 481. 7–14 (PL 119. 955 B).

conceded that, although the removal of Ignatius from office had been by synod in full canonical form, nevertheless they would honour the see of St Peter by granting a rehearing. The legates heard and saw nothing in Ignatius to persuade them that he must be the right person for Rome to be supporting. Against them and their master, Vicar of St Peter, he uttered defiant discourtesies. Their conduct of business achieved a high point in the record of recognition of Roman primatial authority by the see of New Rome. Nevertheless, the legates had failed to gain Illyricum.

Because of the legates' diplomatic failure in regard to Illyricum Nicolas made a show of disowning them, moving them out of their episcopal sees and finding alternative positions. He was well read in the correspondence with Constantinople at the time of the Acacian schism, when the popes had had the greatest difficulties in getting their sentence of excommunication delivered to the patriarch Acacius because of the skill and the gold with which Acacius won over Roman legates. So Nicolas suggested that his two legates had been bribed by Byzantine douceurs and subtlety, simple guileless westerners as they were. Ignatius was the candidate to support: so he was directly informed from Rome that Pope Nicolas recognized him as the true canonical patriarch of Constantinople, subject, however, to one crucial understanding, namely that this recognition depended on his respecting Roman jurisdiction among the Bulgarian churches.[16] It followed that Photius must be set aside, and become the target for vitriolic attacks with charges of naked ambition for power. Poor Photius protested that nothing was less congenial to him than being dragged out of his library to the hub-bub, intrigue, street-fighting, and ceaseless party strife of violent factions in the capital.[17]

At a Lateran synod in 863 Pope Nicolas bluntly declared Photius excommunicate and all his ordinations null and void.[18]

Meanwhile at Constantinople Photius was encountering local difficulties. In August and September 862 Constantinople was shaken by earthquakes, and there were voices in the city to suggest that the tremors were a sign of divine displeasure at the manner in which Ignatius had been treated.[19] The emperor Michael, for all his brilliance, was associated with friends who were playboys and was losing public respect in a way that was adverse to a patriarch closely linked with him. Decisions to order executions, arbitrarily taken during nocturnal drinking bouts, did not make him loved.

---

[16] That is stated by Pope John VIII in 874–5: MGH Epp. vii. 294–5; see Dvornik, *The Photian Schism*, 101.

[17] Photius, *ep.* 290. 49 ff. LW eloquently describes the miseries of high ecclesiastical office.

[18] Nicolas inserted the Acts of the synod in his letter to Constantinople of 13 Nov. 866: MGH Epp. vi. 517–22.

[19] *Vita Ignatii*, PG 105. 525 A.

24

DETERIORATION IN RELATIONS

Bardas and the young emperor Michael were profoundly irritated by Pope Nicolas' support for the to them unendurable Ignatius, and after a lengthy silence the emperor despatched to Rome one of the rudest letters of Byzantine history,[1] suggesting that Roman ignorance of civilized Greek and the Pope's cultural limitations generally had caused incomprehension—the Latin of the barbarian west being in Byzantine eyes no more civilized than the Scythian tongue of tribesmen to the north of the Black Sea.[2] It seemed hardly credible that the Pope, such a stickler for canon law and customary precedent, should set aside the proper decision, taken by a synod attended by as many bishops as the first Council of Nicaea, which removed Ignatius from the patriarchate for which he had shown himself unfit. It was a discourtesy of the Pope to demand a rehearing of a case already closed, especially as there was no dogmatic issue at stake which might have justified Roman concern. The independent authority of the Greek churches was shown by the 'sixth council' (i.e. the Quinisext canons?). Old Rome was now senile, and vitality in the Church was with New Rome, sanctified by relics of great saints. The high privileges of Old Rome were in any event bestowed by the canon law of synods, and there was no ground for autocratic assumptions. The reputation of Rome for upholding orthodoxy had fallen in the east since its cool, at best tepid, attitude to the combat with iconoclasts in which the Greek churches had fought with distinction, especially the patriarch Methodius who had ended their dominance while Rome merely looked on. The emperor concluded with a peremptory order that Nicolas should send to Constantinople Theognostos, whom Ignatius had appointed as authority over the many Greeks in Rome, a body increased by refugees from the

---

[1] The content of the emperor's offensive letter can be deduced from Nicolas' reply: *ep.* 88 (MGH Epp. vi. 454–87 = PL 119. 926–62).

[2] The Byzantines were long conscious of the limitations and restricted vocabulary of Latin as compared with Greek. The emperor was only stating more aggressively than usual an opinion commonly found in the sophisticated world of high culture at Constantinople. At the first session of the Council at Constantinople in 879, Bishop Zacharias of Chalcedon grieved that the Roman Church had been in thrall to 'an alien and barbarian tongue'. On eastern knowledge of Latin see Bruno Rochette, *Le Latin dans le monde grec* (Coll. Latomus, 233; Brussels, 1997).

anti-Ignatian harassment in and near Constantinople. The emperor's letter went so far as to threaten action if Nicolas did not yield.

To the Pope much of the emperor's language was insulting. He had to resolve somehow to avoid returning insult for insult.

For his correspondence Nicolas enjoyed the service of Anastasius, a learned man who knew Greek and who had at one time aspired to be pope. He could assist Nicolas with the provision of trenchant prose in reply to the emperor.

Nicolas had been on the point of sending the emperor a friendly and fatherly remonstrance, asking for action to remove the intruder Photius, when the imperial messenger arrived by ship at Ostia in the late summer of 865. The Pope was offended by the emperor's failure to recognize the dignity of Roman primacy which he proceeded to trumpet. Primacy depended not on conciliar canons but (a) on the juridical inheritance of the Lord's commission to Peter entrusting to him the power of the keys and (b) on Rome's possession of the relics of Peter and Paul; (c) Rome's privileges were recognized and enshrined in edicts by earlier emperors including Constantine, Constantius, Theodosius I, and Valentinian III, whose names were gratefully commemorated at mass. (Even Nicolas appears to have thought emperors of more authority than councils.) The sixth canon of Nicaea I marked no increase in previous Roman jurisdiction, but merely used Rome's extra-provincial powers as a model to justify those of Alexandria. By virtue of powers inherited from Peter and Paul the pope had the right (*ius*) to summon or to welcome at Rome monks and clergy from any diocese. Emperors had no proper concern with monks other than to ask for their prayers. Iconoclasm was condemned by popes long before the time of Methodius (843). Hadrian's legates had presided at the second Council of Nicaea in 787. New Rome's claims to sacredness relied on stolen relics. Its failing in integrity was shown up by unscrupulous alterations made by Greek translators in papal letters to Byzantium. Many bishops of Constantinople had been heretics condemned by name at Rome. Nicolas here catalogues the monothelete sympathizers censured at the Sixth Council in 681 but cannot bring himself to include Pope Honorius. Absurdly Michael calls himself emperor of the Romans; but he knows no Latin, the Romans' language, sanctified by the trilingual inscription on the Cross.[3] This point was disputed in the Slav mission of Cyril and Methodius in argument whether Latin was so sacred a language that the liturgy must not be in Slavonic. Nicolas contended that even in Constantinople Latin was a holy liturgical language: 'It is

---

[3] At Charlemagne's Council of Frankfurt in 794 (PL 97. 198 D) a censure was agreed on those who believed that prayer ought to be in only three languages—evidently Greek, Hebrew, and Latin from the inscription on the cross. (Comparable is the African Donatist claim that Christ is honoured only in Latin and Punic: Augustine, *Tract. in Joh.* 21. 3.)

reported that at stational masses in the Greek liturgy the Epistle and Gospel are read first in Latin and then in Greek translation.' (It is extraordinary that Nicolas should have supposed the Greek lections to be translated from an original, more sacred Latin.) The report was not wildly incorrect since on Easter Day in Hagia Sophia the gospel was read in both Greek and Latin, as can be seen in Mateos's edition of the liturgy,[4] partly paralleled at Rome where on Holy Saturday lections were first in Greek then in Latin, as appears in *Ordo Romanus* 23 and 26–7 (iii. 272 ed. Andrieu). Pope John VIII ruled that among the Moravian churches sacred texts should be translated into Slavonic, but he wanted mass to be in Latin (*ep.* 255).

Nicolas complained that the council at Constantinople in 861 had been dressed up as if its main object was to suppress iconoclasm while in reality, as events showed, it was designed to get western support for removing Ignatius from the episcopal throne. By conceding a rehearing of his case, the emperor was implying that the first trial lacked justice. As for Ignatius' exarch of Greek monks in Rome, Theognostos, there could be no question of handing him over to endure the tortures inflicted on the supporters loyal to Ignatius: 'If he reports adverse things about Photius, he says only what everyone is saying and thinking.'

The crux for Nicolas, however, lies in the emperor's blindness to the unique and supreme primatial jurisdiction of Peter's successor in the Roman see. Nicolas freely quotes from the Symmachian forgeries of 500 asserting the absoluteness of papal supremacy. He prays that the emperor may be granted divine illumination to understand 'the mysterious and arcane secret, how great and of what nature are the privileges of the Roman bishop, conferred by an ineffable providence'. The Roman see is the head (*caput*), mother of all churches.

The conclusion of the Pope's letter wraps the steel in a little more velvet. Both Photius and Ignatius should travel to Rome, with their respective supporters, each to present their claims before the tribunal of the Pope as supreme court of appeal. Naturally this must imply that the negative judgement of Rome on Photius pronounced in 863 would be wholly open to revision. To assist with the process the emperor should send the original texts of the papal letters to the synod of 861, the originals of the first deposition of Ignatius in 858, and of the Acts of the synod of 861. But let it be clear that whatever the outcome of the investigation, there could be no question of any reinstatement of Gregory Asbestas, the grounds for whose condemnation are 'zeal for the Lord's house and for the privileges of the Roman see'.

---

[4] *Le Typicon de la Grande Église* (Rome, 1963), 94–5.

The opaqueness of this last judgement on Gregory Asbestas inevitably provokes the question whether Nicolas' unstated reason for negativity was simply that recognition of Gregory's good standing would disastrously weaken any case for questioning the validity of Photius' consecration. He mentions no specific complaint.

Nicolas' synodical excommunication of Photius in 863 was naturally unacceptable at Constantinople at both palace and patriarchate. But he conveyed the substance to the Armenian Catholicos, Zacharias,[5] warning him not to negotiate about reunion or the truth of Chalcedonian Christology and of Leo's Tome with a patriarch not recognized by the see of St Peter, by whose apostolic relics bishops of Rome were annually renewed in authority. (He was writing soon after St Peter's day, 29 June.) In 866, after the abrasive exchanges with the emperor Michael, Nicolas renewed his proposal of 865 that Photius and Ignatius should send legates to Rome for a re-examination of the whole affair. This implied that the negative decision on Photius at the Roman synod of 863 was still a matter about which Nicolas was open to negotiation.[6] Yet at the Byzantine patriarchate it could be understood only as a bid for more Greek recognition of Roman autocracy. In any event the proposal was cast in terms which presupposed that the probable outcome was a decision in Ignatius' favour.

It is hard to avoid noticing that the Pope was consistently cool to Photius without entirely closing the door. Perhaps there remained some outside chance that Photius would think communion with Rome so valuable a source of support, and so good for the unity of the universal Church, that it would be worth sacrificing Byzantine control in the infant Bulgarian Church and in Illyricum. Nicolas may also have realized that the Roman position in relation to Bulgaria was not strong; and in the final outcome it turned out to be the case that the Bulgars reverted to Constantinople and away from the west. Only thus could they retain independence.

Since John Chrysostom's time, patriarchs of Constantinople had been aware of the need for missionary work among the tribes to the north of the Black Sea and beyond. The restiveness of the Russians with their damaging raid of 860 underlined the urgency. Soon Photius was able to send them a bishop. He was much preoccupied with missionary work to Slavs and Bulgars. His own ancestry no doubt made him especially interested in the Armenians, and he wrote letters to them arguing for the orthodoxy of the Chalcedonian Definition of 451. He was devoted to the memory of St Gregory the Illuminator as his letter to an Armenian potentate makes evident (*ep.* 284). The relics of St Gregory had been found at Constantinople in his

---

[5] Nicolas, *ep.* 87 (MGH Epp. vi. 451–4; not in Migne).
[6] *Ep.* 88 (MGH Epp. vi. 480. 21 ff. = PL 119. 954 C ff.).

time. A mosaic portrait of St Gregory was to find a place in the tympanum of St Sophia.

For a considerable period after Nicolas' denunciation of him Photius quietly got on with his work, ignoring the Lateran synod. He had support from the emperor Michael III and Bardas and many of the bishops. In November 866 Nicolas discharged a salvo of nine letters to dignitaries at Constantinople, vehement for his authority. Meanwhile at Byzantium there was anger at the expulsion of Greek missionaries from Bulgaria as the Bulgarian Khan negotiated with the Pope.

Photius received letters from a few western bishops such as John of Ravenna promising support against Nicolas (which in the event John failed to give).[7] Ravenna, a city with a once intimate relationship to the eastern empire, had a long history of asserting autonomy. In 861 Nicolas imposed excommunication on John if he failed to submit. At that time John was humbled but only for a period. The Ravenna spirit of independence from Roman jurisdiction is a theme running through the *Liber Pontificalis* of Ravenna written during the ninth century by Agnellus.

Western restiveness with Nicolas' autocratic style and the emperor's mounting anger over Latin success in Bulgaria and the expulsion of Greek clergy heightened the tensions to the point of an explosion. Photius would formally state the case for holding Rome and indeed the Frankish west implicated in serious errors, among which the principal points were the *Filioque*, the requirement of celibacy for inferior clergy, and above all the deliberate refusal of the Pope and the Frankish bishops to acknowledge the second Council of Nicaea to be the seventh ecumenical council, thereby undermining Byzantine suppression of iconoclasts.

To Photius Nicolas gave the impression of being intolerant towards differences of custom. He seemed to think that because Rome did so the Greeks ought to fast on Saturdays, and impose celibacy on parish priests, and should bring their venerable and ancient liturgies into conformity with those of the west. But Photius himself could not readily tolerate the Franks' reserve towards the second Council of Nicaea expressed in the Roman and Frankish insistence that they could recognize only six general councils. In his iconophile eyes the west was comforting iconoclasts, whose doctrine was no indifferent matter but a threat to the tradition and being of the Church. It was also time to assert that the *Filioque* was an even greater threat to the authority of sacred tradition and was rank heresy, defying an ecumenical council.

---

[7] Photius, *ep.* 2 LW, his encyclical of 867, expresses anger with Rome. *Ep.* 2. 322 reports that he had received a synodical letter from Italy in which the bishops complain of Nicolas' autocratic ways. Byzantine missions to the Slavs are discussed by P. Schreiner, *Byzantinoslavica*, 56 (1995), 525–34.

On Holy Saturday, 29 March 867, Photius celebrated the installation of a mosaic icon of the Mother of God in the apse of St Sophia. The emperor Michael III and his adopted son Basil were present. In his homily (17 in Mango's translation) Photius justified the picture as mediating the prototype to the devout contemplating her image.

25

THE CASE AGAINST THE LATINS:
PHOTIUS' *MYSTAGOGIA*

In an age when it was undisputed that a bishop of Rome was not in principle incapable of fostering heresy, Photius had a case against Nicolas. Or was it against the entire west?

Photius' argument against the Latins had no difficulty in demonstrating that there had been no ecumenical council later than 381 which in any way authorized a modification of the Constantinople creed, and that this council had achieved recognition as the second in the series of ecumenical councils and therefore as committing the entire Church, not merely the eastern part of it. The Latin reply was already implicit at the Council of Chalcedon of 451, namely that councils subsequent to Constantinople in 381 had certainly received creeds and dogmatic definitions which were other than the Nicene creed of 325, to which the Council of Ephesus (431) had solemnly forbidden additions; indeed the Council of Constantinople itself made several such additions—which was the reason why the Council of Chalcedon had invoked its authority to ward off criticism that its Christological definition fell foul of the Ephesian ban. For the Latin west of the time of Nicolas, the ruling of the Council of Ephesus did not mean a precisionist exclusion of explanatory enlargement of an accepted authoritative text (which in any event could not apply to the Constantinople creed as distinct from that of Nicaea) but rather an affirmation that there is and can be no alteration of the deposit of faith which is always the same in content. The enormous authority attaching to the writings of Augustine throughout the west ensured that Latin theologians could not think of the doctrine of the Trinity as excluding the participation of the Son from the coming forth of the Spirit from the Father as originating cause of all. A succession of western texts from the fifth century onwards attests the influence of Augustine's argument that without the *Filioque* the orthodox doctrine is defenceless against Arianism.

Photius, however, was unimpressed by the western appeal to Ambrose, Jerome, and Augustine. Latin theologians had a filial duty to follow the example of Noah's sons who covered their father's nakedness when he became inebriated (PG 102. 351 A). Of Augustine's writings Photius had no knowledge. Of Jerome he had no more than a hostile report on his work against the Pelagians, in which Jerome was called 'Aram' (*Bibliotheca* 177). Of Ambrose he probably knew only what he could read in Paulinus' biography, translated into Greek in Photius' time (above, p. 131), probably with the motive of vindicating the elevation of a layman to be bishop and patriarch.

Photius' Mystagogia[1]

Photius' theological conviction was a confident judgement that the western understanding of the Trinity was indistinguishable from the modalist heresy of Sabellius; that is, that there is but one God who is known under three aspects denominated Father, Son, and Spirit; the plurality of threeness is in our minds rather than in the being of God or in any individual manifestation of that being. The west after all conceded that the Son is begotten from the Father alone. If so, what is the objection to saying that the Holy Spirit proceeds from the Father alone? (*Mystagogia*, title, in PG 102. 279–80). Western theologians were confusing what in the holy Trinity is shared in common with what is distinctive to the individual hypostases, which must never be mixed up (ch. 30: 102. 316 AB). The Son and the Spirit are caused by the Father who is the unique ultimate source of all that is (3: 281 BC). Asserting the Son to have a share in the procession of the Spirit implies that Father and Son are a single hypostasis, divided up (14–15: 293–6). If we say that the Spirit comes from the Father by virtue of the Father's divine nature rather than his distinctive hypostasis, then we end by making the Spirit, whose divine nature is one with the Father, participate in his own coming to existence (47: 325 AB). An alternative line of Photius' attack is the opposite of the charge of Sabellianism. In ch. 37 (317 A), the sophisticated argument is proposed that if the Son is begotten from the Father while the Spirit is from both Father and Son, then because the three hypostases are equal, the Spirit will in turn produce some fourth hypostasis—or even more without limit.

A basic error in western trinitarianism is to suppose that there are two first principles; or that while the Father is sufficiently perfect to beget the Son, he is not able to cause the Spirit to have being without the help of the Son, which must be incompatible with divine perfection (7: 288 BC).

Photius could concede that the Spirit proceeds through the Son in his temporal mission in the created order (13: 388 AB) but not in his actual eternal being.

[1] Photius' *Mystagogia* is printed in PG 102. 279–392; it was also edited by Hergenröther. It is translated into English by J. P. Farrell (Brookline, Mass., 1987), the version being better than the introduction. I have not seen a French translation by the late Patric Ransen. For a clear exposition of Photius' attack on the *Filioque* see Markos A. Orphanos, 'The Procession of the Holy Spirit According to Certain Greek Fathers', in the Athens journal *Theologia* for 1979, also published separately.

Perhaps even more serious, the *Filioque* not merely lacks conciliar authority; it is a defiance of it.

In developed form Photius' case against the *Filioque* was to be stated very late in his life. In his *Mystagogia* the nerve-centre of his argument is that the *Filioque* is in conflict with the Lord's statement (John 15: 26) that the Spirit 'proceeds from the Father', with successive ecumenical councils, and with previous papal authority as well. The doctrine was what concerned Photius, as much as the adding of a word to the liturgical creed. He felt sure that the Lord and the Council of Constantinople were denying that the Son participates in any way or degree in the coming forth of the Holy Spirit, and he therefore made bold to make his own gloss on the creed by saying the Spirit proceeds from the Father *alone*.[2] The western tradition for him was flouting the authority of the Second Ecumenical Council of 381, whose creed was acknowledged by the Council of Chalcedon and therefore received formal ratification from Pope Leo the Great. (Photius' defence of Chalcedonian Christology against vocal Monophysite critics in his own time led him to stress on many occasions how much the whole Church owed to Pope Leo.) The same creed was similarly affirmed by the Fifth Council in 553 (at its sixth session) and therefore approved by Pope Vigilius when he assented to the council. Likewise the Sixth Council in 680–1, which received approval from Pope Agatho. At this point in the *Mystagogia* Photius' catalogue of popes and councils breaks off; he evidently knew of no papal confirmation of the second Council of Nicaea by Hadrian I. But in a letter to the archbishop of Aquileia written 883–4,[3] the argument of which is closely parallel to that in the *Mystagogia*, he was able to quote Hadrian I's letter to Tarasius in which the Pope qualified his disapproval of Tarasius' elevation by accepting his orthodoxy in assent to the six ecumenical councils and thereby implying approval of the Constantinopolitan creed of 381.

Yet Photius' panegyric on past popes suddenly turns into attack directed against an unnamed Roman bishop (*Mystagogia* 88–9). The creed without *Filioque* was accepted by John VIII—'my John'—and by his legates at the pro-Photian council of 879 (Photius felt warmly towards the Pope who vindicated him, who in 882 had been assassinated), and by his successor Hadrian III (884–5). But now there is a reversion to error. Is this delinquent Pope Marinus (882–4), one of the legates at the anti-Photian Council of 869? (The emperor Basil did not welcome his elevation as being against canon law forbidding translation.) Or is Photius' bogey Formosus (891–6), sent by Nicolas to Bulgaria and no philhellene? More probably the target is Stephen V, who

---

[2] *Ep.* 291. 46 LW. Photius was not the first Greek to add the polemical 'alone'. See above, p. 92 n. 21 on Michael Synkellos, and p. 28 on Theodoret.

[3] *Ep.* 291 expresses amazement that western theologians claim to follow Augustine, Ambrose, and Jerome, in defiance of the Lord and ecumenical councils.

in 885 asserted the *Filioque* to rest on papal authority above all councils, and so instructed the Slavs.

Photius at the end of his life saw Rome weakening still further. The draft polemic is therefore against the Frankish bishops who have departed from the old western tradition, attested by the popes of the past, and an implicit demand that the Roman see should no longer tolerate this deviation from what he has shown to be its own traditional doctrine. It is intolerable that Frankish or Roman missionaries should mislead the new Bulgarian and Slav converts into thinking the Greek doctrine of the holy Trinity to be erroneous in a material point.

As the argument developed, Photius passed from authority to reason, urging that the *Filioque* necessarily implies two distinct causes or sources within the Divine Being, and yet that the west has also confused the distinctions between Father, Son, and Holy Spirit in a way that discloses the latent modalism or Sabellianism which the Greek east has long suspected in western divinity. The *Mystagogia* when restated late in his life represented Photius' final anger with the west, but the substance of the argument was clearly being stated twenty-five years earlier. It is hard not to think that disillusion with Pope Nicolas and his successor Hadrian II was influential. For when he achieved recognition from Rome with Pope John VIII in 879–80, the *Filioque* was going to be marginal, only indirectly on the agenda for discussion.

A question to which the answer cannot be securely known is whether Photius may have been influenced in the direction of cautious reticence by the influence of Dionysius the Areopagite, whose writings he accepted as authentic productions of St Paul's convert at Athens.

The party at Constantinople and in the monasteries of Bithynia remaining attached to Ignatius and resentful of Photius' intrusion as patriarch depended for their canonical argument on the appeal to the see of Rome and therefore on the proposition that the bishop in the Petrine office possessed a power to bind and loose superior to that of any other bishop or church in Christendom. The Ignatian faction wanted to acknowledge with gratitude the support which the west, except in the time of Pope John VIII near the end of his pontificate, had given to their conviction that Photius was simply unacceptable. Photius' attack on the western *Filioque* was therefore an indirect but not less potent onslaught on the authority of the see which was the primary lifeline of the Ignatian dissenters at his back.

No extant text from the Ignatian milieu discloses whether their leaders at any time expressed a view about the *Filioque*. It is no doubt inherently likely that they would have wished to think it capable of being satisfactorily glossed with the explanatory unction applied to it some 250 years earlier by the great hero in the Monothelete controversy, Maximus Confessor. By a paradox

Photius' attack on the western doctrine of the procession of the Spirit was destined to become part of the standard arsenal of Greek polemic. Yet long after both Ignatius and Photius had passed from the scene there was to remain a critical tradition at Constantinople which frankly regretted what Photius had said and done, and which was ready to point out that among the saints venerated by tradition Ignatius received a degree of honour which was not commonly granted to Photius. The Photian party in effect bequeathed that long-lived suspicion and hostility in the Greek east towards theologians who were 'Latinizing', *Latinóphrōn*. Ignatius' record shows that he was not as pro-Roman as some of his supporters.

26

PHOTIUS' BREAK WITH NICOLAS: NICOLAS INVOKES HINCMAR'S HELP: BASIL THE MACEDONIAN: PHOTIUS DEPOSED

In 867 Photius despaired of reaching an understanding with Nicolas at Rome. But perhaps he could enlist help even from the Franks. Frankish missionaries had also been required to leave Bulgaria open and free for Roman catechists. The withdrawal of the Franks is unlikely to have been welcome to King Louis II. The report diffused by Photius' enemies declared that (no doubt in collusion with the Byzantine emperor) he tried to buy the support of the German emperor in alliance against Nicolas by awarding him the title 'emperor of the Romans'. That would mean a parity of rank with the eastern emperor. Louis would unquestionably have welcomed this extraordinary act of recognition from Byzantium, coming with the authority of a synod ratified by the emperor Michael himself.

The authenticity of the story is decisively vindicated by the extant letter written by Louis II to the emperor Basil in 871, replying in sharp terms to Basil's protest at his assumption of this title. Louis defended his title with an argument already used by Pope Nicolas: a Greek emperor ignorant of Latin had no respectable claim to be called 'emperor of the Romans'. Moreover, Louis appealed to the sanction of approval from the bishop of Rome, St Peter's successor. Anointing and crowning by the Pope in St Peter's Rome were surely enough to establish who was justified in assuming the title 'Augustus imperator Romanorum'.[1]

Encouraged by letters received from Italy reporting opposition to Pope Nicolas, including a letter from an Italian synod perhaps more concerned about the challenge to Lotharius' divorce than about the Pope's eastern policy, Photius decided in spring 867 that he would summon a synod and take a firm stand. To impart to the synod ecumenical status he sent out an encyclical (*ep.* 2) addressed to the eastern patriarchs of Alexandria, Antioch, and Jerusalem (all now in Arab-dominated territory). He informed them of suc-

[1] Louis II's letter to Basil is printed in MGH Epp. vii. 385–94. On sensitivities concerning the titles emperor and king see J. M. Sansterre, *Byzantion*, 61 (1991), 15–43.

cesses in converting Bulgarians to the faith, Armenians to (Chalcedonian) orthodoxy, and even providing the Russians, 'a race notorious for murder and cruelty,' with a bishop so that they now acknowledged (east) 'Roman' sovereignty. (The reference to Russian cruelty is reminiscent of the terrifying report on the barbaric English received by Augustine of Canterbury in 597.) Photius had sent out missionaries, evangelists, and catechists to the Slav peoples, and this was giving substance to the patriarchal epithet 'ecumenical'. The commissioning of a bishop to the Russians was a policy continued by Ignatius after the emperor Basil had succeeded in achieving a peaceful alliance with them. In short, Photius had been able to establish a Byzantine Commonwealth beyond the ordinary frontier.

But tragedy had intervened. The missions had been ruined by western intruders behaving like 'savage beasts'. They had enforced fasts on Saturdays, condemned by Apostolic Canon 64 and Trullan canon 55. They demanded presbyteral celibacy, condemned by canon 4 of the mid-fourth-century Council of Gangra. They restricted to bishops an exclusive right to give chrism in contravention of old Greek custom. The western observance of the Lenten fast was deplorably lax. Above all they taught the *Filioque*, 'which merits a thousand anathemas'.

Accordingly a council had become a necessity and, through their apocrisiaries the patriarchs could pronounce a formal judgement.

Photius' council assembled at Constantinople in August or September 867. The opportunity was probably taken to celebrate the new icon of the Mother of God which in the presence of the two emperors Michael and Basil had been installed in the apse of St Sophia on 29 March, Holy Saturday (Photius, *hom.* 17 ed. Mango). The proposed agenda set out in Photius' prior encyclical included a declaration that Nicolas was no longer recognized as legitimate bishop of Rome on the ground that he was tolerating the *Filioque* in the Frankish churches.

Photius evidently felt exasperation at the way in which the bishop of Rome had been treating him. Never had he denied the primacy of the see of St Peter and St Paul. Unlike Ignatius he had been consistently courteous. His sermon at the conclusion of the synod, with many words to honour the emperor Michael, amazes at first sight (*hom.* 18) by its silence about the *Filioque*. He denounced classical heresies, but not a squeak is heard about the Latin doctrine of the Trinity being diffused among the neophyte Bulgars perhaps risking their eternal ruin.

The emperor Michael also had no reason to think kindly of Pope Nicolas since their acrimonious correspondence. The silence about the *Filioque* can be explained if Basil the Macedonian had advocated caution. It would not seem prudent to invite confrontation with the liturgical custom of a powerful part of the west. The discourse is a panegyric on the two emperors whose support has secured the cause of Orthodoxy as expressed in the classical councils. Both emperors signed the Acts of the council.

The east Roman move to enlist support against Pope Nicolas not only in the Greek churches but also among the Franks provoked a vehement and deeply anxious reaction from Rome. On 23 October 867, at a time (he said) when 'the calamities of the world and daily pressures' were particularly severe, Nicolas despatched a long letter to Hincmar of Reims, evidently recognized to be the most potent and influential voice in the Frankish episcopate. Hincmar was asked to circulate copies to other bishops in the realm of Charles the Bald and to gather a synod to respond to a Greek onslaught directed not merely against Nicolas' church but against all churches that used Latin. Hincmar was provided with a list of the Greek accusations, the worst of which was the offensive requirement that Roman legates must offer statements of their orthodoxy as a condition of being received (the Roman Church being without blemish: *ep*. 99. 106). Nicolas offered Hincmar no help with argument to defend the *Filioque* other than the claim that he could cite illustrious authorities and would do so were it not contrary to all precedent, 'either in written documents or in oral memory', for a bishop of Rome to justify his orthodoxy. Hincmar was asked to mobilize a general rebuttal from the western churches in answer to Photius the self-styled universal patriarch, who had been getting support from the other eastern patriarchates. The west should not be impressed by that, for patriarchs at Alexandria and Jerusalem suffering under severe Muslim harassment could not be expected to dissent from the east Roman emperor whose military strength offered their sole hope of relief.[2]

Accordingly at Worms in 868 a synod of bishops rejected the Greek complaints against the west, and asserted unqualified support for the papacy. Bishop Aeneas of Paris despatched an encyclical, happy to be asserting the dignity of the Church 'where St Denis first presided, consecrated archbishop of Athens by St Paul and then made apostle of all Gaul by St Clement', warning all catholic worshippers of the Greek onslaught on western liturgical forms and customs, including lies such as that at Easter western clergy put a lamb on the altar. Happily, unlike Constantinople, 'Rome has never had a heretical bishop', and it is false that Liberius deviated from the faith.[3]

Photius' attempt to enlist western support by driving a wedge between some of the Franks and the papacy went so far as the sending of an embassy

[2] Nicolas, *ep*. 100, MGH Epp. vi. 601–9 (PL 119. 1152).
[3] PL. 119. 1201–12. Mansi xv. 865–86. W. Hartmann, *Das Konzil von Worms 868* (Abhandlungen der Akad. d. Wiss. zu Göttingen, phil.-hist. Kl. 105, 1977); summary in id., *Die Synoden der Karolingerzeit in Frankreich und in Italien* (Paderborn, 1989), 301–9. Aeneas' letter is printed in MGH Epp. vi. 171 ff. (PL 121. 685–90).

to Louis II and his wife Ingelberge. But in 867 Louis suffered a bad defeat at Cassino from the Muslim commander at Bari, an event that could well have led the people in Rome to think a Byzantine army might protect them better than a Frankish force. By the defeat Louis lost honour and some influence in Italy. Photius was misled into overestimating the strength and diffusion of western opposition to Nicolas. Dissidents at Rome certainly existed, and could be relied on to suppose the Byzantine patriarch a source of support to them. Being learned in the Acts of past councils, Photius would certainly have known that Justinian's Fifth Council (553) had reacted to Pope Vigilius' initial refusal to go along with the censure of the Three Chapters by declaring him personally excommunicate—then qualified by the emperor's acute formula that thereby no breach of communion was created with St Peter's see, only with its temporary occupant.[4] It could have been a useful precedent; but the destruction of the records of 867 in 869 makes it impossible to know how Photius argued at this point. At Constantinople he could be sure of having good support for deploring western infiltration into Bulgaria. And he would enjoy approval from iconophiles for his active restoration of icons, seen today in the apse of St Sophia, after a long period of inactivity perhaps caused by the need to teach and train craftsmen in mosaic. On both these points, however, any difference between himself and Ignatius was but a hairline crack. More significant was the certainty that a move against the Pope could rely on the support of the offended emperor Michael. The instabilities of Photius' position were to be suddenly disclosed by the political weakness of his emperor.

Basil the Macedonian

It was soon to become clear that Photius crucially lacked the wholehearted support of Basil the Macedonian, who had become Michael's adopted son and then joint emperor, an adventurer of intense ambition and high ability. In April 866, ostensibly to forestall a plot against Michael, perhaps to ensure his own survival, he had personally killed Bardas, thereby clearing an obstacle on his own way to the top.[5] It was a flaw in Photius' plan that he had not made certain of Basil's approval for his synod and its agenda. He may have banked too much on the fact that the Acts of the synod had been signed by both Michael and Basil (which later Basil had to explain away as done in a

---

[4] *ACO* IV i. 202. 12 ed. Straub: Vigilius' name is to be deleted from the diptychs, 'unitatem vero ad apostolicam sedem et nos servamus et certum est quod et vos custodietis'. The text cited is Justinian's letter to the bishops in council.

[5] Gyula Moravcsik, 'Sagen und Legenden über Kaiser Basileios I.', *Dumbarton Oaks Papers*, 15 (1961), 61–126. On moves to secure legitimacy for Basil see Michael McCormick, *Eternal History* (Cambridge, 1986), 152–9.

nocturnal state of inebriation; so he told Roman legates). A second mistake was more intelligible. Pope Nicolas had been treating pro-Ignatian Greek monks in Rome as authentic representatives of the true voice of the Church at Constantinople. Photius replied in kind. Dissident monks from Rome, evidently in collusion with an opposition party in the western capital, came to Photius and were treated as representing the better and saner part of the Roman Church. Similarly there happened to be in Constantinople traders who were members of the churches at Alexandria, Antioch, and Jerusalem and had brought letters for the emperor. It is not certain that the letters brought were from the respective patriarchs. They may equally well have come from the Arab governors granting permission to travel and commissioning them to negotiate for the exchange or ransom of prisoners of war. The latter responsibility was explicitly the primary reason for the presence of a legate representing the patriarchate of Antioch at the anti-Photian Council of 869. Concepts of ambassadorial representation seem to have been less tight and less juridical in the east than in the west. Visitors in a sense represented their churches even if they brought no letters of credit showing their mandate from their patriarchs. In Byzantine ecclesiology it is common to find the dignity of the bishop of Rome secondary to and derived from the dignity of his church, and in effect more dependent on that than on St Peter. Photius acted as if he had received formally mandated legates, empowered to speak for their patriarchs. Thereby the synod could claim the still vague and elusive epithet 'ecumenical'. With this support the synod placed Pope Nicolas under anathema, unworthy to stand in the Petrine succession. Communion with him personally was suspended.

Photius will have known from the correspondence of Theodore of Studios that at the second Council of Nicaea in 787 Tarasius had delegates from Alexandria, Antioch, and Jerusalem whose authority to speak for their patriarchs was at least as precarious. Nevertheless Photius' method of gathering support seemed to his critics to lack integrity. In any event, the decision to make censure of the Pope an attack on the western church on a broad front was bound to provoke criticism. Immediately after the synod Photius sent legates to Italy to convey the synod's decision. They were recalled by Basil's intervention, and on 23 September 867 Basil murdered the emperor Michael.

Michael had an anxious-making habit of ordering the execution of officials and friends without trial—decisions taken during sessions of hard drinking. Perhaps Basil decided that he had better get rid of the emperor before an intoxicated Michael's irrational commands could single out himself. In any event, Basil could not be unaware that the emperor had lost respect. Unedifying stories were widely circulating about the emperor's private life and riotous friends, including blasphemous parodies of church ser-

vices which people blamed Photius for failing to stop.[6] Two of Photius'
homilies (13 and 14) attack malicious slanderers who, since they are also
given to fasting, are probably monks: 'The sheep condemn their shepherd
and the passengers their captain.' The fact that Basil denied his part in the
conspiracy (as reported in the *Liber Pontificalis*) shows that the murder had
vocal critics, and among these Photius may well have been one, which
would have contributed to estrangement between him and the emperor. A
Short History attributed to Psellos[7] says that Basil sacked Photius for criticizing the murder. Roman tradition in the time of Pope John VIII reported that
Pope Nicolas (by then already sick and dying) derived satisfaction from
Michael's death, which to him was an act of divine retribution for his insults
to the Roman see.

A major breach between east and west, such as Photius' synod of 867 had
precipitated, entailed political consequences, not merely an ecclesiastical
squabble in the sacristy. Byzantine military and political clout in Italy would
have been diminished by the visceral feeling generated against 'the Greeks'.
The emperor Basil might well have felt that the patriarch was expecting him
to bear the responsibility. The restoration of communion between Rome
and Byzantium in 518 had been the prerequisite condition for Justinian's
Gothic war to reabsorb Italy into the east Roman empire. Basil's calculations
in September 867 may have been similar. If Byzantium was to retain
influence in Italy, Photius' hotheaded act had to be reversed, and quickly.
Luckily there was available an alternative patriarch known to have papal
support, and who had the prudence not to disclose how far he would reciprocate.

---

[6] *Vita Ignatii*, PG 105. 528 A; lurid details in Theophanes Continuatus 5. 22–3. High officials
who refused to obey the emperor Michael's order to share in a gross parody of church ritual were
sent to execution (*Acta* of council 869, 7th session). Photius depended much on Michael, and the
publicity damaged him. Some of his letters complain of friends who forsook him such as Paul of
Caesarea, who switched to Ignatius (ep. 175 LW). On legates of the eastern patriarchs see J. M.
Sansterre, 'Les représentants des patriarcats au concile photien d'août-septembre 867', *Byzantion*, 43
(1973), 195–226.

[7] Ed. W. J. Aerts (Berlin and New York, 1990).

27

BASIL I: IGNATIUS RESTORED
THE SYNOD OF 869: POPE HADRIAN II

In the Greek churches of the ninth century many would have reservations about a patriarch not in communion with the patriarch of the west. The Ignatian faction were probably not the only papalists in the Greek churches.

The concept of a pentarchy of five patriarchs exercising jurisdiction as a collective body over the universal Church presupposed that the patriarchs were in communion with one another, and was hard to reconcile with notions of Greek or Latin autonomy. Michael's death had immediate consequences for Photius, and the patriarch's standing was disastrously diminished, to the unconcealed delight of the Ignatian faction. The Ignatians were unremitting in praise of the ascetic mortifications of their hero and in disparagement of Photius, who was portrayed as a worldly prelate whose real interests lay in old pagan books. On accession it was a simple matter for Basil to require Photius' resignation, to replace him at the patriarchate by Ignatius, and to send the news quickly to the Pope.

Not that the alliance of Basil and Ignatius would mean a modification of Byzantine policy about the Bulgarian churches. But communion with Rome could be restored.

Meanwhile Pope Nicolas had his difficulties in the west and had fallen sick. Clergy sent to Rome by Hincmar of Reims found him weighed down with anxieties and gravely ill. On 13 November 867 he died, before Basil's message arrived.[1]

Posterity looked back on Nicolas I as a figure of stature, of high significance for the great institution he was called to serve. He inherited from some of his predecessors a reserve and suspicion towards occupants of the see of New Rome. At the time of the Acacian schism the popes thought Greek patriarchs, even when they were Chalcedonian, were compromising with monophysite heresy, and the same impression was given in the seventh century in the exchanges about monothelete ecumenism. It was new for the

---

[1] Annals of St Bertin s.a. 867. A letter from Anastasius Bibliothecarius to Ado of Vienne of December 867 describes a faction at Rome determined to overthrow the policies of Nicolas: MGH Epp. vii. 400–1.

papacy to come into conflict with an 'ecumenical patriarch' who was unimpeachably orthodox and who, on the ground of both scripture and tradition, had reasoned doubts about the orthodoxy of the pope and his western churches. There was also some shock for Nicolas and his legates to discover that the eastern Church held the Roman see in high honour but as the president or dean of the pentarchy of five patriarchs whose collective will embodied authority in the universal Church, not, therefore, as possessing sovereignty and power of direction or jurisdiction over the four other patriarchs. The 'insolence' of Photius' synod in 867 was bound to produce reaction and a Roman demand for recognition of papal jurisdiction in relation to Constantinople and all the eastern patriarchates.

The Roman see's supremacy over eastern patriarchates was expressly asserted in the Donation of Constantine (above, p. 99), a document of which by 869 the Roman curia was aware, though there is no evidence of its invocation at the time.

For Nicolas' successor Hadrian II the political and diplomatic situation was delicate. A faction among powerful figures at Rome had opposed his election. Anastasius, antipope in 855, letter-writer for Nicolas, later papal librarian and archivist, reports a powerful group wanting an abandonment of Nicolas' policies. The change principally required was probably concerned with Lotharius' divorce, but papal Byzantine policy may have been a factor as well.

After initial hesitations, it became clear that Basil the emperor was not keeping Photius in office.[2] Hadrian announced his programme of remaining in line with Nicolas, and, significantly, first proclaimed this to an assembly of the Greek monks in Rome, the majority of whom were for Ignatius. So in spring 869 Hadrian held a synod in Rome reaffirming a negative judgement on Photius and declaring all his ordinations invalid. The synod was attended by a high officer of the emperor Basil and Ignatius' apocrisiary to Rome, Bishop John of Sylaeum and Perge in Pamplylia (PL 129. 114), from whom no doubt came a copy of the offending Acts of the synod of 867 to be solemnly consigned to the flames. Hadrian's decisions were conveyed to Constantinople by legates briefed to establish that if the patriarch Ignatius and his suffragans wished for restored communion with St Peter's see, this also entailed submission in jurisdiction, not merely in doctrine.

Hadrian assumed that as St Peter's heir he possessed such power to bind and loose as to be able to overrule past conciliar decisions and to make any fresh synodical consideration superfluous.

---

[2] Photius, *ep.* 86 LW and *Vita Ignatii*, PG 105. 540. The Acts of Constantinople 869 survive as a whole in the Latin version by Anastasius and are in printed council collections (Labbé, Coleti, Mansi xvi). See Daniel Stiernon, *Constantinople IV* (Paris, 1967); H. Grotz, *Erbe wider Willen: Hadrian II. (867–872) und seine Zeit* (Vienna, 1970).

Ignatius' reinstatement was not likely to be universally accepted in the east unless it received authority from a synod with strong Greek representation. So at Constantinople there had to be a fresh council to go over the same ground, ratifying the expulsion of Photius—self-condemned as schismatic on the ground of having excommunicated Pope Nicolas. A handful of metropolitans who had been ordained not by Photius but by either Methodius or Ignatius attended, and a phalanx of senior bureaucrats and senators. A royal interpreter was on hand to translate Latin when required. The vocabulary of ecclesiastical invective was deployed, especially describing Photius as a new Dioscorus (the Alexandrian bishop who had declared Pope Leo I excommunicate and thereby brought on his head his own deposition at the Council of Chalcedon in 451).

There remained a problem concerning the Acts of Photius' bellicose synod of 867; copies of the Acts were in circulation, and their destruction had to be ordered. Photius' personal copy was found ornately bound in gold, silver, and silk, the script being the finest calligraphy. It was solemnly burnt. The content of the Acts gave impetus to the destruction. The Acts of 867 had been signed by both Basil and Michael, the emperors, and by numerous senators and bishops. Photius was accused of forging the signatures.[3]

Photius was also charged with inventing bogus non-commissioned legates for the eastern patriarchs. At the Council of October 869 elaborate procedures were gone through to vindicate the legitimacy and authenticity of the representatives attending from Alexandria, Antioch, and Jerusalem. The legate from Antioch spoke no Greek. In each case the actual permit to attend necessarily came from the Muslim Arab governor, and was conditional on obtaining from the emperor the release of Arab prisoners of war. Ecclesiastical authority was doubtful.

The central decisions of the council were to concur with Hadrian's Roman synod anathematizing Photius and declaring all his ordinations invalid. The handful of Greek metropolitans present began to feel that their church was being subjected to humiliation by the west, above all when the Roman legates required them to sign a document affirming unreserved obedience to all decisions of the Roman see as the supreme teacher of truth. To sign was a condition of restored communion. Privately some bishops conveyed to the emperor Basil and to Ignatius that this was a unreasonable humiliation for the ecumenical patriarchate, making it 'servant to a mistress'. In a Watergate-like incident the signed papers were stolen from the lodging of the Roman legates; but this created such a fuss that they had to be rapidly recovered and returned. After the council, however, the Roman legates tak-

---

[3] Among Photius' papers critics found a volume collecting synodical *acta* censuring Ignatius; it was illustrated by Gregory Asbestas with images portraying Ignatius as a condemned criminal, a son of perdition, and Antichrist: Nicetas, *Vita Ignatii*, PG 105. 540 D–541 A.

ing ship from Durazzo in the Adriatic encountered Slav pirates who took their text of the conciliar Acts and all the signed papers, a fact which strongly suggests that the pirates were specifically hired for this purpose by the emperor. So it came about that the Acts of 869–70 survive not in the Greek original but in a Latin translation by Anastasius, who travelled to Italy by a different ship on another route. In 871, in a sharp exchange of letters between the Byzantine emperor Basil and the Frankish emperor Louis II, where Basil complained of the Frankish use of the title 'Roman emperor' which belonged only to himself, Louis's reply specifically mentioned the resentment in Italy that the Byzantine navy had done nothing to protect the Roman legates from pirates and that the documents which they lost had hitherto not been restored.[4] Perhaps the 'pirates' were part of the Byzantine navy.

From Ignatius the Roman legates obtained a confession of papal primacy ('caput ecclesiae') but without spelling out the 'small print' of universal jurisdiction, and also got into the Acts the reading of Pope Nicolas' original letter to the emperor Michael asking for restored jurisdiction in Illyricum, Calabria, and Sicily. The legates wisely did not press this point. The Arabs in Sicily and south Italy would require Byzantine forces to provide a realistic counterattack. It would have seemed enough to obtain assurances of obedience to the papacy. Twice summoned before the synod, Photius remained largely silent. His sole mark of office was a staff, taken from him by one of the Roman legates.[5] They expected the synod to nod grateful assent to a decision already taken by Pope Hadrian II. But they soon found that Ignatius and the emperor were insisting on a proper hearing. Photius could not be condemned unheard without the gravest questions being asked afterwards. Some of his episcopal supporters were allowed to state a case for the defence, in particular raising difficulties about the canonical status of the Roman claim to decide everything. Were the legates appealing to the Council of Serdica, which, though known, did not possess recognized ecumenicity for the Greeks? Where in the Apostolic Canons or in the canons of accepted general councils could Roman claims to autocratic powers be justified? Pope Nicolas' argument against the validity of Photius' consecration as patriarch rested on disapproval of the elevation of a layman. But custom had frequently been allowed to override local canon law, and 'disapproval does not make an ordination invalid'. The Pope objected that the bishops who had consecrated

---

[4] The basic narrative of the council is in *Liber Pontificalis* 108. Anastasius records this in a special note inserted in his translation of the Acts: Mansi xvi. 29. The burning of the Acts of the synod of 867: Mansi xvi. 22 D. Pirates: *Liber Pontificalis* 108. 59; MGH Epp. v. 392. For an illuminating discussion of the two ecclesiologies in conflict at the council see P. Stephanou, *Orientalia Christiana Periodica*, 39 (1973), 363–407.

[5] Mansi xvi. 97 D.

Photius were acting in obedience to the wishes of the emperor Michael. That may or may not be regrettable, but the fact does nothing to prejudice the validity of the sacramental act.

The Roman legates retorted that 'the bishop of Rome has power to judge all other bishops'. They claimed an absolute papal sovereignty. To that claim Photius' supporters asked if so absolute an infallibility could be reconciled with the acknowledged error of Pope Honorius, placed under anathema by the Sixth General Council ratified by Pope Agatho. The Roman legates defended Honorius, and questioned the validity of the embarrassing anathema pronounced 'by Greek bishops after his death'. In not disallowing a condemnation of Honorius Pope Agatho had surely not committed his successor Hadrian II. Besides, Honorius' case was wholly different. He was charged with heresy. Pope Hadrian could allow that an accusation of heresy was 'the one matter on which an inferior bishop might accuse a greater.'[6]

One implication of the Roman legates' answer is surely that the *Filioque* was not a question put before the synod by Photius' supporters in 869–70, and indeed that perhaps even the formal conciliar Acts of the Council of 867 found a way of being reticent on the subject, which would be in line with the silence of Photius' extant sermon at the conclusion of that assembly.

Another implication is that the Roman legates sought to rescue the authority of Pope Honorius by disparaging that of the council which censured him, thereby anticipating an argument of the seventeenth century and later.

In reply to Photius' letter informing Pope Nicolas of his succession to the patriarchate in 858, Nicolas had accepted his full orthodoxy without question. His reservation was technical, based on his alleged elevation from lay status. So two pro-Photius bishops summoned to the council pleaded that the sacramental validity of Photius' consecration had been acknowledged, at least implicitly, by Pope Nicolas himself. Their plea received a measure of impartial support from the body of senators, but the Roman legates would hear nothing of the argument. Appeals to canon law by the Photian bishops were set aside. The judge in such a matter was the present bishop of Rome; and by his anathema on Nicolas Photius had put himself outside the Catholic Church. The final verdict against him was signed with the greatest possible solemnity by following a papal precedent, already used in 646 when Pope Theodore condemned the patriarch of Constantinople for monothelete sympathies, namely that the ink was mixed with drops of consecrated eucharistic wine.[7]

---

[6] In Gerson and conciliarists of the Council of Constance, it is a commonplace that a pope can lapse into schism or heresy; see Glorieux's edition of Gerson, vi. 42–3.

[7] *Vita Ignatii*, PG 105. 545 (not noted in Anastasius' translation of the *Acta*). Theophanes AM 6021, i. 331 de Boor. Gregory VII's *Dictatus Papae* put in sharp form the necessity of agreement with the Roman see: 'quod catholicus non habeatur qui non concordat Romanae ecclesiae'.

The council approved twenty-seven canons. The first upheld the tradition of the holy fathers and of orthodox councils whether 'ecumenical or regional' (a formula which provided an umbrella for the authority of the Council of Serdica). The second affirmed the irrevocability of the decrees of Nicolas and Hadrian against Photius. Icons were to be venerated on a level with Bibles (canon 3). Photius' consecration was wholly invalid, so that all ordinations by him were also null and void (canon 4). The Acts of his synod declaring Nicolas deposed had been burnt. The twelfth and twenty-second canons condemn the nomination and consecration of bishops in cases of nomination and pressure from the government. No lay ruler may have any influence or power in such matters. These last rulings became momentous when canonists of the time of Pope Gregory VII wanted synodical authority to oppose lay investiture, and probably nothing in the Acts did more to ensure that in the west the Council of 869 came to be ranked as the eighth ecumenical council.

That, however, was not an estimate which would command unanimity.

The latent tension between papal autocracy and conciliarity was partly resolved by an ambiguous canon (21) that when a council is called to consider a question on which the Pope has already given a decision, its role is to clarify, but never to contradict or, like Photius, to condemn the supreme pontiff. Naturally this canon bore directly on the council which agreed it.

The Bulgars

Supported by the emperor Basil, the bishops found it easier to reach agreement on ejecting Photius than on the issue of jurisdiction in Bulgaria. At the last session of the council a Bulgarian deputation appeared to express gratitude for their evangelization by Greeks and for the bishop and clergy recently sent from Rome. But they needed to know whether they belonged to Rome or to Constantinople. The biography of Pope Hadrian II in the *Liber Pontificalis* preserves a painful account of sharp exchanges between the Roman legates and the representatives of the eastern patriarchs, whose inferiority to the Roman see was vehemently asserted.[8] The Roman legates protested that they had no authority from Hadrian to take part in an open discussion, and that no decision should be taken prejudicial to the Roman Church; the council's duty was to concur in the Roman verdict, based on the presence of Latin clergy among the Bulgarians. The legates flourished a letter, not previously produced, in which Pope Hadrian II recognized Ignatius as patriarch on the express condition that he agreed to send no Greek missionaries to the Bulgarian churches. Ignatius declined to declare his assent

---

[8] *Liber Pontificalis* 108. 46 ff. (ii. 182–5 Duchesne).

immediately; he wished to support the honour of the Roman see, but was not to be treated like a child or like a senile dotard. To Hadrian's anger he had already sent the Bulgars a bishop.

The Bulgarians undermined the legates' case by observing that the land where they now lived had been conquered from the empire of Constantinople. Evidently they thought it right that they should look to the Greek churches for guidance. The representatives of the eastern patriarchs were unimpressed by the Roman legates' argument that the political interest of the empire was irrelevant to questions of ecclesiastical jurisdiction, and insinuated that the popes' interest was shared by and dependent on the Franks.

In disillusion the legates turned angrily on Ignatius, holding him responsible for insulting the apostolic see. The emperor Basil, however, was obviously in control and could not imaginably have been content to see strong Latin influence in so close a neighbour of warlike inclinations. In 871 Pope Hadrian wrote directly to Basil demanding withdrawal from Bulgaria of the Greek archbishop and clergy. It would remain far from clear that Hadrian actually ratified the Council of 869–70.[9] In any event it was declared null by Pope John VIII, justifying his action by asserting the superiority of popes to councils.

At the same time as the Pope was telling the emperor to keep his church out of Illyricum, Basil was writing abrasively to the Frankish king Louis II, protesting against his use of the title 'emperor of the Romans'. Louis naturally retorted that his imperial title had the supreme sanction of St Peter's successor, the bishop of Rome. To this Basil contended that the Roman see alone was insufficient authority unless joined by the consent of the four eastern patriarchs.[10]

It is noteworthy that a Russian bishop attended the council.

The Bulgarian decision to look to Constantinople rather than Rome had evident and awkward consequences for Roman influence in the Balkans. The erosion of Roman authority in this region deprived the churches in this area of a strong principle of coherence and bequeathed a legacy of rival nationalisms or regional patriotisms which has long continued to haunt the eastern Orthodox churches.

---

[9] MGH Epp. vi. 759–61 (PL 122. 1309), cf. John VIII, *ep.* 177 (MGH Epp. vii. 142) on Photius' reinstatement. A letter from Pope John VIII to the emperors Basil, Constantine, and Alexander (Basil's sons) survives in Latin and Greek versions, where the Latin is clear that Hadrian ratified the Acts of 869–70, and the Greek version omits this (MGH Epp. vii. 171, cf. 185–6). Both versions declare that John VIII invalidated the council. In the seventeenth century Patriarch Dositheos of Jerusalem was certain that Hadrian had not confirmed the Council of 869: *Τόμος Χαρᾶς*, ed. K. Siamakes (Thessaloniki, 1985), p. 413; my thanks to Dr George Dragas for obtaining a copy of this convenient and well-presented edition. The work was first printed in 1705.

[10] MGH Epp. vii. 384–94 prints Louis's riposte.

Hincmar's report on the 'eighth ecumenical council' in the St Bertin Annals for 872 records that, to gain Roman approval, the Greeks conceded decrees on the adoration of images 'contrary to their own Synod'. At its seventh session the council reasserted the Roman view of Pope Nicolas on icons that they should not be destroyed. At the tenth session, the third canon approved honour and reverence to icons of Christ, the Virgin Mary, angels, apostles, prophets, martyrs, and holy people. Hincmar felt (or hoped) that this said significantly less than the canons of Nicaea II, no more in fact than Gregory the Great on the devotional value of pictures for those who cannot read. At least in Anastasius' Latin version the council agreed to add Nicaea II to the councils ranked as ecumenical. The emperor Basil, scenting danger here, persuaded the council formally to condemn a diehard iconoclast, Theodore Crithinos, a refugee from Arab-occupied Sicily active against icons in Constantinople, who had preceded Gregory Asbestas as bishop of Syracuse, before Methodius restored icons in 843. In face of Roman and Frankish hesitations, the council needed to show itself sound and to allow no revival of iconoclasm. It is very possible that the elimination of the emperor Michael and the fall of Photius seemed a chance for iconoclasts in Constantinople to make a bid to recover their position.

Ignatius was reinstated but not at ease. Many bishops and clergy remained loyal to Photius. The conciliar ruling declaring Photius' ordinations invalid caused huge difficulty. It was hard to staff the churches effectively and with the appropriate quality without looking to those ordained by Photius. Soon Ignatius was writing to Hadrian asking to be allowed to reinstate in office two of exceptional quality who had owed their orders to Photius; he was sharply rebuffed. Ignatius saw no reason not to be sending Greek missionaries to Bulgaria, and Latin missionaries were being turned out in favour of the Greeks, all of which increased the tension. Ignatius could profess strong belief in Roman primacy and supremacy at the council, but found his pastoral responsibilities impossible on the terms imposed by Rome.

In Ignatius' judgement it was out of the question to treat Photius as invalidly consecrated and therefore incapable of conferring valid orders. Early in 873 Hadrian's successor Pope John VIII (872–82) was offended to discover that many Greek clergy sent to Bulgaria by Ignatius owed their orders to Photius. He gave Ignatius thirty days to get his missionaries out of Bulgaria on pain of excommunication.[11] To the extent that the Roman curia had dreamt of finding in Ignatius a more cooperative colleague than Photius, it was now becoming clear that this had been illusion from the start.

Against this background Ignatius was no longer disposed to allow Roman claims to Bulgaria to be a controlling factor in settling the factional rivalry

---

[11] Ibid. 62–3, 278, 296.

between his supporters and those of Photius. Reconciliation with Photius was gradually achieved. After being expelled from office in 867 Photius had suffered frightful humiliations—imprisoned in an isolated monastic cell, refused access to friends, worst of all deprived of all books; even churches and martyria which he had founded and endowed with pious intentions were dismantled. He pleaded with Basil to remember the hands that had anointed him at his coronation and ministered to him the sacred elements at the liturgy. The plea was heard, and he emerged to become tutor in liberal arts to the illiterate emperor's sons.[12] The mutual hostility of the Ignatian and Photian parties seems to have been unabated; Ignatius' supporters were horrified by the reconciliation. But as Ignatius sickened with old age, he received kind pastoral visits from Photius. Without difficulty he assented to Basil's wish that after his demise Photius should once again resume office as patriarch.

[12] Theophanes Continuatus 5. 44.

28

PHOTIUS RESTORED. POPE JOHN VIII. THE COUNCIL OF 879

Even before Ignatius breathed his last aged 80 on 23 October 877 (his funeral being marked by manifest devotion among the *plebs*, *Vita Ignatii* 557 D), Basil opened correspondence on this delicate matter with Pope John VIII. Arab attacks in south Italy were making the time propitious for persuading the papacy to listen respectfully to the eastern emperor. John VIII had previously written twice to the Bulgarian Khan Boris warning him against the Greeks, but now his tone had to change with the Saracen menace in the south.[1] Early in 878 his expedition to hold a synod at Troyes in Francia was intended to raise Frankish military support against the Arabs, but was fruitless. He was going to be dependent on Byzantine force provided by the emperor Basil.

In the reinstatement of Photius there was a canonical difficulty which the Ignatians mentioned to Pope John, namely that at the Council of 869 Photius had been treated as a schismatic layman whose ordination was wholly invalid: so how could he be restored to the patriarchate? The emperor Basil assured the Pope that in 869 Photius had humbly resigned his office in writing, and there was no question of him being treated as other than a bishop.[2]

A difficulty for the emperor Basil was to gain from Pope John an unconditional confirmation of his consent to the reinstatement of Photius. Basil's position was strong in that the Pope, who was deeply committed to resisting the Arab advance, could check the invaders only with Byzantine help. The Frankish king Louis II had been suffering defeats. Arabs held Bari and were besieging Ragusa (Dubrovnik). So John was glad to send legates to the east in response to invitations from Basil, who was proposing ecclesiastical reconciliation to continue under Photius as much as under Ignatius. However, the legates arrived to find Ignatius dead and Photius already securely installed, a *fait accompli* rather than a matter to be negotiated. Could the legates at that stage succeed in proposing approval of Photius' reinstatement provided that

---

[1] *Vita Ignatii*, PG 105. 560, 567; Annals of St Bertin, s.a. 872. A letter from Photius to Leo archbishop of Calabria (*ep.* 297 LW) answers questions about procedure when wives of clergy are raped by the barbarians, or Arabs ask for baptism.

[2] MGH Epp. vii. 380–1.

he apologized for past errors and consented to leave Bulgaria to Latin missionaries? The formula was intended to save the honour of Popes Nicolas and Hadrian II and at the same time to reassert the Roman bid for Bulgaria as originally stated by Nicolas, since that issue was the nub of the dispute about Ignatius.

Hope of an apology from Photius was wholly unrealistic. Aware of his leading role in sending the Greeks Cyril and Methodius to the Moravians and in the mission to the Bulgarians, conscious of having established a bishop among the Russians and of some success in reconciling the Armenians to the Christology of Chalcedon, he looked back on a 'tragic sad history' in which he had suffered injustice, endurable only because of his trust in the intercession of the *Theotókos*.[3] And on Bulgaria he conceded more than Ignatius.

At the Council of 869 a bishop on Photius' side, Zacharias of Chalcedon, had submitted instances in church history where the decisions of past synods had been amended later. Pope John would restate this argument with western examples: had not a canon of Carthage allowed the restoration of Donatist clergy even though a previous conciliar act condemned them? Pope Innocent I condemned Bonosus' ordinations and then allowed them later. John Chrysostom and Flavian of Constantinople were condemned by synods but then reckoned to be saints in the calendar. So the new synod in 879 had the power and authority to declare the anti-Photian synod of 869–70 to be null and void, with (of course) papal concurrence. In a letter addressed to leading anti-Photian senators and bishops (Metrophanes of Smyrna, John of Sylaeum, and Stylianos of Neocaesarea) on 16 August 879 Pope John exhorted them to be united to Photius, for 'the Church has power to loose what was bound,' and Pope Gelasius once said that 'no bond is unbreakable except for those who persist in error'.[4] Nicolas' objection to sudden lay promotion had been wise caution, and the present pastoral situation made it necessary to relax the negative view.

John had to find a way of abandoning the hard line of Nicolas and Hadrian without conceding that they had been wrong. On the information given to them they were right, and no one should suppose otherwise. But they were fed with misleading information and would have judged very differently had they been well informed. The invalidation of the Council of 869 depended on the papal power to bind and loose. Roman legates were embarrassed to find this already decided.

---

[3] Photius, *epp.* 183. 37; 188. 19; 291. 407.

[4] MGH Epp. vii. 186–7. The Acts of the Council of Constantinople, 879–80, first printed in Dositheos' *Tόμος Χαρᾶς*, are edited in Coleti xi and Mansi xvii. 371–526 from Hardouin's edition of a text in Vatic. gr. 1115 (printed 1714). Some differences occur between Pope John's register extant in a Cassino Ms (s. xi) and his letters in the Acts, not necessarily to the demerit of the Greek form. See Johan Meijer, *A Successful Council of Union: A Theological Analysis of the Photian Synod of 879–880* (Analekta Vlatadon, 23; Thessaloniki, 1975), 40–1.

Rome Approves Photius

A revisionary Council at Constantinople opened on 14 November 879, Photius sharing the presidency with the three Roman legates and then the legates representing the patriarchs of Alexandria, Antioch, and Jerusalem. Three hundred and eighty-one Greek bishops attended, including a bishop Agatho of the Moravians and two bishops from the Bulgarian territory. Honeyed words were the order of the day. As the leading pro-Photian, Bishop Zacharias of Chalcedon blamed the disastrous divisions in the Church on the slanderous accounts given to the Roman see by the enemies of the patriarch; he saw the council as making possible a reinstatement of Rome's credit after a series of seriously mistaken decisions. The legates could plead misinformation. Zacharias observed the absurdity of the Ignatian leaders Metrophanes of Smyrna and Stylianos of Neocaesarea, who fed Rome with slanders to enable them to use the popes as tools in their conspiracy, and even now continued appealing to Roman authority when Pope John and Photius were establishing the best of relationships. John sent a pallium and other vestments for Photius, all displayed before the council. The Roman legates at the second session on 17 November chanted Latin psalms, a translation being provided by the head of the imperial bureaucracy, Leo. Letters were read from the three eastern patriarchs, denouncing as frauds and crooks those who had pretended to represent them or their predecessors at the Council of 869–70; one such legate, Thomas of Tyre, had begged forgiveness. The concern to plead for the release of Arab prisoners of war continued, however, with the legates of 879. The Muslim governors had evidently made that a condition of their permit to attend. All three eastern patriarchs recorded the sufferings they endured, 'terrible tyrannical acts', under their Arab masters. All three boldly asserted that they had never failed to recognize the legitimacy of Photius as patriarch, a claim which presumably need mean no more than that when he was in office they acknowledged him to be so and not when he was not.

Pope John's concern, to persuade Photius to allow Rome jurisdiction in Bulgaria, was delicately handled. Photius reminded the Roman legates of his answer to Nicolas, that this was a matter for the emperor to decide. Procopius of Caesarea (Cappadocia) looked forward to the time 'when God restores the empire's old frontiers and the emperor can then decide diocesan boundaries with serenity'.[5] The promotion of laymen to be bishops in one jump remained painful to the Pope and his legates. On this the Greek bishops were reluctant to make an absolute rule: 'Christ did not come to earth

---

[5] That even in 879 the papacy had not given up hope of Bulgaria is explicit in the *Acta*: Mansi xvii. 453 B.

only for the sake of clergy.' Different customs prevail in different regions: 'let Rome observe its own customs, and we ours.'[6] There was agreement that bishops retiring to become monks could not (like Ignatius) then return to their dioceses; also that laity who struck or imprisoned bishops (which had recently occurred) were to be held excommunicate.

The sixth and seventh sessions contained language that surprised a medieval Greek. Here Photius had no difficulty in persuading the Roman and other patriarchal legates to accept that the second Council of Nicaea could be reckoned the Seventh Ecumenical Council. The *Filioque* remained in his mind potentially contentious. A marginal note in one (Vatican) manuscript of the Acts rejects these last two sessions as spurious 'forged to imply that the *Filioque* was the cause of the schism' (Mansi xvi. 474 cf. xvii. 527–30). To Hardouin this was intended to give plausibility to sessions I–V, which he thought equally false. The west was sure the Council of 879 never took place (e.g. Andrew, archbishop of Rhodes, at the Council of Ferrara/Florence, Greek Acts 135).

Although the content of the Acts becomes so favourable to Photius as to raise questions, the probability is strongly in favour of their originality and (qualified) authenticity. The subsequent letters of Pope John VIII to the emperor Basil indicate that while he accepted the council's decisions, he remained unhappy at the version of his letters. The pro-Photian bishops had evidently had a fairly free hand from the Roman legates in the drafting of the record. But that the Council of 869 was cancelled was known to Deusdedit and to Ivo of Chartres; and a short treatise found by Dvornik ascribed to Patriarch Euthymius (907–12) presupposes knowledge of the sixth and seventh sessions.

A Greek note (printed by Hardouin vi/1 (1714), 331, thence in Coleti or Mansi xvii. 511) declares that Photius himself forged the sixth and seventh sessions. This presupposes the negative attitude to him found in patriarch John Bekkos at the time after the Council of Lyon (1274) with the judgement that east–west schism was not justified, least of all on the ground of the *Filioque*. This term or concept is never spelt out in the Acts. The Roman legates cheerfully agreed that no addition might be made to the 'Nicene' creed (by which the council meant that of Constantinople, 381). The proposal was qualified by a clause 'provided that the Devil starts no new heresy'.

---

[6] The theme that different customs do not amount to breach of communion is developed by Ratramnus (PL 121. 304–10), and became commonplace, e.g. in Guibert of Nogent, *De sanctis et eorum pignoribus* 1 (PL 156. 610 CD). John VIII may have been echoing Gregory the Great, for whom liturgical diversity was no obstacle to unity at the level of faith; e.g. *Reg.* 11. 56a, MGH Epp. ii. 334, 3 'una fides . . . diversae consuetudines'. Gregory the Great's authority had been much invoked by Nicolas I. During the pontificate of John VIII Gregory's life was composed by John the deacon.

At the final session the council acclaimed the universal jurisdiction of Photius as ecumenical patriarch. Pope John VIII he had saluted as 'our brother and spiritual father', while the Roman legates called John 'the apostolic and ecumenical pope'. Byzantine rhetoric was not given to understatement. At the fourth session (5 December 879) the Roman legates are recorded as saying 'The pure soul of Photius is so inspired that like the sun he illuminates all creation, even while resident at Constantinople', and illustrated their point by instancing the presence of representatives from the eastern patriarchates and of Basil bishop of Martyropolis (Maipherqat) in Mesopotamia. The presence of a bishop of the Moravians and missionary bishops in Bulgarian territory could have provided further evidence of Photius' energetic programme of diffusing Christian faith and Byzantine culture among the northern neighbours of the empire. A Greek bishop acclaimed Photius as being 'charged with spiritual oversight of the entire world', to which the Roman legates commented 'We too who inhabit the ends of the earth, we have heard that said.' They complimented Photius as world-famous, known 'not only in Gaul and Italy, and not only where Greek is understood but among the most savage barbarian races'. Perhaps some of that fame was derived from the diffusion of gossip about the confrontation with Pope Nicolas. More probably the generous words refer to his encouragement of missionary work beyond the northern frontier.

The council approved a canon to the effect that anyone placed under censure by Pope John would be likewise treated by Photius, and anyone censured by Photius in any diocese whatever would be similarly treated by the Pope. That was to imply a supremacy of the ecumenical patriarch over the other eastern patriarchs within the east Roman empire, and a parallel jurisdiction with the Roman see with equal power and dignity in their respective spheres of influence.

These claims affected the understanding of the Serdican canon on Roman appellate jurisdiction. The twelfth-century canonist Balsamon expounded them to mean that an equal authority was possessed by the patriarch of Constantinople.

The reinstatement of Photius to the patriarchate after the death of Ignatius led Photius into a situation where cooperation with the emperor Basil I was necessary to survival for himself and tranquillity for the Church in the capital. Photius' old missionary policy towards the Turkic and Slav populations on and beyond the frontiers of the empire, whereby through baptism and catechism these peoples were also brought within the sovereignty of the east Roman emperor, could be continued. In the treatise on the administration of the empire authored by the emperor Constantine Porphyrogenitus (905–59), it is recorded that under his grandfather Basil I Slav tribes, including Croats and Serbs, were baptized and incorporated in the empire. This is also said by Leo VI in his *Tactica*,[7] where it is avowed that Christianization was linked to military ends of defence. In this mission to Dalmatian Slavs Photius can only have been central. He would also have pleased Basil by his drafting of a handbook of guidance to Basil's son Leo on how an emperor ought to act. He even wrote poems in his honour.

In the Acts of the Council of 879–80, therefore, it is natural to find Photius obviously riding high on waves of support from the palace. He had been the principal agent in the enlargement of Byzantine political influence not only to the north-east but also to the north-west in Dalmatia, thereby decisively bringing the sovereignty of New Rome to the Adriatic coast. Even the representatives of Rome, anxious to please the emperor, could acknowledge that Photius merited a salute for his sponsorship of missionary labours among the southern Slavs. The Acts show no mitigation of Roman authority by the legates.

The terms used, nevertheless, by the Roman legates imply a minimizing and therefore to Rome acceptable interpretation of the title 'ecumenical patriarch' accorded to bishops of Constantinople since the mid-fifth century (as in the Acts of the Council of Chalcedon), but vehemently objected to by Pope Gregory the Great. Anastasius the papal librarian had removed teeth from the title by expounding it to mean 'patriarch of Christians in a part of the Roman empire', and not implying any latent claim to a universal or worldwide jurisdiction.[8]

However, at Constantinople there will have been stronger exegesis. Under the emperors Basil and Leo VI a law-book was produced, commonly called *Epanagoge*.[9] The preface defines the powers of the ecumenical patriarch and lays down for example, that local provincial synods are subject to ratification by him. Photius drafted the preface. He had learnt something from Nicolas I. It was evidently implied that the ecumenical patriarch rather than the east Roman emperor ranked as head of the Church. For Basil's son Leo the Wise that was to be offensive and unacceptable. He would show that the emperor was the teacher of God's Church.

[7] Constantine Porphyrogenitus, *De administrando imperio* 29, ed. Gy. Moravcsik and R. J. H. Jenkins, rev. edn. (Dumbarton Oaks Texts, 1; Washington, DC, 1967), 124–5; commentary volume ed. Jenkins (University of London Press, 1962), 93 ff. Leo VI, *Tactica* 18. 101 (PG 107. 969). Patriarch Nicolas I (*ep.* 17 Jenkins–Westerink) seeks to avert Byzantine war with Bulgaria about 921 by telling Symeon of Bulgaria that by baptism the Bulgarians have 'become Romans', and (*ep.* 20, p. 132) that Christ has set the Roman emperor as his representative on earth to be lord over all other princes. *Ep.* 25 advises Bulgars to be as courteous as Arabs when writing to the 'Romans'; *ep.* 28 deplores the Bulgarian habit of treating ambassadors as hostages.

[8] MGH Epp. vii. 417. 17–26 (a letter to Pope John).

[9] The preface to the *Epanagoge* or *Eisagoge* is reedited by A. Schminck, *Studien zu mittelbyzantinischen Rechtsbüchern* (Frankfurt a. M., 1986), 4–10. Photius' authorship was established by J. Scharf, *Byzantinische Zeitschrift*, 49 (1956), 385–400, cf. 52 (1959), 68–81. Brief discussion in A. E. Laiou and D. Simon, *Law and Society, Ninth and Tenth Centuries* (Dumbarton Oaks, 1994).

No greater triumph for Photius than the Council of 879–80 could be imagined. As he put it, Rome had returned to communion with the ecumenical patriarchate (Mansi xvii. 380 A). Moreover, he now enjoyed unqualified support from the emperor Basil and his sons. Cooperation between emperor and pope was indispensable to both parties in maintaining a united Christian front faced by a militant Islam pushing northwards from north Africa into Sicily and the Adriatic as well as into Asia Minor and the Aegean.

The restoration of communion between Photius and the Roman see was personal to himself, but had consequences in the office which he held as patriarch. The benevolence and warmth of Pope John VIII towards him certainly touched him deeply. He could not deliver what the Pope wanted in Bulgaria. That fell outside his powers, even though to the west it could hardly have appeared so. But he could at least undertake not to send Greek bishops into Bulgaria, as his predecessor Ignatius had done. The agreement not to intervene himself could obviously be circumvented by making alternative arrangements, should that be pastorally necessary. He succeeded in persuading the Roman legates to accept Nicaea II to be ranked with the six ecumenical councils common to east and west, and that was the first occasion when official representatives of the Roman see had said that. (It did not mean that thereafter western writers would all agree on 'seven councils'.)[10] The terms used at the sixth session of the council forbidding addition to the creed were capable of being interpreted in more than one way. Anyone knowing the background would be aware that the *Filioque* was the issue at stake, but nowhere was the *Filioque* explicitly brought up by Photius or his Greek bishops as a serious error which Rome had been tolerating in the Frankish churches. And no mention was made of the awkward fact that the 'Nicene' creed, cited in full, was the Constantinopolitan creed of 381 which had self-evidently made significant additions to the creed of 325.

The anti-Photian Council of 869 claimed to be the eighth ecumenical council. Since John VIII and the Council of 879 had declared it null and void, the place was vacant for the pro-Photian council to claim that title. However, by the chance that Anastasius' Latin version of the Council of 869 survived in the west, and that canonists seeking papal authority for the monarchy asserted by Gregory VII found rich matter in Pope Nicolas I's letters, the lasting western picture of Photius from the twelfth century onwards, though not earlier, became that of a schismatic. (In 1436 the Council of Basel took it for granted that a new Pope accepted the 'eight ecumenical councils'.)

---

[10] 'Seven' recurs in Deusdedit 236, while Ivo has eight.

At the fourth session of the Council of Ferrara in 1438, following a speech by a Greek pro-unionist, Andrew Chrysoberges archbishop of Rhodes, Giuliano Cardinal Cesarini appealed to see the *Acta* of the eighth council, meaning that of 869. There came an immediate correction from Mark Eugenicus observing that the synod of 879–80 under Pope VIII had cancelled the earlier synod of 869 under Pope Hadrian and reinstated Photius, so that the later council is properly called the eighth (Syropoulos, p. 334 Laurent; Greek Acts 90–2).

Nevertheless, Latin critics of Photius noticed in time that Greeks did not continue to reckon the Council of 879–80 as ecumenical. It is evidence in favour of the authenticity of the last two sessions that Pope John, while accepting Photius' reinstatement (against the Council of 869), disliked some things his legates had said and the doctored record of his letters to Constantinople.

Boris of Bulgaria won what he wanted: a patriarchate for an independent Bulgarian Church. This would take its affinity from the orthodoxy of Constantinople, not from Rome. Even so, its liturgy was not Greek but Slavonic. The determination to stay independent was certainly political: a letter from Photius to King Boris informing him of the death of the emperor Basil on 29 August 886 reveals that hostilities had already revived between the Bulgarians and Constantinople.[11]

Photius adopted a policy of generosity to the minority of bishops who felt that to recognize Photius as patriarch was to be disloyal to the memory of Ignatius. After all, their case had been clear, that at no point was it possible to recognize as canonically legitimate the consecration of an intruder when the patriarch he had replaced was still living and still claiming legitimacy; if that left thorny questions about the validity of ordinations, as indeed it did, the problem was for him and not for them to solve.

At the Council of 879–80 a delegation of bishops was despatched to call on a leading Ignatian, Metrophanes of Smyrna, asking him to come to the synod and state his reasons for refusing to acknowledge Photius. He declined to come, pleading that he was too unwell to walk and talk. The plea was dismissed by the council as insincere. But Photius was not discouraged in his policies of conciliation. A mosaic portrait of Ignatius, extant today, was placed in the 'great church' of St Sophia side by side with divines of the greatest eminence, signifying that the deceased patriarch was now reckoned among the saints with whom Photius and all his clergy and people held com-

---

[11] Photius, *ep.* 287 LW. On the early history of the Bulgarian patriarchate see H. D. Döpmann, 'Zum Streit mit Byzanz um das erste bulgarische Patriarchat', *Byzantinische Forschungen*, 18 (1992), 101–10. Nicolas I's argument that the patriarchal title at Constantinople was conferred by the emperor might well have been used by the Bulgarian Khan to justify the conferring of the title on his principal bishop.

munion.[12] The generous mosaic is explained when one considers the enormous popularity of Ignatius, who continued to be invoked by the sick and troubled. He was understood to be the causative source of cures to the ill; Nicetas' *Life of Ignatius* ended with a catalogue of his miracles. In one speech at the Council of 879–80 Photius had occasion to explain that Ignatius and he had become close friends without any rivalry between them.

After Photius' death another leading Ignatian, Stylianos Mapa of Neocaesarea, decided to surrender and unite in communion with the patriarch of Constantinople. That is stated in the Life of St Euthymius.[13] One can feel sure that this capitulation will have occurred after Photius had for the last time lost office and had been put into early retirement by the emperor Basil's adolescent son Leo VI. That removal could have been indispensable if the Ignatian body was to be reconciled.

On the first Sunday in Lent at the annual commemoration of the restoration of icons in 843 under Patriarch Methodios, it became customary for acclamations to recall Orthodox patriarchs, including 'Ignatius and Photius the most holy orthodox and famous patriarchs, eternal be the memory.'[14]

---

[12] See C. Mango, *Materials for the Study of the Mosaics of St Sophia at Istanbul* (Dumbarton Oaks Studies, 8; Washington DC, 1962), fig. 62 and pp. 51 ff. Ignatius was joined not only with Methodios but with John Chrysostom, Cyril, Athanasius, and Ignatius of Antioch. With Methodios he is commemorated in the Typikon of the Great Church in Patmos cod. 266 (s. x), not later than 890. Photius also has a place but in another manuscript.

[13] *Ed. pr.* C. G. de Boor (Berlin, 1888); ed. with good and full commentary by Patricia Karlin-Hayter (Brussels, 1970).

[14] So Michael Cerularius, PG 120. 730 D.

29

THE EMPEROR LEO VI THE WISE:
PHOTIUS DEPOSED

Basil's death brought a second fall to Photius. Basil's unruly son Leo was 19; rumour had it that he was begotten by Michael III, Basil's wife being Michael's mistress both before and after his marriage. To Photius he owed not only good tuition but also support when report of a plot to murder him led an angry Basil to imprison Leo and to threaten blinding. Dissident Ignatians remained unreconciled. In hope of appeasing them, perhaps also to assert imperial authority over the Church against a too powerful patriarch, Leo brutally ousted Photius and installed in the patriarchate his own adolescent brother Stephen. An appointment of one so youthful was to be rivalled in the west when in 1012 a faction at Rome elected the twelve-year-old Gregory VI. The homily that Leo VI addressed to assembled senators and bishops at the installation survives with other homilies from the didactic emperor. The tone to the bishops was threatening. In the outcome the boy was pious and did rather well. In view of his high understanding of his office as both emperor and priest, Leo claimed to be able to decree dogma without a synod.[1]

As Stephen had been ordained deacon by Photius, it was necessary to persuade Ignatians that Photius' ordinations were valid, and therefore Photius had been canonically consecrated.

The *Life of Euthymius* describes a tangle of intrigue. Photius was coerced into resignation and exiled to solitary confinement in a monastery at the Hiereia. His relatives suffered ferocious harassment. In his cell he returned to books and revised his *Mystagogia* with additional anti-western force. He died in or soon after 893.

The Ignatians did not fail to observe that after Photius and those ordained by him were ejected in 870, the emperor Basil enjoyed military success,

---

[1] Edited with French translation by J. Grosdidier de Matons, *Travaux et mémoires*, 5 (1973), 200–7. Leo's belief that a synod is not really necessary when the emperor has defined it in his *Novel* 17 (PG 107. 456 CD). Some of the prescribed acclamations to the emperor recorded in Constantine Porphyrogenitus, *On Ceremonies*, 1. 73 would do nothing to diminish the sense of being in the highest position in the Church. That sacking Photius was a necessary prelude to reconciling the Ignatians is stated in a note on Stylianos' letter to Pope Stephen V printed in MGH Epp. vii. 374–5.

capturing Tefrik in the east and Bari in the west, conquering Lombards, and taking Taranto from the Arabs; moreover that when after Ignatius died Photius was restored with those ordained by him, the empire lost Syracuse and all Sicily. The memory of this was still being recalled in 920 in a letter of the patriarch Nicolas I (*ep.* 75, ed. Jenkins–Westerink).

Photius' removal from high office gave scope for critics and opponents to stock the archives with hostile documentation against him. Probably about 905–10 a *Life of Ignatius*, bitter and cruel to Photius, was composed out of party pamphlets by Nicetas David; but it was a sign of the policy of reconciliation that his ordinations were not declared invalid. Leo, however, needed to ensure Roman acquiescence in the demotion of Photius. In 899 a council attended by Roman legates recognized the legitimacy both of Photius' sacking and of his ordinations as patriarch and, to this apparent contradiction, added successful reconciliation of the Ignatians led by Stylianos Mapa of Neocaesarea. Were a critic to insinuate that Leo was being too obsequious to the papacy, any such suspicion was answered by an imperial homily on the Holy Spirit with a long attack on the *Filioque* (PG 107. 133–53). In the catalogue of Byzantine protocol composed in 899–900 by Philotheos and entitled *Kletorologion*, it is expressly noted that at the Council of 879 the Roman legates, Bishop Nicolas and Cardinal John, were accorded precedence 'above all the class of magistroi', and that 'bishops from Rome take precedence over our bishops'.[2] There may well have been high officials at the court or the patriarchate who were raising their eyebrows at the degree of dignity being accorded to Old Rome.

Leo VI's relations with the patriarch and bishops were to become complicated by his four successive marriages, disagreeable to Greek canon law. The emperor, however, was able to win support from Rome, western canon law being more flexible. This did not endear papal authority to the Greek episcopate. The *Life of Euthymius* explains that as patriarch he found a way to exercise 'economy'. But there was still opposition from Arethas of Caesarea, and much sharper criticism came from Nicolas, who was patriarch 901–7 and 912–25.

Later memory at Byzantium recalled Pope Formosus (891–6) as being no friend to the Greek churches, perhaps indeed, it was said, he was the first to proclaim the *Filioque*, or at least to teach it in private while admitting no

---

[2] Philotheos is edited by N. Oikonomides, *Les Listes de préséance byzantines des IXe et Xe siècles* (Paris, 1972); see p. 161. This text is also in Migne, PG 112. 1353 C. On Leo's sermons see now Theodora Antonopoulou, *The Homilies of the Emperor Leo VI* (Leiden, Brill, 1997). On secular aspects see Shaun Tougher, *The Reign of Leo VI* (Leiden, 1997); and Steven Runciman, *The Emperor Romanus Lecapenus and his Reign* (Cambridge, 1929), ch. 2: Constantine Porphyrogenitus, *De cerem.* 1. 23 says that Leo was tonsured. His *Novels* legislate on many church matters, clergy, monks, feast days, ordinations, and other internal affairs. See M. Mitard, 'Le pouvoir impérial au temps de Léon VI', in *Mélanges Charles Diehl* (Paris, 1930), i. 217–23.

change in the creed. There is no sufficient evidence that in Formosus' time there was renewed schism, though the *Mystagogia* was an obvious justification for it if there was a move in that direction. Formosus had earlier served the Latin mission in Bulgaria, and is unlikely to have forgiven Greek criticism of the Latin catechism. But Photius' irate reference in *Mystagogia* 84–5 to an unnamed pope going back on his predecessors by proclaiming the *Filioque* is probably a hit at Pope Stephen V, who in 885 told the Slav churches that this truth rested on papal magisterial authority overruling all synods to the contrary (above, p. 145).

John of Damascus (PG 94. 1421 A) was not excited about *Filioque*. The *Mystagogia* of Photius was in effect addressed to his fellow Greeks. There is no evidence that the work found western readers until almost three centuries later. The earliest Latin theologian to have read the work was Hugo Etherianus in the twelfth century, who had lived in Constantinople in the time of the emperor Manuel I (PL 202. 227 ff.). After Photius and Leo VI (p. 183), there was to be a long Greek silence on the subject of the *Filioque*, until the eleventh century.

30

GREEK CRITICS OF PHOTIUS: PHOTIUS HONOURS IGNATIUS' MEMORY

Before long the *Mystagogia* would attract Greek critics who asked how Photius could pen such vehement invective against the west when in his synodical letter announcing his appointment as patriarch to Pope Nicolas he had said no word of criticism of western trinitarianism, and when at the Council of 879–80 he had kissed and embraced the Roman legates with enthusiasm and had at no point confronted the Latins with the frightful heresy of which the *Mystagogia* accused them. How could he conclude the council by a shared eucharist with a Latin cardinal in Hagia Sophia? The *Mystagogia* became the charter for the anti-Latins at Constantinople. Yet peace and communion between Old and New Rome continued for 160 years after Photius' time. Meanwhile, by the accident that the Acts of the anti-Photian Council of 869–70 were available in the Latin version of Anastasius the librarian, there was preserved in the west a lasting portrait of Photius largely negative and schismatic, which the *Mystagogia* could reinforce, especially because a Latin theologian was bound to feel its picture of the western tradition to be a malicious caricature. Apart from a few exceptions (including, however, Ivo of Chartres), the medieval west did not remember that the so-called eighth ecumenical Council of 869–70 was declared null by John VIII. What Latin canonists delighted to find was the *fortissimo* assertion of papal autocracy and supremacy over emperors in matters spiritual in the letters of Nicolas I; and the toughest of those letters were hostile to Photius.

The Byzantine world was one in which faction was endemic, whether on religious issues or on wholly secular matters. It was peculiarly unfortunate that a conflict of interest between rival missionary endeavours in Bulgaria conducted with high-minded motives became entangled in a local party dispute, which in turn brought the see of Rome into the conflict. That bequeathed a legacy of tension between those at Byzantium wanting to invoke Roman authority and those for whom Nicolas I's language about the absolutism of papal supremacy was bizarre and unacceptable. On the western side, Pope Nicolas' concern about Roman revenues and jurisdiction over the new churches of Bulgaria inevitably presented an ambivalent picture, easily interpreted as those perennial anxieties about money and power which permeate human institutions, including the Church (1 Pet. 5: 2).

Pope Nicolas emerges from the story with a mixture of motives, many high and sublime. Fed with anti-Photius information by Ignatius' agent in Rome, Theognostos, he could not easily have grasped that Ignatius was even more unlikely than Photius to give him what he wanted. The bargain which he proposed over jurisdiction in Illyricum was rooted in the honest belief that the once Latin-speaking provinces in the Balkans by ancient tradition belonged to Rome, and that it was his duty to reassert ancient customs and rights. He clearly believed that the story of Bardas' affair with his daughter-in-law was probably true, and that Ignatius had been a courageous patriarch to repel the Caesar from communion in a most public and humiliating manner. By implication (never explicitly) Photius was treated as a compromiser with sin and sleaze in high places. Hence Nicolas' systematic disparagement of Photius, a far more considerable figure than he was ever to acknowledge, and, until all patience broke down in 867, consistently courteous to him and to the primacy of honour which for the Greeks he embodied.

Even the modern historian of the schism least sympathetic to Nicolas (F. Dvornik) is clear that Photius' anathema upon Pope Nicolas in 867 was a major error of political judgement, so far as concerns the unity of the Church as well as the interests of the Byzantine realm. The immediacy of the emperor Basil's decision to get rid of him from the patriarchate shows that at the time this was clearly discerned in the palace in Constantinople. But Photius cared deeply for strict orthodoxy, a subject on which many entries in his *Bibliotheca* show him to be highly expert. He felt profoundly offended that the bishop of Rome, successor of St Peter, should be claiming a degree of infallible jurisdiction over the entire Church, east and west, when he was in the pocket of the Franks and was too weak to correct them on two matters of passionate importance to the Greek churches, namely icons and the *Filioque*. The Greek churches were accustomed to treating the bishops of Rome as in themselves a sufficient embodiment of the entire western Church. When the empress Irene decided to summon an ecumenical council to correct iconoclasm, no western bishop other than Pope Hadrian was consulted or invited to be represented. Therefore to disagree with the Roman see was in principle to be dissenting from the entire Latin west then dominated by the Franks. Disastrously Photius made exchanges with Nicolas I into a total confrontation between the Greek east and the Latin churches.

Pope John VIII and Photius restored communion. Nevertheless the *Mystagogia* of Photius is thunderous in fierce criticism of the *Filioque* being encouraged by the Franks and conceded by the contemporary papacy. That was to herald troubles to come, not merely between east and west but also between pro- and anti-unionist Greeks, the question being whether Photius was consistent with himself.

Already in Photius' lifetime Anastasius the Roman librarian was protesting that the Latins were being misrepresented as teaching that the Son is an originating cause or *principium* of the Holy Spirit. He wrote this in the year 874.[1] Anastasius here reflected the shift in Roman attitude to a more irenic relationship with Constantinople after the death of Pope Hadrian II. He regarded the difference between east and west on this point as comparable to the little terminological differences sorted out by Athanasius of Alexandria at his Council of 362, when he showed that diversity or even direct incompatibility of vocabulary did not necessarily have to mean contradiction at the level of faith. Even Anastasius, after being ghost-writer for Nicolas' most militant letters, had learnt a more peaceful way.[2]

At the Council of 879–80 Photius received decisive support from Pope John VIII in a letter to the emperor Basil (*ep.* 207, MGH Epp. vii. 167–86, cf. *epp.* 208–10) and achieved what he most needed for his own standing at Constantinople, namely a reinstatement acknowledged by Roman legates certain of being ratified by their master and thereby of restored communion with the west. Pope John VIII coupled his support for Photius with a restatement of the Roman demand for jurisdiction in Bulgaria. There remained difficulties for him at home. The Greek churches will already have had anti-Latin voices ready to accuse him of gross dogmatic compromise politically motivated. The accusations of the *Mystagogia* or of his letter to Aquileia (*ep.* 291), that the west was committing the sin against the Holy Spirit and so had fallen into the 'ultimate blasphemy', could well have been impelled by the need to show Greek critics how utterly principled and uncompromising he really was. Both Latins and Greeks could allow for some flexibility, which Greeks called 'economy' and Latins 'dispensation'. Photius had to allow to critics that he had exercised economy, though it was only provisional. Or had he betrayed the point that objection to the Latin *Filioque* was at bottom little more than a pretext for asserting eastern independence?

Photius' *Mystagogia* is an irate work by an irritated angry man. It is unlikely to have been drafted during the lifetime of John VIII, and the silence about

---

[1] MGH Epp. vii. 425. 22.

[2] Anastasius' chequered career is traced by G. Arnaldi in *Dizionario biografico degli Italiani*, iii (Rome, 1961), 25–37, and by P. Devos in *New Catholic Encyclopedia*, i (New York, 1967), 480–1. On his role as translator and as papal archivist and letter-writer see G. Lähr in *Neues Archiv*, 47 (1928), 416–68, and D. Lohrmann, *Das Register Papst Johannes' VIII.* (Tübingen, 1968), 239–58. A masterly account in W. Berschin, *Greek Letters and the Latin 'Middle' Ages* (Washington DC, 1988) 162–3. On the Council of 869–70 see C. Leonardi, 'Anastasio Bibliotecario e l'ottavo concilio ecumenico', *Studi medievali*[3], 8/1 (1967), 59–192. Ivo of Chartres cites this council as the eighth: *Decretum* 5. 122; *Panormia* 3. 8 (PL 161. 364 and 1151). But he knew the Council of 879 declared its decisions invalid: *Decretum* 4. 76; cf. *Panormia* 8. 149. See G. Hofmann, 'Ivo von Chartres über Photios', *Orientalia Christiana Periodica*, 14 (1948), 105–37. The Acts of 879 were also known to Deusdedit 616.

the *Filioque* in 867 except for the prior encyclical suggests that the argument had not been worked out at that stage of his career. Probably the text belongs to his last years after he had been finally expelled from the patriarchate by the emperor Leo VI. Much of the argument is summarized in his letter to the archbishop of Aquileia. The occasion of that letter can only be conjectured. Perhaps at Aquileia there was pressure from the Frankish side to introduce the *Filioque* liturgically, and Photius hoped to prevent that. One recalls that in the 860s he received letters of support from north Italy in his combat with Pope Nicolas. Aquileia was not far from Ravenna where successive bishops had an insuppressible desire to be more independent of Roman jurisdiction; but in the Three Chapters controversy Ravenna had supported the Council of 553 under Justinian and with Pope Vigilius' assent.

At the anti-Photian Council of 869–70 the problem of *Filioque* was not raised either by Photius or his supporters. Surprisingly in the pro-Photian Council of 879–80 the problem was raised only in an oblique form by restating a prohibition of the Council of Ephesus (431) against adding to the Nicene creed, which paradoxically was what the Council of Constantinople in 381 had done. In 879 Photius put no question to John VIII's legates about toleration of Frankish heresy. After Photius had lost the patriarchate, it would have cost him nothing to publish a manifesto that orthodoxy mattered to him more than power.

Nicetas, archivist of Nicaea about 1100, compiled a catalogue of schisms between east and west. He expressly recorded that the reunion with Rome achieved under Photius was 'vulnerable to criticism', since the issues raised in Photius' encyclical were left 'unexamined'. 'After much shouting reconciliation was facile.'[3]

The biographies of the missionaries Cyril and Methodius record that in their mission they were molested by 'the cohorts of Latins'—no doubt Frankish clergy from Regensburg and Passau.

As we have seen, a very possible context precipitating the anger of Photius' *Mystagogia* (and his letter to Aquileia) was the aggressive intervention of Pope Stephen V (885–91) soon after his elevation to the Petrine see, by which he forbade the infant Slav churches to use Slavonic for their liturgy and, at the same time, directed them to use the *Filioque*. The *Filioque*, he held, was assured by papal authority superior to that of any conciliar consensus of bishops or any ruling by a mere council that no addition might be made to the creed. Moreover, the Slavs must observe the Roman rule of Saturday fasts.[4]

---

[3] PG 120. 720 A, 717 C.

[4] Stephen V's commonitorium to a delegation of his clergy sent to the Slavs and his letter to the Slav king Zventopolcus are printed in MGH Epp. vii. 352–8. Discussion by G. Lähr in *Neues Archiv*, 47 (1928), 159–73. The Pope insisted on the *Filioque*, Saturday fasts, and Latin mass. This

For the ninth-century patriarch the two primary issues were the Roman claim to a supra-conciliar sovereignty over the entire Church on earth, not merely to a patriarchal responsibility with direct jurisdiction over the west, and, linked with this, the arrogance, as it seemed to the Greek east, of making an addition to the creed sanctioned by an early ecumenical council and ratified by successive bishops of Rome in the past.

Nicetas' *Vita Ignatii* records healing miracles at Ignatius' tomb (PG 105. 561), and his intercession was invoked by the praetor of Sicily when the Arabs attacked (564 A).

After his death Ignatius had been 'canonized', especially marked by the admission of a mosaic portrait of him among the saints on the wall of the great Church of Holy Wisdom in Constantinople. His supporters ensured that the hagiographical tradition was kind to him, whereas it would long remain hesitant about the standing of Photius. When at the time of the Council of Florence the anti-western leader Mark of Ephesus appealed to the arguments of Photius' *Mystagogia*, he was criticized by the pro-unionist Gregory Mammas (patriarch 1443–53) with the observation that while Ignatius' name stood in the calendar of the synaxary on 23 October, 'Photius has never been among the saints.' In fairness it has to be remarked that while Photius' name is not found in many manuscripts of the Greek synaxary, there are some where it occurs. The hesitation was a reflection of the success of the Ignatian publicists. Moreover, as Nicetas of Nicaea would point out in the tenth century, Photius appeared hopelessly inconsistent for both denouncing and then holding communion with the west: 'He was a better patron of schism than of ecumenism.' Even George Scholarios, who was prominent at the time of the Council of Florence and after the Turkish conquest of 1453 became patriarch, thought it true to say that 'Photius made use of the difference concerning the procession of the Spirit as a pretext for dividing the Churches. That he then reconciled them was due to private interest.' This negative opinion is surprisingly echoed by Nectarius the seventeenth-century patriarch of Jerusalem (1682). Among the Greek rather than the Slav churches, there has been a much more adulatory

---

intervention alienated the Slav mission of Cyril and Methodius from Rome, not least because Stephen's policy (unlike John VIII, *ep.* 255, MGH Epp. vii. 224) opposed a Slavonic liturgy, and moved their work to the eastern Orthodox realm under the aegis of the Bulgarian churches. A group of Stephen V's letters was translated into Greek *c.*900 intended to show that Photius was never absolved by Rome and his ordinations were invalid: MGH Epp. vii. 371–84. The letter to Pope Stephen V from Stylianos Mapa of Neocaesarea favours forgiveness to those who were ordained by or held communion with Photius, but on the analogy of the acceptance of Dioscorus' supporters after Chalcedon in 451, or penitent ex-iconoclasts after 787: MGH Epp. vii. 379. 19 ff.

stream, especially stemming from opposition to the emperor's policies of union with the west at the Council of Lyon, 1274.[5]

The exchanges between Photius and the Popes Nicolas and Hadrian II are slightly less painful to read than those of 1054, but they mark a climax in a long process of estrangement with many anticipations and foreshadowings: first, when discourteous and unbrotherly language was used during the Acacian schism from 484 to 518 which, with a change of emperor, ended in Pope Hormisdas' successful insistence that the Greek churches acknowledge the Petrine authority of the papal office, with the corollary that communion with Rome entails obedience to papal directives and jurisdiction; then in Pope Vigilius' role in the controversy over the 'Three Chapters'; thirdly, in the prickly dispute between Rome and Constantinople in Gregory the Great's time concerning the title 'ecumenical patriarch' (a title which Photius, surely deliberately, abstained from using in all correspondence with the west); fourthly, in the ultimately successful struggle of late seventh-century popes against monothelete qualifications to the purity of 'two-natures' Chalcedonian Christology, culminating in Agatho's imposition of a western formula, silent on the *Filioque*, at the Sixth Council of 680–1; fifthly, the awkward exchanges about the privileges of New Rome and priestly celibacy at the Council *in Trullo* of 692; sixthly, in the hesitant *via media* which successive popes attempted to pursue between iconoclasts and iconophiles—a middle course which seemed inescapable when the papacy was dependent on the anti-Byzantine Franks for property and liberty.

Through all disagreements there was no stage at which the eastern and western protagonists understood themselves to lead two separate Churches. There could be only one Church, even when strong dissensions arose on matters more than diversities of custom and liturgy. The west pervasively assumed the Greek churches to be too beholden to the east Roman emperor. The east (operating with a basic assumption that Church and State were two different aspects of the same society) disliked claims for universal papal jurisdiction, especially when the papacy was dependent on Frankish power which the Byzantines suspected, with reason, to have large territorial ambitions in their part of the world. The Orthodox east honoured Petrine authority in the Roman see but never conceived that papal authority could

---

[5] Photius has an entry in the tenth-century Synaxary of Constantinople on 6 February. See M. Jugie, 'Le culte de Photius dans l'église byzantine', *Revue de l'Orient chrétien*, 23 (1922–3), 105–22 for a catalogue of references. Invocations of Photius 'the most holy patriarch' by the opponents of the union at Lyon appear in some of the documents printed by J. Darrouzès, *Dossier grec de l'union de Lyon* (Paris, 1976), especially pp. 574–88, a *synodikon* probably by George Moschobar pronouncing anathema on all critics of Photius, among whom the patriarch Bekkos was a leader.

be qualitatively distinct from the collegial consent of the patriarchs and of the episcopate in council.

Nevertheless the alliance of the Franks with the papacy was momentous in its consequences for the authority of the popes at least in relation to the western barbarian kingdoms. Charlemagne's establishment of a western empire asserting a claim to be Roman and equal in standing to the east Roman world owed not a little to the link with the successor of St Peter. The benefits of the alliance were mutual, and with the decline of the Franks an unhappy period followed for the popes of the tenth and early eleventh centuries until the dramatic reassertion of Roman authority by Pope Gregory VII (Hildebrand). In the ninth century the dependence of the papacy on the Franks, coupled with the political distrust of Frankish military ambitions at Constantinople, formed a constant framework for the ecclesiological differences. Moreover, just as the papacy, the centre of gravity of the Latin west, derived a large increase in its authority and prestige from the successive missions to the Anglo-Saxons and to the Germanic peoples, so also the patriarchate of Constantinople was enhanced in dignity by the missions fostered by Photius to the Bulgarians, Slavs, and Russians. Photius contributed much towards the creation of the Byzantine Commonwealth described by the late Sir Dimitri Obolensky in a famous book under that title.

Photius was not the first Greek churchman to raise objection to the western *Filioque*. That initiative, foreshadowed in the fifth century by Theodoret's criticism of Cyril, first came with the monotheletes during the seventh century, and their objection no doubt helped to make western leaders such as Pope Agatho remarkably silent on the subject. The episode of controversy between Theodore of Canterbury and Wilfrid of York may have been on the margins of this friction. Nevertheless, it is not until the *Mystagogia* of Photius that the western *Filioque*, sung liturgically by the Frankish churches and not objected to by ninth-century popes after Leo III, becomes a virtual article by which the Latin churches are seen to fall. Photius was probably out of office when his passionate denunciation was diffused in the form in which we now have the text, and the immediate effect was not great. But he had planted a delayed-action bomb with enormous destructive potential. Surprisingly the *Mystagogia* does not pronounce 'anathema', the word of ultimate condemnation. But then the *Filioque* was not synodically defined western dogma in his time.

By 1100–1200 the popes and their theological advisers may have begun to assume that the *Filioque* was a truth which the Greek east would in time come to accept, at least as an act of obedience to the universal authority of the see of Rome. Pope Innocent III would find that the Bulgarian Khan, perhaps in reaction to the western conquest of Constantinople by the Fourth Crusade in 1204, was glad to acknowledge papal sovereignty, and that the correspondence between them at no point suggested the existence of a dogmatic difference needing to be sorted out.[6]

At Constantinople or Nicaea no such optimistic estimate could easily be found. The *Filioque*, so far from being vindicated by the supreme authority of St Peter's successor, was the principal factor discrediting the absoluteness of that authority.

---

[6] Innocent III, *Reg.* 6. 142–4 (PL 215. 155–8).

31

LIUDPRAND OF CREMONA
IN CONSTANTINOPLE

In the century following the patriarchate of Photius, relations between Constantinople and Rome or the west generally fluctuated in close correspondence with political factors, and political concerns became a more potent factor than religious or theological matters. The Carolingian kingdoms passed into decline, and in the west power shifted to the Saxons under King Otto I. He inherited the Frankish determination to establish a western empire, making use of the papacy's blessing to give it the name of Roman, but with an ambition to enjoy the prestige imparted by alliance, if possible a marriage alliance, with the imperial house at Byzantium. Tenth-century diplomacy regarded young princesses as exploitable instruments for sealing pacts of friendship. There were precedents for Otto's aspiration.

A vivid picture of the situation in the mid-tenth century is provided by Liudprand, a Lombard who became bishop of Cremona by 962.[1] His stepfather was a successful ambassador to Constantinople in 942; he obtained Greek fire to help the Italians in repelling Arabs invading from Africa, and in 949 sent Liudprand on an embassy to the emperor so that he could learn Greek. Liudprand moved from north Italy to the Saxon court of King Otto, whose star was rising rapidly, and there became a friend of the ambassador from the Caliph in Spain, Recemund bishop of Elvira, at whose instigation he wrote his famous *Antapodosis*, 'Tit for Tat'—a collection of anecdotes,

---

[1] Liudprand's works are edited by J. Becker for MGH, 3rd edn., 1915 repr. 1977. A sermon was first printed by B. Bischoff, *Anecdota Novissima* (Stuttgart, 1984), 20–34. The *Legatio* (principally drawn on for the text above) is edited with translation, commentary, and bibliography by Brian Scott for Bristol Classical Press (London, 1993). An older English translation by F. A. Wright (London, 1930, repr. 1993) includes *Antapodosis* and the *Chronicle of Otto*. His work is illuminated by modern studies: e.g. by Karl Leyser, 'Ends and Means in Liutprand of Cremona', *Byzantinische Forschungen*, 13 (1988), 119–43; J. Koder and T. Weber, *Liudprand von Cremona in Konstantinopel* (Vienna, 1980); M. Rentschler, *Liudprand von Cremona, eine Studie zum ost-westlichen Kulturgefälle im Mittelalter* (Frankfurt a. M., 1981); J. N. Sutherland, *Liudprand of Cremona* (Spoleto, 1988); R. Levine, 'Liudprand of Cremona, History and Debasement in the Tenth Century', *Mittellateinisches Jahrbuch*, 26 (1991), 70–84. See also J. D. Howard-Johnston (ed.), *Byzantium and the West 850–1200* (Amsterdam, 1988), 119–43; K. Leyser, *Communications and Power in Medieval Europe: The Carolingian and Ottonian Centuries*, ed. T. Reuter (London, 1994).

many of violence and sex in high places. The work contains grisly portrayals of the Hungarian attacks on north Italy, where the standard of living was beyond barbarian dreams, or of Slav boys castrated at Verdun market for sale to Moorish princes in Spain. Liudprand himself bought a few to be gifts to the east Roman emperor, where by long tradition eunuchs were valued, either as chamberlains in the palace or as castrati singers in choirs.

In the *Antapodosis* Liudprand's account of his reception by the emperor at Constantinople is favourable. But in the 960s relations between King Otto of Saxony and the east Roman emperor deteriorated. Otto was determined to rule the whole of Italy. He dealt sharply with Lombard dukes in the south and with Pope John XII (955–64) who had crowned him 'emperor of the Romans' at St Peter's but whose private life was unregenerate and an unedifying scandal. As Otto advanced southwards, he moved into Apulia and Calabria, territory which the Byzantine emperors regarded as under their sovereignty.[2] Otto observed that some barbarian kings had enhanced their status by arranging dynastic marriages with Byzantine princes or princesses. He was ambitious to do the same. So in 968 Liudprand, chosen no doubt because of his linguistic skill, was sent on embassy to the emperor Nikephoros Phokas (963–9) at Constantinople in hope that he could negotiate a political marriage between Otto's son, lately raised to imperial status, and a princess of the imperial house. The probable candidate for the duty of bride was a young girl named Anna, daughter of Romanos II (emperor 959–63) and 'born in the purple chamber' of the palace. The suit was wholly unsuccessful. (The princess Anna was later betrothed to Vladimir of Kiev and thereby brought the Russians into the Orthodox Christian fold, converting her husband to Christianity.)[3]

At Constantinople, where from previous visits Liudprand had 'Greek friends', the reception was arctic. For the months spent in the capital he found himself closely guarded, at times under house arrest, as if Otto was in collusion with seditious enemies of Nikephoros Phokas who could be intriguing for a change of emperor. This emperor was in fact to die at an assassin's hand in the following year. He could have good reason to fear

---

[2] *Legatio* 7.

[3] Otto's matrimonial proposals to east Roman emperors are discussed in a symposium on the Greek empress Theophano, edited by Adelbert Davids (Cambridge, 1995). See also A. von Euw and P. Schreiner, *Kaiserin Theophano, Begegnung des Ostens und Westens um die Wende des ersten Jahrtausends: Gedenkschrift des Kölner Schnütgenmuseums*, 2 vols. (Cologne, 1991), 385–96. Otto II eventually married Theophano in the time of John Tzimiskes (ruled December 969–January 976) who was her uncle. Constantine Porphyrogenitus (*De administrando imperio* 13), observing that barbarian embassies normally seek imperial robes, or Greek fire, or marriage with a princess, advises on discreet ways of refusing all three. Earlier in the tenth century Patriarch Nicolas I sought to persuade the Bulgarian Khan to abstain from aggression by offering him gold and royal robes (*ep.* 31, p. 214 Jenkins–Westerink).

Otto's intentions especially if the news had leaked to him that he was arranging for a Latin bishop to be consecrated and travel to Kiev. In anger and resentment Liudprand wrote the account of his embassy to instil in his royal Saxon master the maximum distrust of Byzantine intentions.

The conflict about sovereignty in Apulia and south Italy complicated the task for the embassy. The ecumenical patriarch asserted his jurisdiction there by mandating the bishop of Otranto, raised to the rank of an archbishopric, to consecrate bishops for several Apulian sees. He also directed that the liturgy must be in Greek, not Latin.[4] The popes were bound to think nominating for sees so near to Rome was or ought to be a papal right. Otto had attempted to capture Bari, and certainly made trouble there for the defence. The Byzantine emperor Nikephoros Phokas was sure to regard Otto as putting pressure on him by intimidation.

Nikephoros did not tell Liudprand directly that the young Otto II was socially unacceptable, a malodorous Saxon 'clothed in furs and skins'.[5] But the princess Anna being 'born in the purple' was beyond the reach of a Saxon monarch. Nikephoros made it clear that he would be willing to stretch a point and consent to the marriage only on the impossible political condition that Otto would restore east Roman authority not merely in Apulia but also in the once Byzantine cities of Ravenna and Rome and the lands between.[6] Liudprand sharply refused to endorse an assurance given to the emperor by some ambassadors from Otto, who came to Constantinople a year before him, that the Saxon king would never do anything to injure the Byzantine interest.

But from the moment of his arrival Liudprand knew that the imperial court was not pleased to see him. The bishop of Cremona felt insulted at being lodged with his party in a particularly draughty palace of ice-cold marble. When he was invited to a meal with Greek bishops, their austere lifestyle did not impress him, and the food, heavily seasoned with garlic and onion, was not to his taste. To be invited to supper and be offered nothing more than a lettuce (no doubt on a fast day) proved the inferiority of the entire eastern episcopate. Moreover, the Greek bishops had no servants to see to their shopping and to serve their meals. Retsina was for him a horrid drink. Liudprand made no allowances for the fact that there was a severe famine at the time of his stay in the capital. He resented the Greek assumption that Germanic barbarians were impoverished and uncultured. The Byzantine court seemed to him shabby and living on a distinguished past.

The disagreement turned on divergent views of authority in Church and State. Liudprand was told that 'the stupid Pope' failed to comprehend that Constantine the Great, whose successor Nikephoros was, had transferred to

---

[4] *Legatio* 62.   [5] Ibid. 53.   [6] Ibid. 15.

New Rome the entire sovereignty over the Roman empire and brought to Constantinople all the senate and nobility, leaving in old Rome a mere underclass of riff-raff such as lived there now.[7] In another context Liudprand himself could concede that the barbarian west too held in utter contempt the rabble of Old Rome.[8] Above all, the point was repeatedly made that the Byzantine court felt much offended that, following the precedent of the Franks, the Saxon king had assumed the title 'emperor of the Romans' and, worse still, had addressed Nikephoros as 'emperor of the Greeks'.[9]

The offence was aggravated when Byzantine spies discovered Liudprand to have bought substantial lengths of purple silk, claiming it was for ecclesiastical vestments, when it was obviously intended for Otto and his son to wear as imperial insignia. Purple silk of top quality was reserved for the emperor and his empress at Constantinople. Inferior cloth, however, was marketed in the west by merchants from Amalfi and Venice. Nevertheless, Liudprand found his purchase confiscated.[10]

In Byzantine eyes the Frankish and then the Saxon kings were a power to be reckoned with, but their standing was not more than that of a particularly important barbarian. Constantine VII Porphyrogenitus had laid down that Byzantine princesses were not to marry foreigners, though an exception might be made in favour of Franks; he wanted to justify obtaining a Frankish bride for his son Romanos II.[11] When eventually in 971 a Byzantine bride was brought to the west for Otto II, she was Theophano, niece of John Tzimiskes (murderer and successor of Nikephoros Phokas), a disappointment to the west because she was not 'born in the purple' and therefore, as the western chronicler Thietmar of Merseburg put it, not the 'virgo desiderata'.[12]

Liudprand's ecclesiastical career had given him some familiarity with theological problems of biblical interpretation and with church history, when even among highly placed clergy in both east and west there could be woeful ignorance on this subject. He found himself engaged in disputes about the exegesis of biblical texts used by the Byzantines in the interest of diminishing the dignity and standing of western barbarians like himself. He was frankly

---

[7] *Legatio* 51. Balsamon (in RP i. 148–9) reports that several patriarchs of Constantinople, including Cerularius, unconvincingly claimed this transfer. Paul Alexander argued that the Byzantines were not adapting the Donation of Constantine: *Religious and Political History and Thought in the Byzantine Empire* (Aldershot, 1978), ch. IV, pp. 14–15. Balsamon interpreted them otherwise (above, Ch. 15 n. 2).

[8] *Legatio* 12.   [9] Ibid. 47, and 50.   [10] Ibid. 53–5, 65.

[11] Constantine Porphyrogenitus, *De administrando imperio* 13, ed. Moravcsik–Jenkins 70–2; commentary volume, 67.

[12] See n. 3; Thietmar, *Chronicon* 2. 15 (ed. MGH SRG ix. 56). Greek canonists ruled that the anointing at Tzimiskes' coronation sufficed to confer absolution for the murder of his predecessor: RP iii. 44.

told that the then Pope, to whose authority he was appealing to justify his master's high imperial title, was notorious for gross simony, trading in the Holy Spirit for money. The charge was evidently a barbed reference to the debauched life of Pope John XII, who was believed to have financed his too numerous mistresses at the Lateran palace by the sale of episcopal consecrations. Contemporary kings exerting their power to nominate bishops were similarly offering appointments to those willing to pay well. Rodulfus Glaber could comment astringently on the practice (*Hist.* 2. 6. 11–12).

Nevertheless, Byzantine poisoned arrows discharged against the west did not include any reference to the western doctrine of the Trinity.

To the Greek accusation of papal immorality Liudprand retorted that 'all heresies' had taken their rise in New Rome. For instance, grave heresy concerning the resurrection fostered by the patriarch Eutychius had needed correction from Pope Gregory the Great; and a century earlier bishop Ennodius of Pavia had come to the eastern capital to bring to an end a serious degree of unorthodoxy.

Nikephoros and his bishops were not convinced of western orthodoxy, and made their point by inquiring what synods were recognized by Liudprand and the western churches. Liudprand's list was, with one exception, embarrassingly Greek: Nicaea, Chalcedon, Ephesus, Carthage, Antioch, Ankyra, and Constantinople. Which council in the capital he did not specify. The sharp comment came at once: 'You forget to mention Saxony.' Not much had been done there to maintain the orthodox tradition. The sneer no doubt referred to the Frankish Council of Frankfurt in 794, which mortally offended Greek iconophiles by its comfort for unrepentant iconoclasts. The ecumenical patriarch ironically excused Liudprand by saying the Germanic Council was too recent for its decisions to reach the Greek churches and to be known to their canonists.[13]

At table with the emperor and his senior bureaucrats Liudprand found himself forced to listen to a catalogue of insults against 'Latins and Germans', who were generally labelled 'Franks'.[14] If the *Filioque* was mentioned, he abstained from recording it. Nor do we hear of complaints about clerical celibacy, Saturday fasts, lax observance of Lent, or the Latin restriction of confirmation to bishops (cf. below, p. 205).

Byzantine memory about 1100, represented by Nicetas, archivist of Nicaea, understood that patriarch Sergius II (1001–19), who enjoyed peace with Pope John XVIII (1004–9), came to disagree with Rome for reasons which Nicetas could not discover. Nicetas thought it could be a dispute about sees, i.e. primacy.[15] The same information was known half a century earlier to patriarch Peter of Antioch in his correspondence with Michael

---

[13] *Legatio* 21.   [14] Ibid. 33.   [15] PG 120. 718 D.

Cerularius, who was abruptly told by Peter not to regard the question of naming in the diptychs as a weighty matter.[16] A possible cause of disagreement was offence taken if, for the first time at Rome, the *Filioque* was inserted into the creed at the coronation of the emperor Henry II on 14 February 1014 under Pope Benedict VIII (1012–24). That the creed was incorporated in the mass for the first time at Rome is precisely attested by Berno, abbot of Reichenau, who was a protegé of the emperor Henry of Saxony and was present at the ceremony.[17] He says nothing about the *Filioque*, but that it was part of the creed is a presumption based on a virtual certainty that the Saxon churches were already accustomed to it as was also the monastery at Reichenau on Lake Constance (Bodensee). In other words, Berno would have been more likely to comment on its omission than on its inclusion, had he commented at all on the matter.

But it does not seem plausible to suggest that this singing of the *Filioque* precipitated a grave breach between Constantinople and Rome. If anything in that ceremony offended a representative of the eastern emperor, it is more likely to have been the Pope's investiture of the Saxon emperor with the golden orb, symbol of world authority. Henry II was no friend to the east Roman empire, and in 1018 was encouraging a revolt against Constantinople in Apulia, a revolt not the less irritating for being unsuccessful.

All things considered, a more persuasive ground for explaining the breach reported by Peter of Antioch and Nicetas is the decision of the east Roman emperor in 1019 to install a Greek archbishop for the Bulgarian churches at the see of Ochrid. It was one thing to have a Bulgarian in that see, but an episcopal agent of east Rome was a political hazard for Rome in the west.

At Byzantium the old sovereignty over provinces in south Italy and Sicily remained an assertion that New Rome was the capital of the old Roman empire extending to the western half of the Mediterranean world, not only to the Greek-speaking provinces. The visibility of the emperor's authority in Greek-speaking Sicily, Calabria, and Apulia was enhanced if ecclesiastical jurisdiction was conterminous with political control. In 1024 a Greek embassy came to the see of Rome with rich presents and gold offered to sweeten an agreement under which the popes would recognize the authority of the bishop of Constantinople as parallel within the east Roman empire to the primacy held in the west by the bishop of Rome. The formula proposed declared that the Church of Constantinople should be recognized as

---

[16] PG 120. 796. The correspondence concerning the quarrels of 1054 is conveniently read in the edition of C. Will (Ch. 9 n. 5). Peter of Antioch's letters are in Will. A good monograph by Mahlon H. Smith, *And Taking Bread . . . Cerularius and the Azyme Controversy of 1054* (Paris, 1978).

[17] PL 142. 1060–1. When Berno asked why the Roman Church had not included the creed after the Gospel at the eucharist, he received the reply that it had never been defiled by the dung of heresy, and that other churches needed to chant the creed more often. Berno adds that he does not know whether Rome still keeps the creed in the mass or not.

'universal in its own sphere' just as the Roman see possessed universal authority extending 'throughout the world'. The negotiation is never mentioned by Byzantine historians, but is recorded by the western chronicler Rodulfus Glaber.[18] Initially the Roman see was impressed by the cash on offer, but the leaking of the proposal produced a furore in the west, and Pope John XIX found himself receiving much vehement advice that he should not concede virtual equipollence to his colleague at Constantinople. The notion that a division of responsibility for the Church should closely correspond to the political division of power between east and west was in principle objectionable to western minds.

[18] Rodulfus Glaber, *Hist.* 4. 1. 2–4, pp. 172–6 France.

32

THE NORMANS IN THE SOUTH: CARDINAL HUMBERT: THE COUNCIL OF ROME (1059): UNLEAVENED BREAD

The inhabitants of southern Italy had for some considerable time past been accustomed to the presence of Arabs coming from north Africa and trading, at times raiding, but not always a dangerous threat. They could well have found the Arabs less uncomfortable neighbours than either the Byzantine authorities or the aggressive Normans, both of whom wanted to dominate the area.

Rising tension over political and ecclesiastical control in south Italy and Sicily mounted sharply with the arrival of invading Normans in the eleventh century. They were unwelcome both to the papacy and to the eastern empire, and alliance between emperor and pope was a possible answer. The patriarch of Constantinople, Michael Cerularius (1043–58), who had a political past and owed his promotion to the emperor Constantine IX Monomachos, wrote a friendly letter to Pope Leo IX proposing cooperation in opposing 'the Franks'. No reply came.

The aggressive Normans in Apulia stopped Greek services and imposed the use of Latin and western liturgies. In 1053 papal and Byzantine forces separately suffered serious defeats. Leo IX was taken prisoner. Nevertheless the Pope could hardly regret Latin usage in churches. In the east, in Constantinople, and western Bulgaria, the news of the closure of Greek services in Apulia and Calabria caused anger.

The Norman intruders were not likely to have been sympathetic to popular Greek piety, which had its own favourite saints and icons. Perhaps some reconciliation was available in the shrine of one Latin saint in south Italy, Dominic of Sora, at whose tomb miracles of healing were attested.[1]

A Latin custom which seemed strange and indeed very wrong to the Greek churches of south Italy was the use of unleavened bread (*azyma*) at mass. The western churches had become confident that this must have been apostolic custom. In fact Ambrose, *De sacramentis* 4. 4. 14 'meus panis est usitatus', supported by a sermon of Augustine (*S. Guelf.* 7), makes it certain that

---

[1] See F. Dolbeau in *Mélanges Éc. Franç. Rome, Moyen Âge*, 102/1 (1990), 7–78; C. V. Franklin, *Mediaeval Studies*, 55 (1993), 285–345; J. M. Sansterre, *Revue Mabillon*, NS 7 (68) (1996), 20–1.

late in the fourth century the west was using leavened bread. It is not known when the change was made. Perhaps the intention was to distinguish the sacred species from bread at home. The Apostle's words in 1 Cor. 5: 9 may have influenced the shift.

The absence of leaven had practical merits. It avoided falling crumbs which distressed the faithful. If the host were reserved for the sick, it did not quickly become putrid. But Greeks were not sure it was bread, and some were sure that without leaven it was not. If not, then God's will was being flouted.

The earliest western witness to *azyma* is Alcuin, in one of his letters (137) in 798, but his reference does not suggest that in his time it was a recent innovation. *Azyma* emerged as contentious because Greek and Roman rites existed side by side in Sicily and Magna Graecia. By coincidence the dispute arose at Constantinople at a time when there was an influx of Armenians to posts in the capital and when the emperor and the bishops were forcing conversion on dissenting Armenians, who also used *azyma*. The Orthodox case, even when helped by Studite polemic,[2] was weakened if the coerced Armenians could point to identical customs in Latin churches at Constantinople. At least against the Latins the Greeks did not need to find fresh arguments.

Visitors to Constantinople from south Italy were offended by Greek insistence on ordinary bread. In a letter to Peter patriarch of Antioch (at one time among the higher clergy at Hagia Sophia) Patriarch Michael Cerularius, in office from 1043, reports that he had suffered hard words from a high-ranking soldier Argyros, a Lombard from Bari, who had had to be repelled from communion because of his protests favouring *azyma*.

A strong statement in favour of unleavened eucharistic bread comes early in the ninth century from Fulda and the pen of Rabanus Maurus, *de Institutione Christiana* i. 31 (PL 107. 318–19), a work in which he also insists on the *Filioque* as a disputed proposition. The Fulda monks were evidently being told to follow the Frankish lead against the east. Another insistence is on standing for the liturgical Gospel.

Early in 1053 an open letter was sent to John the Greek bishop of Trani (north of Bari), by Leo archbishop of Ochrid, particularly warning him against the grave error of using bread for the eucharistic liturgy which was unleavened (*azyma*): if unleavened, it was not actually bread and, if it was not bread as commonly defined and understood, was the eucharist being done as Christ intended? In short its validity was at least doubtful. At Archbishop

---

[2] Nicetas Stethatos' anti-Armenian pamphlet is printed by J. Hergenröther, *Monumenta graeca ad Photium eiusque historiam pertinentia* (Regensburg, 1869, repr. ed. J. M. Hussey, Farnborough, 1969), 139–54.

Leo's express request, John of Trani had copies made for circulation to the Pope and to other Italian bishops.[3] It is a reasonable presumption that Leo expected the Italian episcopate to support his judgement that unleavened bread was Judaistic and unsuitable for the sacrament of the new covenant.

Leo of Ochrid had previously been archivist at St Sophia, and was the first Greek-speaker to be bishop of his see in Bulgaria. His past gave him close links with Constantinople. It was assumed that behind the bishop of Ochrid lay the mind of the ecumenical patriarch Michael Cerularius. That is a possible hypothesis, but is not necessarily so. At least it is certain that the patriarch agreed with him. The reaction in Constantinople to the news from Apulia was to close churches using the Latin rite,[4] thereby hurting numerous traders from Amalfi, Pisa, Venice, and Genoa. That was bound to provoke anger at Rome. Leo IX was a reforming pope. Reformers seldom like deviations from a norm. There is usually a preference for uniformity.

Cardinal Humbert

The imprudent closure of Latin churches in Constantinople was bound to foul the nest in the delicate diplomatic negotiations between emperor and pope to achieve an alliance capable of checking the land-hungry Normans in southern Italy, where they were unwelcome to both contracting parties.

On behalf of Pope Leo IX a tough remonstrance was drafted by his able and aggressive old friend, Humbert,[5] formerly archbishop in Sicily but brought into Leo's administration as bishop of the minor see of Silva Candida and a Cardinal. Berengar of Tours, whom Humbert was soon to harass, called him a 'stupid Burgundian'. Lanfranc said he came from Lotharingia (Lorraine). In Sicily he would have had contact with Greek churches and clergy but had evidently not been impressed. His text for Leo complained of Greeks calling Latins *azymitae* as if this were the name of a heresy. The Greeks at Constantinople should remember that in or near Rome numerous Greek monasteries and churches were vulnerable to retributive action.[6] He brushed aside as irrelevant logomachies all theological questions (an allusion to the *Filioque?*), and proclaimed loud and at length the absolute supremacy of St Peter's successors in the see of Rome. The recognition of this supreme jurisdiction was vindicated for Humbert and Leo by the Donation of

---

[3] Will 56–64. Anton Michel, *Humbert und Kerullarios*, 2 vols. (Paderborn, 1924–30), ii. 282–9 demonstrated that Leo of Ochrid was the author of the encyclical, not Cerularius.

[4] Will 76ᵇ34; 80ᵇ37.

[5] For Humbert's authorship see the proof in Michel, *Humbert und Kerullarios*, i. 44. For a general account of Humbert see Ute Blumenthal s.v. in *Theologische Realenzylopädie*, xv (Berlin, 1980), 682–5. On the chronology of events see M. Kaplan, *Byzantinoslavica*, 56 (1995), 147–57.

[6] Will 81ᵃ3.

Constantine, from which Humbert's text included substantial citations.[7] Moreover, the Roman Church had never deviated from orthodoxy whereas there was a long list of heretical bishops of Constantinople. Humbert supposed that Honorius was one of these.[8]

At one point Humbert declared that he could produce a list of more than ninety heresies, all of which had emerged from the eastern churches. His number was derived not from Augustine, who catalogued eighty-seven, nor from Epiphanius, whose list of eighty corresponded to the number of Solomon's concubines in Song of Songs 6: 8, but from the 'semi-Pelagian' writer Praedestinatus.[9] The Greek 'deletion' of the *Filioque* seemed to Humbert to be derived from the heresy of the fourth-century Pneumatomachi led by Macedonius bishop of Constantinople; for he found it in 'the creed of Athanasius', Epiphanius, and Cyril of Alexandria. Above all, with his own ears he had heard the *Filioque* decisively affirmed by the mouth of the reigning supreme pontiff, Leo IX, during a conference at Bari: Peter had spoken.[10] Humbert would himself raise the issue to accuse the Greeks.

The mood at Rome under Pope Leo IX was one strongly favouring reform. A few years later in 1059 the Pope, fortified by the militant support of Humbert, would hold a major council in Rome hoping to clear up the widespread practice of simony. Important and wealthy laymen were a necessary source of support to anyone with an ambition to be a bishop, and if money did not pass before the election it was commonly expected afterwards by way of reward and thanks for indispensable assistance. Two other matters loomed large on the council's agenda. It seemed urgent to bring to an end the decisive voice of the emperor in the election of a new pope, a power of veto with a long history. At the same time there was a growing determination to enforce the celibacy of the clergy. This could be a particular source of friction in southern Italy and Sicily, where Latin clergy could be in close proximity to Greek parish priests who were allowed to have wives and children. That could never be an easy juxtaposition. A canon of the Roman Council of 1059 strictly prohibited laity from hearing mass celebrated by a priest possessed of either a wife or a concubine. That would no doubt create practical difficulties in rural areas in the west where villagers could be anxious for their wives and daughters if the local priest had no woman living with him, whether formally married or not (usually not), and also for impecunious bishops who relied on the annual fines paid by priests to allow the practice to continue.

---

[7] Will 70^{b} ff.   [8] Will 68^{b}43 ff.; 142^{a}26.   [9] Will 78^{a}2 ff.
[10] Will 68^{b}44; PL 53. 587–8, identified by Michel, *Humbert und Kerullarios*, ii. 410–15.

The council's enactments reflected a concern to mark a sharper line of separation between clergy and laity.

The same council forced Berengar of Tours, archdeacon of Angers, to assent to the affirmation that change wrought by eucharistic consecration is not merely spiritual (which sounded subjective) but also physical, so that what communicants crush with their teeth is the corporeal reality of Christ's body, not a symbolic representation conveying that reality. Berengar's enforced confession was written for him by Humbert. It became a matter for prolonged debate in catholic schools of theology and canon law whether Humbert's text was no less heretical than the doctrine of Berengar. Under Gregory VII there was a rehearing of Berengar, ending in a considerably modified confession.

Humbert admired the manner in which Pope Nicolas I had dealt with Photius,[11] ordering (so Humbert understood) the closure of St Sophia until such time as he was obeyed in his command that Photius stand down and be replaced by a reinstated Ignatius. By its inherent nature as the unity of Christ's Body the Church was unbreakable; nevertheless its continuance in unity depended on unquestioning submission to the bishops of Rome.[12] As for the Greek challenge to the western use of unleavened bread, that tradition depended on unerring authority. Was the Church of St Peter to learn, as long as a thousand and twenty years after the Lord's Passion, how this redemptive act ought to be commemorated?[13] To suggest that the correct use lay concealed from St Peter would be incredible impudence. The arrogance of the bishops at the eastern capital of Constantinople was evident from their claim to possess an authority superior to that of the older and Petrine patriarchates of Alexandria and Antioch.

Humbert had made the decision to conduct his campaign on the ground of authority, but with propositions that were axiomatic to him and highly contentious to the minds of the eastern churches.

Each opposing side in the controversy about *azyma* regarded the other as manifesting culpable disrespect for authority. To the Greeks the Lord had commanded the use of 'bread' for this supremely sacred rite; to use unleavened bread, even if there might be good pastoral reasons advanced, was not obeying the Lord's will. Moreover, unleavened bread was Judaistic, a Passover rite belonging to the old covenant. The bread and wine of the Last Supper were the inaugurating signs of the new covenant, and Old Testament precedent could not imaginably be invoked to enforce the form of rite used under the New.

---

[11] Humbert, *Rationes de S. Spiritus processione a Patre et Filio*, ed. ibid. i. 97–111.
[12] Will 66–7.   [13] Will 68. 21 ff.

The debate turned in part on the difference in chronology between St John and the Synoptic gospels, vigorously debated in the second century and later. The eastern churches finally came to follow St John in holding that the crucifixion of Jesus was on 'the preparation', which implied that the Last Supper was not an actual Passover meal using unleavened bread. The west preferred to follow the Synoptics in the judgement that the Last Supper was indeed the Passover meal and therefore followed all the precepts of the Torah. The Lord who came to fulfil the Law, not to destroy it, would certainly have used *azyma*.

Latent in the apparently trivial ceremonial quarrel was a deeper issue concerning the relation of old and new covenants under the Christian dispensation. The western participants in this controversy thought the eastern position improperly disparaged the word of God in the Old Testament.

Initially the one and only issue put forward by Leo archbishop of Bulgaria was that of unleavened bread, *azyma*. But an undercurrent stemming from the influential monastery of Studios had a longer list of anti-Roman complaints. The background of this may have been located in tension between the Studite monks and their patriarch Cerularius, who had vexed them by endeavouring to stop the monks wearing special belts. Reconciliation with the patriarch was achieved partly by the participation of the monk Nicetas Stethatos in the campaign against eucharistic unleavened bread, partly by the patriarch encouraging the veneration of Nicetas Stethatos' favourite saint, Symeon the New Theologian, who had once been censured by the patriarchal synod for the risky doctrine that authority in the Church lay with charismatic spiritual men, not with the ordained. In 1052 the patriarch brought the saint's relics back to Constantinople.

For his part Nicetas Stethatos wrote a short treatise widening the dispute about *azyma* to include Rome's Saturday fasts and priestly celibacy, so mistakenly regarded at Rome as universally compulsory.[14] A weak point in his case was the claim that since the canons of the Quinisext assembly *in Trullo* of 692 were deemed to have the authority of the Sixth Council, these canons could also be held to be ratified by Pope Agatho. At least he was better informed than his patriarch Cerularius who supposed that the 'Sixth Council' (*sic*) had excommunicated Pope Vigilius for his arrogance in refusing to join with their assembly.[15] This error, however, may simply be a different numeration of ecumenical councils.

---

[14] Will 127–36. Nicetas' *Opuscula* and *Letters* are edited by J. Darrouzès (Sources Chrétiennes, 81; Paris, 1961). See in general the article on him by F. Tinnefeld in *Theologische Realenzyklopädie*, xxiv (Berlin, 1994), 463–4.

[15] Will 178. He was gently corrected by Patriarch Peter of Antioch.

33

POPE LEO IX'S LEGATION
TO CONSTANTINOPLE (1054):
HUMBERT AND CERULARIUS

The dispute about the eucharistic bread moved Pope Leo IX to send to Constantinople a small but potent legation led by Cardinal Humbert. He had the special merit that his education had included study of Greek. He was also by nature and inclination pugnacious, and expected any patriarch of Constantinople to be devious and untrustworthy. He was accompanied on his embassy by Frederic, chancellor of the Roman Church, and by Peter archbishop of Amalfi. Since the merchants of Amalfi had substantial trading interests in the eastern capital, the Pope had to assure the emperor that there was no call for suspicions of the archbishop's possible intentions. At Beneventum the three legates conferred with the Byzantine general Argyros,[1] a soldier of Latin church sympathies who had, during a five-year stay in Constantinople, earned the gratitude of the emperor by saving his life. He was rewarded by being appointed *katepáno* or generalissimo in command of Byzantine forces defending south Italy. During his stay at the eastern capital, he had crossed verbal swords with the patriarch by urging the case for unleavened bread. Arguments against the traditional Greek usage of ordinary bread were familiar to him.

The legates arrived at Constantinople about the time that Pope Leo IX in Italy died (19 April 1054), and presented themselves at the palace to be received there with honour and respect. The papal letter addressed to the patriarch Michael was delivered, and the patriarch found to his alarm that the seal had been broken and then replaced. Perhaps alien matter never authorized by the Pope had been added or substituted. Cerularius suspected the hand of Argyros in this, and felt the gravest doubts whether the offensive matter he was reading could really be the authentic text of Leo IX. He feared that his old enemy Argyros had conspired with Humbert to turn the issue into a personal attack on himself.

---

[1] A summary life of Argyros in Vera von Falkenhausen, *Untersuchungen über die byzantinische Herrschaft in Süditalien vom 9. bis 11. Jhdt* (Wiesbaden, 1967), 187 ff.

Meanwhile Humbert discovered that copies of an anti-western pamphlet by Nicetas Stethatos, of the monastery of Studios, were circulating. He was able to get hold of a copy of the pamphlet and to compose a Latin refutation. It might be judged a betrayal of some sense of weakness that his piece had more vulgar abuse than considered reasoning, such as telling the Studite monk that a critic of enforced celibacy would be at home in a brothel.[2] He found a sympathetic ear in the emperor (though he must have had reason to regret that the patriarch of Constantinople exercised more power over the Church than the emperor), and the palace forced Nicetas to withdraw his attack and see it burnt.

The political situation required the emperor to be anxious to avoid offending the representatives of the Roman see. If the east Roman empire was to retain its influence in south Italy and Sicily in face of the Norman moves to take over all this territory, there was only one authority capable of restraining the invaders, and that was the Pope. The Pope for his part also looked to the east Roman emperor to safeguard Roman interests against the Normans. Humbert may well have felt that with the emperor's support, he could use abrasive words in dealing with the patriarch. There was no subject on which he was not naturally abrasive.

Humbert defended the use of unleavened bread on the ground that Christ himself had certainly used it at the passover meal, the Last Supper. For him it was immemorial western tradition. The carelessness of Greek churches in regard to the eucharistic bread was, in Humbert's view, demonstrated by a general lack of reverence in regard to the unconsumed remains at the end of the liturgy, commonly buried in the ground or thrown into a well.[3]

It is a striking fact that in the first instance the controversy turned on pastoral and liturgical practice, not on a major dogmatic question. Only after the initial exchanges about *azyma* did the dispute move to other matters, with the *Filioque* coming into the debate almost as an afterthought.

Humbert was also repelled by the Greek liturgical custom of dividing the host with a knife, and dipping it in the wine.

In any event the use of ordinary bread baked at the bakery by unclean hands seemed to him distasteful and insufficiently reverent towards the unique character of this bread to be offered and consecrated.

Remains at the Eucharist

Humbert's protest against the burial of the consecrated remains is the earliest known evidence of east–west tension on this subject. The New Testament

---

[2] Will 136–50. Peter Damian entitled his exhortation to priestly continence 'Liber Gomorrhianus' (PL 145. 159–90), dedicated to Pope Leo IX.

[3] Will 109.

provided no guidance in regard to the proper use of the consecrated elements not consumed during the community liturgy. All believers knew that this was no longer common bread, and the cup no longer to be treated as ordinary wine; by God's act in answer to the Church's prayer and by virtue of the word of Christ himself the species were invested with special dignity. But two broadly distinguishable customs emerged.[4]

On the one hand, in Tertullian's time about AD 200 or in the *Apostolic Tradition* of Hippolytus,[5] sacred bread was taken home, where baptized laity were commanded to take steps to ensure that it was not eaten by an animal or by a pagan. The host was there in case of grave illness or an unforeseen deathbed. It was soon customary to give the eucharist to a dying person, in anticipation of the heavenly feast of which it was a pledge and foretaste.[6] It became common for the species to be carried like an amulet hanging round the neck[7] to assure protection on a dangerous journey—most journeys in late antiquity being hazardous from bandits or storms. Carried in this manner by a bishop or priest, the sacred gift was immediately available if called for by the sick and dying.[8]

When a church was suffering persecution, the deacons' responsibility included the taking of the eucharistic bread to members of the community languishing in prison or sick, in pledge of their membership of Christ's Body.[9]

In time, private and domestic reservation came to seem dangerous because of the risks of profanation or even magic, so that the proper place came to be under the priest's control at the church, in medieval times (as directed by the fourth Lateran Council, 1215, canon 20) under lock in a safe. Even so, there were reports of theft for superstitious and magical purposes.

A further factor which made reservation pastorally desirable was the large growth in numbers especially during the fourth century and later. At the memorial of an apostolic martyr, such as the shrines of St Peter and St Paul in Rome, or at the holy places in Jerusalem and Bethlehem, the flood of pilgrims at a high festival could become too great to make possible any accurate estimate of the numbers of communicants. The presiding clergy

---

[4] The subject has received magistral treatment from Otto Nussbaum, *Die Aufbewahrung der Eucharistie* (Bonn, 1979).

[5] Tertullian, *Ad uxorem* 2. 5; Hippolytus 37.

[6] e.g. Paulinus, *Vita Ambrosii* 47 (PL 14. 43); 'Cluniac Customs', by Udalric, writing about 1086 (PL 149. 653).

[7] An early instance is the letter of the eastern bishops at the Council of Serdica in 342 (CSEL 65. 55). Ambrose's unbaptized brother Satyrus in a ship wrecked on rocks obtained a consecrated species from a baptized fellow traveller, bound it in a cloth, and saved his life: *De excessu fratris* i. 43 (CSEL 73. 230–1).

[8] Ivo of Chartres, PL 161. 165.

[9] Justin Martyr, *Apol.* 1. 65, 67. Pope Damasus wrote a memorial epigram on a deacon Tarsicius who lost his life being arrested when he was taking the eucharist to a sick Christian.

needed consecrated bread and wine in reserve to avoid the embarrassment of far too much or far too little for the size of the congregation.

On the other hand there was also strong feeling that the community eucharist should always be using elements consecrated there and then, just as the children of Israel in the wilderness were miraculously provided with manna and forbidden to keep it beyond the actual day of its being given for consumption. The Old Testament directions for the celebration of Passover (Exod. 12) included repeated injunctions that no food should be left unconsumed—if not eaten, then consumed by fire. The president of the early Christian eucharist would either follow this model by committing the consecrated remains to the fire or he would reverently consume the remains himself (or ask the help of baptized laity, never catechumens).[10]

Reservation of the sacred elements is therefore ancient. In the west the extra-liturgical adoration of Christ in the signs of his presence is not established before the twelfth century and came to be much fostered by Cistercians and Franciscans. This mode of adoration became so influential a form of personal devotion for the individual that authority, for instance the Council of Trent (XXII 6), needed to stress the fundamental importance of communicating, not merely of being present in the church at the time of the offering or of seeing the host being elevated. Elevation is first attested late in the twelfth century, soon marked by an acclamation. A problem attaching to the elevation was simply that for some the seeing became a substitute for reception in communion. Hence the explicit insistence of the Council of Trent that the purpose of consecration is *ut sumatur*, that the consecrated host be received. Then elevation was right and acceptable.

In Humbert's time in the eleventh century a reverent consuming of consecrated remains was normal and prescribed in current western canon law. But western churches were already beginning to keep the remains under protection in a safe in the sacristy. Medieval clergy were aware that there were high risks of superstition if the host became treated as an amulet like a holy relic or a lucky charm. Herbert of Clairvaux mentions with apprehension peasants who carried the host like a talisman in hope that it might bring them wealth and health, and who commonly suffered disappointment.[11]

Humbert felt outraged when Greeks told him that a eucharist celebrated with unleavened bread was Judaistic and invalid.[12] He was no less offended that at least some Greeks rebaptized Christians who had received Latin baptism; that was to regard Latin Christians as falling outside the frontiers of the one Church (though it might be argued that they had received a baptism of desire). As for Greek accusations about the *Filioque*, Humbert's bizarre belief

[10] Hesychius of Jerusalem, *in Levit.* 2. 8 (PG 93. 886–7).
[11] PL 185. 374. On elevation see P. Browe, *Jahrbuch f. Liturgiewissenschaft*, 9 (1929), 20–66.
[12] Will 141.

was that the Greek Church had deleted the *Filioque* from a creed which orig-inally contained it under the influence of the fourth-century heretics who denied the full divinity of the Holy Spirit, Pneumatomachi.[13]

At Rome Cardinal Humbert had reordered the papal library and archive and knew Pope Nicolas I's correspondence with Photius. It seemed a model to follow.

Pope Leo IX initiated correspondence not with the ecumenical patriarch Michael but with the emperor, Constantine IX Monomachos. Towards the patriarch he expressed hostility and some degree of contempt. The Pope had been told a rumour that Michael had not passed through the proper sequence of orders before being consecrated to the episcopate; in short, perhaps he was yet another instance of a 'neophyte' being promoted in a manner that the papacy disapproved. It was understood in Rome that he was still using the offensive title 'ecumenical patriarch' to which Gregory the Great had stated objections nearly five centuries earlier. Moreover, had he not asserted his authority over the older and Petrine patriarchates of Alexandria and Antioch in a way that could only presuppose overweening ambition?

When Pope Leo IX decided that he must send a legation to Constantinople, the patriarch received no letter to inform him that he should expect the legates who were received by the emperor and lodged at the palace. Michael Cerularius was systematically ignored: none of the normal courtesies were shown in his presence, and throughout the action the con-duct of the legates presupposed that he was expected to be the defendant on a grave charge and the legates were both prosecutors and judges. Customary protocol was offensively ignored. The patriarch did not even receive a polite bow.

Neither Cardinal Humbert nor Patriarch Michael could be described as learned in theology or in church history. Confrontation without concession or discussion was the chosen method of Humbert. At the same time Michael Cerularius appears an ambitious man, fussy about secondary matters, not in the least inclined to classify any point of divergence between east and west under the category of *adiaphora*, things indifferent. At least he had not dis-covered that Latin churches had come to use language about divine purifica-tion of souls hereafter which to Greek ears sounded like the universalist heresy of Origen. But his ambition for his see is sufficiently attested by Balsamon's report (above, Ch. 3 n. 7) that he interpreted the Donation of Constantine to mean that the supreme authority over the world Church

---

[13] Will 153[b]15. Ockham was similarly sure that the Council of Nicaea condemned failure to say that the Spirit proceeds from the Son with the Father. Because the Greeks are heretics and schis-matics, their emperor cannot be deemed legitimate, and it is wrong to deny that the apostolic see has power to transfer the imperium from the Greeks to the Germans. *Allegationes de potestate imperi-ali*, ed. H. S. Offler, *Opera Politica*, iv (Oxford, 1997).

bestowed by the emperor on the Roman bishop was now transferred to Constantine's New Rome.

Before taking orders Michael Cerularius[14] had had an unsuccessful career as a political adventurer involved in a conspiracy. A common Byzantine penalty for such indiscretion was retirement to a monastery (among others even Anna Comnena suffered in this way). Michael's move to become a monk and priest was an escape, the monastery a confinement. But his ability and his unbending intransigence attracted the favour of the emperor Constantine IX Monomachos (1042–55). The emperor was able to impose him on reluctant clergy and made him take up the office of patriarch. At first he followed his emperor's admonition to be conciliatory in correspondence with Rome and Roman legates. But Humbert's autocratic style was hard to take; he had succeeded in conveying the clear impression that it was a categorical Greek duty to have clean-shaven clergy, to adopt *azyma* as the usage of the Last Supper, to require celibacy of the inferior clergy, not merely of bishops, and to clear their name of heretical association by 'restoring' the *Filioque* to the creed. So confident was the ill-informed Humbert that the *Filioque* had been suppressed by the Greeks, not added by the Latins, that he boldly took the initiative in introducing the subject.

On 16 July 1054 the three Roman legates went to St Sophia at the normal early hour of the liturgy and, after a brief speech, placed on the altar a bull of personal excommunication against the patriarch and his adherents.[15] On leaving the building they shook the dust off their feet in accordance with the gospel. The document began with praise of the emperor and the good people of the city. Then came attack. Michael Cerularius was accused of daily diffusing heresy. It was absurd for the Greek churches to suppose that true baptism and true eucharistic sacrifice had been preserved only by them. To rebaptize Latins was Arian or Donatist. To allow priests to marry was like the erotic Nicolaitans (Apoc. 2: 15). Rejecting unleavened bread implied rejecting the Old Testament law. They have deleted the *Filioque* from the creed, do not allow infants dying within a week of birth to be baptized, forbid menstruating women to communicate (a ruling not unknown in the west, but rejected by Augustine of Hippo), and repel from the eucharist shaven Latins. Michael, 'falsely entitled patriarch', scorned Pope Leo's admonition, refused colloquy with the legates, and denied them a church for

---

[14] The best biography of Michael Cerularius (or Kerullarios) is by F. Tinnefeld, *Jahrbuch der österreichischen Byzantinistik*, 39 (1989), 95–127. The older book by Michel, *Humbert und Kerullarios*, has valuable matter but has not at all points persuaded readers. In his portrait Cerularius is demonized. Psellos described Michael as hostile to study and learning: Michel ii. 476–81. See also R. J. H. Jenkins and E. Kitzinger, 'A Cross of Michael Cerularius', *Dumbarton Oaks Papers*, 21 (1967) 235–40.

[15] Will 150–4.

Latin masses, calling Latins *azymitae*, which in effect was to anathematize the apostolic see. 'Anathema Maranatha' (1 Cor. 16: 22) was pronounced upon him, on Leo of Ochrid, on Michael's *sacellarius* Constantine, who had trampled with his feet on the Latins' host of *azyma*, and on all their followers. (Leo of Ochrid no doubt offended them by being in Bulgaria, which had been unsuccessfully claimed by Nicolas I and Hadrian II.) Amen, amen, amen. Humbert's conclusion shows that he felt entitled to assume the assent of his master, Leo IX, and of whoever might be his successor. The anathema was pronounced in the name of the dead pope.

Humbert's curse lay only on Patriarch Michael, Leo of Ochrid, and their immediate supporters, not upon the whole eastern Church. Nevertheless by the extreme prominence which he had given to the *Filioque*, the Greek denial of which was in his eyes a failure to recognize the supreme authority of St Peter's Roman successors, Humbert impelled the patriarch to reread Photius' examination of this intricate subject and especially his encyclical letter of 867.

The document placed on the high altar at Hagia Sophia had been removed by the subdeacons 'on duty for that week' and handed back to the western legates who threw it on the ground. It passed through many hands but was eventually to come into the possession of Cerularius. He had a Greek version made and reported the dramatic events to the emperor. The legates had already left the city and travelled fifty miles, but were recalled by the emperor. They refused to explain their action to the patriarch or the resident synod; but the emperor declined to use any force on persons of ambassadorial standing. However, the people in the city were demonstrating in the patriarch's favour. An imperial letter to Cerularius authorized him to pronounce anathema on the authors and to burn the translation with full solemnity, the original Latin document being preserved in the archives. Condemnation in full synod followed four days later on Sunday 24 July in the presence of the people, whose support for Cerularius seems to have been solid.[16]

The emperor had evidently realized that his hopes for an alliance with the papacy to check the Normans in south Italy were now altogether dead. Italian land was passing out of the control of the eastern empire.

Cerularius took care about his response. There was no excommunication of the Pope, though eventually it came to be supposed that that was what the patriarch had done. The tone of Photius' encyclical was echoed. When the synodical riposte began by speaking of the west as 'the land of darkness', there was a conscious reminiscence of language used by Photius. But theology was not Michael's forte. The blame was attributed to the Byzantine general in

[16] Will 155–68.

southern Italy, Argyros,[17] whose meeting with Humbert at Beneventum had envenomed the entire confrontation. Humbert had been in consultation with Argyros on his way to the east, and would certainly have learnt from him to think of Michael Cerularius as a politically dangerous person. Humbert did not conceal his conviction that he was engaged in conflict with an agent of Antichrist.

Both sides released fearful catalogues of errors and misdemeanours committed by their opponents. In his charge sheet Humbert even included an accusation that the Greek churches not only promoted eunuchs to be bishops, which was in some cases true, but had actually consecrated a woman.[18] It is unlikely that this echoes a very early variant of 'Pope Joan', whose story is not met until the mid-thirteenth century. (As her corbel head among the popes in Siena cathedral shows, it was widely believed in the west, until proved fictitious by the Protestant Blondel.)

On his side Michael sought to enlist support from the other eastern patriarchs of Alexandria, Antioch, and Jerusalem, especially Peter of Antioch. Peter III of Antioch received a lengthy letter enumerating the intolerable faults of Rome and the west: *Filioque*, insistence on priestly celibacy for inferior clergy, *azyma*, and a failure to give proper reverence to relics and icons of the saints. In their eating the western Christians were indifferent about the Apostolic Decree of Acts 15. They encouraged clean-shaven clergy. The Latins also allowed clergy to be combatants in war, and tolerated dangerous liturgical formulae such as 'You alone are holy' (*Tu solus sanctus*) in the *Gloria in excelsis*, episcopal rings, laxities in the Lenten fast—all these were symptoms of their departure from authentic tradition. To Cerularius it seemed a coolness in western devotion and Christology or Mariology that where the Greeks spoke of *Theotókos*, Mother of God, the Latins usually said no more than *Sancta Maria* (*Deipara* was in use but much less common.)

Peter Patriarch of Antioch

Peter III of Antioch (1052–6) deplored Michael's letter and held a strongly unionist position.[19] Michael was directly told that he should not regard differences of custom as Church-dividing; they were secondary. The only painful and weighty questions were Latin refusal to accept communion when the celebrant was married and, above all else, the mistake of the *Filioque*.

He did not accept that the bishop of Rome possessed autocratic powers over the eastern patriarchates. He held an honoured primacy in a pentarchy

---

[17] Will 160ᵃ28; 167ᵃ2, 14; 175ᵃ5; 177ᵃ30.
[18] Will 68ᵃ12. Patriarch eunuchs included Methodius and Ignatius. [19] Will 189–204.

but he judged the *Filioque* indefensible. The Latins, he thought, had lost their copies of the first Council of Nicaea during the long period when they were ruled by the Vandals, who may have taught them Arian ways. He noted that the Greeks did not accept 'You alone are holy' in the *Gloria in excelsis*, though he conceded that it was capable of an orthodox exegesis. He felt strongly that while unleavened bread was a serious western mistake, its use did not render a mass invalid.

Nevertheless, he wrote, the western Christians

are our brothers, even though from rusticity or ignorance they often lapse from what is right when they follow their private choice. We ought not to expect barbarian races to attain the same level of accuracy that we ask of our people.[20] They make many mistakes, but the remainder of our criticisms do not touch fundamental doctrine. The charge of neglecting to honour icons and relics is unintelligible when one recalls that Rome has the tombs of Peter and Paul, and that Pope Hadrian with the other patriarchs presided (through legates) over the seventh council to anathematize iconoclasm. Moreover, Frankish visitors to the East are to be seen showing every respect to our icons. Consider the injury that schism inflicts on the Church. I would not ask for more than correction of the creed.[21]

Peter of Antioch had also had correspondence with the patriarch of Grado,[22] partly to tell him that to use *azyma* indicated a rite of the Old, not the New Testament, but also to protest that he had no right to the title 'patriarch'. Indeed Rome and Alexandria had popes, Constantinople and Jerusalem had archbishops, and the one and only real patriarch in the pentarchy was at Antioch.

Michael Cerularius did not convince all canonists that the Council of Constantinople in 381 had intended New Rome's privileges to be the equal of Old Rome's.[23]

Peter of Antioch radically disagreed with Michael Cerularius. He had no intention of removing the Pope's name from the diptychs of his church and patriarchate. What had lately occurred at Constantinople was deplorable and shocking, but exchanges of calculated offensiveness between Cerularius and Humbert did not amount to a formal breach between the Latin and Greek churches. The fracas did not appear to Peter sufficient ground for refusing to acknowledge the Pope's honour as first bishop of the universal Church; moreover, Leo IX had had the right ideas about Antioch's dignity as a Petrine see. Each year on the Sunday after the feast of the Exaltation of

[20] From his reading of Nicolas I's letter to the emperor Michael (above, p. 148) Humbert took his expressions of resentment at Byzantine superciliousness towards Latin as a barbarous language, and reproduced the remark that at Byzantium church lections could be in Latin. He added Latin acclamations (Will 78[b]1–3) which he had evidently witnessed.

[21] Will 198.   [22] Will 205–28.

[23] See the scholion on Photius' *Nomocanon* in RP i. 148.

the Cross (14 September) it was customary to read the Acts of the Sixth Council containing a panegyric on the person and office of Pope Agatho; there was a model for the east to continue.[24] Peter recalled that when Sergius II (1001–19) became patriarch of Constantinople, the Pope's name was being included in the diptychs. He (Peter) had been unable to discover why that had later been dropped.[25]

If the break in the custom occurred during Sergius' patriarchate, which is unclear, this could possibly have been related to the Bulgarians receiving from Constantinople a Greek to be archbishop of Ochrid in 1019. In that appointment there was no consultation with Rome.

In Peter's view Rome had a leading place in the pentarchy. His advice to Michael was that he write to Rome a courteous letter explaining the difficulties felt by Greeks in some western practices. The answer might well come that the east was misinformed; or that he disowned what some others had been saying and doing.[26]

When in 1052 Peter of Antioch had taken up his office as patriarch, he had sent a copy of his synodical letter, including a statement of his orthodox beliefs, not only to the other eastern patriarchs but also to Pope Leo IX. That was in accordance with old custom, though it had apparently fallen into disuse.

Peter of Antioch's admonition to Michael Cerularius was grounded in the concept, inherited from Justinian, of a universal Church guided and maintained in the truth primarily by the pentarchy of five patriarchs, in which decisions were made by their consensus, but in which the bishop of Rome was responsible for a particular see, not for the worldwide body which he shared with the other four patriarchs.[27] His authority lay in the west, and he carried authority in the Greek east or in the Slavonic world only in so far as the east and the west walked together in harmony. That was a very different notion of the nature and order of the Church from that presupposed by Cardinal Humbert.

For that reason it must be thought unlikely that Peter of Antioch would have succeeded in achieving a quiet, rational, and brotherly examination of differences with the over-excitable Cardinal Humbert. He had received a letter from Pope Leo IX enlisting his friendly support in the conflict with Patriarch Michael,[28] confident that at Antioch where believers were first called Christians, he had not the least wish to depart from the agreed decree of all holy fathers that the holy Roman and apostolic see is the head. The apostolic sees of Rome and Antioch should maintain concord; in Peter's see the faith cannot fail. Pope Leo states his concern as that of defending

[24] Will 192. Acts of the Fifth Council were customarily read on 20 July (Will 167ᵃ 30).
[25] Will 193ᵃ7. [26] Will 201.
[27] Will 211–12 (to the patriarch of Venice and Grado). [28] Will 168–71.

Antioch's privileges as third see of Christendom. Each should maintain its rights and privileges as fixed by our fathers. Pope Leo adds his profession of orthodox faith, including the *Filioque* emphatically repeated, with special dignity for the first four general councils and a like respect for the fifth, sixth, and seventh. (Leo makes no mention of the anti-Photian Council of 869.) The main motive of the Pope's letter appears to be to encourage the patriarch of Antioch to reassert the dignity of his see above that of the upstart at Constantinople.

There was a minor practical difficulty that Peter knew no Latin and had to send the Pope's letter to Constantinople to obtain a (poor) translation.

Juridically the action of Cardinal Humbert in delivering the bull of excommunication was invalid.[29] Pope Leo IX had died on 19 April and that meant an automatic ending of Humbert's mandate to do what he was sent to Constantinople to do. In high summer, especially if one used the route by the isthmus of Corinth, a journey from Rome to Constantinople did not require more than six weeks and with favourable winds could be completed in less.[30] The time between Leo IX's death and Humbert's delivery of the bull on 16 July entirely allows for a special courier to carry the news from Old Rome to New. The patriarch Michael Cerularius will have known of the crucial fact, for in all probability before 16 July the news had reached Constantinople.

Humbert was thereby impelled to deliver his hammer-blow as soon as possible. Granted that the outcome was not in the full and formal sense a schism, it was nevertheless a declaration of cold civil war in the Church, an inauguration of mutual deep freeze.

When not many days later Michael Cerularius was writing his rebuttal of the bull, he did not omit to say that Leo IX was dead. He made nothing of the canonical point that Humbert therefore had no mandate to act. He was not enough of a canonist to grasp the useful point. But in any event he had ceased to be particularly interested in achieving reconciliation; he had reason to feel that he and his church and office had been treated in an insulting manner. The uncultured barbarians from the west could be ignored, once his anathema on the bull, synodically proclaimed, had been approved.

In any event, the emperor had lost hope of the Byzantine–papal alliance, and in the ecclesiastical field Patriarch Cerularius had defeated Humbert, who had evidently overestimated the power of the emperor to control his principal bishop and the determination of the emperor to use the hope of an anti-Norman alliance as a weapon in the argument.

[29] A. Herman, 'I legati inviati da Leone IX nel 1054 a Constantinopoli', *Orientalia Christiana Periodica*, 8 (1942), 209–18.

[30] See e.g. *ACO* II iv. 180.

The exchanges of 1053–4 make painful reading. The emperor Constantine Monomachos was self-evidently right that the Byzantine interest in south Italy was likely to be better safeguarded by being courteous to the Pope and his legates than by intransigent hostility. But the patriarch Michael had been wholly ignored by Humbert, and it is hardly surprising that a quiet discussion of differences was never achieved. The patriarch had the support of a considerable proportion of the city population, and there were moments when the Roman legates needed to be behind the walls of the imperial palace to be sure of their personal safety.

At the level of theological discussion, both sides felt the issues to be a threat to their own traditions. Roman negotiation with the Greek churches had for a long time past rested on the assertion of Petrine authority, which the bishops of Rome claimed to have as no other patriarch or bishop had. When Leo I sent his Tome to Flavian of Constantinople, he expected the Councils of Ephesus (449) and Chalcedon (451) to ratify it, to show the orthodoxy of the Greek episcopate by that ratification, but not to regard its propositions as contributions to a free discussion. When early in the sixth century Popes Symmachus and Hormisdas sought a way to end the thirty-five-year-long Acacian schism, what they asked of the eastern church was submission to papal authority. They were unable to provide a clarification of the intricate problems underlying the Christological dispute. Cardinal Humbert's strength in his own eyes, but weakness in the view of the eastern patriarchs, whether alienated as was Michael Cerularius or friendly as was Peter of Antioch, lay in his underlying axiom that obedience to papal authority was the key to unlock all the disputed matters.

At Constantinople Roman claims to universal jurisdiction were bound to seem implausible when the city of Rome had ceased to have political importance. Michael Cerularius was patriarch of a great church where the bishop of Rome was not commemorated in the diptychs, and was astounded to learn from Peter of Antioch that in other eastern patriarchates the Pope was in their diptychs. Indeed the patriarchs of Jerusalem and Alexandria were reported to have celebrated the liturgy using *azyma*. Cerularius at Constantinople thought no Greek patriarch had named a pope in his diptychs since pope Vigilius, misdated to the time of the Sixth Council (680) which he refused to attend because of his opposition to a condemnation of the Three Chapters. It was a surprise to him to discover that patriarchs of Antioch did not necessarily do what patriarchs of Constantinople were doing (or not doing). It must have left him astounded to be told by Peter of Antioch that only a generation previously the patriarch Sergius II had been commemorating the Pope at Constantinople, and that Peter had no notion why that had come to an end.

From that exchange it is reasonable to suppose that it would be illusion to think of Michael Cerularius' words to be committing a monolithic Greek or

Russian Orthodoxy. The exchanges between Humbert and Michael were personal to themselves. Their historical importance lies rather in what most people assumed to be the case. Churches are out of communion with one another if they come to think and feel that they are. The events of 1053–4 were more symptomatic of a state of mind than a primary cause. And it is a matter of some delicacy to estimate how far the ecclesiological divergence was used as a political weapon in the dispute about Byzantine sovereignty in south Italy. That the political dimension of east Rome's sovereignty in south Italy had much to do with the story is certain.

The affair of 1054, in which the patriarch had in effect frustrated the political hopes of the emperor and virtually coerced the palace into supporting his rebuff to Humbert, left Michael Cerularius in a position of power in the capital. In 1057 he was able to give decisive help to raise a seditious general, Isaac Comnenus, to be emperor, with the assurance that any pollution incurred by usurpation was removed by the sacred ceremony of coronation. But within two years patriarch and emperor had come to quarrel about the degree to which Isaac could control the financial affairs of monastic houses; Isaac removed Cerularius from Constantinople, accusing him of treason. Psellos represents the patriarch as dangerously democratic, relying on his power with the city mob to assert his authority in defiance of the emperor. Cerularius died on 21 January 1059. He was never to achieve admission to the Greek calendar of saints.[31]

---

[31] For a brief political portrait of Michael Cerularius see Michael Angold, *Church and Society in Byzantium under the Comneni 1081–1261* (Cambridge, 1995), 22–7.

34

PETER DAMIAN: GREGORY VII: THEOPHYLACT OF OCHRID

Pope Alexander II (1061–73) took office at a time of high tension with the German emperor Henry IV, and faced an antipope, a rich German who became bishop of Parma and as pope took the name of Honorius II. To strengthen his position Alexander sought support at Constantinople and asked the emperor (Constantine X Doukas) if normality could be restored. The emperor asked the patriarch to write to Pope Alexander.

Peter Damian mentions a letter written about 1062 by Patriarch Constantine III Lichoudes (1059–63) addressed to Pope Alexander II asking for solid witnesses in texts of holy scripture which would vindicate the *Filioque*. Peter Damian faced the problem that 'almost all Greeks and some Latins' say the Spirit proceeds only from the Father. His reply is partly to observe that to say the Spirit proceeds from the Father is entirely correct, but does not imply 'not from the Son', partly to quote Ambrose, Augustine, Jerome, and Gregory the Great. The Latin Fathers are fortified 'for those who know only Greek and no Latin' by citations from the 'Athanasius' creed and a version of the Nicene-Constantinopolitan creed ascribed to Cyril of Alexandria.[1]

It is hard to imagine that Peter Damian's little tract could have done much to reassure anxious Greeks in the patriarch's circle. Nevertheless, the fact of the correspondence is evidence that on the Greek side there was no wish to regard all doors to the west as slammed shut. The reference to the existence of Latins convinced that the Greeks were right about the *Filioque* is particularly instructive. It would have been easy for contemporaries of Cardinal Humbert to contemplate the vehemence of his style in dealing not only with the Greek patriarch but also with Berengar of Tours and to feel that he had an unfortunate way of going to indefensible extremes.

---

[1] PL 145. 633–42. A guide to recent work on Peter Damian by S. Freund, *Revue Mabillon*, 68 = NS 7 (1996), 239–300.

Gregory VII

In 1071 the eastern empire suffered a massive double blow. Its last lands in south Italy were lost, and in eastern Asia Minor the main Byzantine army was crushingly defeated by the Turks at Manzikert.

In July 1073 the new Pope Gregory VII (Hildebrand) received a friendly letter from the emperor Michael VII Doukas at Constantinople, brought to Rome by two monks. Gregory sent a most courteous reply by the hand of a prestigious legate, Dominic patriarch of Grado and Venice, in which he expressed the warm hope that between Constantinople and Rome the old concord might be restored. Five months later Pope Gregory was writing to King Henry IV revealing his plan for an expedition to the east intended to protect Christian pilgrims who had been suffering massacres from Islamic zealots, but which would also have a beneficent effect upon the church of Constantinople, which, 'though dissident from us on the Holy Spirit, looks for concord with the apostolic see'. Moreover, it may be valuable in restoring orthodoxy among the Armenians, 'almost all of whom depart from the Catholic faith' and need convincing of the correctness of the Fourth Ecumenical Council at Chalcedon. Another letter from Gregory praises the Armenians for their use of unleavened bread in the eucharist and for their ignoring of Greek Orthodox criticism.[2]

Pope Gregory VII nursed the ambition to assert the uniqueness of Rome's bishop as St Peter's vicar, with the corollary that he had the right to demand obedience not only in the Church but also from secular rulers. The prince of the apostles was given power to bind and loose not only in heaven but also on earth. Accordingly, military force could be deployed in the cause of St Peter's vicar, using swords and spears to enforce submission.

Gregory VII was a pugnacious pope, resorting to the arm of authority in his determination to end simony and to enforce priestly celibacy. He acquiesced in Norman ambitions to take over east Roman lands not only in south Italy and Sicily but also on the eastern side of the Adriatic. That was bound to have unhappy consequences for Latin relations with the Greek empire and its churches. Gregory particularly wished to establish his jurisdiction over the eastern churches, because he was confronted by a rival pope, Clement III, and had many western critics.

Clement III continued to create a problem for Gregory's successor Urban II (pope 1088–99). One of Urban's first acts was to write to the archbishop of

---

[2] Gregory VII, *epp.* 1. 18, 2. 31, 8. 1 ed. Caspar. On papal attempts to reconcile the Armenian Church to Roman unity see Peter Halfter, *Das Papsttum und die Armenier im frühen und hohen Mittelalter* (Cologne, 1996). Agreement was signed between Pope John Paul II and Catholicos Karekin I in December 1996. In general see H. E. J. Cowdrey, *Gregory VII* (Oxford, 1998).

Canterbury, Lanfranc, warning him against notions of being independent.[3]
In Deusdedit, Urban had a competent canonist capable of defending Roman
primacy against critics who were sneering at such authority as 'windy
rhetoric'.[4] But Deusdedit saw that an approach to the eastern churches from
Rome had to be conditional on a positive evaluation of the authority of the
Greek patriarchates. In launching the first crusade by his speech at Clermont
in 1096 Urban had in mind not only the protection of harassed pilgrims to
the Holy Land but also a show of force that would impress the eastern empire
and facilitate peace.

Theophylact of Ochrid

At this time there were highly placed Greek ecclesiastics who regretted the
east–west tension. Prominent among these was Theophylact,[5] a native of
Euboea who came to Constantinople to study under the polymath and
philosopher Michael Psellos, became a deacon of St Sophia, and about 1090
was promoted to be archbishop of Ochrid. He did not feel able to dissent
from the Greek consensus that the Latin churches had involved themselves
in numerous errors. Of these the *Filioque* was unquestionably the worst. Less
serious were *azyma*, which in his view, though mistaken, did not invalidate
a mass, priestly celibacy provided it were not enforced upon the east, and
similarly Saturday fasting. He thought it ridiculous that 'when we Greeks
find fault with the *Filioque*, they shake St Peter's keys at us'. (Theophylact had
evidently met the contention that by virtue of his supreme power over the
Church the bishop of Rome possesses authority not merely to confirm general councils but to supplement and correct them.) 'Nevertheless differences
of custom and usage are no sufficient ground for schism. Experience shows
that arguing about *azyma* and Lenten fasts gets nowhere. The Greeks should
be accommodating and make concessions to the ignorant western barbarians, hoping that in time they will correct their errors to conform to the apostolic tradition stemming from Jerusalem.'

[3] PL 151. 286.
[4] See the preface to his canon-collection, ed. V. Wolf von Glanvell (1905); an account of
Deusdedit's ecclesiology in A. Becker, *Papst Urban II. (1088–1099)*, 2 vols. (Schriften der MGH, 19;
Stuttgart, 1964–88), ii. 50–62.
[5] Will 229–53. Theophylact made use of the letters of Peter of Antioch. On his correspondence
see Margaret Mullett, *Theophylact of Ochrid* (Aldershot, 1996), D. Obolensky, *Six Byzantine Portraits*
(Oxford 1988), 34–82.

35

POPE URBAN II:
ANSELM OF CANTERBURY AT BARI

The moderation in Theophylact's tone reflected something of the situation between Constantinople and Rome at this time. Two rival popes were competing for recognition at Constantinople to strengthen their claims in the west. Urban II was conceiving the idea of a great crusade in which Latins and Greeks could cooperate in recovering Christian possession of the holy places. To this end he needed good relations with Greek churches, and in 1089 held a papal council in southern Italy at Melfi. At this council there was discussion of Latin–Greek relations, but the records of the exchanges do not survive. However Basil, the Greek metropolitan of Reggio (Calabria), wrote to patriarch Nicolas III reporting on an interview he had with Pope Urban during which Urban proposed a *quid pro quo*: if he were to be recognized as lawful pope by the Greek churches then he would recognize the customs and the bishops of south Italy and presumably protect them from molestation by Normans. Bishop Basil declined the proposal since it entailed his submission to papal jurisdiction.

In the same year the emperor Alexios received a letter from Urban II complaining that his name was not being included in the diptychs at the eastern capital and that Latins living in the Greek empire were being excluded from communion if they attended a Latin mass. Patriarch Nicolas held a synod and sent a gentle reply, encouraging Urban to hope he could deprive his rival Clement III of the support for which he had been negotiating with some success. Urban asked the emperor if perhaps there was a schism of which no one had told him; to the best of his knowledge there had been no canonical decision to that effect. Urban evidently did not know or chose to ignore the fact that in 1054 the initiative in the exchanges had been substantially on the Latin side. He received the answer that indeed there was no schism, but there were points of canon law (*kanonika zetēmata*) needing attention. Adopting a moderate position, the Greeks felt that they were exercising some 'economy' or less than rigorous application of their canon law.[1]

---

[1] Four documents in Greek concerning this encounter were first generally used after their publication, from British Library MS Add. 34060, s. xii–xv, by W. Holtzmann, *Byzantinische*

The Greek patriarch and bishops accepted their emperor's view that no state of schism existed. However, if they were to restore Urban's name to the diptychs at Constantinople, the patriarch's synod would ask the Pope to remedy a defect in their documentation. The Pope had sent no enthronement-letter (*inthronistika*) setting out his orthodox beliefs. This custom had once been general, and is found in the correspondence of Pope Gregory the Great. It continued in the Greek east but, since Nicolas' brush with Photius, it had effectively ceased to be normal practice for popes to assure eastern colleagues of their orthodoxy, though Deusdedit certainly regarded it as a good custom of the Church. Pope Leo IX in 1054–5 had set out to patriarch Peter of Antioch his assent to the great ecumenical councils. But the implication of telling Urban that the patriarch of Constantinople could insert his name in the diptychs only after being assured of his orthodoxy by a written statement was bound to alarm those in the Roman curia most conscious of papal supremacy as stated, for example, in Gregory VII's *Dictatus Papae*. Apart from the principle of authority at stake, there could be embarrassing consequences. What would be said if Urban either did or did not include the *Filioque*? Whether among Greek critics or among those in the west determined to follow Humbert's line of militant aggression, he would provoke hostile comment whatever he said.

In the ninth century Pope Nicolas I had registered profound vexation at Greek demands for assurances of orthodoxy from his legates. So now the Greek demand for a statement of Pope Urban's belief was sure to be regarded by curial advisers as a conversation-stopper. It did not expressly ask for a view of the *Filioque*, but that lurked in the background. However, from Malaterra's history of Count Roger in Sicily (*Historia Sicula* 4. 13)[2] it is clear that the principal reason for a rift lay in the different customs in regard to *azyma*. Malaterra reported that the emperor responded humbly to the Pope's protest, replying to his letter with an epistle inscribed with ink of gold, inviting the Pope to come to Constantinople for a disputation between learned Latins and Greeks with the intention that there should be one custom in the one Church of God. Unhappily the journey was impracticable. The episode, however, is an indication of Urban's awareness that, if a crusade were to be launched to expel the infidels from possession of the Christian holy places and to protect western pilgrims, good relations with the eastern Church would be of the first importance.

Zeitschrift, 28 (1928), 38–67. Unknown to him three of them were printed earlier by E. Boulismas of Corfu in 1876. Revised texts with translation and commentary are in Becker, *Papst Urban II.*, ii. 206–71. The Latin representatives at the meeting held in Nicaea in January 1234 also complained that a Latin resident in the Greek east suffered excommunication by the Greek parish priest because he attended a Latin eucharist: text edited by H. Golubovich, *Archivum Franciscanum Historicum*, 12 (1919), 430.

[2] PL 145. 633–42.

It was difficult for the patriarch of Constantinople to stop arguing about unleavened bread when he and his bishops were continuing an unremitting, not always unsuccessful endeavour to reconcile the Armenians, and were convinced that Armenian abandonment of *azyma* was, together with the acceptance of the Chalcedonian definition, a prerequisite of union. About 1063 the then patriarch Constantine III Lichoudes ordered the Syrian and Armenian liturgical books to be burnt (according to the report of Michael the Syrian 15. 2, ed. Chabot). In the 1170s Patriarch Michael III of Anchialos was inviting the Armenian Catholicos to union and proposing conditions, still including the correction of *azyma* in his list.[3] Western *azyma* remained objectionable to the ecumenical patriarch as late as 1895.

Already in Gregory VII's concept of legitimate force in defence of lands occupied by Christians in a remembered past, there is a theme of 'Christendom' as a territorial region in Europe and perhaps north Africa needing defence by Christian powers. Nicolas in 865 had written of the sword entrusted to a king at his coronation, representing power delegated through the pope to be used against infidels.[4] The possibility of an armed crusade was already long current when in 1095 at Clermont Pope Urban II issued his great call. But the despatch of a large armed force to the east would need good support from the Christians of the east, and if satisfactory relations were to be established, there would have to be discussions between Latins and Greeks concentrating on the central Greek complaint against the Latins, the *Filioque*.

So at Bari in 1098 Urban presided over a synod of Latin and south Italian Greek bishops, the agenda being Greek objections. They were meeting round the shrine of St Nicolas of Myra, whose relics had been brought to Bari eleven years previously when Lycia was occupied by the Turks. The main spokesman for the western cause was its greatest and most acute mind, Anselm archbishop of Canterbury. He was asked by the Pope to 'fight' in defence of the Roman Church against the Greek criticisms. His book 'On the Procession of the Holy Spirit' serenely states his arguments which, as one would expect, are based more on careful reasoning than on authoritative proof-texts from patristic authors, though Augustine is constantly behind the arras.

The report by William of Malmesbury says that Pope Urban invited Anselm to occupy a seat beside the archdeacon of Rome with the words that the archbishop of Canterbury is 'like the pope of another world' (*quasi alterius orbis papa*; Mansi xx. 948). The essential points are that to deny the participation of the Son in the procession of the Spirit suggests openness to Arian

---

[3] PG 133. 269.

[4] *Ep.* 34, MGH Epp. vi. 305. 5–6 (PL 119. 914 D): 'usum machaerae quem primum a Petri principis apostolorum vicario contra infideles accepit'.

conclusions, and that since that would be unacceptable to Greeks they must surely concede that the addition to the creed is explicative of true doctrine. The difference between Latin and Greek is not in dogma but in just one more of the accepted liturgical diversities, and if the *Filioque* were chanted in the liturgy by only one province in the Church, it would be faultless in that practice.

Anselm of Canterbury's encounter with the Greeks also lies behind his little treatise on the use of unleavened bread at mass. The Greeks are mistaken if they deny validity to a eucharist celebrated with unleavened bread, which was used by Christ and the apostles. But the difference of usage between Latin and Greek is not one of substance: both use bread. On the essential point they are in substantial agreement. The argument of this treatise must presuppose that at Bari some Greeks had restated the contention of 1054 that *azyma* cannot be real bread and are therefore not to be used.[5]

Discussions at Bari cannot have done much to promote unity between Rome and Constantinople. In 1112 Pope Pascal II (1099–1118) wrote an aggrieved letter to the patriarch of Constantinople complaining that for some years past no letters or messengers from Rome had been accepted. At a conference in the capital in 1112 attended by Archbishop Peter Grossolanus of Milan on his way to the Holy Land, the Greeks explained that different customs such as shaven clergy or bishops' rings were minor matters, but major issues were western scorn for married priests, lack of veneration for icons, *Filioque*, and above all the unjustified Roman claim to be the mother of all churches.[6]

In the origins of the first crusade a mixture of motives is likely to have been present. Pope Nicolas I had articulated the notion that while war between Christians is wicked, it is legitimate against infidels, and this thesis had enabled Gregory VII to support Christian military action in Spain. In the east the emperor needed help, and pilgrims were being harassed. So Jerusalem was the goal. Moreover as (armed) pilgrimage, crusading qualified for the remission of penitential penalties.

The radical flaw in the crusading movement emerged quickly after the capture of Jerusalem (1099). Evidently the crusaders could not achieve a lasting protection for pilgrims unless they actually occupied the land. Some of the land on the way there was desirable in itself, apart from any religious considerations. What was to the high-minded an expedition to the holy places was to the less high-minded a chance to capture property of the Byzantine

---

[5] Anselm's writings on the Procession of the Holy Spirit and on *azyma* are printed in the second volume of Schmitt's edition. Anselm's role at Bari is briefly described in Eadmer's *Historia Novorum*, ed. M. Rule (Rolls Series, 1884).

[6] On the meeting of 1112 see J. Darrouzès, *Revue des études byzantines*, 23 (1965), 54–8, in a study of successive twelfth-century debates on Roman primacy.

empire. Soon after the capture of Jerusalem the Latin clergy were treating the Greek clergy and people as second-class members of the one Church needing to correct their mistakes and to learn better from papal authority.

At Constantinople the impression bequeathed by Cardinal Humbert and other western visitors was one of incredible arrogance. Western churchmen did not seem to think they had anything to learn in the east, and this high-handed style did more to cause alienation than any other factor. To demand that the eastern Christians should abandon their immemorial custom of using ordinary bread at the eucharist was shocking. It offended western visitors to find that at the consecration of the elements, Greeks did not add water to the cup until after the bread and wine were sanctified, though it answered a problem which perturbed theologians in the eleventh-century west, namely whether the water added to the wine was also changed at consecration together with the wine.[7] (Current usage is to consecrate a mixed chalice, warm water being added before communion.)

Western clergy coming to Constantinople talked as if most patriarchs had been heretics, and received the usual witty retort that to start a heresy requires a high degree of intelligence and the bishops of Rome had all been too thick in the head to propose one.[8] The papal claim that their see was 'mother and mistress' did not fit the eastern understanding of 'sister churches', and the contention that if the Church were to be one body, it had to have a single earthly head left the Greeks baffled with incomprehension. The Latin argument remained that Christ's vicar was Peter and the popes were Peter's vicars. The east thought that that concentrated in one bishop an authority which was shared by all bishops collectively.

At the back of these exchanges lay two problems emerging at the Council of Chalcedon in 451. The Roman chancery had reinterpreted and rewritten the first clause of the sixth canon of Nicaea (325), which justified provincial jurisdiction for Alexandria over Libya and the Pentapolis besides the provinces of Egypt by analogy with undefined extra provincial powers traditionally exercised by Rome and Antioch. At Chalcedon the Roman legate, Paschasinus of Lilybaeum in Sicily, cited this sixth canon with the prefatory sentence: 'The Roman Church has always had primacy.' This form passed into the pseudo-Isidorian canons. It was the form known to Anselm bishop of Havelberg who died in 1158 as archbishop of Ravenna.

A second problem was the 'vote' (not strictly a canon, though later reckoned as such) of the bishops at Chalcedon at a session from which the Roman legates absented themselves reaffirming the canon of Constantinople (381)

[7] Durandus of Troarn, PL 149. 1389 C. On the difference between Latin and Greek whether water should be added before or after consecration, see Anselm of Havelberg, PL 188. 1241 C. On Latin objections to Greek custom see Balsamon's commentary on Trullan canon 32 (RP ii. 377–8).
[8] PL 188. 1223 C.

regarding the precedence and jurisdiction of Constantinople as New Rome. Chalcedon understood Constantinople to have 'equal' precedence, but in the second place after Old Rome, to which the council assigned the first place of honour as the imperial city. Pope Leo I hated the implication that Roman authority depended on (*a*) conciliar decision and (*b*) the civil standing of his city. Chalcedon continued by giving to the bishop of Constantinople power to ordain metropolitans in 'the Pontic, Asian and Thracian Dioceses' (Diocese being a secular term for a group of provinces) and all bishops among the barbarians. Some bishops in Asia Minor disliked centralizing limitations on an older provincial autonomy. Their independence of choice and action was being eroded.

To western observers of the twelfth century it seemed possible that the various patriarchates of the Orthodox Greek communion did not really possess any strong bonds of coherence. In Anselm of Havelberg one even meets the suggestion that a tendency towards independent national churches, which the Chalcedonian vote evidently ought to have been taken to restrain, was in practice ultimately rooted in the degree of autonomy which the Council of Chalcedon hesitantly conceded to provincial metropolitans, even though the choice and ordination of the metropolitans themselves was to be centralized at Constantinople. Provincial autonomy could in the end be a recipe for near-chaos.

36

ANSELM OF HAVELBERG

Anselm of Havelberg was to play a marginal role in east–west relations. Admittedly his record cannot be described as an outstanding success. But he tried.

The ambitions of the Norman king Roger in Sicily alarmed both Constantinople and the German emperor Lothair III. Lothair wanted an alliance and sent to Byzantium this courteous and able Premonstratensian, chosen perhaps not only for his diplomatic skills but also for his ability to cope with the long-controverted ecclesiastical questions, should they happen to arise during the negotiation. They did. On 10 April 1136 a public disputation began in the Church of St Irene, but soon attracted such a crowd of listeners that it had to move into Hagia Sophia nearby. Anselm had with him supporters from Italian cities also interested in the political problem but notable for their knowledge of Greek. They were James of Venice, translator of some of Aristotle's logic, Moyses of Bergamo, a competent grammarian and so linguistically fluent that he could act as interpreter, and Burgundio of Pisa, aged only about 25 (he died in 1193) but skilled in Greek since for some time during his boyhood he had lived in the Pisan quarter of the city.[1] Later he was to make for Pope Eugenius III (1145–53) translations of John Chrysostom on Matthew's and John's gospels, and also parts of Justinian's *Digest* from the great manuscript then at Pisa, later to be carried off as booty to Florence. He also translated John of Damascus.

Like Maximus Confessor in the seventh century, Anselm of Havelberg was aware that misunderstandings between Greek east and Latin west often originated in faulty grasp of each other's language: 'Some Latins are misled by Greeks' words, for they hear only the words, not the sense, and think the Greeks are affirming what they are not, and denying what they do not deny.'

Anselm's partner in debate was Nicetas archbishop of Nicomedia, one of a prestigious group of twelve official Teachers who chose him to be their spokesman. He was of high standing, being spiritual director to Anna

---

[1] See Peter Classen, *Burgundio von Pisa* (Sitzungsberichte der Heidelberger Akademie 1974, 4); Gudrun Vuillemin-Diem and M. Rashed, 'Burgundio de Pisa et ses manuscrits grecs d'Aristote', *Recherches de théologie et philosophie médiévales*, 64 (1997), 136–98.

Comnena.[2] Some fifteen years later Anselm composed a freely developed account of the conversations, based partly on memory, partly on notes by shorthand writers, but substantially adding new matter, evident from the attribution to Nicetas of statements derived wholly from Latin sources such as the *Liber Pontificalis* (e.g. *Dial.* 3. 7, PL 188, 1218 A). He dedicated his work to the then Pope Eugenius III, partly to foster more Latin toleration of the Greek churches, partly to vindicate himself after unkind suggestions that he had inadequately stated the western case for the *Filioque, azyma,* and, above all, papal monarchy. His preface pointedly declares submission to 'apostolic authority' to be a 'necessity of eternal salvation'.[3]

The *Dialogues* in three books begin from western anxieties about the rivalries in the recent multiplicity of religious orders. Anselm's thesis, derived from Augustine and Gregory the Great, holds diversity of usage to be compatible with unity of faith. He was a disciple of Norbert bishop of Magdeburg, founder of the Premonstratensians. The anxieties he sought to allay were widespread, for the fourth Lateran Council in 1215 prohibited new orders (canon 13, reaffirmed by the Council of Lyon, 1274, canon 23). The Lateran Council felt no difficulty about different rites within a substantially identical faith (canon 9).

Book II asks if the differences between east and west are compatible with one faith, the neuralgic points being the western doctrine of the procession of the Spirit from Father and Son and the eucharistic bread. On a shadowy margin lay painful questions about Greek hesitations towards Latin baptism.

On the *Filioque* Nicetas declares the eastern position to be that if such an addition were to be accepted in the Orthodox churches, it must have the authority of a general council backed by the authority of the Pope and allowed by emperors. It would need to be shown to be consonant with reason, scripture, and conciliar tradition. They wholly rejected 'two first principles' (*duo principia*). Nicetas sees no possibility of reconciliation if the

---

[2] The reliability of this statement is confirmed by Paul Magdalino, *The Empire of Manuel I Komnenos 1143–1180* (Cambridge, 1993), 325. Anselm of Havelberg's *Dialogi* are in PL 188. 1139–1248. The first book of the three was edited by G. Salet for Sources Chrétiennes 118 (Paris, 1966); he did not live to complete his work. A French translation of the second Dialogue, mainly on *Filioque*, is in *Istina*, 17 (1972), 375–424, by P. Harang. See also P. Classen, *Ausgewählte Aufsätze* (Sigmaringen, 1983), 472–3; G. R. Evans, *Analecta Praemonstratensia*, 67 (1991), 42–52; J. T. Lees, 'Charity and Enmity in the Writings of Anselm of Havelberg', *Viator*, 25 (1994), 53–62; J. W. Braun, 'Studien 2. Überlieferung der Werken Anselms von Havelberg', *Deutsches Archiv*, 28 (1972), 133–209. Jay T. Lees, *Anselm of Havelberg: Deeds into Words in the Twelfth Century* (Leiden, 1998) has a full discussion. Important on the sources and character of the Dialogues is H. J. Sieben, *Die Konzilsidee des lateinischen Mittelalters (847–1378)* (Paderborn, 1984), 153–79.

[3] Anselm of Havelberg's opening statement lays great stress on his obedience to 'apostolic authority' not merely out of humility but also 'for my eternal salvation' (PL 188. 1140 BC). His relationship to the Pope is 'obedientia absoluta' (1139 B).

sole western authority for adding to the ecumenical creed of the Council of Constantinople is that of the Roman see, respected as that is.

Anselm's reply disowns two first principles. There is no proposition in scripture or the Nicene creed forbidding one to say that the Son has a partnership in the proceeding of the Spirit from the Father. No text says 'from the Father alone'. Greeks cannot invoke John 15: 26 and say no addition may be made to scripture, when the Nicene creed self-evidently made such additions. Adding the *Filioque* is a clarification, not a different dogma of the Trinity. It belongs in that developing area which the first Church could not grasp but into which the Paraclete has led (John 16: 13), much as Gregory Nazianzen could argue for the consubstantiality of the Holy Spirit. Ancient councils were good, and manifest a development of doctrine under the Spirit's inspiration with a growth in understanding. Ancient fathers supporting the *Filioque* include Cyril of Alexandria, and not only the Latins Ambrose, Jerome, and Augustine. To illustrate the point that an orthodox creed can come from a pope without a council, Anselm can cite Pope Leo IX (*Dial.* 2. 21–2), with a tactful omission of Leo's *Filioque*. When Nicetas asks Anselm's opinion of 'proceeding from the Father *through* the Son' (*per Filium*), held by some Greek Fathers, Anselm replies that he has never heard such language and sharply cites a negative paragraph from Hilary of Poitiers, *De Trinitate* 12, an author well respected in the east. The discussion of *Filioque* ends, perhaps more cheerfully than the argument would suggest, with the confidence that if one sets aside 'stupid Greeks and arrogant Latins' (2. 26, 1208 D)' and 'if only' we can have a general council, mutual agreement could be reached; and then the Greek Christians could accept the *Filioque*.

The third Dialogue concerns the sacraments, especially the western use of unleavened bread in the mass, a custom which for Anselm represents 'universal tradition' since the Last Supper. Above all, to continue using leavened bread is defiance of Rome's authority, 'mother and mistress of all', a supremacy created by no councils but by the Lord in the gospel saying 'Thou art Peter. . .', and sealed by the martyrdom of Peter and Paul. While Alexandria and Antioch are also sees associated with Peter, Rome alone has been endowed with the special privileges of never departing from the true faith (any suggestion that Pope Liberius did so is expressly denied) and of exercising supreme universal jurisdiction. By contrast, bishops of Constantinople have made a home for heresies like a sewer (3. 6), and only repeated papal interventions have saved the situation (3. 12). Roman usage is therefore to be copied by all other churches (1217 A). Anselm can cite pseudo-Isidore (1226 B).

Nicetas finds this monarchical doctrine too strong. The great patriarchates are 'sisters', among whom Rome has first place and can be appealed to in cases of doubt. But Roman primacy does not antedate the seventh-century decree granted by Phocas to Pope Boniface III (attested in *Liber Pontificalis* 68). The authority of New Rome is older, determined by the Council of Constantinople in 381. Moreover, without the assent of the Greek bishops in ecumenical councils, the authority of Rome would have been nothing. It is rewriting history when Anselm claims immemorial usage of *azyma* at Rome; the use of leavened bread (*fermentum*) is attested as authorized by Popes Melchiades and Siricius (from *Liber Pontificalis* 33 and 40). Moreover, Nicetas has verified that Greek monks at Grottaferrata use leavened bread without scandal to the Roman pontiff (3. 13 end). Probably the apostles used either leavened or unleavened bread indifferently (3. 14). Despite the attachment of long custom, Greeks could be willing to take the same view, Nicetas thinks:

this indifference continued without controversy until the violent invasion of the 'Roman empire' by Charlemagne. From that time dates the Latin use of blasphemous words about leavened bread, and in retort 'we call them heretics and hold no communion with them, saying *azyma* are unworthy of the altar'.

Nicetas protests that he is not denying Rome's first place among the patriarchates; but 'in asserting monarchy, Rome separated from us'. 'If the Roman pontiff arbitrarily pronounces without consulting us, that is not brotherly . . . In the creed we confess the universal Church, not the Roman Church.'

These words hurt Anselm. They sounded ironical to his ear, and he replies with an unqualified assertion that the bishop of Rome is vicar of Peter and of Christ. The upholding of orthodox faith in the Greek churches was not, as Nicetas claims, the achievement of Greek bishops but of the popes. The Council of Nicaea, he is sure, was summoned wholly on the initiative of Pope Silvester, not Constantine.

As a tailpiece Anselm has a complaint. There is a western grievance that when a Greek marries a Latin wife, 'which often occurs among persons of high rank', before the marriage 'you anoint her with oil and wash her entire body, and to the west that appears as rebaptism.' Nicetas, tactfully perhaps, does not explain that western error about the Trinity makes at least some Greeks uncertain about the validity of Latin baptism, a problem that will be mentioned in canon 4 of the Lateran Council of 1215. His answer is to deny that this is rebaptism; it is no more than a purification applied when outsiders join Greek society. (The difficulty in distinguishing it from the baptismal rite being so great, it is obvious that most Greeks understood the rite as at least a conditional baptism.) In the eyes of Anselm rebaptizing is a heretical Greek practice, inherited from the Arian bishop Eusebius of Nicomedia, who, he supposes, 'rebaptized Constantine the Great after Pope Silvester had conferred orthodox baptism at the time of his conversion'. Anselm rewrites fourth-century history to suit his theory.

The two protagonists end confident of the future because the ancient fathers, both Latin and Greek, enjoyed consensus. Hope for reunion on ground of the shared agreement of Latin and Greek Fathers becomes a standard argument of ecumenists, recurring in bishop Robert Grosseteste in the early thirteenth century, and prominent at the Council of Florence in the brief union of 1439.

Moreover, Anselm presents both sides as speaking with courtesy and modesty. Nicetas more than once compliments Anselm upon the evidently unusual absence of arrogance in his Latin manner and matter. Nevertheless reflection must observe the intransigence of the partners. Neither yielded a centimetre of ground on the controversial areas debated.

Nicetas is given the last word: 'Our disagreements are not in great but in very minor matters and, though not a help to charity, are no hindrance to the salvation of souls.' At a future general council, he repeats, all difficulties can be sorted out and solved. That was no doubt true of *azyma*, but less obvious in the case of the two ecclesiologies in confrontation.

37

CRUSADES: FALL OF CONSTANTINOPLE (1204): INNOCENT III: BALSAMON

Pope Urban II intended the crusade(s) to be both a support to Christians in the east, with the rider that they were simultaneously to be brought to reconciliation and pristine unity with the Roman see, and also a means of defending western pilgrims to the holy places.[1] In practice relations between crusaders and the east Roman emperor steadily deteriorated until, it must be said, the western forces became more influential than the Turks in achieving the destruction of the Byzantine empire. Commercial interests played a part, with rivalry developing between Venice and Constantinople for control in the Adriatic, and western merchants trading in the eastern capital became the object of steadily mounting odium, culminating under the anti-Latin emperor Andronicus in 1182 in a massacre of foreigners in the city. Three years later the Normans captured Thessalonica and subjected the inhabitants to ferocious deaths and tortures, vividly described by an eye-witness, Eustathius.[2] The 1180s were a disastrous decade both for the empire and for the crusading forces in the Holy Land, who suffered grave defeat from Saladin and the loss of Jerusalem. Byzantium came to need an alliance with Saladin to protect the empire from western invaders and the erosion of power in the Balkans generally. The secular weakness of the German empire in the 1190s was soon compensated for by the advent of a great and ambitious pope, Innocent III (1198–1216), who longed to overcome the separation of the eastern churches from his jurisdiction. He happened to coincide with a passionately ambitious Doge of Venice, Enrico Dandolo, who saw Venetian interests threatened by the eastern empire and therefore dreamt of military action to make it Venetian property, thereby warding off Italian rivals, Pisa and Genoa.

---

[1] See Becker, *Papst Urban II.* On Urban in south Italy, see Robert Somerville, *Urban II* (Oxford, 1996).
[2] Text and annotated English translation by J. R. Melville Jones, *Eustathios of Thessaloniki* (Byzantina Australiensia, 8; Canberra, 1988), H. Hunger, *Die Normannen in Thessalonike* (Graz, 1955).

Innocent III

In 1198–9 Innocent III corresponded with the patriarch of Constantinople, John Kamateros, and with the Greek emperor Alexios III. The launching of another crusade was in the Pope's mind, and there was also an interest in building a fresh alliance between Constantinople and the Papacy to put a check on German (Hohenstaufen) ambitions to unite Germany with Sicily. To the patriarch, Innocent affirmed the necessity of the Pope's Petrine primacy, so that to be out of communion with the Pope was to be outside the Church which is the ark of salvation. This Roman primacy existed by divine creation, and had such universality of jurisdiction ('plenitude of power') that its dignity made Rome the 'mother of all churches'.

Pope Innocent was confident that he was not only successor of Peter but also vicar of Christ so as to be 'the Christ of the Lord', admittedly lower than God but certainly higher than men, 'who judges all and is judged by none'. For 'Christ left to Peter not only the entire Church but also the entire world to govern'.[3] It followed that the papacy had all authority to transfer the empire from the Greeks to the Franks.

Innocent's powerful claims for his supremacy in the Church had an important underpinning in the great collection of western canon law compiled a few decades earlier by Gratian of Bologna in his 'Harmony of Discordant Canons'. Gratian was neither ignorant nor disparaging towards the eastern patriarchs, but his conception of the universal Church was that of a pyramid with the papacy at its apex and with all other authority derived therefrom. Gratian articulated Church law in a tight juridical form with precise rulings from the past, in particular papal decretals many of which he derived from Pseudo-Isidore, the ecclesiology of Nicolas I and Gregory VII. The patriarchs of Constantinople understood the nature of the Church's structures in a more collegial way. At the same time patriarchs of Constantinople wanted the east centralized in their see.

Patriarch Kamateros replied with a declaration of welcome for union. But the universality claimed for centralized Roman authority was not the eastern understanding: 'Christ's flock has many shepherds, and the mother of all is Jerusalem.' It was not the Greek east that had rent the unique garment of Christ, but Rome by adding *Filioque* to the creed in defiance of scripture and of the decisions of councils assented to by papal legates as attested by their signatures. The words of Christ in Matthew 16 do not specify that the Roman Church is the head, the universal and catholic mother of all churches everywhere throughout the entire world; nor had that been decreed by any ecumenical council. St Peter's preaching and martyrdom in the city of Rome

[3] PL 217. 657–8, 215. 759 CD. For Innocent III's writings see PL 214–17.

was an insufficient basis for primatial claims of the kind being made. Certainly the Roman Church had a primacy, founded on the pentarchy; it is 'first among honoured sisters'. The supreme head of the Church is not Peter or the Roman Church but Christ himself. The honour of Rome is derived from its former possession of emperor and senate, neither of whom resides there now.[4]

Balsamon

The stance of the patriarch of Constantinople was also underpinned by the work of canonists, and in particular by the labours of Theodore Balsamon, who had risen at Hagia Sophia to the influential posts of Nomophylax and then Chartophylax.[5] He was consecrated to be patriarch of Antioch for the years 1185–91, but the residence of a Latin patriarch at his see forced him to live in Constantinople. This circumstance did nothing to endear the Latins to him. His commentary on the canon law recognized by the Greek churches, namely the authorities defined by the second canon of the Council *in Trullo* of 692, contains some sharply anti-Latin observations: 'their words are smoother than oil (Ps. 55: 21), Satan having hardened their hearts.' He was sure that the Latins had seceded from the authentic tradition, and that the powers, for example of appellate jurisdiction, given to the papacy by the canons of western Serdica had been wholly transferred to New Rome. The old capital had passed under the power of barbarians. The true Romans were subjects of the Christian emperor at Constantinople. The laws of the emperors stood in Greek canon law where papal decretals stood in the west.

The Latin Patriarchate

The fourth crusade of 1204 turned its attack on Constantinople, led by the Venetians and the French (not Normans), with catastrophic, long-lasting consequences for relations between eastern and western Churches. In the west Villehardouin saw it as a chapter of accidents, not initially intended, but of course it would not have occurred had there not been anti-Greek anger, memories of the anti-Latin massacre in 1182, and belief that schismatics could rightly be compelled to unity. Pope Innocent III had never suggested that the crusaders should assault the city, but when the great capital fell, he did not hide his delight at the outcome. The schismatics had been brought

---

[4] A. Papadakis and A. M. Talbot, 'John X Camateros Confronts Innocent III', *Byzantinoslavica*, 33 (1972), 24–41.

[5] On Balsamon see Clarence Gallagher, *Church Law and Church Order* (Aldershot, 2002), 153–86, V. Grumel, *Revue des études byzantines*, 1 (1943), 250–70. Most of his writings are in PG 119. 137–8; the commentaries on canon law conveniently in RP.

low, and now they would all be required to take an oath of loyalty to the Pope, with a fulfilment of a long-held western dream, mightily offensive to Greeks, a Latin patriarch installed at Constantinople. By force of arms unity between Rome and Constantinople had been restored. Rome could even recognize the bishop of New Rome to have the rank of 'patriarch'—at long last.[6] The crusading soldiers had admittedly inflicted massive damage on looted churches, removing gold and silver vessels, overturning altars, throwing holy relics into the sea, trampling on icons of saints, even using churches to stable their horses. Such actions were not calculated to impress Greek Christians with the devotional sensitivity of those whom they took to be representatives of the western churches inviting them to union in obedience to the will of God. The Greeks retorted by declining to celebrate the eucharist at any altar which had been used for the Latin rite unless it were first washed and disinfected. It was a manifestation of the rancour reflected in western treatment of Greek churches and clergy that once a year (westerners mistakenly believed) the bishop of Rome was declared excommunicate. But well before 1204 there was a groundswell of anti-Latin feeling. The measure of mutual hostility can be exemplified in the Life of patriarch Leontius of Jerusalem (1110–85) who found himself forbidden by the Latins to visit Jerusalem except incognito and unofficially, so that he was not allowed to celebrate the liturgy at the Holy Sepulchre, and had to meet a death threat.[7]

More formidable was the canonist Balsamon. He regarded Rome's claim to universal jurisdiction as utterly invalidated by the heresy of the *Filioque*, and interpreted the Donation of Constantine as conferring just such a jurisdiction on the see of Constantinople. Balsamon judged that Latin prisoners and other westerners who sought to receive communion in Greek churches must first renounce Latin 'heresies and customs' (i.e. *Filioque* and *azyma*).[8] At least he did not recommend rebaptism, which was a question in the cases of Nestorians, Armenians, and Syrian Jacobites, but all these, so he held, could be admitted on renunciation of their heresy and on receiving chrism.[9]

Balsamon deeply resented Latin claims that the *Filioque* embodied no disagreement in dogma from the Greek tradition, and that unleavened bread in the eucharist was nothing to get excited about since both Latin and Greek customs were valid. 'The Latins have separated from us, but use very oily language.'[10] He was decisive in his opinion that those Greeks who believed the east to be wrong not to be in communion with the see of Rome failed to

---

[6] Fourth Lateran Council 1215, canon 5 (i. 236 ed. Tanner). Awareness of the crusaders' ambition for a Latin patriarch enforcing *azyma* at the eucharist appears in 1147 in Manganeios Prodromos in verses soon to be edited by E. M. and M. J. Jeffreys.

[7] Leontius' Life is edited with English version and notes by D. Tsougarakis (Leiden, 1993).

[8] RP iv. 463.   [9] Ibid. 473.   [10] Ibid. 521.

realize that a difference in dogma was at stake.[11] The western claim to be in agreement on all essentials was for him simply false.

Balsamon would surely have found it hard to echo Nicetas' language to Anselm of Havelberg about sister churches. At least the western church was for him a fallen sister. The attitude of the westerners outside Rome can be judged from the *Chronicon Maius* of Matthew Paris. He was notoriously no admirer of Innocent III. But for him it was sheer arrogance for the Greek church to be claiming to be a sister church rather than a daughter,[12] an opinion which was being echoed from Rome in 1997.

Pope Innocent III's fourth Lateran Council of 1215 complained (canon 4) of the pride and hatred of Greeks towards Latins, illustrated by Greek refusal to offer the eucharist on an altar previously used by a Latin priest without first washing it clean from defilement, and by Greek rebaptism of Latin converts. How different were the assumptions about authority is seen in the fact that the canons of the Lateran Council are decisions taken by Innocent III rather than conciliar acts. The assembly of bishops is advisory. Greeks did not think that way.

[11] RP ii. 695.   [12] Ed. H. R. Luard, iii (London, 1876), 386, s.a. 1237.

38

EAST–WEST DEBATES AT NICAEA
AND NYMPHAION

The Greek centre of government moved with the patriarchate to Nicaea, to remain there until 1261. The weakness and low morale of the east Roman empire was not lost on hungry adventurers in the west, who wanted to capture more of the old empire if they could. The emperor John III Vatatzes (1222–54) calculated that the survival of the remains of his empire must depend on restoration of communion with Rome, thereby depriving warlike Normans of a motive for further hostilities. Five Franciscans on pilgrimage had been taken hostage, but were released on accepting a commission, on returning to the west, to ask the Pope to send legates for a discussion of the issues. Patriarch Germanos' letter to the Pope invited the correction of mistakes. Gregory IX accordingly sent in May 1233 two Franciscans (one English, one French) and two Dominicans from France. They passed through Constantinople on their way to Nicaea, where they arrived on 15 January 1234. We owe to one of the four a vivid and impassioned account of their experiences.[1]

The papal envoys were warmly received by emperor and patriarch. When they asked to be taken to the principal church of the city for prayers, they found themselves being shown a smaller church where the first Council of Nicaea was held, with frescoes illustrating that assembly. Next day with the patriarch they were asked if they came as legates to a council, as the patriarch evidently hoped, and explained that they had no powers to negotiate but were merely messengers to the patriarch personally, not to a council. Their commission was not to debate doubtful matters but rather to deal with Greek doubts in amicable conversation. In the faith and practice of the Roman Church there was nothing open to review or question. Doctrines defined

---

[1] Ed. H. Golubovich, *Archivum Franciscanum Historicum*, 12 (1919), 428–65. Blemmydes' document refuting the *Filioque* is edited in Greek by P. Canard, *Orientalia Christiana Periodica*, 25 (1959), 310–25, Blemmydes' autobiography is edited by Joseph A. Munitiz in the Greek series of Corpus Christianorum, 13 (Turnhout, 1984); his annotated English version in Spicilegium Sacrum Lovaniense, études et documents 48 (Leuven, 1988). See also his paper 'A Reappraisal of Blemmydes' First Discussion with the Latins', *Byzantinoslavica*, 51 (1990), 20–6, with remarks on the document on the *Filioque*.

with divine authority called for obedience, not discussion. The western aim was to invite the Greek churches to submit to papal authority, as they once used to do. The central question would be whether the *Filioque* and unleavened bread constituted a reason for withholding obedience. The four emissaries then obtained the use of a church for Latin mass next morning, which was attended by Franks, Englishmen, and other Latins living at Nicaea. One of these Latins after mass wept as he told the envoys that for attending this mass his Greek priest excommunicated him. The priest in question with other clergy were sent to apologize to the Latin emissaries, for an act done in naivety, not out of malice. The friars asked the patriarch to grant them pardon.

On 19 January disputation began in the emperor's palace. The westerners wanted *azyma* to be taken first. They felt specially confident on that question; the Dominicans at Constantinople had persuaded the Greek abbot of St Mamas to offer no objection to unleavened bread.[2] The friars felt the Greeks were on the run. But the Greeks insisted that the primary issue was the procession of the Holy Spirit. The friars were sure that on neither topic was there real disagreement. This immediately led the old and infirm patriarch to be awkward and to ask if some addition had been made to the creed, as he had heard to be the case. Next morning, after mass and the canonical hours, disputation was resumed, with the patriarch telling 'one of his wise men' to read Cyril of Alexandria's insistence on no addition to the Nicene creed. For the westerners, Cyril constituted no authority, but in any event the west had made no alteration in the faith; and where could the Greeks find authority for their statement that the Spirit does *not* proceed from the Son, which really is an addition to the Nicene creed? When the Greeks then read the creed of Constantinople (381), the Latins immediately observed that this creed added to the Nicene creed of 325, a point which much embarrassed the Greek spokesmen until they conceded that it was not an addition in so far as it was expressing the truth. The envoys could quote Cyril's joining of the Son with the Father in the procession of the Spirit. They had brought an arsenal of texts from Constantinople. To deny the *Filioque* was not precisely the Greek position, explained a philosopher; it was rather that the Greeks do not say 'and from the Son'. The philosophers made the emperor anxious; he deplored resort to syllogisms in stating articles of faith.

On the evening of Tuesday, 24 January 1234 the friars were called to the patriarch's house, where they were handed a long document stating the Greek case. They had supposed the questions to be simple and had not expected a written statement. They debated whether they would receive this

---

[2] The Athos manuscript, Iviron 381, fo. 100ʳ, preserves the apology he made to authority: see Laurent, *Regestes*, 1287.

'ridiculous text'. The Greeks observed the scorn of the Latins, and withdrew the text, to compose a revised document delivered to the friars' lodging at bedtime. On 25 January the friars celebrated mass and said their office before working on a Latin version of the Greek document. Word came that the patriarch felt unwell (the friars seem to have thought this a diplomatic illness), and the emperor wrote apologizing for failing earlier to tell the friars that the talks were off. But after a main meal the friars were called to the patriarch's house for debate on the Greek document, though they felt unsure of the correctness of their hasty translation.

From the autobiography of Nikephoros Blemmydes (at heart favourable to union) it is certain that he was the author of the Greek document.[3] He reviewed the Latin arguments for the *Filioque*. It cannot be argued from the consubstantiality of the Spirit with the Son, for the Father is also consubstantial. Nor can it be argued on the ground that the Son sends the Spirit upon the creaturely order. Yet the scripture speaks of the Spirit as being 'of the Son', and, in the Latin view, that must mean that the Spirit proceeds from both Father and Son. Blemmydes thought the Latin arguments wholly unpersuasive. From first principles one cannot deploy logical argument. Christ has said, without syllogism, that the Spirit proceeds from the Father. However, this authoritative utterance is also logically coherent. Blemmydes deploys his clear comprehension of Aristotelian logic. But the crux of his argument is that with the Latin *Filioque* the Son shares with the Father in the origination of the Spirit's procession, and that loses the individuality of the hypostases in the holy Trinity. In the divine Triad, the Monad is not prior to the threeness: that is, not first Monad then a Dyad, and finally a Triad. The Latins make the first principle a Dyad.

The emperor, discerning a rising hostility in the friars, thought Blemmydes' document would merely generate contention. He asked the friars to give their presentation. One of the friars who knew some Greek produced a book by Cyril of Alexandria with a sentence on 'the Spirit of Christ', and observed that Theodoret, to whose criticism of Cyril the Greeks now appealed, had been condemned at the Fifth Council (553). The friars uttered anathema on all who deny the *Filioque* and withdrew.

On 26 January the friars wanted to talk about unleavened bread in the eucharist, especially since the emperor was to leave Nicaea on the following day. The Greeks, however, appeared most reluctant to talk about this subject and seemed to the friars to be almost conducting a filibuster to avert serious discussion. The patriarch finally said that the question was intricate and a proper answer could not be given without a conciliar decision with full participation of the patriarchs of Jerusalem, Alexandria, and Antioch. The

---

[3] Blemmydes, autobiography, 2. 25–40.

friars replied that their commission from the Pope was not to any council, and was to no patriarch other than the presiding Greek bishop. So they would retire to Constantinople. At the patriarch's request they would stay there until mid-March when they would hope to have an answer to take back to Rome. After mass early next morning they went to take their leave of the emperor, and found him with the patriarch. Hope of reconciliation (they said) depended on submission to Rome. When the emperor asked whether, if the Lord Patriarch is willing to obey the Roman Church, the Lord Pope will restore to him his rights, they gave the sharp reply that 'if the patriarch gives obedience and what he owes to his mother, we believe that with the Lord Pope and the entire Roman Church he will find greater mercy than he expects.'

As March ended the friars at Constantinople received a disturbed letter from the patriarch Germanos inviting them to come to Leschara (unidentified location) where a council was to be held. The emperor also wrote saying a ship was ready to transport them, intended also to take his envoys to the Pope. At that time the Latin empire of Constantinople was extremely weak, without money or means of defence, ringed by enemies. If the friars could negotiate a truce with the Greek emperor Vatatzes, the Latin authorities at Constantinople would wish them to accept the invitation. So they went to Leschara and thence on to Nymphaion, east of Smyrna, where the Greek emperors had a palace. (Substantial ruins of the palace survive today.)

Discussions began on 17 April and their temper was from the start difficult. It did not help that the palace had no copy of the Bible. When the friars wanted a speedy debate, they were met by a paper with thirty anti-Latin propositions which were hardly to be answered in haste.[4] Moreover, the patriarch of Antioch had not yet turned up. The friars again asked for *azyma* to be discussed first, but the patriarch insisted that the procession of the Holy Spirit be clarified. A philosopher-monk explained that for Greeks the Holy Spirit was the prior question. The Greeks wanted their answers put in writing, whereas the friars saw this as a delaying tactic and pressed for oral replies. The patriarch alarmed them by suggesting that the written record of the previous discussions at Nicaea be read in full. The friars felt that they were being deceitfully treated. They were evidently aware that the Greeks were on far stronger ground with the *Filioque* than with *azyma*.

---

[4] J. Darrouzès, *Revue des études byzantines*, 21 (1963), 50–100 edits an astonishing catalogue of Latin errors by Constantine Stilbes, bishop of Cyzicus. His list includes much more than *Filioque*, *azyma*, and papal autocracy, not to mention items from Cerularius' indictment. The catalogue includes indulgences (no. 33), and outrage at the sack of Constantinople (76 ff.), 'for which no sanctions have been imposed on the criminal malefactors' (98).

The Latins seemed to speak with two voices, asserting the validity of both traditions, Greek and Latin, yet regarding the Greeks as being in error on *Filioque* and *azyma*. The Greeks did not think either Latin tradition valid.

On 26 April the archbishop of Amastris on the Black Sea coast asked the friars if the Pope intended to maintain the existence of two parallel traditions in the Greek and Latin ways of celebrating the eucharist. (If so, could he accuse the Greeks of being in the wrong in their customs?) The friars felt the question was somehow a trap, and denied their competence to interpret the Pope's letter. The friendliness of the earlier discussion at Nicaea rapidly evaporated, with Greeks cataloguing the crimes and sacrilege of the sack of Constantinople in 1204, the friars enumerating Greek offences in denying validity to a sacrament using unleavened bread, in cleansing altars after use for a Latin mass. Each party believed that the other side had deleted their leader, pope or patriarch, from commemoration in their respective diptychs, thereby certainly implying him to be excommunicate and a heretic. The patriarchal archivist denied that the Greeks excommunicate the pope. The friars denied that the patriarch had at any time been in Roman diptychs.

The emperor Vatatzes realised that the conference was fast passing out of control. The archbishop of Amastris explicitly rejected the possibility of mass with *azyma*, to be met by the awkward question from the friars whether he meant canonically forbidden or intrinsically impossible. The Greeks were sure that leavened bread had once been used at Rome, since St Peter could not have given one tradition to the west and another to the east. The Pentarchy must be agreed. A written document condemning *azyma* was handed to the friars, signed by the archivist in obedience to the patriarchs of Constantinople and Antioch. The friars answered with a written text declaring that 'anyone who believes that the Holy Spirit does not proceed from the Son is in the way of perdition', citing in support Athanasius, Cyril, Ambrose, Jerome, and Augustine, and condemning appeal to Theodoret's criticism of Cyril as an invocation of a heretic censured at the fifth council. This written text defending the *Filioque* was then supported by an oral statement declaring that 'bread' could be either leavened or unleavened, so that both usages were valid. And the Greeks should please not appeal to St John's gospel against the other three gospels on the question whether the Last Supper was the Passover meal.

The emperor put the sad question whether compromise might be possible. Perhaps the Latins could drop the *Filioque*, and the Greeks accept the validity of *azyma*. That kind of procedure was customary with secular princes. So it was a question to the friars if perhaps the Pope would yield a little. 'Not an iota', was the friars' reply. The Greeks must make a formal declaration that *azyma* are as valid as leavened bread, and they ought to confess the *Filioque*.

The meeting ended with each side condemning the other for heresy. The emperor gave the friars leave to depart. They left without a salute to the patriarch and council and were recalled, but only to say in anger that patriarch and council mattered nothing to them. They had six days' voyage to Constantinople after crossing a desert land, facing mountain bandits. After six or seven miles the emperor's army officer arrived on horseback. The friars turned back to their lodging and gathered their books. The archivist came and abstracted the Greek paper on *azyma*, but failed to remove the translation already made.

The patriarch issued a formal synodical statement on the procession of the Holy Spirit from the Father, mediated through the Son to the created order; the *Filioque* was utterly unacceptable. A strong anti-Latin statement could help in the difficult task of maintaining unity among the different Orthodox 'national' groups. It was also a warning shot against those Greeks who (like the emperor) wanted an accommodation with the Roman see. In 1245 a council at Lyon was to describe the emperor Vatatzes as 'the enemy of God'.[5]

The Latin friars more than once accused the Greeks of proceeding disingenuously, especially in the patriarch's repeated attempts to persuade them to participate in a formal synod. It is not evident that they were justified in drawing this conclusion even from their own account of the matter. It is, however, certain that the two sides were not sufficiently equipped in each other's language and did not understand one another as soon as the debate became in the least technical. The protagonists felt it to be their duty to achieve total defeat and refutation of their partners in debate. No concession was possible by either party. Naturally enough the Greeks remained angry and resentful at the Latin occupation of Constantinople, and this political background could hardly fail to colour their attitude. The Greeks also thought that with Blemmydes' carefully argued document they had presented a reasoned case against the *Filioque*. The friars repeated preference for talking about *azyma* may well be taken to imply that they felt on stronger ground there than on the doctrine of the Trinity. Blemmydes' arguments were in fact formidable, and though the friars were not without some comprehension of Aristotle's logic they cannot be said to have answered the Greek case. For them both *Filioque* and *azyma* rested ultimately on supreme and universal jurisdiction in the Roman see. That implied an ecclesiology which the Greek east did not share.

[5] Ed. Tanner, i. 282.

39

PURGATORY

There was an aftermath to the Franciscan visit to Nicaea and Nymphaion. At a Greek monastery near Otranto one of the friars, named Bartholomew, met the Metropolitan of Corfu, George Bardanes, and the conversation turned to the destiny of the departed. What, asked the friar, did Greeks believe to be the destiny of souls dying before they had completed the penance imposed by their confessor? The friar held what had become the normal Latin view that immediately on death souls receive their reward, the damned to hell, the just to paradise, the imperfect to purification in Purgatory. To Bardanes that seemed indistinguishable from Origenist universalism denying everlasting punishment. Bardanes could grant that the imperfect need purification, but absolutely rejected the notion of any place of purgation, with material fire, and pains which carry expiation for faults. The friar was sure that Pope Gregory the Great (*Dial.* 4. 39) taught these last doctrines. (Augustine was uneven and hesitant on the subject.)

A record of the discussion was made, and its circulation precipitated vigorous reactions since it disclosed a further hitherto undiscovered subject of disagreement between the Latin and Greek churches.[1] Western theologians were sure the Greeks erred in holding that destiny is decided at the general judgement, not at death. Perhaps because of Augustine's hesitations, there was no unanimity that purgatory is a place or what its precise nature would be. At successive encounters in Lyon (1274), Florence (1439), and then at Trent (1563) no exact definition was given.

The report of the debate about purgatory which has survived from the Otranto meeting gives the Greek side, but a Latin account certainly went at once to Rome. Within a few months Pope Innocent IV (1245–54) heard of trouble in Cyprus between Greek and Latin clergy, and sent rulings to his cardinal legate Odo in the island. Some Greeks were already 'obedient to the apostolic see'. Greek rites and usages which did not endanger souls could be tolerated. Greek clergy should follow Roman customs in unctions at baptism; their custom of anointing the entire bodies of baptizands should be

---

[1] The text of the record is edited by M. Roncaglia, *Georges Bardanès métropolite de Corfou et Barthélemy de l'ordre franciscain* (Studi e Testi Francescani, 4; Rome, 1953), one of the three manuscripts being dated 1236 (Barberinus gr. 297).

tolerated if it could not be abolished without scandal. But only bishops should give chrism in confirmation. Unction intended for the sick should not be used for reconciling penitents. The host should be reserved for up to fifteen days, not for a year, and mass should not be celebrated after the ninth hour. Priests were to say matins before, not after mass. Women must not serve the altar. Married priests could hear confessions. There must be no restriction on the number of marriages, if spouses die; but second marriages were not to be blessed. The Greeks must acknowledge that fornication is mortal sin. The longest paragraph teaches purgatory. Speaking against the Holy Spirit cannot be forgiven in this age or in the age to come (Matt. 12: 32) implies that some other offences can be remitted after death; 1 Corinthians 3 teaches purification by fire for believers whose good works are inadequate. Now the Greeks do not deny purification of souls after death, but have no name for the place which the Latins call *purgatorium*, 'the name we wish them to use in future'. The fire is transient and only small and minor sins are thereby purged, not crimes or capital offences.[2]

Innocent IV evidently wished to be concessive towards the Greek churches. Nevertheless he confessed himself puzzled that the Greeks could acknowledge Roman authority to provide a judge in controversies of faith but would not grant the Pope power to add the *Filioque* to the creed.[3]

---

[2] Mansi, *Concilia*, xxii. 581–2. Papal refusal to support Patriarch Nicolas I in his campaign against Leo the Wise's fourth marriage much offended rigorist Greeks: Nicolas, *ep.* 32 (ed. Jenkins–Westerink).

[3] Text in Antonino Franchi, *La svolta politico-ecclesiastica tra Roma e Bisanzio (1249–1254)* (Rome, 1981), 195–6; L. Wadding, *Annales Minorum*, ii (Lyon, 1628), 148–9.

40

MICHAEL PALAEOLOGUS' RENEWED QUEST FOR UNITY: POPE GREGORY X: COUNCIL OF LYON: BEKKOS

On 25 July 1261 Constantinople was recovered for the Greek empire by the usurper Michael Palaeologus, aided by the Genoese. The city remained precarious, and there was no lessening of western ambition to recover Jerusalem (taken by Saladin in 1187) and to dominate the eastern Mediterranean. Charles of Anjou from bases in Naples and Sicily assembled a fleet to reconquer the capital, but his ships were lost in an Aegean storm. The emperor Michael, squeezed between Arab and Latin threats, sought urgent negotiations for unity with successive popes.[1] In 1263 he was assuring Urban IV (1261–4) that there was no disputed point on which he did not submit to Rome's verdict, and Urban replied that all issues between the Greek and Latin churches came down to obedience to papal authority. A mediating role was played by a bilingual Greek from Dyrrachium (Durrës/Durazzo), Nicolas, who became bishop of Cotrone (Crotone) in Calabria. He adapted an anthology of citations in defence of the Latin *Filioque* dependent on the collection attested in the manuscript Parisinus gr. 1115, and paid a clandestine visit to the emperor Michael. He made a poor Latin translation which Pope Urban sent to Thomas Aquinas, who made the anthology the basis for his tract refuting Greek errors (*Contra errores Graecorum*) vindicating the *Filioque*, papal primacy, *azyma* in the eucharist, and the Latin doctrine of purgatory. This became programmatic for the Latin stance in negotiation. Michael being politically weak, the papacy could be tough and uncompromising.

Urban's successor, Clement IV (1265–8), prescribed assent to a formula of faith: the Greeks had to accept the *Filioque*, purgatory, seven sacraments, papal primacy with Rome's appellate jurisdiction; all powers of eastern patriarchs were derived from Rome. There could be no council at which there was open discussion or a new definition of dogma. Clement added in a subsequent letter that the emperor had great power over the Greek clergy and

---

[1] For a magistral account of the emperor Michael's ecumenism see D. J. Geanakoplos, *Emperor Michael Palaeologus and the West* (Cambridge, Mass., 1959)

should simply coerce his subjects into union. Neither pope nor emperor needed to provide reasoned argument.

The emperor Michael did not have as much power as the Pope supposed. His usurpation and murder of the legitimate young emperor Vatatzes brought excommunication from the patriarch Arsenius, who was thereupon forced to resign but whose party remained troublesome even after his death. Moreover, Michael's policy was to look west rather than east, to see virtually insuperable difficulties in repelling the Turks in Asia Minor, and to aspire to integrate the old east Roman empire so closely into the western powers that, as under Justinian, Constantinople could once more be a New Rome, not merely the empire of the Greeks. That policy was to cause anxiety among his subjects, and if it entailed submission of his Church to the bishop of Rome, opposition was bound to be formidable.

About 1272 a conciliatory essay proposing a programme for conciliar harmony was produced by Humbert, a Dominican from Romans near Valence in the Dauphiné. He knew Greek and understood the eastern standpoint. He thought it impossible that one could envisage two churches, western and eastern. Christ did not say, Upon this rock I will build my churches. The Nicene creed affirms one holy catholic and apostolic Church. If one Church, reason demands a focus in a single leading bishop. Therefore the Greek churches should be persuaded to repent of schism. Humbert traced the history of gradual widening of the gap: the disagreements over Constantinople in 381 and at Chalcedon in 451; the Acacian schism ending in Hormisdas' humiliation of the Greek bishops; Pope Martin and the Lateran Council; the Quinisext critique of western customs; the cool western attitude to the second Council of Nicaea on icons; the tension about the Bulgarian mission. Humbert thought the history important, especially the offence caused by the coronation of Charlemagne, a matter on which Latins were regrettably ignorant. They ought to learn Greek, should treat their legates with respect, cease to distrust the Greeks, and not demand obedience from them. The Greeks should be asked to reciprocate by not washing altars after Latin priests have celebrated there, and not requiring a Latin woman marrying a Greek to renounce western rites. It should be frankly conceded that the Roman Church needed cleaning up, and that in western cathedrals the attendance of canons at the canonical hours had become deplorable. One 'notorious fornicating prelate' could not be further tolerated. In short the agenda of the coming council needed to include the reformation of morals. The luxurious life-style of cardinals needed checking. Excessive saints' feasts were resented by lay merchants and traders. Some bishops were corrupt. Sellers of indulgences and relics ought to be suppressed.[2]

---

[2] Humbert's *Opusculum Tripartitum* is edited in Edward Brown, *Appendix ad Fasciculum rerum expetendarum et fugiendarum* (London, 1690), 185–228; discussion in a monograph by E. T. Brett (Toronto, 1984).

The Council of Lyon

Pope Gregory X announced in March 1272 that in 1274 a general council would meet in May at Lyon. In the autumn he sent an invitation to the patriarch of Constantinople, Joseph I, and informed the emperor Michael Palaeologus of his intentions. The Roman conditions for unity were those stated by Clement IV, but the legates were privately told to present them so as to make them appear flexible. The actual formula of submission to Rome was not rigid. Gregory's principal hope was to win support for a crusade, a plan welcomed by Michael with the proviso that he would need to calm adverse forces at home. Michael believed that in practice papal claims to appellate jurisdiction and commemoration in the diptychs would cost next to nothing, and that it was a trivial price to pay for Roman restraint on Charles of Anjou, King of Sicily and ambitions to recapture Constantinople. But Greek theologians judged the Latin *Filioque* heretical; John Bekkos, archivist at Hagia Sophia, was imprisoned for expressing this opinion. The patriarch Joseph, Michael's sister, and some prominent military figures joined forces in the anti-unionist cause: nothing was more likely to incur divine displeasure than a compromise of the authoritative Orthodox tradition popularly identified with Byzantine patriotism. What Michael was proposing implied a loss of Orthodox identity: were they to 'lose themselves to gain the Pope'? Patriarch Joseph put it more correctly: he was wholly in favour of union if Rome corrected its errors. No serious Christian could then be against union.

Joseph was sure the 'Italians' were heretical not merely mistaken, though in the exercise of 'economy' he would say this only in private, not to their face. Moreover, he was sure that on *azyma* they were in collusion with the Armenians. The Pope had given no assurances that Greek customs would be preserved. The Latins had falsified texts of Cyril of Alexandria to defend the *Filioque*. Past experience had shown that the Latin crusaders, far from being a support to the Greeks in checking the invading Arabs, were themselves an equal danger on the other flank. Communion with Rome could be accepted only in the way that Photius had done this when he found the 'Italians' professing the same creed at the sixth session of the Council of 879–80.

Pope Gregory's Council at Lyon opened on 7 May 1274, and began with the problem of fund-raising through tithes to finance a crusade to recover the Holy Land.[3] The western attendance was large, including the king of Aragon

---

[3] The constitutions of the Council of Lyon are printed with English translation in vol i of Tanner, based on the collection by G. Alberigo, *Conciliorum oecumenicorum decreta*[3] (Bologna, 1973). An Orthodox story of the Council in Geanakoplos (p. 246 n. 1 above), a Roman Catholic estimate in J. Gill, *Byzantium and the Papacy 1198–1400* (New Brunswick, 1979); id., 'The Church Union of the Council of Lyons (1274) Portrayed in Greek Documents', *Orientalia Christiana Periodica*, 40 (1974),

and many abbots and priors. The Greek delegation encountered a severe storm in the Aegean which sank one of the two ships with large loss of life and rich presents for the Pope; the other ship reached Modon, and the delegates arrived at Lyon on 24 July, the council being already in session. Patriarch Joseph was not among them, but the ex-patriarch Germanos III came with Theophanes, metropolitan of Nicaea and, more important than they, the emperor's Grand Logothete (or First Lord of the Treasury and Prime Minister), George Acropolites, a layman who had been orally empowered by the emperor to swear before the council, on his behalf, that he professed the faith of the Roman Church and recognized its primacy. Representation of the Greek churches was so thin that the assembly could hardly enjoy confidence in the east. Almost all the western bishops thought the submission to Rome to be motivated solely by temporal considerations, i.e. to check Charles of Anjou. That was in fact what the emperor had frankly said. Pope Gregory was satisfied that the declaration was sincerely intended. The *Te Deum* and the Nicene creed with the *Filioque* were both chanted in Latin and then the Greek legates with bishops and abbots from Sicily repeated twice in Greek.

George Acropolites had no written document to show the Pope his plenipotentiary powers, but he brought a bull in golden ink from the emperor, affirming assent to the *Filioque*, to the Latin doctrine of purgatory (as that had been explained to him by a Greek Franciscan at Constantinople), and papal primacy. However, the emperor requested leave to allow the Greek Church to say the creed 'as it did before the schism and until today, and that we may keep to our rites as used before the schism'.

The emperor's letter frankly explained that some Greeks needed more time to reflect, but agreed to the primacy of Rome as attributed to that see in antiquity in accordance with the terms of the ancient conciliar canons. The emperor's son Andronicus also sent a letter declaring his agreement with his father.

There was no discussion in council concerning *Filioque* or purgatory. The Pope himself was no theologian, but had Albert the Great and Bonaventure present (the latter died during the council). Thomas Aquinas was invited but died on the way. The formal constitution professed the procession of the Spirit from the Father and the Son 'not as from two first principles but as from one, not by two spirations but by one single spiration which has always

5–45; J. Darrouzès, *Dossier grec de l'union de Lyon* (Paris, 1976); A. Franchi, *Il Concilio II di Lione (1274) secondo la Ordinatio Concilii Generalis Lugdunensis* (Rome, 1965); the symposium, *1274, année charnière* (Paris, 1977). B. Roberg has written two monographs on the Council (1964 and 1990), with a supplement of texts from Paris and Durham in *Annuarium Historiae Conciliorum*, 21 (1989), 103–46. Letters to and from Gregory X are collected by A. L. Tautu, *Acta Urbani IV, Clementis IV, Gregorii X* (Codex Iuris Canonici Orientalis, Fontes[3], V/I; Vatican City, 1953).

been believed by the holy Roman Church, mother and mistress, and is also the faith of both Latin and Greek fathers.'

The wording of this constitution, first published with others early in November 1274, directly rebuts the accusation inherited from Photius that the *Filioque* implies two first principles or ultimate causes. It is impossible to know whether it may have undergone some rewriting in the papal chancery subsequent to the council.

In his *Summa Theologiae* (II, 18 qu. 122 memb. 1 art. 2) Albert the Great records that at Lyon the Greeks were compelled to grant that fornication is mortal sin.[4] This did not reach the formal constitutions, and may have been the result of conversation outside synodical proceedings. The topic may have had indirect bearing on Humbert of Romans's demand for the removal of 'a notorious fornicating prelate'. On July 3 Pope Gregory in council demanded and obtained the resignation of Archbishop Henry of Liège on account of his 'excesses'.

Bekkos

Michael suddenly found a highly intelligent supporter and convert to his cause in John Bekkos, whose prison studies of Cyril of Alexandria showed him to have good authority in a Greek father of high standing using the language of *Filioque*.[5] His florilegium defending the *Filioque* had 123 citations from Cyril. Against the anti-unionists' appeal to the *Mystagogia* of Photius, Bekkos' studies, especially in the Acts of the Council of 879 convinced him that Photius' arguments against the *Filioque* were coloured by personal resentment against Nicolas I and Hadrian II (with some of their successors), and that his acceptance of communion with Rome in 879–80 without demanding of the papal legates any formal disavowal of western heresy betrayed recognition of this truth. For anti-unionists Photius was a heroic saint monstrously maligned, whose troubles were simply caused by Roman ambition in Bulgaria. Bekkos' argument that Photius had been in the wrong in the displacement of Ignatius as patriarch and that his character was deeply flawed aroused profound anger; this was deemed worthy of synodical anathema (after the emperor Michael's death). It was to become important to Orthodoxy to put Photius on a pedestal as faultless, so to repel the danger-

[4] *Opera Omnia*, xxxiii (Paris, 1895), 396.
[5] Bekkos' writings are printed in Migne, PG 141; discussion by J. Gill, *Byzantina*, 7 (1975), 251–66. The historian Pachymeres provides a vivid contemporary portrait of Bekkos and his problems. Important texts in Darrouzès, *Dossier grec*, esp. 430 ff. On Pachymeres see A. Laiou, *Constantinople and the Latins* (Cambridge, Mass. 1972), 32–7. Bekkos' vast florilegium from Cyril (PG 141. 613–724) much influenced Bessarion and Isidore of Kiev in their acceptance of the Florence union (1439); see B. Meunier, *Annuarium Historiae Conciliorum*, 21 (1989), 147–74.

ously plausible thesis of Bekkos that the *Filioque* was no more than a pretext for wrongfooting Rome, and therefore that the schism had no justification.

It is scarcely possible to believe that Pope Gregory X was uninformed about the strength of anti-papal opposition at Constantinople. At Lyon he had obtained the submission of the emperor, but not of the current patriarch Joseph, who in the event refused his assent and had to resign. The emperor brought in Bekkos to succeed him five months later, which imposed on the new patriarch a stormy career. Greek distrust of the power-hungry Latins was deep. But no less formidable was the scepticism of Gregory X's successors and other Latin bishops concerning the sincerity of the emperor Michael and his son Andronicus. Successive popes after Gregory's time continued to demand individual oaths of submission not only from the emperor Michael and his son but also from all clergy; none was to be exempt from the requirement to affirm the *Filioque*. Such a demand ensured fanatical anti-western feeling, and bishops who assented to the union found numerous laity refusing to accept the sacraments at their hands and describing them in pamphlets in abusive terms. By invoking the principle of 'economy', whereby an unsatisfactory situation may be tolerated for the sake of achieving in time something better, a substantial body of bishops and clergy conformed to the emperor's unionist policy, and the historian Pachymeres reports on the debate which this caused, with the opponents of the Council of Lyon denying that this principle could properly be invoked to justify a compromise with heretics. As one might expect, the principle of economy enabled many clergy and laity to support the emperor's unionist policy either without commitment or even merely to advance their career at the court.

The emperor Michael was utterly frank in telling his bishops to have harmony with the Latin west on the persuasive ground that this was a condition of the empire's survival. The threats of Charles of Anjou remained, and in Epirus and northern Greece, where Charles acquired allies, there was no enthusiasm for the prospect of being dominated by a westward-looking emperor at Constantinople. Bulgaria, courteously persuaded by Innocent III to recognize papal primacy without any questions about the *Filioque* or eucharistic bread, was also reserved towards the policies of Michael and was on friendly terms with Latin patriarchs.

On Mount Athos Michael's soldiers are said to have set fire to the intransigent Bulgarian monastery Zographou; monks were killed and books destroyed. The emperor acquired a reputation for tyrannical government. Sustained pressure failed to win the hearts of the opposition, especially among the laity, women being prominent.

Charles of Anjou's influence with the French Pope Martin IV (1281–5) brought a papal excommunication of the emperor Michael, to which the emperor retorted by having the Pope's name deleted from the commemoration in the diptychs. With Michael's death (11 December 1282) and the accession of his son Andronicus, Bekkos' fall was a matter of days. He was tried (unedifyingly) and imprisoned for the remaining fourteen years of his life. But political factors had already ruined the peace process of Lyon.

The *Filioque* was the only dogma on which the Council of Lyon gave a ruling. Bekkos and his emperor had a strong case for contending that this issue was secondary or even marginal: was the Spirit proceeding from the Father *and* the Son or *through* the Son? But Bekkos was no Latinizing theologian; his ecclesiology was fully Byzantine. He regretted putting the *Filioque* into the liturgical creed, but thought it legitimate theology.

In the west the Council of Lyon was deemed 'ecumenical' on the ground of the pope's presidency. No eastern patriarch was there or represented but those attending included Latin patriarchs of Constantinople and Antioch, and it was celebrated as a council which achieved a long-desired union with the separated Greeks who had refused to acknowledge papal primacy of jurisdiction. At Constantinople that achievement was far from clear. A defence of the *Filioque* composed by George Acropolites was consigned to the flames after Michael's death. How peripheral he thought the theological issue to be appears from the fact that earlier he had written a pamphlet, based on Photius, on the error of this doctrine.[6]

A retrospective judgement on the exchanges before, at, and after the Council of Lyon has to notice the degree to which Latins and Greeks could each conceive of union and communion only if the other were wholly converted to the 'opposed' standpoint. Except in the writings of Bekkos, Greek scrutiny of theological issues was almost trivial. Those willing to make concessions offered only those which in their view cost nothing or, at least on the Greek side, were worth granting in order to save the eastern empire. Bekkos himself felt that there could be no alteration of Greek customs such as chrism being given by presbyters, consecration by invocation of the Holy Spirit (epiklesis), and leavened bread in the eucharistic liturgy. The notion that the bishop of Rome's Church is 'more orthodox than ours' he thought false. The Latin *Filioque* was capable of acceptable explanation, but Bekkos did not think it should be inserted into the creed in the Greek liturgy. The Latin purgatory was also unobjectionable. The crux for Bekkos lay in recognition that Latins and Greeks could share the same faith and express it in different idioms—not a widely held view on either side of the divide. Yet some such understanding was implicit in the shared proposition that the great Fathers of the ancient Church, both Greek and Latin, enjoyed consensus. A few years

---

[6] The early anti-Latin tract is edited by A. Heisenberg in the second volume of his Teubner text (1903), with a biographical introduction. W. Blum's introduction to his German translation of Akropolites' Chronicle is valuable (Stuttgart, 1989).

after the Council of Lyon, Duns Scotus (*Ordinatio* 1 d. 11 n. 9) could write that the contradiction between Greeks and Latins concerning the *Filioque* is more apparent than real. No one could treat the doctrines of Basil, Gregory, Cyril, Jerome, Augustine, and Hilary as heretical.

The intention in the achieving of reunion at Lyon in 1274 was to make possible Greek and Latin cooperation in a coming crusade. The plan to recover the Holy Land was soon abandoned, but not that of a crusade to recapture Constantinople. That required a decision by the Pope to declare the emperor Michael Palaeologus to be excommunicate, and therefore a legitimate target for attack by Charles of Anjou. In 1281 the Byzantine army succeeded in repelling the invaders, and in the following year the 'Sicilian Vespers' destroyed the basis for Charles's military ambitions. The emperor Michael died on 11 December 1282, unloved by his church and people. His successor Andronicus abandoned Michael's union policy, and the threat of western campaigns against Constantinople did not die down. Meanwhile the Turkish advance into Asia Minor was unrelenting, and from 1354 they moved into Europe. The west remained intransigent that nothing could or should be done to rescue Constantinople inhabited by dissident schismatics. The notion that the west might itself have an interest in stopping the Turks made virtually no entry into the Latin mind until Islamic forces were penetrating Serbia, Greece, and Bulgaria (1393), and even then western military aid was to be conditional on submission to the pope. On the Greek side there was always a cool reserve fed by the memory of western armies and merchants coming to the east to conquer land and to capture the best trade.

Barlaam

Barlaam started life in a Greek Orthodox family in Calabria in the south of Italy—a region where for a long time the juxtaposition of Latin and Greek had been a source of tension (above, pp. 200 ff.). He became a monk and was well educated to be competent in Greek philosophy and theology. He moved to Thessalonica and became a professor at Constantinople. He could tell bishop Demetrius of Thessalonica that as a general council was hard to gather, 'the mother of churches' had power to rule or correct in a secondary issue (i.e. *Filioque* or *azyma*), and in any event the relative authority of pope and general council was not disputed.

In 1334, when the patriarch of Constantinople desired to reopen the possibility of a good understanding with the Latins, Barlaam was selected to speak for the Greek orthodox position especially on papal primacy and the *Filioque* in dialogue with two Dominican bishops, one French the other English. He was sure of Latin errors and probably from this period of his life came his anti-Latin tracts found in manuscripts in many European libraries and expertly edited by Antonis Fyrigos (Studi e Testi, 347–8; Vatican City, 1998).

These texts show him to be familiar with Aquinas and Denys the Areopagite and to derive from Photius' *Mystagogia* his criticisms of the *Filioque*. He first discerned affinity between Denys and the late Neoplatonists such as Proclus, drawing however the mistaken conclusion that these Neoplatonists were Christians like Denys.

The Dominican bishops evidently impressed him and probably sowed the seeds of his later conversion to the Latin cause; though he admired their logical skill he did not think they proved their case. He remained hegumen of a Constantinople monastery until 1341. He occasionally served the emperor Andronicus III on embassies to the west. Some Greeks were alienated by his criticisms of the theory and practices of the Palamites, whose language about visions of divine light seemed to him Messalian. Censure of his criticisms by synod at Constantinople led him to turn west and at Avignon he was received by Pope Benedict XII. He told Benedict that if Greeks were to be successfully persuaded to accept papal power and doctrines they would need the authority of an ecumenical council. Moreover, it was a diplomatic error to make western military aid dependent or in any way conditional on the submission of the Greek Church. Action by the west to check the relentless tide of Islam ought to come first. The Greeks were repelled by the Latin view that there could be no discussion of western doctrines such as the *Filioque*, and that once papal authority had decided such matters, the only proper course was obedience (PG 151. 127 CD, 1331–42)

Reflection convinced Barlaam that the *Filioque* was no proper justification for a schism splitting the universal Church; the matter seemed to him clearly unrevealed and beyond the power of human reason to decide. His practical solution was to recognize that the question can only be in the realms of transcendent mystery. It would be recognizing the authority of the ecumenical Council of Constantinople if in the liturgy the Church recited the creed in its original form of 381 ('proceeding from the Father') while allowing theologians to affirm the participation of the Son in their informal lecturing and discussion without being accused of heresy. Syllogisms cannot elucidate this issue. We do not know and do not need to know. The Church was once united even when some affirmed the *Filioque* and others affirmed the Spirit proceeding from the Father alone. Now, Latins and Greeks constitute factions where the parties begin from divisive language before they have acquired any powers of thinking. A pamphlet to this effect Barlaam addressed to the Pope in very obsequious language.[7]

---

[7] The Greek of this pamphlet is printed from a Vatican manuscript by C. Giannelli in *Miscellanea Giovanni Mercati* (Studi e Testi, 123; Vatican City, 1946). See T. M. Kolbaba, 'Barlaam the

The emperors realized that their position had become impossible. Emperor Manuel II (1391–1425) was clear in the famous dictum that the only viable policy was to talk to the west positively about reunion but not to forget that the Greek people nursed attitudes to the Latins which made it hopeless (Georgios Sphrantzes 2. 13).

The authority of the Latin churches in conversation with the Greek east was spectacularly weakened by the election in 1378 of two rival popes. Successive attempts to reduce their number to one were unsuccessful and produced three popes. The only available expedient for solving the problem was a general council. This implied the view of theologians and canonists of the thirteenth century that a general council possessed an authority superior to that of a pope, on the ground that, if a pope could fall into heresy, then only a general council could rectify the situation and suspend him from his sublime office. In the time of Photius it was almost non-controversial at Rome that Pope Honorius could have fallen into heresy by supporting monotheletism, but such heresy was a unique and quite exceptional situation. The case of Honorius did nothing, therefore, to undermine normal papal powers to guide the church through disputes. The conciliarists of the thirteenth century could distinguish between the pope and the Catholic Church as separate entities, the one local, the other universal. The papalist cause was strengthened by reaction to the hazardous claim of some on the conciliarist side that papal power had to give way to that of the state embodied in the king or emperor.

This alarming thesis in the form that even in spiritual matters the state is supreme was strenuously argued in 1324 by Marsilius of Padua, *Defensor Pacis*. He even went to the length of denying that St Peter had died in Rome, a thesis that sounded congenial to radical Protestants in the sixteenth and seventeenth centuries; the demonstration that Peter's martyrdom in Rome is historically highly probable (in the absence of any other ancient claimant) was argued by the learned Anglican John Pearson in the 1660s. He thought it imprudent when Protestants imagined that (unjustified) scepticism was an easy short cut to invalidating Roman Catholic claims.

The Council of Constance (1414–18) forced either resignation or withdrawal of recognition on the three popes in office and chose a fourth, Martin V. There was then a problem: the council affirmed the superiority of a general council to the Pope, and envisaged the government of the Church being in the hands of a succession of councils in which bishops would be seated, as at Constance, according to their national groupings. At Constance the concession to national patriotism created other problems, evident when news of

Calabrian: Three Treatises on Papal Primacy', *Revue des études byzantines*, 53 (1995), 41–116 (edition, translation and commentary); id., *The Byzantine Lists, Errors of the Latins* (Urbana and Chicago; University of Illinois Press, 2000).

the Anglo-French battle at Agincourt in 1415 left the French bishops unwilling to cooperate with the English delegation. But the assertion of conciliar superiority to the Pope weakened papal capacity to provide the glue needed by a universal body. Martin V saw that appeals from the pope to a general council would create vast practical problems of which cost would only be one. In 1460 Pope Pius II, himself a former conciliarist, forbade any such appeal by the bull *Execrabilis*. On the other hand, the concentration of the idea of a Catholic Church embodied in a single bishop entailed a problem if and when that one bishop acted or spoke in a way morally outrageous, e.g. to Martin Luther. He was scandalized by the deception of the laity in the sale of indulgences (necessary if St Peter's was to be built) as if they could bring remission of penalties for sin.

At the Council of Constance the Hussites of Bohemia were a major anxiety with their demand for communion in both kinds, and the council ensured that the problem was rendered insoluble by burning Jan Hus after the emperor had promised him safe conduct (which the bishops did not feel bound to honour in the case of a heretic). On 6 July 1415 he died reciting the creed, and overnight became a national hero.

The German emperor Sigismund was in touch with the eastern emperor Manuel, who sent to Constance a learned bilingual envoy Chrysoloras; he died during the council's proceedings. Martin V also had some correspondence with the emperor Manuel. Not long before his death in 1431 Pope Martin summoned a council to meet at Basel with Cardinal Cesarini to be its president. He specifically named among the council's responsibilities the *reductio* or return of the Greeks as well as the reconciliation of the Hussites to the catholic fold. However, the bishops at Basel used very conciliar terms for their invitation to the emperor and patriarch, implying a more collegial understanding of authority than papalists liked.

In consequence the Council of Basel was unwelcome to the new Pope, the Venetian Eugenius IV (1431–47), who was to have great difficulties in maintaining his position in Rome. Property disputes caused a virtual state of war with the Colonna family. He sought refuge from the riots by moving to Florence and on to Bologna. Within a few months of his accession he decided to dissolve the Council of Basel, but was then confronted by a denial that he had the power to do such a thing to a duly called general council which had the support of a majority of the cardinals and of several kings. The bishops at Basel sought negotiations with the Greeks in 1433. At the same time they were engaged in attempting reconciliation with the Hussites of Bohemia, deciding in 1437 to restore the eucharistic cup to the laity, and also agreeing on reforms in the practical operations of the Roman curia. The bishops and royal representatives at Basel wanted to end papal claims to appoint to important offices in the Church and also to restrain the payment of 'annates'. The council had, however, the problems that the one established central agency for any action in the western Churches was the Roman curia which they disliked; and how was a pope without annates to survive financially?

Eugenius realized that his weak position both at Rome and in relation to the assembly at Basel would be transformed if he were able to compete successfully for the trust and cooperation of the Greek emperor and patriarch. He decided to call a rival council in Italy. This met at Ferrara in January 1438. The substantial Greek delegation arrived at Venice early in March, having hesitated whether to go to Basel or to Ferrara. The Venetians advised them to go to their own Eugenius. The old Greek patriarch was aware that his bishops might not be intellectually strong enough to cope with the sophisticated western theologians expert in Aristotelian logic, and in preparation for the meeting two highly cultivated Greeks were consecrated to be bishops, Bessarion to Nicaea, Mark Eugenicus to Ephesus.

41

THE COUNCILS OF BASEL AND
FERRARA/FLORENCE: POPE EUGENIUS IV

The Council of Basel

The Council of Constance had been able to tidy the disorder of the papal
schism (1378–1415) by affirming the principle that a general council by its
nature represented all Christians and so possessed an authority superior to
that of single bishops of Rome. It had successfully removed three rival popes
from office and appointed a member of the powerful Colonna family in
Rome, Martin V, as sole bishop of Rome. Its most famous decree ordered
that general councils ought to occur frequently. Conciliarists did not think
the worldwide church well administered by a concentration of power in the
Roman curia. A conciliarist council was held at Pavia, but moved to Siena
1423–4. At Basel a further conciliarist council was assembled with the support of the Holy Roman Emperor Sigismund. Pope Martin V had nominated
an apostolic legate to preside. He was Giuliano Cardinal Cesarini, whose
appointment was confirmed by Martin's successor Eugenius IV, nephew of
Pope Gregory XII. He did not get on with the Colonna family, who made
Rome too uncomfortable for Eugenius to live and work there. He did not
think the conciliarist principle could justify the calling of a general council.
That, he thought, was his responsibility. But if such a synod was to be held,
the Pope's main objective would be to use it to destroy conciliarism. Unlike
the Basel bishops Eugenius did not believe that the unity of a worldwide
Church could be maintained without the centralized authority of the Roman
see. Against the conciliarist claim to embody a more universal representation
of the whole Church, Eugenius could reply (Greek Acts 26) that he with the
patriarch, the emperor, and all patriarchs and all cardinals constituted the universality of the Church; and that although the Basel bishops had been invited
to Ferrara not one had come.

Since the unsuccessful Council at Lyon in 1274, which was in reality more
like an individual conference between the archbishops and the eastern
emperor's lay representative, aspiration to achieve consensus between Latin
west and Greek east had in no sense died away. A critical question remained
whether Greek bishops were ready to accept the Roman see's primacy of

universal jurisdiction. It did not seem natural to them to do so, and past experience did not make it easy to think the western church understood and tolerated the different customs of the east. Memories of the past, especially the bitterly remembered Fourth Crusade, did not encourage anyone to believe this.

There was bound to be a problem in the tradition of eastern ecclesiology, expressed in Justinian's doctrine of a Pentarchy, authority being vested in the collective consensus of five more or less equal patriarchs, each of whom was essential to a fully ecumenical authority in the whole Church. The Pentarchy idea was not obviously welcome to bishops of Rome since it was incompatible with the notion underpinned by the forged Donation of Constantine assigning to the Roman see powers superior to the other four patriarchs in the east. Moreover both east and west assumed that all those taking their seats in an ecumenical council were neither schismatics nor heretics. In 1420 there were still not a few Latins who regarded the eastern churches as being in schism from the Catholics by their independence from the catholicity-defining see of St Peter. Authentic tradition was defined for the Greeks as the doctrine of seven ecumenical councils ratified by the east Roman emperor, as Constantine had done for Nicaea, Theodosius I for Constantinople I, Theodosius II for Ephesus I, Marcian for Chalcedon, Justinian for Constantinople II, Irene and Constantine VI for Nicaea II (787), an assembly that the west took time to evaluate.

The *Filioque*'s insertion in the creed might well lack full ecumenical authority by being an addition to the creed sanctioned (tradition said) by the Council of Constantinople in 381, which simply affirmed that the Spirit proceeded from the Father and said nothing of the Son's participation. The bishops at the Council of Lyon had wisely denied that they were affirming two independent first principles in the procession of the Spirit from the Father and the Son. That was how Photius had (mis)read the *Filioque*. Some determinedly Orthodox Greeks such as Mark Eugenicus had no doubt that the western *Filioque* was a heresy, not a tolerable liturgical diversity, but putting a serious question to the validity of Latin baptisms in the name of the Trinity. At Florence the Russian bishop Isidore of Kiev thought it deplorable that this had not been openly discussed. These questionings among Orthodox clergy persisted for a long time—even until modern times.

As we have seen there were other issues under contention such as the proper bread to be used in the Eucharist or whether clergy might be clean-shaven. But there was also a basic axiom common to Latin and Greek, that the tradition of the Fathers was sacrosanct. This axiom is found boldly asserted in the fourteenth-century historian and critic of Palamas and the Hesychasts, Nicephorus Gregoras, who sharply declares (10. 8, Bonn edition i. 518), that he has to stand immovable, echoing the apostle's words that neither death nor life nor height nor depth nor any other creature can justify him in abandoning a defined path of patristic tradition. Any council which invited the acceptance of changes from what the ancient Fathers had decided must be a futile waste of time and money and a threat to the Church's coherence.

Ecumenical synods cannot be other than costly. At Basel a question looming rather large was how to fund such an assembly attended by numerous Greeks and perhaps a Russian or two. The rich city of Avignon offered to provide the needed resources drawing on the royal treasury with the favour of the French king, provided that the council could be located in their city. Since the eleventh century, good causes in the western Church had been funded by issuing popular indulgences, hazardously announced as providing 'remission of sins' for those who bought them. This custom was regarded with deep misgiving by Peter Abelard and by lesser figures. Many medieval manuscripts preserve tracts anxiously complaining that it must be illusion for the laity to think they could buy remission of sins with cash even for so worthy a cause as the building of St Peter's. Martin Luther said very little on this subject that was not already commonplace. But the Basel bishops, anxious to be able to provide shipping from Constantinople to Venice and to welcome their guests with accommodation and hospitality, saw no reasonable or simple way of raising the necessary funds other than by a popular indulgence glossed 'for the remission of sins'; and this went ahead with no consultation with Pope Eugenius. They expected their guests from the east to include not only the patriarch but even the Roman emperor himself; all this was bound to require a level of hospitality which could not be cheap or shabby if the Latins were to hold their heads high.

The conciliarism of the Basel assembly was unwelcome to Pope Eugenius IV, though at first he acknowledged it and confirmed his predecessor's appointment of Giuliano Cardinal Cesarini as its president. But the conciliarist principle stated at Constance that a general council possessed greater authority than a bishop of Rome, which had given the assembly at Constance the assurance and power to declare three popes deposed, was abhorrent to Eugenius. He was resolute in decreeing the dissolution of the Basel council. This naturally enraged the bishops in synod, who denied that the Pope possessed the power to do this. They made sharp criticisms of Eugenius and in July 1437 the Basel bishops resolved on 'implacable resistance to the end' formally accusing him of contumacy in rejecting the decree of Constance.

They passed formal charges threatening him with deposition. They complained of slackness in liturgy and in the maintenance of important church buildings. At Praeneste near Rome and in a church near Bologna the condition of great buildings had been so neglected as to become ruinous.

So it fell to the council to insist that clergy should be more reverent in the conduct of services. Their surplices must be clean. All should rise for the *Gloria Patri* and observe a pause in the middle of verses in saying the Psalms and there was criticism of those who at mass do not say the creed to the end or who even omit the Preface and the Lord's Prayer (session XXI). They also demanded a purge of widespread tolerated concubinage (XX). They despatched a letter to the Pope and his cardinals. The document was tough and demanded his submission within sixty days, failing which he would be deposed.

The synod approved a profession of faith to be made by every candidate to the papacy. It would include respect for conciliar authority.

The reforming ecclesiology of the Basel bishops could not be congenial to Pope Eugenius. Because the supreme jurisdiction of the Pope was upheld by a number of curial cardinals, the council demanded that Eugenius promote no one to be cardinal while the Council at Basel was still in session (evidently they had in mind the possible drafting of a decree on the subject of cardinals' duties, qualifications, and function). The bishops laid down a principle that cardinals were costly to the Church, and their number must be moderated.

Conciliar Ecumenism

The Basel bishops wrote a friendly letter to the Patriarch of Constantinople inviting the Orthodox bishops to join an ecumenical synod. They received an answer especially friendly:

We note your reverent care for the whole of Christianity and especially for us. We have often written and sent many legations about restoration of unity as is well known to all. Yet circumstances have not allowed us to achieve the desired end. We seek for an ecumenical council which is unanimous and attended by all persons who must be there [i.e. not like the meeting at Lyon in 1274]. We send three legates: Demetrius Palaeologus Maeotides, the distinguished abbot of St Demetrius' monastery, and a layman Dishypatos [Latinized as Dissipatus]. These legates will explain everything in our mind, please grant them your full confidence.

The western bishops were properly impressed to be receiving as a legate a Palaeologos, evidently a brother of the emperor himself. But the patriarch made one crucial point disturbing to the Basel council, namely the patriarch required the bishop of Rome to be present at the synod. This condition would bring the proposal into line with the doctrine of the Pentarchy, Rome being one of the five patriarchs whose consent was necessary to ecumenical decisions. Western conciliarists had not been thinking in this way. It was to Eugenius' advantage that the Greeks assumed this doctrine of authority. If he had also been able to conceive of the equality of all five patriarchs, the union of 1439 would have been more successful.

When Pope Eugenius called his ecumenical synod to meet at Ferrara, conveniently close to Venice, the Basel bishops dismissed that assembly as 'a conventicle of schismatics', and excommunicated Eugenius on 25 June 1439. His union with the Greeks a month later was crucial for him as well as for the emperor and the dying patriarch. Pope Eugenius rapidly saw that the painful rivalry between himself and the Basel conciliarists was being resolved in the council's favour by the patriarch's acceptance of the Basel invitation to an ecumenical council. The Basel council had promised to send to Constantinople 300 crossbowmen and 15,000 ducats towards the reinforcement of the city's defences. The Pope may have thought it unfitting that he should send help of so military a character. We do not hear of any rival offer, though he sent to the patriarch a rival embassy.

The bishops at Basel were aware of the humanist tradition. Twice in their documents they approve a re-enactment of a constitution approved by the Council of Vienne in 1311–12 that stipends should be provided to supply teachers of studies in Hebrew, Arabic, Greek, and Chaldaean (i.e. Aramaic, the language of much of the Book of Daniel). Evidently nothing had actually been done in this regard though the council had specified who was to be asked to pay (Tanner i. 378).

The Pope needed to ensure that the patriarch also received an invitation under his papal authority which a believer in the Pentarchy might well be likely to accept. This council should be in Italy. The Basel bishops soon heard rumours of a council being called to be in Florence or Savoy or Udine in the north-west. They saw this as a rival schismatic proposal to hinder their own reforming work.

Meanwhile the Greeks were sailing north up the Adriatic, their voyage delayed by storms. From stops on the Dalmatian coast (emperor and patriarch did not easily sleep on board a moving ship) they learnt that the Pope was awaiting them at Ferrara and that the emperor Sigismund had died in Hungary. This was bad news for the emperor hoping for military aid from Sigismund. The discomforts of their voyage lasting two months convinced them that there could be no question of travelling on to Avignon, as was being much pressed by the king of France, whose gold would meet the high cost of the Greeks' transport and hospitality; this was to become in time a heavy burden for Eugenius deprived of income by the decisions at Basel suspending annates.

The Greeks finally arrived at Venice early in February. Not until they reached Venice was a decision required between the rival invitations to Basel or to Ferrara, to council or to pope. The Venetians advised them to make political capital out of the competition for their favours. The emperor Sigismund had written to the east Roman emperor advising him to go to neither. This had also been the opinion of John of Ragusa when the Basel council sent him as a legate to Constantinople. The Greek emperor hoped the princes at Basel would move to Ferrara, and he was disappointed that they did not come. He relied on them for protection against the Turkish threat; for him princes could be more valued than bishops.

Venice to Ferrara

Italian cities, especially Venice and Florence, had come to provide a desirable and safer home for many learned Greeks from Constantinople. The route was used by Greek scribes and owners of valued manuscripts of Aristotle and Plato, and other notable classical writers. We hear of one Italian grandee arranging for his cooks to hear readings in Aristotle's *Ethics* translated into Italian.[1]

At Venice the emperor was greeted by the Doge at the fort of St Nicolas on the Lido. The main party went on to Ferrara by river; the emperor, who had been on rough seas for much of the Adriatic, preferred to make the short journey on dry land. The ill octogenarian patriarch also went by land on horseback, honoured by an escort of two cardinals. The Venetians crowded the water in small boats; to welcome the Roman emperor was no minor event for them. On arrival in Ferrara, the patriarch Joseph delivered a speech formally consenting to the synod meeting in Ferrara at St George's church; this averted possible tension about the validity of the proceedings. He lamented unhappy divisions and prayed for union. Meanwhile there was a problem in that the 700 Greeks, though not few, were outnumbered by the Latins and wanted the two churches to be counted as equals, not valued merely by number. Emperor and patriarch discussed this privately with Pope Eugenius.

The agenda could not be unfamiliar; it was sure to consist of the questions which had been in the forefront for some centuries past: the recently surfacing question of purgatory; the eucharistic species, leavened or unleavened; the *Filioque* first disputed in the 640s; and (not unrelated) the teaching authority and jurisdiction of the bishop of Rome. For Eugenius Greek admission of his primacy, especially his universal jurisdiction, was more important than the theological questions under dispute.

On the east's pentarchic notion of authority an ecumenical council was as unthinkable without the bishop of Rome as it was in the west. But the Greeks had never easily thought of Rome as possessing a universal jurisdiction; that would be power not merely strong influence. In the past the west had not treated the different customs of the east with much respect. There had been

---

[1] See the fascinating collection of such improbable facts in Nigel Wilson, *From Byzantium to Italy* (London, 1992); this migration has also been studied by O. Kristeller and by D. J. Geanakoplos, *Greek Scholars in Venice* (Cambridge, Mass., 1962).

argument on such delicate and refined problems as the moment of eucharistic consecration. Was this change dependent on the Lord's Words of Institution, the tradition going back to Ambrose of Milan late in the fourth century? Or did it depend on the prayer invoking the Holy Spirit—'the Epiklesis'—as was assumed in all ancient Greek liturgies? That consecrated bread was not the same as unconsecrated and possessed a distinct dignity was a shared conviction. Argument was on whether the bread was leavened or unleavened. At the Council of Ferrara/Florence this last issue had to be discussed but had not been disputed at conciliar level (eg. at Lyon) since the Council of Bari in 1099, with Anselm declaring that there was no question of invalidity in the use of leavened bread, though this was not now western custom. The west still thought it better to use unleavened bread. Practicalities at the distribution made it more edifying.

At Ferrara there was very soon fairly serious debate about purgatory, especially on whether the fire was to be taken literally, as western divines seemed to think; before long, however, the most painful subject of disagreement was felt to be the Latin addition of the *Filioque* to the ecumenical creed. Mark Eugenicus, bishop of Ephesus, was clear that this lay at the root of the schism, all other questions being secondary. The Greeks, led by Mark, remained convinced that this addition had been a great mistake. To Mark and others it was gross disrespect for sacred authority to change the text of the creed of the Second Ecumenical Council. He was of course unaware that at the time the west had been cold to all decisions made by that council.

At an early stage in the proceedings Mark of Ephesus laid it down as a principle that, even were the *Filioque* proved to be true theology, he would never accept it. Such a matter was for him decided exclusively by authority, not reason, and authority (other than a decision by the Pope) was obviously against the addition (Greek Acts 57).

There were also sensitive matters of protocol. In the church at Ferrara the Pope was enthroned in the northern part of the building with a throne for the German emperor below him; then came the cardinals. There was sensitivity about the rank of different ecclesiasical officials when the two bodies were put together. Latin custom, even for emperors, was to kiss the pope's foot. The Greek patriarch was not going to agree to do this and his refusal was dramatic. A kiss of peace was one thing, kissing a foot quite another. These matters reflected the mutual distrust that was sadly to haunt the council.

The Greek patriarch had had misgivings about the western promise to pay the Greeks' expenses of travel and lodging. He thought it possible that the Greek bishops might feel obliged to agree with the Latins if the Latins had been their hosts throughout. As there was a period during the council when the Greeks were not receiving the agreed financial support for subsistence (at one point they had had no support for five months), they may well have thought that this was practical pressure being put upon them by the Latins. It was possible that the suggestion attributed to the patriarch belonged to that context. But the shrewd old man could have foreseen the possibility as a danger to be guarded against: so at least says the anti-unionist Greek diary of Syropoulos—often a reliable reporter.[2] We owe to Syropoulos a touching description of the pain felt by the Greeks as they looked at the walls of San Marco in Venice plastered with Greek loot from St Sophia at the time of the Fourth Crusade.[3] These treasures in the west had been stolen by barbarians.

The two sides faced mountainous problems, notably the deep and visceral dislike for all Latins shared by the people of Constantinople with their vivid memory of the Fourth Crusade. Their trade had been taken out of their hands by Venice and Genoa. The sack of 1204 had initiated half a century of occupation and very intolerant Latinization of their churches and liturgies when they were coerced into confessing the *Filioque*, and into using unleavened bread, by a west ready to justify the attack with the argument that the conquest had brought a merited force to coerce a bunch of schismatics, which as Pope Innocent III persuaded himself was restoring communion between old Rome and Constantinople with a Latin patriarch in the Greek capital acknowledged by the west, as his predecessors had not been for a long time past.

The writer Nicolas Mesarites (who held the post of Skeuophylax at the church of the Pharos and was to be ordained Metropolitan of Ephesus and Exarch of the province of Asia, later translated to Nicaea) was credited in 1207 with a diary of conversation with Roman legates who asked what might be the root cause for Greek alienation from the Latins: he was thought to have answered that beside the *Filioque* the Greeks could not accept the claim of the bishop of Rome to exercise universal jurisdiction, with power to appoint to major sees.[4] The Greeks thought every bishop to be a successor of St Peter and that the unity of believers inhered in their faith in Christ more than in the bishop of Rome with his canon law.

The extent and depth of the alienation is manifest in the canons of the Fourth Lateran Council under Pope Innocent III (1215). Canon 4 entitled 'on the pride of the Greeks against Latins', deplored rebaptizing Latins as if Catholic baptism were invalid and not offering a Mass on an altar previously used by a Catholic priest without first washing it (above, p. 236). After the

---

[2] p. 120. Laurent, whose edition (Rome, 1971) has replaced the incompetent edition of R. Creyghton (The Hague, 1660), in any event a rare book.

[3] pp. 220 ff. Laurent; Greek Acts 6–8.

[4] That the diaries of Nicolas Mesarites are less than an authentic document by him was persuasively argued by G. Spiteris, *Orientalia Christiana Analecta*, 204 (1977), 181–6. The forgery cannot have been hard to compose.

Roman Church, mother and mistress of all, come the Eastern Patriarchs in the order Constantinople (Rome had at long last accepted Constantinople in the second place), Alexandria, Antioch, and Jerusalem, each receiving a pallium from Rome in conferment of authority.

Not all the Greeks were suspicious of western ideas. The patriarch had been anxious to come to Italy with a team of well-equipped theologians and had specially ordained not only Mark Eugenicus to the see of Ephesus but also Bessarion to the see of Nicaea. Bessarion was in favour of the union and got on very well with the prominent Italian scholar and general of the Camaldolese order, Ambrogio Traversari, able in both Greek and Latin. Bessarion owned a remarkable collection of old manuscripts, which, eventually after the council was past and Eugenius had made him a cardinal, he donated to Venice so that they form a very important element in the Biblioteca Marciana (see Mioni's catalogue). Bessarion's utterances in the council were received with deep respect. His texts of Basil (*contra Eunomium* and *De Spiritu Sancto*) had persuaded him to think well of the formula that the Spirit proceeds from the Father through the Son.

Another Greek layman of high intelligence, George Scholarios, whose writings are a major source of information, argued at the council in favour of the union. After the council ended, Mark Eugenicus succeeded in persuading him to change his mind, thereby qualifying him to be supported as the first patriarch of Constantinople under the Turks; he took the name of Gennadios. He became convinced that to accept the union was to become Latin. An argument for union probably emerging from discussions between Bessarion and Traversari was based on the concord of the ancient Church Fathers, both Greek and Latin.[5] In the patristic age Latins and Greeks recognized each other as orthodox and equally authentic members of the same Church communion.

During the summer of 1438 a potentially lethal plague attacked Ferrara. The outcome was an inevitable move which Eugenius was able to fix with Florence. The Pope only needed to convince the Greeks that Florence would be suitable. They were depressed and longed to go home having been so long away and being owed five months' financial support. Moving to Medici Florence would at least solve that problem. The emperor could not be persuaded to allow their desired return to Constantinople. At first the Greek bishops were reluctant to move but were persuaded by the emperor revealing that only Florence had the resources to keep the Pope solvent and therefore to support the Greek guests. Cosimo de' Medici paid for horses and boats to transport all the bishops and supporters; the great city was glad to have them. Florentine artistic achievements made the city famous.

---

[5] Greek Acts 425–6; Syropoulos, p. 438. Laurent.

Florence

The midwinter move of the council from Ferrara over the hills to Florence was not entirely simple. They arrived in February 1439, the Pope on 25 January. Florentine humanists were pleased to welcome Greeks for their learning and trade potential. One of this Greek team brought by the emperor was the Platonist Gemistos Plethon, whose religion was nearer to that of pagan late Platonists than to Christianity. As the Greek Lent had begun, there was no feast of welcome for the emperor. Reluctantly discussion of the *Filioque* was resumed on 2 March. At the same time experience suggested that private discussion in small groups would be the best way to achieve union, some of the debates being highly technical with Aristotelian terms shared by both Latins and Greeks. Mark Eugenicus discerned that the Latin *processio* did not have a precise Greek equivalent.

Subtle argument followed, debating the meaning of a passage in Epiphanius, then a text of Basil of Caesarea. The recorded discussions turned to the technical exegesis of the conciliar texts, especially Basil and Athanasius, the Latin reading being presented by the Dominican Montenero, Mark Eugenicus replying. Montenero stressed that the Latins admit only one cause (the Father) for the procession of the Spirit. The Greeks cited a passage from the letter to Marinos from Maximus Confessor, an author of authority fully recognized by both parties (PG 91. 133–6), Maximus observing that the western *Filioque* was paralleled in Cyril of Alexandria's commentary on St John's gospel. Montenero's strength lay in scripture, describing the Holy Spirit as the Spirit of the Son; Leo the Great (PL 54. 402 A) had 'the Spirit proceeds from both'. Others cited were Pope Damasus' Tome, texts of Hilary, Ambrose, and especially Augustine, also Pope Hormisdas and his formula of faith which, under imperial pressure, was accepted by many Greeks at the time (in 519). The catalogue continued with Gregory the Great, Boethius, Isidore of Seville, and more than one of the Councils of Toledo, after whom Montenero turned to Greek Fathers. The western clergy did not include a serious student of eastern Christianity with its tradition of spirituality and liturgical life.

The Greeks were not impressed by the western resort to Aristotelian syllogisms instead of to patristic authorities. This point was sharply put by a Georgian bishop. But the Greeks were impressed by the patristic citations, especially Greek Fathers quoted by Montenero, who was equally able to hold his own in metaphysical arguments, a field in which the Greeks relied on Mark Eugenicus and Scholarius.

Both sides shared the axiom repeated by Bessarion (PG 161. 543–624) that the saints of antiquity were sound and correct in their faith. It followed that texts of the Latin Fathers should have cogency for the Greeks but it was embarrassing that the Greeks were unable to verify their belief that texts quoted by Latins in favour of the *Filioque* were corrupt and interpolated.

The case favouring union, which was supported by Scholarius, was given a sudden fillip by news that a Turkish attack on Constantinople was imminent.

One Latin argument supporting the *Filioque* was that even if it was forbidden by the Council of Ephesus I (431) to add to the creed, the west did not worry since the *Filioque* was not an external addition but a classification or inward development internal to the Nicene creed (Greek Acts 141–2); just as the first Council of Ephesus approved the word *Theotókos* but did not insert it into the creed as that would be an addition.

At Florence no Greek recalled objection to the *Filioque* based on its advocacy by anti-Byzantine Franks. Their weakness was that the Latins could cite early Latin Fathers like Augustine in favour of the doctrine. The emperor discerned difficulty in debate on the truth of the double procession. He proposed that this be entrusted to a committee of twelve Latins and twelve Greeks.

Meanwhile the debate concerning the *Filioque* became complex and contested. If the Spirit derives being from the Father and the Son, is that from the Godhead as the three in the Trinity share one deity?

At the next session Mark of Ephesus preached a sermon on the exposition of Basil. Montenero expounded an ancient copy of Basil brought from Constantinople by Nicolas of Cusa. Montenero rashly suggested that a characteristic of Greeks was to corrupt texts. Mark could immediately answer with the notorious case of Pope Zosimus, who in 418 cited a canon of Serdica as if it were a canon of Nicaea.

The Greeks regarded the discussion as mere words, opposing formulae, not real issues. They lacked the controversial equipment to be in theological combat with well-educated Latins, and their patriarch in particular lacked comparable intellectual fire so that his bishops felt themselves to be weakly led. In this respect Mark Eugenicus of Ephesus was a prominent exception.

Ephesus was an important centre for pilgrims venerating St John in the noble church built in his honour under Justinian on the hill nearby Seljuk. Syropoulos' diary includes disparaging evaluations of the abilities of his fellow Greeks, except for Mark Eugenicus, with whose anti-unionism he largely concurred. On the *Filioque* the winning formula for Maximus Confessor was that the *Holy Spirit* proceeds substantially from the Father through the Son (PG 90. 672 C).[6] Maximus did not clearly state both Father and Son to be cause of the Procession of the Spirit; the preposition 'through' implied 'known to the Church militant', whereas to say 'proceeding from

---

[6] Patriarch Tarasius had said much the same but had vexed the Franks by doing so (Ch. 12 n. 8).

the Father and the Son' suggested a procession in the eternal order of being. The Greeks did not want to lose that distinction. Mark Eugenicus expressed the negative opinion that if a form of words for the *Filioque* were discovered to be acceptable to both sides the Latin interpretation would not be orthodox. He could not recognize that Latins and Greeks were expressing the same meaning but in different words of Latin idiom.

The next stage in the council was the draft union decree. The patriarch was now very sick which exempted him from participation in the drafting. The emperor, however, had a leading role. On 10 June 1439 the old patriarch died and was accorded a notable funeral and tomb in S. Maria Novella; his last remembered words were clear that union was indispensable for the salvation of Constantinople. Syropoulos saw his death as a disaster for the unionist cause. Discussion in synod thereafter turned on the question whether 'and the Son' meant the same as 'through the Son' and then on the easier question of western *azyma*; this eucharistic question led on to the problem when the change in the species took place, and the choice between Epiklesis of the Spirit and the Lord's words of institution. This difficult problem was followed by dispute whether pope or emperor would have his name at the head of the signatures to an act of union. The emperor conceded this to Eugenius whose reaction was that surely the Latins did not need to ask any further concession from the Greeks (*Acta Latina* 256. 30 or Greek Acts 453). The *Filioque* was accepted as having the support of saints, some of whom said 'proceeding from the Father and the Son', others saying 'from the Father through the Son'. It was boldly claimed that the expression differed but the meaning was the same since the Greeks do not exclude the Son from the Spirit's proceeding eternally from the Father's essence, while the Latins do not exclude the Father from being the one principle (or ultimate cause) for the inspired procession of the Spirit. The Holy Spirit proceeds eternally from Father and Son and both Latins and Greeks affirm this in the same sense, with one soul.

Mark of Ephesus immediately denied that this could be acceptable. The Russian Isidore qualified assent by interpreting 'through' the Son to mean 'from' the Son. Mark could not swallow this. He could only agree to union if the Latins excised *Filioque* from the creed. Isidore cited Bekkos (PG 41. 61 c), not an author highly respected by Greek critics, for whom he was the arch-Latinizer. Cyril of Alexandria he cited as agreeing with the Latins. That was no minor figure to cite.

Scholarius, admirer of Aquinas and aware that contemporary Byzantine thinkers could offer no rival, helped Bessarion to answer the pro-Latin archbishop of Rhodes, Andrew Chrysoberges. Scholarius had been appointed by the Emperor in 1436 to begin preparatory studies for the council; he was convinced with Cesarini that Greek and Latin Fathers were in agreement.

He put to Bessarion the thesis that this agreement of ancient Greek and Latin Fathers offered a model for the council's union. In any event he was sure that the Latins' 'double procession' was true.

After the Florence union was signed, Scholarius regretted his role in its making; perhaps he had come to realize the profound misgivings of the Greek bishops who had voluntarily signed their assent. He realized that the Greeks had only accepted the union under political pressure from the emperor and his ambition to save his city. He did not regard the *Filioque* as orthodox, and he was opposed to intercommunion with Latin clergy, and his eucharistic faith was expressed by the term *metousia*, 'change of being'. He was critical of the established Latin custom of not offering the laity the chalice.[7]

The Definition

On 6 July 1439 the Council of Florence agreed on a doctrinal definition, headed by the names of Eugenius IV and the Greek Emperor John Palaeologus. It would be difficult for dissident Greeks to defy their emperor, and for dissident Latins to defy the Pope who some of them felt was being soft in the demands being made of the Greeks (a view voiced by the Spaniard Torquemada). Critics from the Council of Basle did not support the Florence union; the dissenters were not only Greeks.

On the procession of the Spirit, it was defined as affirming both being 'from the Father and the Son' and being 'from the Father', the two formulae bearing an identical meaning on the ground of scripture and many citations from both Latin and Greek Fathers. The Latins affirmed that the Father is the ultimate cause of the procession of the Spirit and wholly denied separate causes. All Christians should believe in the Spirit proceeding from the Father and the Son. Those who die in mortal sin go down to hell for punishment, the penalties being unequal. The primacy of papal jurisdiction was affirmed on the ground that the Roman pontiff is successor of Peter and Vicar of Christ, head of the whole Church and teacher of all Christians, possessing full power to rule and govern the whole Church, as contained in the Acts of ecumenical councils and in the sacred canons.

The ranking of patriarchs defined by the canons was expressly without prejudice to their privileges and rights. The primacy of the see of Rome was thereby qualified to be as defined by canon law. Eugenius' primacy was enhanced by the arrival on 13 August 1439 of legates from the Armenian Church who affirmed Eugenius to be St Peter and so also to be 'mother and mistress of all the faithful'. This was much stronger language than Greeks had

---

[7] C. J. G. Turner, 'Scholarius and the Union of Florence', *JTS*, NS 18 (1967), 83–103.

been accustomed to. On 4 September 1439 Eugenius issued a round condemnation of the criminal schismatic meeting at Basel and decreed excommunication of the bishops continuing there and on the principal citizens of that city, ordering all merchants to cease trading. As the Basel meeting refused to dissolve, it was declared invalid and its decisions in no way Acts of an ecumenical council but merely those of a spurious conventicle. The Pope's censure at the Basel assembly was supported by Cardinal Cesarini, who had had to withdraw from Basel and move to Ferrara.

The Florence affirmation of papal supremacy shattered the conciliarism of the bishops at Basel, though the conciliarist ecclesiology was evidently influential in the Reformation Divines in seventeenth-century England, especially in Richard Field, *Of the Church* (1606). The Greeks, having signed the Union and longing to return to Constantinople, soon departed for their ships at Venice. Mark Eugenicus had refused to sign. When the Pope was informed he replied 'Then we have achieved nothing.' The argument that Mark would surely submit to the decision of an ecumenical council was one he could not accept without being convinced that the decision was proved orthodox by scripture and orthodox tradition irreconcilable with the *Filioque*. From this position stated at the start, he never deviated.

Mark was well educated and well informed in patristic texts, therefore he was influential. On the return journey numerous Greeks withdrew their assent to the Union definition and they felt confirmed on reaching Constantinople. The Florentine concord aroused a storm of dissent. The Greek rejection of Roman jurisdiction was influential on King Henry VIII of England, who thought it could justify his determination to transfer papal powers to his own position as head of the Church of England. His daughter Elizabeth amended the title to 'supreme governor'.

The successful completion of the Union was naturally a source of deep satisfaction for the Latins, other than the Pope when he learnt of Mark Eugenicus' intransigence. In the Union agreed in July the Latins had won all disputed points, above all the *Filioque* and Roman primacy, which the Greeks were persuaded to accept. The western bishops and Pope Eugenius wanted a thanksgiving Eucharist, which the Greeks then attended without participating. There was no Greek reception of the sacred elements. (That the Greeks were offered them is not recorded.) No one thought of a joint concelebration. During the signing the emperor's dog beneath his chair howled in disapproval.

To both Greeks and Latins it was axiomatic that the saints of the ancient church were in unquestioned communion and therefore both orthodox. So Bessarion (PG 161. 543–624) denied that there could be disagreement among them. All agreed that the saints were inspired and thereby protected from error. If this was seriously affirmed, it should be simple to achieve union

(Isidore, Greek Acts 400). Mark Eugenicus accepted the axiom and then deduced from that that the ancient saints could not imaginably have said the Holy Spirit proceeded from both Father and Son. The texts cited by the Latins must have been corrupted, he thought (Greek Acts 408). The Council of Ephesus (431) had solemnly forbidden any addition to or alternative to the Nicene creed of 325. This was repeated at Chalcedon (451) and at the Sixth Council in 680–1. The Greeks were accustomed to defining Orthodoxy as the faith of the seven ecumenical councils, without further gloss or detail. Here were the Latins manifestly defying the creed of Constantinople (381) by an addition in evident contravention of the ruling of the Council of Ephesus 431 led by Cyril of Alexandria. It seemed paradoxical that the Latins and Latinizers such as Bessarion could be quoting Cyril in support of the *Filioque*.

The Council of Florence has seemed to the Latin west to be the ideal moment of ecumenism when the Greeks formally signed their agreement, but then withdrew their assent as reflection induced qualms, because of the political pressure from the emperor or the conviction of Mark Eugenicus that the Union was Latinizing, a painful accusation in the light of past experience. There were also Greeks who had serious doubts about the emperor's belief that the west should send strong military force to repel the attacking Turks. Naturally after 29 May 1453 many Greeks would think this to be God's judgement on them for a religious compromise at Florence in July 1439. Past experience warned the city that a military force from the west was likely to want to take over the city as the Venetians had done in 1204.

Armenians in Poland Reconciled

After the reconciliation of the Greeks there remained a question whether the Armenian Church could also agree on the same terms of Union. The Armenians on Sundays and Holy Days were to add the *Filioque* (Greek Acts 424). An approach had been made to them by the Council of Basel, and it was important that Pope Eugenius IV should not fail to write also. The Armenian delegates partly from Poland presented themselves at Genoa and were given a fine reception by the Doge. They went on to reach the Pope on 24 May 1439 and travelled to Florence. Eugenius commended them to John of Montenero OP. They arrived at Florence at the end of July arriving a few days after the Union agreement on 6 July. The Decree for the Armenians instructed them in Thomas Aquinas' doctrine of the Seven Sacraments and noted that they accepted the ecumenical Councils of Nicaea, Constantinople, and Ephesus I (431) and by custom did not add water to wine in the chalice. But they claimed to accept all synods accepted by Rome. However, they did not accept the doctrine of Pope Leo I and the Definition of Chalcedon. The Armenians at Lemberg (Lwów, L'viv) united with the Roman Catholics.[8] Union was established with the Copts of Egypt in 1442.

The consequence of the decision of bishops in Poland to accept the terms of the union agreed at Florence was that this became the ground on which these churches of Ruthenia were in communion with the see of Rome. The Roman curia would therefore rank them as Uniates, a category treated with cool reserve by the strict Orthodox of Russia.

[8] Cf. A. Balgy, *Historia doctrinae catholicae inter Armenos unionisque eorum cum ecclesia Romana et Concilio Florentino* (Vienna, 1878).

EPILOGUE

The Council of Florence came near to success: so near and yet so far. The decisions gave nothing to the Greeks for on every point of contention they were required to accept Latin positions. It was easy for them to come away feeling that the council had only reinforced the schism which it was designed to heal. To the present day Orthodox historians can seldom think of the exchanges of 1054 with the clash of Cardinal Humbert and the ecumenical patriarch Michael Cerularius as the moment when communion was severed. They are more likely to think of the decisions made at Florence or of the sack of Constantinople in 1204 as the time when the divorce of Latin west and Greek east came to be made permanent.

The confrontational style of the debates did not help the ecumenical cause. Each side was defending its own fortified position. At one point at Florence a Latin pro-unionist quoted Aristotle to support his opinion that in what is universally agreed, dissent is a sign of falsehood (Greek Acts 108). If there is dissension one party must be wrong.

In the third century Origen replied to Celsus, a pagan critic of the Church, who pointed to the many sects of Christianity which had an uneasy mutual relationship with one another. Origen observed that in all serious subjects there will be some difference, as for example in medicine. And philosophers seldom find agreement easy.

A genuine ecumenical agreement had to win the hearts and minds of those on both sides who had reservations. There were fears and layers of conscious or subconscious hatred inherited from centuries of separation and ignorance. In the *Acta* one cannot discern that the two sides in the debate wished to express a Christian love for one another or a strong sense of sharing in the Christian past to which they appealed.

What keeps pro-unionists from losing heart is the ineradicable belief that division brings evils in its train—evils to which we become insensitive by habit. Patient listening can uncover deep and wide agreement concealed by the polemics of the past. The most obvious characteristic shared in common by the anti-unionists on both sides in ecumenical conversation, whether at Florence or elsewhere, is that interpretation of the past defines the limits of what is possible in the present.

BIBLIOGRAPHY

ALBERIGO, G. (ed.), *Christian Unity: The Council of Ferrara–Florence 1438/9–1989* (Leuven, 1991).

ALEXAKIS, A.. *Codex Parisinus Graecus 1115 and its Archetype* (Dumbarton Oaks Studies 34: Washington, DC, 1966).

ANASTOS. M. V.. 'The Transfer of Illyricum, Calabria and Sicily to the Jurisdiction of the Patriarchate of Constantinople', *Studi bizantini e neoellenici*, 9 (1957). 14–31.

BÄUMER. R.. *Das Konstanzer Konzil* (Wege der Forschung, 415; Darmstadt, 1977).

BAYNES. N. H.. *Byzantine Studies and Other Essays* (London, 1955).

BECKER. A.. *Papst Urban II. (1088–1099)*, 2 vols. (Schriften der MGH, 19; Stuttgart, 1964–88).

BENEŠEVIČ, V. N., *Ioannis Scholastici Synagoga L Titulorum* (Abhandlungen der Bayerischen Akademie der Wissenschaften, philosophisch-historische Abteilung, NF 14; Munich, 1937).

BERTHOLD, G. C., 'Maximus Confessor and the *Filioque*', *Studia Patristica*, 18/1 (1985), 113–17.

—— 'Cyril of Alexandria and the *Filioque*', *Studia Patristica*, 19 (1989), 143–7.

BISCHOFF, B., *Manuscripts and Libraries in the Age of Charlemagne*, trans. and ed. M. Gorman (Cambridge. 1994).

—— and LAPIDGE, M., *Biblical Commentaries from the Canterbury School of Theodore and Hadrian* (Cambridge. 1994).

BOULNOIS, M. O., *Le Paradoxe trinitaire chez Cyrille d'Alexandrie* (Paris, 1994).

BREYDY, M.. *Études sur Saʿīd ibn Baṭrīq et ses sources* (Leuven. 1983).

BRYER. A., and HERRIN. J. (eds.), *Iconoclasm: Papers Given at the Ninth Spring Symposium of Byzantine Studies, University of Birmingham* (Birmingham, 1977).

CASPAR, E. L. E., *Geschichte des Papsttums von den Anfängen bis zur Höhe der Weltherrschaft*, 2 vols. (Tübingen, 1930).

CECCONI, E., *Studi storici sul concilio di Firenze* (Florence, 1869).

CHADWICK, H., 'The Origin of the Title "Oecumenical Council"', *JTS*, NS 23 (1972), 132–5.

—— *Boethius: The Consolations of Music, Logic, Theology, and Philosophy* (Oxford, 1981).

—— *History and Thought of the Early Church* (Aldershot, 1981).

CHENEY, C. R., *Selected Letters of Pope Innocent III concerning England* (London, 1953).

CHRYSOS, E., *Ἡ ἐκκλησιαστικὴ πολιτεία τοῦ Ἰουστινιανοῦ* (Analekta Vlatadon, 3; Thessaloniki, 1969).

COLETI, N., *Sacrosancta concilia ad regiam editionem exacta*, 23 vols. (Venice, 1728–33).

CONSTABLE, G., and HUYGENS, R. B. C. (eds.), *Apologiae duae* (CCCM 62; Turnhout, 1985).

CONTE, P., *Il Sinodo lateranense dell'ottobre 649* (Vatican City, 1989).

DAGRON, G., *Empereur et prêtre* (Paris, 1996).

DARROUZÈS, J., *Dossier grec de l'union de Lyon* (Paris, 1976).

—— *Notitiae episcopatuum ecclesiae Constantinopolitanae* (Paris, 1981).

DESCARREAUX, J., *Les Grecs au Concile de l'union, Ferrare-Florence, 1438–1439* (Paris, 1970).

DUCHESNE, L. M., *Les Églises séparees*, 2nd edn. (Paris, 1905); English trans. of 1st edn. by A. H. Mathew, *The Churches Separated from Rome* (London, 1895).

DVORNIK, F., *The Photian Schism: History and Legend* (Cambridge, 1948).

—— *Early Christian and Byzantine Political Philosophy: Origins and Background* (Dumbarton Oaks Studies, 9; Washington, DC, 1966).

—— 'Photius', *New Catholic Encyclopedia* (New York, 1967), xi. 326–9.

—— *Byzantine Missions among the Slavs* (New Brunswick, 1970).

FERRUA, A., *Epigrammata Damasiana* (Rome, 1942).

FINKE, H., *Acta concilii Constanciensis*, 4 vols. (Münster in Westfalen, 1898–1928).

FLICHE, A., *La Réforme grégorienne* (Leuven, 1937).

FOUYAS, METHODIOS G., Ἡ ἐκκλησιαστικὴ ἀντιπαράθεσις Ἑλλήνων καὶ Λατίνων· ἀπὸ τοῦ μεγάλου Φωτίου μέχρι τῆς συνόδου τῆς Φλωρεντίας, *858–1439*, 2nd edn. (Athens, 1995).

FRANCHI, A., *Il Concilio II di Lione (1274)* (Rome, 1965).

GEANOKOPLOS, D. J., *Emperor Michael Palaeologus and the West 1258–1282: A Study in Byzantine–Latin Relations* (Cambridge, Mass., 1959).

GERSON, JEAN, *Œuvres complètes*, ed. P. Glorieux, 10 vols. (Paris, 1960).

GILL, J., *Quae supersunt actorum Graecorum Concilii Florentini*, 2 vols. (Concilium Florentinum: documenta et scriptores, B v; Rome, 1953).

—— *The Council of Florence* (Cambridge, 1959).

—— *Eugenius IV: Pope of Christian Union* (London, 1961).

—— *Personalities of the Council of Florence* (Oxford, 1964).

—— *Byzantium and the Papacy 1198–1400* (New Brunswick, 1979).

HALLER, J. (ed.), *Concilium Basiliense: Studien und Quellen*, 8 vols. (Basel, 1895–1936).

HALLEUX, A. DE, *Patrologie et œcuménisme* (Leuven, 1990).

HARDOUIN, J., *Conciliorum collectio regia maxima*, 12 vols. (Paris, 1714–15).

HELMRATH, J., *Das Basler Konzil, 1431–1449* (Cologne, 1957).

HERRIN, J., *The Formation of Christendom* (Oxford, 1987).

—— ' "Femina Byzantina": The Council in Trullo on Women', *Dumbarton Oaks Papers*, 46 (1992), 97–105.

HOFMANN, G., *Acta Latina Concilii Florentini* (Concilium Florentinum: documenta et scriptores, B vi; Rome, 1955).

HOFMEISTER, PH., 'Der Streit um des Priesters Bart', *Zeitschrift für Kirchengeschichte*, 62 (1943), 72–94.

HUSSEY, J. M., *The Orthodox Church in the Byzantine Empire* (Oxford, 1986).

JEDIN, H., *Bischöfliches Konzil oder Kirchenparlament* (Basel, 1963).

—— and DOLAN, J. (eds.), *Handbook of Church History*, iii: *The Church in the Age of Feudalism* (London, 1969); trans. Anselm Biggs from *Handbuch der*

Kirchengeschichte, iii: *Die mittelalterliche Kirche*, i: *Vom kirchlichen Frühmittelalter zur Gregorianischen Reform* (Freiburg im Breisgau, 1962).

KARLIN-HAYTER, P., 'Activity of the Bishop of Constantinople outside his *paroikia* between 381 and 451', in *Kathegetria: Essays Presented to Joan Hussey* (Camberley, 1988), 179–210.

KREUZER, G., *Die Honoriusfrage im Mittelalter und in der Neuzeit* (Stuttgart, 1975).

LAUCHERT, F., *Die Kanones der wichtigsten altkirchlichen Concilien nebst den Apostolischen Kanones* (Freiburg im Breisgau and Leipzig, 1896; repr. Frankfurt am Main, 1961).

LAURENT, V. (ed.), *Les Mémoires du grand ecclésiarque de l'Église de Constantinople Sylvestre Syropoulos sur le Concile de Florence (1438–1439)* (Concilium Florentinum: documenta et scriptores, B ix; Rome, 1971).

MANGO, C. (trans. and comm.), *The Homilies of Photius, Patriarch of Constantinople* (Dumbarton Oaks Studies, 3; Cambridge, Mass., 1958).

MANSI, J. D., *Sacrorum conciliorum nova et amplissima collectio*, 55 vols. (Florence etc., 1759–1962).

MARKUS, R. A., *Gregory the Great and his World* (Cambridge, 1997).

MEYENDORFF, J., *Imperial Unity and Christian Divisions: The Church 450–680* (Crestwood, NY, 1988).

—— *Rome, Constantinople, Moscow: Historical and Theological Studies* (Crestwood, NY, 1996).

MICHEL, ANTON, *Humbert und Kerullarios*, 2 vols. (Paderborn, 1924–30).

MOHLER, L., *Kardinal Bessarion als Theologe, Humanist und Staatsmann: Funde und Forschungen*, 3 vols. (Paderborn, 1923–42).

MORRALL, J. B., *Gerson and the Great Schism* (Manchester, 1960).

NICOL, D. MacG., *Byzantium: Its Ecclesiastical History and Relations with the Western World, Collected Studies* (London, 1972).

—— 'The Papal Scandal', in Derek Baker (ed.), *The Orthodox Church and the West* (Studies in Church History, 13; Oxford, 1976).

—— *Studies in Late Byzantine History and Prosopography* (London, 1986).

—— *The Last Centuries of Byzantium 1261–1453* (Cambridge, 1993).

NICOLAS CHONIATES, *Chronicon*, ed. I. Bekker (Corpus Scriptorum Historiae Byzantinae; Bonn, 1835).

NOBLE, T. F. X., *The Republic of St Peter* (Philadelphia, 1984).

OBOLENSKY, D., *The Byzantine Commonwealth* (London, 1971).

ORPHANOS, M. A., *The Procession of the Holy Spirit according to Certain Greek Fathers* (repr. from *Theologia*, Athens, 1979).

QUELLER, D. E., *The Fourth Crusade* (Philadelphia, 1977).

RHALLES, G. A., and POTLIS, M., Σύνταγμα τῶν θείων καὶ ἱερῶν κανόνων τῶν τε ἁγίων καὶ πανευφήμων Ἀποστόλων καὶ τῶν ἱερῶν οἰκουμενικῶν καὶ τοπικῶν Συνόδων καὶ τῶν κατὰ μέρος ἱερῶν Πατέρων, 6 vols. (Athens, 1852–9).

RIANT, P. E. (ed.), *Exuviae sacrae Constantinopolitanae: Fasciculus documentorum minorum ad Byzantina lipsana in Occidentem saeculo XIII. translata spectantium, et historiam quarti belli sacri imperiique Gallo-Graeci illustrantium*, 3 vols. (Geneva, 1877–1904).

RICHARDS, J., *Consul of God: The Life and Times of Gregory the Great* (London, 1980).

ROBERG, *Die Union zwischen der griechischen und der lateinischen Kirche auf dem zweiten Konzil von Lyon* (Bonn, 1964).

ROCHOW, ILSE, *Kaiser Konstantin V. (741–775)* (Berliner byzantinische Studien, 1: Frankfurt am Main, 1994).

RODULFUS GLABER, *Histories*, ed. John France (Oxford, 1989).

RUNCIMAN, S., *History of the Crusades*, 3 vols. (London, 1951–4).

—— *The Eastern Schism: A Study of the Papacy and the Eastern Churches during the XIth and XIIth Centuries* (Oxford, 1955).

SCHWARTZ, E., *Publizistische Sammlungen zum acacianischen Schisma* (Abhandlungen der Bayerischen Akademie der Wissenschaften, philosophisch-historische Abteilung, NF 10; Munich, 1937).

SIEBEN, H. J., *Die Konzilsidee des lateinschen Mittelalters (847–1378)* (Paderborn, 1984).

STIEBER, J., *Pope Eugenius IV: The Council of Basel and the Secular and Ecclesiastical Authorities in the Empire* (Leiden, 1978).

STUMP, P. H., *The Reforms of the Council of Constance (1418–1418)* (Leiden, 1993).

TANNER, NORMAN P., *Decrees of the Ecumenical Councils*, 2 vols. (London and Washington, DC, 1990).

VRIES, WILHELM DE, *Der christliche Osten in Geschichte und Gegenwart* (Würzburg, 1951).

—— *Rom und die Patriarchate des Ostens* (Freiburg im Breisgau, 1963).

WILL, J. K. C., *Acta et scripta quae de controversiis ecclesiae Graecae et Latinae saeculo undecimo composita extant* (Leipzig and Marburg, 1861; repr. Frankfurt am Main, 1963).

WOLF VON GLANVELL, V., *Die Kanonessammlung des Kardinals Deusdedit* (Paderborn, 1905).

WOODHOUSE, C. M., *Gemistos Plethon* (Oxford, 1986).

INDEX

Index compiled by Meg Davies
(Registered Indexer, Society of Indexers)

CPSIA information can be obtained at www.ICGtesting.com
Printed in the USA
BVOW06s2309220916

462699BV00024B/10/P